Law and Economics

OXFORD IN INDIA READINGS

Readers in Economics
(*Themes in Economics Series*)

Law and Economics

Edited by

Satish K. Jain

OXFORD
UNIVERSITY PRESS

OXFORD
UNIVERSITY PRESS

YMCA Library Building, Jai Singh Road, New Delhi 110001

Oxford University Press is a department of the University of Oxford. It furthers the University's objective of excellence in research, scholarship, and education by publishing worldwide in

Oxford New York

Auckland Cape Town Dar es Salaam Hong Kong Karachi Kuala Lumpur Madrid Melbourne Mexico City Nairobi New Delhi Shanghai Taipei Toronto

With offices in

Argentina Austria Brazil Chile Czech Republic France Greece Guatemala Hungary Italy Japan Poland Portugal Singapore South Korea Switzerland Thailand Turkey Ukraine Vietnam

Published in India
by Oxford University Press, New Delhi

First published 2010

ISBN-13: 978-0-19-806773-3
ISBN-10: 0-19-806773-9

Typeset in Adobe Garamond Pro 10.5/12.75
by Digital Domain IT Services Pvt. Ltd., Kolkata.
Printed in India at Rakmo Press Pvt. Ltd., New Delhi 110 020
Published by Oxford University Press
YMCA Library Building, Jai Singh Road, New Delhi 110 001

Note from General Editors

Each volume in this series brings together a selection of important contributions on a particular theme, comprising excerpts from books and previously published journal articles. The need for publishing these *Readers* arises from the fact that over the years economic journals have become both numerous and expensive. Most of the journals and a good many of the books have gone beyond the reach of scholars and students in developing countries. It is for them that these volumes are primarily meant. The topics selected for these volumes are also those which are of particular interest to them.

The present series of *Readers* is a companion to the series on *Themes in Economics,* which is already being brought out by Oxford University Press. While the two series have the common objective of providing easy access to research in particular areas to students and teachers in developing countries, their contents are different. The *Themes* volumes carry freshly written survey articles while the *Readers* put together already published work which has stood the test of time.

KAUSHIK BASU
PRABHAT PATNAIK

Contents

Acknowledgements

The publisher acknowledges the following for permission to include articles in this volume:

Notre Dame Journal of Law, Ethics and Public Policy for "Wealth Maximization Revisited", 1985, Vol. 2, pp. 85–105, published by The University of Chicago Law School.

The Journal of Legal Studies for "Why Is the Common Law Efficient?", 1977, Vol. 6, pp. 51–63, published by The University of Chicago Press.

The Journal of Legal Studies for "Toward an Economic Theory of Liability", 1973, Vol. 2, pp. 323–49, published by The University of Chicago Press.

The Yale Law Journal for "A New Positive Economic Theory of Negligence", 1983, Vol. 92, pp. 799–829, published by The Yale Law Journal Company.

Journal of International Trade & Economic Development for "Efficiency of Liability Rules: A Reconsideration", 2006, Vol. 15, pp. 359–73, published by Taylor and Francis Journals.

The Journal of Legal Studies for "When Does the Rule of Liability Matter?", 1972, Vol. 1, pp. 13–28, published by The University of Chicago Press.

Journal of Economics for "Efficient Liability Rules: Complete Characterization", 2002, Vol. 75, pp. 105–24, published by Springer Science and Business Media.

The Journal of Legal Studies for "Taxes and Legal Rules for the Control of Externalities When There Are Strategic Responses", 1980, Vol. 9, pp. 165–78, published by The University of Chicago Press.

International Review of Law and Economics for "Strategic Behavior under Tort Law", 1992, Vol. 12, pp. 377–80, published by Elsevier.

Cornell International Law Journal for "Compacts, Conventions, and Codes: Initiatives for Higher International Labor Standards", 2001, Vol. 34, pp. 487–500, published by Law School, Cornell University.

The World Bank Economic Review for "Child Labor: Lessons from the Historical Experience of Today's Industrial Economies", 2003, Vol. 17, pp. 175–96, published by The World Bank.

The Journal of Legal Studies for "Liability for Harm versus Regulation of Safety", 1984, Vol. 13, pp. 357–74, published by The University of Chicago Press.

Harvard Journal of Law and Public Policy for "Standards, Rules, and Social Norms", 1997, Vol. 21, pp. 101–17, published by Harvard Society for Law & Public Policy, Inc.

Fordham Law Review for "Conflicting Values in Law", 1994, Vol. 62, pp. 1661–73, published by Fordham University School of Law.

Journal of Democracy for "'Democracy as a Universal Value", 1999, Vol. 10, No. 3, pp. 3–17. © 1999 National Endowment for Democracy and The John Hopkins University Press. Reprinted with permission of The John Hopkins University Press.

1

Introduction

Satish K. Jain

Analysis of social institutions, including legal and other institutions of governance, can be done from a normative perspective or from a positive one, although in practice the two are often interconnected. In the context of normative analysis of an institution there are two important questions that one could ask. First, what purposes the institution as it exists is serving; and second, whether there is a divergence between the purposes for which the institution is supposed to exist and the purposes which are actually being served by it. Thus, the focus of normative analysis of an institution would generally be on the divergence or otherwise of actual values realized by the institution and the desired values. Instead of proceeding from the institution to the realized values and comparing them with the desired values one could also proceed the other way round. One could start from the set of desired values and ask how the institution in question should be designed so that the desired set of values is realized through the instrumentality of the institution. A positive analysis of an institution on the other hand would normally attempt to explain why the institution exists in the way it does. In terms of comprehending an institution in its entirety the best possible scenario would be to discover an idea in terms of which the whole of the institution in all its complexity could be explained or understood. Although there are many theories of law, both positive and normative, here we will be exclusively concerned with economic analysis of law.[1]

[1]For an excellent introduction to various contemporary schools of legal theory, see Patterson (1999).

1. METHODOLOGY OF ECONOMIC ANALYSIS OF INSTITUTIONS

One of the central elements of the economic analysis of institutions is that individuals are assumed to be rational, i.e., purposive. It is also generally assumed that individuals are self-regarding. Rationality or purposiveness per se, of course, does not imply self-regardingness. One can be purposive without being solely concerned with one's own welfare. Individuals are generally taken to have well defined preferences over the set of relevant alternatives or outcomes. For instance, it is assumed that a consumer can rank all conceivable consumption bundles in the order of preference, a player in a two-person non-cooperative game can rank all possible outcomes which result as a consequence of the two players choosing various combinations of strategies, and a potential law-breaker can rank all relevant risky prospects in which the possible outcomes are getting away with ill-gotten gains and getting caught and punished. Being purposive, each individual is assumed to choose that course of action which given the circumstances is likely to yield as high an outcome as possible in terms of his or her preference ordering.

Given the institutional structure, the totality of actions taken by all the individuals determines the social outcome. The outcomes generated by an institution can be analyzed from the perspective of different characteristics which the outcomes may or may not possess. For instance, given the legal rules of evidence, one could analyze the outcomes arrived at from the perspective of correctness of the decisions regarding conviction or acquittal of the accused. In economics, the outcomes are almost invariably analyzed from the perspective of efficiency.

2. EFFICIENCY CRITERIA

In economics several different, though closely related, notions of efficiency are used.[2] The most important notion of efficiency is that of Pareto-optimality, which is based on the Pareto-criterion. A social alternative x is defined to be Pareto-superior to another social alternative y if and only if every individual in the society considers x to be at least as good as y and at least one individual considers x to be better than y. According to the Pareto-criterion, alternative x is regarded to be socially better than alternative y if x is Pareto-superior to y. A social alternative

[2]On efficiency criteria see Kaldor (1939), Scitovsky (1941), Arrow (1963), and Sen (1970).

is defined to be Pareto-optimal or Pareto-efficient if and only if there is no feasible alternative which is Pareto-superior to it. That is to say, an alternative is Pareto-efficient if and only if it is not possible to make some individual better-off without making anyone worse-off.

From the definition it is clear that the notion of Pareto-efficiency is defined with respect to a particular set of social alternatives and a particular set of individuals. If the set of social alternatives or the set of individuals changes then the set of Pareto-efficient alternatives would also in general change. In particular, if the set of social alternatives contracts then an alternative which earlier was Pareto-inefficient might become Pareto-efficient; and if the set of social alternatives expands then an alternative which earlier was Pareto-efficient might become Pareto-inefficient.[3] If the set of individuals expands or contracts then an alternative which earlier was Pareto-inefficient might become efficient; and an alternative which earlier was efficient might become Pareto-inefficient.

Most people find the value-judgment of the Pareto-criterion to be rather compelling. It should, however, be noted that the Pareto-criterion can easily conflict with some important value-judgments. Suppose under state x a small number of individuals are better-off compared to state y and the remaining individuals are equally well-off under the two states. While according to the Pareto-criterion state x would be judged to be socially better than state y; it is possible that state y might be judged to be less inegalitarian than state x. In which case the Pareto-criterion would be in conflict with the value-judgment which declares a state to be better than another if the former is more egalitarian than the latter.

If one accepts the value-judgment of the Pareto-criterion, then it follows that the choice of the society or the collective should be from the set of efficient alternatives, assuming of course that the set of efficient alternatives is not empty. Choice of an inefficient alternative would imply selection of an inferior alternative and rejection of a superior alternative as inefficiency of an alternative implies the existence of a Pareto-superior alternative and, therefore, a socially better alternative in the set of feasible alternatives. Thus, for the purpose of making social choices only the sets of efficient alternatives need be considered if the collective subscribes to the Pareto-criterion. It is, however, rather important to note that the

[3]The alternatives which are Pareto-inefficient before the expansion of the set of alternatives must, of course, remain so after the expansion as well; and the alternatives which are Pareto-efficient before the contraction must continue to remain so after the contraction.

acceptance of the Pareto-criterion does not imply that any arbitrary efficient alternative is better than any arbitrary inefficient alternative. If an alternative is inefficient then it merely entails that there exists another alternative which is Pareto-superior to it and, therefore, socially better in view of the Pareto-criterion. Under the Pareto-criterion, only some pairs of alternatives can be compared. It is perfectly possible that a particular inefficient alternative may be non-comparable with a particular efficient alternative in terms of the Pareto-criterion but better in terms of another evaluative criterion. An alternative can be Pareto-efficient and at the same time socially highly undesirable.

One difficulty with the Pareto-criterion is that its scope is rather limited. If there is a person in the collective who prefers alternative *x* to alternative *y* and another person who prefers *y* to *x*, then under the Pareto-criterion *x* and *y* cannot be compared regardless of the preferences of the remaining individuals. Thus, in general, only a small proportion of all pairs of alternatives would be comparable under the Pareto-criterion. Because of this one would also generally expect the sets of Pareto-efficient alternatives to be large. In many contexts, therefore, the notion of efficiency that is used is that which is based on the Kaldor compensation principle rather than that based on the Pareto-criterion. Under the Kaldor-criterion, a change is considered better if gainers can compensate the losers and still be better-off. Actual compensation, however, need not be paid. Intuitively, it seems that if the gainers can compensate the losers and still be better-off then the total wealth after the change must be larger than that before the change. It should be noted that if actual compensation is not paid then there is no consensual basis to the change. The underlying, though often implicit, premise in using this notion of efficiency is that the questions of total wealth and its distribution can somehow be separated. The main drawback of the Kaldor compensation principle lies in the fact that the 'better than' relation generated by it fails to be asymmetric. Under the Kaldor compensation principle, it is possible that of the two social alternatives *x* and *y*, each is better than the other. That is to say, examples can be constructed such that if there is a move from alternative *y* to alternative *x*, gainers can compensate the losers and still be better-off; and also that if there is a move from alternative *x* to *y*, gainers can compensate the losers and still be better-off. One way to resolve this difficulty is to modify the compensation principle along the lines suggested by Scitovsky. Under the Kaldor compensation principle, one infers 'social alternative *x* is better than social alternative *y*' from the statement 'if there is a move from social alternative y to social alternative x then the gainers can compensate the losers and still be better-off'. Under the Scitovsky criterion, one infers 'social alternative x is better than social alternative y' from 'if there is a move from social alternative y to social alternative x then the gainers can compensate the losers and still be better-off; and if there is a move from social alternative x to social alternative y then it is not the case that the gainers can compensate the losers and still be better-off'. Unlike the Kaldor compensation principle, the 'better than' relation generated by the Scitovsky compensation principle is asymmetric; and, therefore, it can never happen that of the two alternatives x and y, each is better than the other. The Scitovsky relation, however, fails to satisfy transitivity.[4] The logical difficulties associated with the Kaldor and Scitovsky compensation principles are particular instances of the Arrow paradox relating to aggregation of individual preferences into social preferences. Another way to look at these difficulties is to see them as manifestations of the fact that the notion of wealth in general cannot be separated from its distribution.

Notwithstanding these difficulties, the use of Kaldor-criterion in economics is widespread. In fact, in the sub discipline of law and economics, efficiency analysis of law has mostly been done using the Kaldor-criterion.

3. EFFICIENT INSTITUTIONS

If an institution has the property of invariably yielding efficient outcomes, as a shorthand expression one can call the institution itself as efficient. One of the important results of economic theory relates to the efficiency of the institution of market. Under ideal conditions, which include perfect competition and absence of externalities, the institution of market has the property of always yielding a Pareto-optimal allocation of resources. That is to say, under the ideal conditions, the allocation of resources which comes about under the institution of market is such that there is no slack in the sense of there being possibilities of improving some persons' welfare without any reduction in those of others. This particular feature of market has fascinated both economists and philosophers. The interaction of self-regarding individuals, concerned neither with the welfare of others nor with the welfare of the collective as a whole, under the institutional structure of market gives rise to the

[4]See Arrow (1963).

unintended consequence of resulting in a Pareto-optimal allocation of resources. Although market is a decentralized institution without a coordinating authority, even then it is able to allocate resources efficiently. If allocation of resources were to be done by a central coordinating authority efficiently, stupendous amount of information, unlikely to be available in any realistic situation, would be required.

If one associates inefficiency with wastage of resources, then the importance of the relationship between the institution of market and Pareto-efficiency becomes clear. In fact, association of inefficiency with wastage of resources makes the importance of having efficient institutions self-evident. If an institution does not have the property of invariably yielding efficient outcomes then in some situations there would be wastage of resources; on the other hand, if an institution is efficient then in no situation would there be wastage of resources. It is essentially because of this kind of understanding that the questions of efficiency or otherwise of institutions have come to acquire such a preeminent position in the economic discourse.

Although the questions of efficiency or otherwise of institutions are interesting, some care must be taken in interpreting the results and evaluating their import. While discussing the notion of Pareto-efficiency it was pointed out that the acceptance of Pareto-criterion does not entail that every efficient alternative is better than every inefficient alternative; and that a Pareto-inefficient alternative which is non-comparable with an efficient alternative in terms of the Pareto-criterion may very well be better in terms of some important value-judgment. From this it follows that it can easily be the case that the outcome which would be yielded by an efficient institution would be socially inferior to the corresponding outcome which would be yielded by an inefficient institution. Indeed, when one is considering selection of a rule or institution from a set of rules or institutions, it may very well be the case that the outcomes which would be generated by an efficient rule or institution would be by and large inferior to the outcomes yielded by an inefficient rule or institution.

4. MARKET FAILURES

Market under ideal conditions allocates resources efficiently. When these ideal conditions are not there the link between market and Pareto-optimality is ruptured. Inefficient allocation of resources under the market mechanism because of non-satisfaction of one or more of the ideal conditions under which market necessarily gives rise to efficient outcomes is construed as a market failure. When there are externalities there is no longer any guarantee that the allocation arrived at under the market mechanism would be Pareto-efficient. When an activity undertaken by a person results in harm to another person, but this harm is not a cost to the person undertaking the activity, a negative externality is said to exist. When a factory emits pollutants and harms those living in the neighbourhood, the costs that the factory imposes on the residents in the neighbourhood are not a cost to the factory if it is not liable for these harms; and consequently the factory emission constitutes a negative externality. The notion of a positive externality is similarly defined. Externalities create a divergence between private and social cost. Suppose the factory mentioned above is operating under competitive conditions, so that the price of the good which is being produced by the factory is equal to its marginal cost. If the factory reduces its output by one unit the net private loss to the factory owner would be zero. What would be lost because of decrease in revenue would be exactly matched by the gain because of reduction in costs. However, the net gain to the society would be positive as the harm due to the marginal unit would be eliminated. It is because of this divergence that socially inappropriate decisions would be taken. The socially optimal amount of good is that level at which price is equal to the sum of marginal harm and private marginal cost. On the other hand, the actual amount which would be produced would be that level of output at which the price would be equal to the private marginal cost. Thus, from a social point of view there would be overproduction of the good manufacturing of which is pollution-generating.

Thus, in the presence of externalities market is not able to allocate resources efficiently. What is required for efficient allocation of resources is that the divergence between private costs and social costs be eliminated. One way to bring about the alignment of private and social costs is to use Pigovian taxes and subsidies to correct problems of negative and positive externalities, respectively. If the factory owner is made to pay taxes equal to the harm inflicted on the people living in the neighbourhood, while deciding on how much output to produce the factory owner is going to take into consideration not only the costs of producing the good but also the harm which would take place as he would have to pay taxes equal to the harm. Thus, while deciding on the amount to be produced he would be taking into consideration the full social costs of his decision and, therefore, would arrive at the socially appropriate decision. Pigovian taxes and subsidies, therefore, constitute one method of solving the externality problem.

5. THE COASE THEOREM

Coase in his celebrated Article 'The Problem of Social Cost' (1960), criticized the Pigovian approach to solving the externality problem. According to him the conclusions that the Pigovian analysis had led to, namely that it would be desirable to make the injurer liable for damage or to place a tax equivalent to the damage, so that the socially excessive harm is eliminated, involve courses of action which 'are inappropriate, in that they lead to results which are not necessarily, or even usually, desirable'. According to him, the nature of the externality problem is reciprocal. If person A's activity is inflicting harm on person B then preventing A from undertaking the harmful activity so that harm to B can be avoided would harm A as he would have to forego the gain accruing to him from the activity. According to Coase, what is required is that the more serious harm should be avoided.

Existence of an externality leads to divergence between private costs and social costs and consequently leads to inoptimal allocation of resources. For optimal allocation of resources the market failure due to externality will have to be addressed. Coase argued, by considering some examples, that even if there are externalities, in certain circumstances, for instance when transaction costs are zero, the market will be able to achieve optimal allocation of resources without any intervention.

Consider an interaction between two parties A and B; and assume that A is contemplating undertaking an activity which would harm B to the tune of 10. If A is liable for the harm inflicted on B then in deciding whether to undertake the activity in question, A is going to compare his gains from the undertaking of the activity with the costs of the activity inclusive of harm to B as being liable the harm to B is a cost to him; and he will undertake the activity only if the gains are at least as large as costs. The decision arrived by him would be socially optimal as there is no divergence between private and social gains and costs. For instance, if the excess of A's gain over costs exclusive of harm to B is 5, then A would decide not to undertake the activity.

Next, suppose that A is not liable to B for the harm from his activity. One might think that if the excess of A's gain over costs exclusive of harm to B is 5, then A will decide to undertake the activity as he does not have to pay for the harm to B. Coase argues that it would not be correct to think along these lines. In fact, according to Coase, A's decision would be the same as before. The net gain to A from the activity is 5; and net loss to B from the activity is 10. There is clearly scope for mutually beneficial agreement between A and B. Assuming that transaction costs are zero, if A is offered a sum greater than 5 and less than 10 by B for agreeing not to undertake the harmful activity then both parties would benefit. Thus, it makes no difference whether A is liable for the harm to B or not. In either case A will undertake the activity if social gains exceed social costs; and will not undertake the activity if social costs exceed social gains.

The logic of examples considered by Coase is generally stated as a theorem. One way to state the Coase theorem is to assert that if transaction costs are zero then the allocation of resources will be efficient regardless of liability assignments. In the examples which Coase had considered in his article the allocation of resources in fact was invariant with respect to liability assignments; as indeed was the case with the example considered above. As a result, the first set of statements of the Coase theorem asserted both efficiency and invariance of allocation of resources with respect to different liability assignments. The invalidity of the invariance claim was soon realized. When the injurer is liable for the harm to the victim the distribution of wealth would be in favour of the victim; and when the harm has to be borne by the victim himself the wealth distribution would be in favour of the injurer. Consequently, if in the context of some activity the liability regime is changed then one set of people would become wealthier and another set of people would become less wealthy. This in general would have differing implications for demands of different goods and in general would result in a different allocation of resources.

There is a very important implication of the logic of the Coase theorem. What the Coase theorem tells us is that in a world of zero transaction costs, even if there are externalities, markets would be able to allocate resources efficiently regardless of the liability assignments. From the kind of examples and considerations which were used to assert the Coase theorem, it follows that if the transaction costs are prohibitively high then the allocation of resources would depend on the liability assignments.[5] In the example which was considered above, it is clear that if transaction costs are so high as to preclude private bargaining then A would not undertake the activity in case he is liable for the harm

[5]For a lucid exposition of the Coase theorem and its implications for liability assignments, see Demsetz (1972)[Article 7 of this Reader]. This article, like all previously published articles contained in this Reader, has been reprinted here without change and in its orignal form.

to B. On the other hand, if he is not liable then he would undertake the activity as it would benefit him to the tune of 5 to do so. When transaction costs were zero, the payments from B made the gain from not undertaking the activity at least equal to 5, which now is ruled out because of the prohibitively high transaction costs.

When transaction costs are high, in the example considered here, imposing the liability on the injurer results in greater wealth than imposing it on the victim. This is because we assumed that the net gain from the injurer's activity is negative (5 – 10 = –5).

One important difference between solving the externality problem by the use of an appropriate liability rule and by the use of Pigovian taxes and subsidies should be noted. Use of Pigovian taxes and subsidies for solving the market failure problem requires the acquisition of relevant information for calculating the appropriate magnitudes of them for aligning private and social costs; and these requirements can be formidable. Use of taxes and subsidies for externality problems also requires interventions in the functioning of markets by the government, implying a larger role for the state than is regarded desirable in some political doctrines. The use of liability rules on the other hand merely implies assignment or reassignment of property rights without any necessity of intervention in the functioning of free markets. This is one important reason for the significance of the Coase theorem for the market ideology.

6. LIABILITY RULES

One of the most fundamental problems of law is how to apportion harms which ensue interactions between injurers and victims. A rule which apportions the harm between the injurer and the victim is called a liability rule. Strict liability and no liability constitute two polar cases. Under the rule of strict liability the injurer is made liable regardless of anything. On the other hand, under no liability the liability invariably falls on the victim. When one person's activity results in harm for another person it would generally be the case that the probability and extent of harm can be reduced by care taken by one or both parties. A rule for assigning liabilities may take into account the actual care levels in relation to the due care levels of the parties. Suppose there is a legally prescribed due care level for a party. If the party's actual care level is greater than or equal to the due care level then the party is called nonnegligent; and if the actual care level is less than the due care level then the party is called negligent. Most of the liability rules which are used in practice make liability assignments dependant on negligence or otherwise of the parties. These include rules of negligence, negligence with the defence of contributory negligence, strict liability with the defence of contributory negligence, and comparative negligence.

Under the rule of negligence the injurer is liable if he is negligent and not liable if he is nonnegligent. If the rule is that of negligence with the defence of contributory negligence then the injurer is liable if he is negligent and the victim is nonnegligent; otherwise the victim is liable. The strict liability with the defence of contributory negligence is like the negligence rule with the roles of injurer and victim reversed. Comparative negligence is like the negligence rule with the difference that if both parties are negligent then the loss is apportioned between the two parties.

If one considers an interaction in which from a social point of view it is optimal for both parties to take positive amounts of care then it is clear that neither strict liability nor no liability would lead to socially optimal results. Consider for instance an interaction such that taking care by either party costs 1, if neither party takes care loss would be 10, if one of the two parties takes care then loss would be 8, and if both parties take care then loss would be 0. It is immediate that taking care by both parties is socially optimal as it minimizes social costs, sum of costs of care and loss. Under strict liability, the victim has no incentive to take care as he would be fully compensated for the loss, whatever it may be. Knowing that the victim would not take care the injurer has the option of not taking care and paying 10 to the victim or taking care at a cost of 1 and paying 8 to the victim. Clearly, he would choose the latter option. Thus, under the strict liability the social outcome which would result would involve total social costs of 9, while the minimum of social costs is 2. Similarly, the social outcome which would result under the rule of no liability would also not be total social costs minimizing.

Next, we consider the negligence rule in the context of our example. Suppose the legally specified care level for the injurer is fixed at the level which costs 1. If the injurer does not take care then he would be liable for 8 or 10 depending on whether the victim is or is not taking care. On the other hand, if the injurer takes care his only cost would be 1, the cost of taking care, as he would not be liable for the victim's loss. Clearly, the injurer would choose to take care. Given that the injurer is taking care, if the victim takes care then his loss would be 0 and if he does not take care then his loss would be 8. Thus, his costs would be 1 when he takes care, and 8 when he does not take care. Thus, a rational victim would take care. Thus, under the negligence rule the outcome which results as a consequence of strategies adopted by rational individuals is such that the social costs are minimized. In the context of the example being considered here, by similar arguments it can be shown that the rules of negligence with the defense of contributory negligence, strict liability with the defense of contributory negligence, and comparative negligence also result in the same outcome as the negligence rule. Thus, all these rules in the context of our example are able to induce both the parties to take socially appropriate levels of care.

The first formal analysis of important liability rules from the perspective of social cost minimization was done by Brown (1973) [Article 4 of this Reader]. In the context of his model, Brown showed that the rules of negligence, negligence with the defense of contributory negligence, and strict liability with the defense of contributory negligence all have the property of invariably inducing both the victim and the injurer to take levels of care which are appropriate from the perspective of minimization of total social costs. He also showed that the rules of strict liability and no liability do not possess this property.

Most results in the law and economics literature pertaining to liability rules have been obtained using frameworks very similar to the one used by Brown. One important assumption which is made in these models is that the due care levels which are specified by courts are appropriate from the perspective of minimization of total social costs. The results on the efficiency of liability rules crucially depend on this assumption. Any given liability rule might result in an inefficient outcome if the due care levels are not chosen properly.

For most of the liability rules which are commonly used the question of efficiency was settled by Brown's contribution. While in practice only a small number of liability rules are used, in theory there is an infinite number of them. In Jain and Singh (2002)[6] the totality of all liability rules are considered from the efficiency perspective and a general characterization of efficient liability rules is obtained. It is shown there that a liability rule is efficient for all applications if and only if it satisfies the condition of negligence liability. The condition of negligence liability requires that: (i) whenever the injurer is nonnegligent and the victim is negligent, the entire loss in case of occurrence of accident must be borne by the victim, and (ii) whenever

[6]Article 8 of this Reader.

the victim is nonnegligent and the injurer is negligent, the entire loss in case of occurrence of accident must be borne by the injurer.

In Brown's model as well as in the subsequent literature on the efficiency of liability rules it is assumed that the activity levels of both the parties are fixed. The reason for this assumption is that if activity levels can also be varied in addition to care levels then there is no liability rule which would invariably give rise to efficient outcomes as has been shown by Shavell.[7]

When there is only one injurer and only one victim, the problem of characterizing efficient liability rules has been completely solved as noted above. However, for the cases when there are multiple injurers or multiple victims only fragmentary results are available. The first results with multiple injurers and one victim were obtained by Landes and Posner (1980).[8] They showed that when there are multiple tortfeasors and one victim the rule of negligence gives efficient results in all cases; but strict liability with the defense of contributory negligence does not. This result is important because it shows that the results obtained in one-injurer-one-victim case do not all go over to the cases when there are multiple injurers. While both negligence and strict liability with the defense of contributory negligence are efficient in the one injurer and one victim case, in the multiple-injurer case only negligence rule turns out to be efficient.

There is a particular subclass of liability rules, namely simple liability rules, which is of some importance. A liability rule specifies the proportions in which the loss is to be apportioned among the parties involved in the interaction in case of harm taking place. In general, the division would depend not only on the negligence or otherwise of various parties, but also on the extent of negligence by the negligent parties. In the case of simple liability rules, however, the liability assignments depend only on the negligence or otherwise of parties. The extent of negligence is not a determining factor in the assignment of liabilities. The rules of strict liability, no liability, negligence, negligence with the defense of contributory negligence, and strict liability with the defense of contributory negligence are all simple liability rules. In fact, most liability rules used in practice belong to the subclass of simple liability rules. An important exception is the comparative negligence rule. For the class of simple liability rules the

[7]See Shavell (1980, 1987).

[8]See also Kornhauser and Revesz (1989) and Landes and Posner (1987).

set of efficient liability rules, when there are multiple injurers and one victim, has been characterized. In Jain and Kundu (2006), it is shown that a simple liability rule with multiple injurers and one victim is efficient if and only if it satisfies the condition of collective negligence liability. The condition of collective negligence liability requires that whenever some individuals are negligent, no nonnegligent individual bears any loss in case of occurrence of accident. The condition of collective negligence liability, in fact, can be shown to be sufficient for efficiency of any liability rule, not just any simple liability rule. However, the question whether the condition is necessary for the efficiency of any liability rule has not been settled. Thus, the problem of complete characterization of efficient liability rules when there are multiple injurers and one victim remains an open one.

The results on the efficiency of liability rules when there are multiple victims and one injurer are very different from the results obtained for multiple injurers and one victim. It can be shown that when there are multiple victims and one injurer there does not exist any liability rule which invariably gives rise to efficient outcomes.[9] From this it follows that when there are both multiple injurers and multiple victims, no liability rule can possibly be efficient for all applications.

7. LIABILITY RULES, PIGOVIAN TAXES, AND TRANSACTION COSTS

When transaction costs are prohibitively high then the liability rules satisfying the property of negligence liability invariably yield efficient outcomes; and the liability rules violating negligence liability condition sometimes give rise to inefficient outcomes. Rules of strict liability and no liability, both of which violate the negligence liability condition, therefore sometimes give rise to inefficient outcomes when transaction costs are prohibitively high. In the context of discussion on the Coase theorem, we saw that under the assumption of zero transactions costs strict liability and no liability both resulted in efficient outcomes in the context of examples considered there. In view of those examples it is fairly clear that when transaction costs are zero both strict liability and no liability will result in efficient outcomes. In fact, it can be shown that when transaction costs are zero every liability rule is efficient for all possible applications.

[9]See Jain (2007).

This very interesting property of liability rules is not shared by the Pigovian tax rule. In Brown and Holahan (1980) [Article 9 of this Reader], it is shown that an efficient outcome under the Pigovian tax rule is not robust with respect to decreases in transaction costs. An example may help illustrate the point. Suppose undertaking of an activity results in net gain to the injurer of 1.5 and net loss to the victim of 1. Under the Pigovian tax rule, when transaction costs are high, the injurer would find it advantageous to undertake the activity and pay tax equal to 1. However, when transaction costs are zero, both parties will be better-off if the activity is not undertaken and a sum greater than 0.5 and less than 1 is transferred to the injurer from the victim. From a social point of view undertaking of the activity is wealth-enhancing; and consequently the outcome achieved by the Pigovian tax rule when transaction costs are prohibitively high is efficient. This efficient outcome, however, ceases to be an equilibrium when transactions costs become sufficiently low.

In the standard tort model within which the question of efficiency of liability rules has been discussed, it is assumed that each party decides on its strategy in ignorance of the choice of strategy by the other party. Brown and Holahan (1980) have also discussed equilibria for certain rules when one party moves first and then the other party moves after observing the choice of the party moving first. They showed that under the rule of negligence with the defense of contributory negligence it makes no difference whether both parties move in ignorance of each other's strategy choice or one party moves after observing the choice of the other. The equilibrium is the same in each case. Under the Pigovian tax rule, however, it makes a difference whether the two parties choose their strategies in ignorance of each other or one party moves after observing the choice made by the other. Brown and Holahan show that when one of the parties chooses its strategy after observing the choice of strategy by the other the outcome that results under the Pigovian tax rule is not efficient.

Endres (1992) [Article 10 of this Reader] has considered the framework of one of the parties choosing its strategy after observing the choice of the other party in a different context. It was mentioned earlier that in the standard tort model within which the efficiency of liability rules has been analyzed it is assumed that due care levels which are specified by courts are appropriate from the perspective of minimization of social costs. If this assumption is not satisfied then there is no guarantee that the outcome would be efficient, no matter which liability rule is considered. Endres considers the rule of strict liability with the defense of contributory negligence. He shows that in case the due care level for the victim is set at a moderately inefficient level, then the equilibrium which is obtained when the injurer moves first and the victim after observing the injurer, is socially superior to the equilibrium which is obtained when both parties move in ignorance of each other's strategy choice.

8. COMMON LAW AND ECONOMIC EFFICIENCY

If we confine our attention to interactions between one victim and one injurer then in view of the results which have been obtained on the efficiency of liability rules discussed above, it would not be inaccurate to say that by and large the rules which are used in common law to apportion liability among the interacting parties involving torts are efficient. Similarly, economic analysis of contract law has shown that the most commonly used damage measure in cases of breach of contract, namely expectation damages, is an efficient damage measure. Expectation damages are defined to be that sum of money which if given to promisee will make him indifferent between contract performance on the one hand and contract breach combined with the award of expectation damages on the other. From a social point of view the net gain to the society of contract being performed is equal to the net gain to the promisee minus the cost of performing by the promisor. Economic efficiency requires that promisor should perform if net gain is positive and breach if net gain is negative. If damages which promisor is required to pay in case of breach of contract are set equal to expectation damages then net gain of promisor from performance will be the same as net gain for the society; and consequently promisor will be motivated by self-interest to take decisions which are appropriate from efficiency perspective. It is clear that if promisor has to pay in case of breach of contact a sum greater than expectation damages then he may find it advantageous to perform even when the net gain to the society is negative. This will happen if excess of cost of performance over net benefit to promisee is less than the amount by which actual damages exceed expectation damages. Similarly, if promisor has to pay in case of breach of contact a sum less than expectation damages then he may find it advantageous to breach even when the net gain to the society is positive.[10]

[10]For an introduction to some of the main results of economic analysis of contracts see Cooter (1985), Cooter and Ulen (2003), Miceli (1997), and Posner (2007), among others.

Apart from efficiency analysis of common law rules, questions relating to choice between liability and regulation have also been analyzed from efficiency perspective. On theoretical grounds Shavell (1984) [Article 13 of this Reader] identifies four determinants of choice between liability and regulation. These are: possibility of a difference in knowledge about risky activities as between private parties and a regulatory authority, lack of capability or otherwise of private parties of paying for the full magnitude of harm done, magnitude of probability that parties inflicting harm would not face the threat of suit for harm done, and magnitude of the administrative costs incurred by private parties and by the public in using the tort system or direct regulation. He finds that the choice between liability and regulation in practice is consistent with the objective of minimizing social costs. In fact, according to him, the general claim of theoretical consistency is further supported by considering the second-order choices society makes as to which aspects of an activity to regulate, given the initial choice that the activity is one that should be subject to regulation.

In view of the above and similar results pertaining to efficiency of laws, procedures and doctrines of common law, some scholars of law and economics have come to the conclusion that efficiency provides a unified explanation for the whole of common law. According to Posner, common law can best be understood by hypothesizing that judges decide cases so as to promote efficiency. Rubin (1977) [Article 3 of this Reader] provides an 'invisible hand' kind of explanation for the efficiency of common law. According to him, the efficiency of the common law, to the extent that it exists, can be explained by an evolutionary model—a model in which it is more likely that parties will litigate inefficient rules than efficient rules. In Rubin's model the evolutionary pressure comes from behavior of litigants, rather than that of judges. He found that when neither party is interested in establishing a precedent there is no incentive to litigate and hence no pressure on law to change; when only one party is interested in precedent then that party will litigate until a favorable decision is obtained; and when both parties have an ongoing interest, there will be pressure toward efficiency.

In connection with the thesis that efficiency provides an explanation for common law, it has been argued that the explanatory role of efficiency is independent of whether efficiency is considered a compelling or even an appropriate value in the context of law. A particularly cogent statement of this position is to be found in Landes and Posner (1987). This point regarding whether an idea constitutes an explanation for law being independent of acceptability or otherwise of the idea is certainly a valid one. The question that needs to be considered is whether on the basis of the results which have been obtained in the law and economics literature one would be justified in claiming that efficiency constitutes an explanation for the common law.

Suppose one is able to establish that: (i) all rules of a legal system satisfy a particular property; and (ii) these rules are the only ones which satisfy the property under consideration. In such a case it is immediate that the property in question constitutes a complete explanation of the rules of the legal system, as a rule is part of the legal system if and only if it satisfies the property in question. On the other hand, if all rules of the legal system satisfy the property but there are other rules, not part of the legal system, which also satisfy the property then it would not be accurate to say that the property constitutes a complete explanation of the rules of the legal system. In such a case the property in question constitutes only a partial explanation of the rules of the legal system. For a full explanation one would need to know the basis on which some rules satisfying the property are included in the legal system and the rest are excluded.

Consider, for instance, the results of economic analysis of tort law. While it has been shown in the law and economics literature that most of the liability rules used in practice are efficient, these rules are not the only ones which are efficient. For a correct and complete explanation one needs to know the basis on which the efficient rules used in practice can be isolated from the set of all efficient liability rules. In this connection it is pertinent to note that the efficient liability rules which are used in practice differ widely in terms of incidence of liability when both injurer and victim are nonnegligent. Although in most cases some version or the other of negligence rule is used, in some contexts the rule of strict liability with the defense of contributory negligence is used. Under the various negligence rules when both parties are nonnegligent the liability for loss falls on the victim; and under the rule of strict liability with the defense of contributory negligence, when both parties are nonnegligent the liability for loss falls on the injurer. Thus, from the perspective of providing compensation to the victims various efficient rules used in practice differ widely. A complete theory of tort law must of necessity provide an explanation as to why in some contexts efficient liability rules are used which put the entire liability on the victim when both parties are nonnegligent; and in some other contexts put the entire liability on the injurer when both parties are nonnegligent.

The results on the efficiency of liability rules are among the most important results of law and economics literature. These results have been obtained by formalizing the notion of negligence in a particular way. The notion of negligence is defined as failure to take at least the legally specified due care. Therefore, an individual is defined to be negligent if and only if his or her level of care is less than the due care level; and nonnegligent if and only if his or her level of care is greater than or equal to the due care level. It is also assumed that the courts specify the due care levels appropriately from the perspective of minimization of total social costs. This way of defining the notion of negligence has, however, been questioned, most consistently and cogently by Grady (1983, 1984, 1989),[11] on the ground that the courts do not determine negligence or otherwise of a party in this way. According to Grady, whether a party is adjudged by the courts to be negligent or not depends on whether the opposite party is able to show the existence of some cost-justified precaution which could have been taken but was not taken. That is to say, a party is considered to be negligent if and only if it can be shown that the party could have averted some harm by taking care which would have cost less than the loss due to harm. If negligence is determined on the basis of existence of a cost-justified untaken precaution then the results on the efficiency of liability rules change radically. It can be shown that with negligence defined as existence of a cost-justified untaken precaution, there is no liability rule which is efficient.[12] If it so turns out that the courts indeed determine negligence or otherwise of a party on the basis of existence or non-existence of a cost-justified untaken precaution, then it would seriously undermine even the thesis of efficiency as a partial explanation for tort law unless one is able to show that the rules used in practice are among the least inefficient of all rules. No such demonstration has been made; and it is highly unlikely that such a proposition holds. In view of the above, it appears that the results of law and economics literature pertaining to common law are not of a nature as to warrant the claim that efficiency provides a unified explanation for the whole of common law or even the lesser claim that efficiency is a major explanatory idea for the whole of common law.

9. LAW AND JUSTICE

Suppose one disregards the above points and accepts the claim that by and large common law is efficient. One question which then arises is

[11]Grady (1983) is included in this Reader as Article 5.
[12]See Jain (2006), Article 6 of this collection.

that of relationship between justice and efficiency, as justice is normally viewed as the predominant value embedded in legal institutions. If there are situations such that justice is possible only at the expense of efficiency then efficiency of law would have the implication of justice not being the predominant value embedded in law. Consequently, anyone who accepts the existence of this kind of situations and also believes that justice is the predominant value embedded in law can accept the thesis of efficiency of common law only in a moderate form and not in the form it is usually expressed. On the other hand, if both the propositions of efficiency of common law and justice as the predominant value in law hold then it must be the case that there are no situations such that justice is possible only by sacrificing efficiency. Non-existence of such situations would make justice non-conflictive with efficiency in the sense that in any situation ends of justice can always be met in a way consistent with efficiency.

Although assuming justice to be non-conflictive with efficiency suffices for consistency of efficiency of common law thesis with the proposition of predominance of justice in law, some law and economics scholars have taken a more extreme position. Posner, for instance, has taken the position that:

> A second meaning of 'justice', and the most common I would argue, is simply 'efficiency'. When we describe as 'unjust' convicting a person without a trial, taking property without just compensation, or failing to require a negligent automobile driver to answer in damages to the victim of his carelessness, we can be interpreted as meaning simply that the conduct or practice in question wastes resources. It is no surprise that in a world of scarce resources, waste is regarded as immoral.[13]

In conformity with the Coasian approach, Demsetz (1972) says that the expressions like blameworthy, at fault, etc. have no useful meanings in economic analysis other than as synonyms for the party who could have most easily avoided the harm due to costly interaction; and that regardless of whether the interaction problem involves damage, accident, or pollution, the qualitative relationship between the interacting parties is symmetrical.

Calabresi (1980), however, favors a moderate approach with respect to efficiency of law claims. He says:

> I find it hard to explain judicial behaviour in America simply in terms of wealth maximization. But I find it equally hard to explain it only in terms of ultimates or principles. In other words, my guess would be that courts do decide policies as well

[13]See Posner (1981). For an exposition and advocacy of the normative criterion of wealth maximization, see Posner (1985) [Article 2 of this Reader].

as principles, and perhaps more often the first than the second. The policies are based, and again I am guessing, on that mixture of efficiency and distribution that in the particular context is thought by the court to be instrumental toward justice and, in particular, does not violate any fairly precisely defined rights or veto points.

Whether that is an appropriate task for that institution is another matter and one that I wish to pass for now. My only thought on that at this point is that such a discussion works better in context than in the abstract. I find it difficult, in other words, to consider that issue apart from the capabilities of other institutions. For that reason, discussions of the role of courts that do not distinguish England from America (let alone both of these countries from Italy and France) seem to me prima facie suspect.

If justice is defined in the way as Coase, Demsetz, Posner, and most law and economics scholars do then the question of there being conflict between justice and efficiency does not arise. On the other hand, if one imputes to justice a meaning close to what is commonly held; then in most contexts if an activity by an individual harms another individual and if the latter individual is not compensated for the harm then such a situation would be regarded as unjust to the latter individual regardless of who might be in a position to eliminate harm at a lower cost. In this connection it is important to make a distinction which is often overlooked in the economic analysis of law. One may want to resolve a conflict between justice and efficiency in favour of efficiency because one may consider efficiency to be more important than justice. But such a resolution does not imply that justice and efficiency are one and the same or that they are not independent values. The position taken by Coase, Demsetz, Posner, and others not only gives primacy to efficiency but also rules out a conflict between efficiency and justice by interpreting justice in a way invariably consistent with the requirements of efficiency. The intuitive notion of justice for most people is such that they would ordinarily find situations of uncompensated harms caused by activities undertaken by individuals other than the victims as unjust, although they might find them to be acceptable on other considerations. But for those who subscribe to the idea of basic rights, such acceptance is not possible when there is a conflict between efficiency and human rights of a fundamental nature.

10. EFFICIENCY AND BASIC RIGHTS

If one considers an activity with negative externalities but in the aggregate socially beneficial then under the wealth-maximization criterion undertaking of the activity would be socially better than not undertaking it. If individuals on whom the costs of negative externalities fall are not compensated for harm then ordinarily as mentioned above it would for most people be a case of injustice as these individuals are made to bear the costs of harm without any fault of theirs. One may, however, condone it on the ground that the situation under discussion involves a trade-off between fairness considerations on the one hand and wealth considerations on the other and that in social contexts such trade-offs are inevitable. In the context of trade-offs between values, it is important to remember that by their very nature basic rights do not permit any trade-offs. In Ronald Dworkin's (1977) terminology they are trumps. Willingness to make a trade-off between wealth and fairness in some situations does not imply willingness to make a trade-off between wealth and basic rights. One may countenance the losses of those suffering negative externalities for the sake of much bigger gains of those undertaking the activity if the losses are merely material losses without any serious consequences for those suffering harm. However, if those suffering harm have a precarious existence, bordering on starvation, where the harm on account of negative externalities can make a difference regarding survival, then obviously the situation is radically different and not at all appropriate for making any trade-off. One cannot make a recommendation for the activity to be undertaken in such a scenario.

The above makes it clear that in the absence of compensation the unmitigated pursuit of economic efficiency in a context like the contemporary context where large numbers of people live a marginal existence and where economic activities have varied and multifarious negative externalities can seriously conflict with basic rights. If compensation is paid to the victims of negative externalities then it might seem that there cannot possibly be any conflict between basic rights and efficiency. While the possibility that there might not be any conflict between basic rights and efficiency when compensation is paid to the victims certainly exists, there is an important reason why even with full compensation for victims the conflict may still be there.

Under the rule of strict liability the victim is always fully compensated. If the optimal amount of care which should be taken by the victim from the perspective of wealth- maximization is zero then the rule of strict liability is an efficient rule; but not in general. In the context of interactions involving negative externalities, efficiency in the sense of wealth-maximization generally requires that care be taken by both potential injurers and potential victims for minimizing social costs. To ensure that both the victim and the injurer involved in the interaction take socially optimal levels of care the rule apportioning liability between them must satisfy the negligence liability condition. Now, if an efficient liability rule is used so that every individual is induced to take socially optimal level of care then in case no harm materializes the victim would end up paying the cost of care; and in case the harm materializes then the victim would end up paying at least the cost of care. Under the various negligence rules which are the most common tort rules the victims would end up paying for their losses as well as for the costs of care. Thus, it is clear that efficiency at the very least requires from the victims socially efficient levels of care. If the victims in question are living a precarious existence, then the efficiency requirements would conflict with basic rights in an essential way.

11. LIBERTY AND DEMOCRACY

The notion of efficiency pertains to outcomes. In this respect, not all values are like efficiency. Liberty, for instance, is primarily a procedural value. There is a close relationship between liberty on the one hand and the core ideas of basic rights, autonomy, and democracy on the other. They all seem to emanate from the normative principle that individuals as well as collectives have a fundamental and inalienable right to determine their own destinies. If certain things concern only a particular individual and no one else then the individual concerned must have the final say with respect to those things; and if certain things concern only a particular collective, whether the collective is the whole of the society or only a part of it, and no one else, then the collective in question must have the ultimate decision-making power pertaining to those things. Once this normative principle is accepted, all the fundamental elements of democratic governance including those of human rights, autonomy, periodic elections, etc. can be seen to be constituting an organic whole, rather than merely a collection of unconnected elements. As Sen (1999) [Article 16 of this Reader] points out, it is important not to equate democracy with majority rule as it consists of much more than merely voting and respecting election results. According to him, for a system of governance to qualify as democracy, among other things, the protection of liberties and freedoms, respect for legal entitlements, and the guaranteeing of free discussion and uncensored distribution of news and fair comment would be required.

Democracy and human rights are of intrinsic value. The significance of what free individuals and collectives decide lies in the fact of free choice itself; what decisions are taken by them being irrelevant from this perspective. There is no presumption that if individuals and collectives are free then their decisions will be 'good' from some particular perspective. But it so turns out that democracy and basic rights are not without significant instrumental value. Sen (1999) argues that political and civil rights play a positive role in prevention of economic and social disasters. As an example, he mentions the remarkable fact that no substantial famine has ever occurred in any independent and democratic country with a relatively free press.[14] Furthermore, Sen argues that there is no convincing general evidence that authoritarian governance and the suppression of political and civil rights are really beneficial to economic development.

We have already seen that efficiency considerations can conflict with basic rights. Single-minded pursuit of efficiency can be inimical to democratic governance as well. Free and global markets together with a minimal State are widely regarded as conducive to efficiency. These, however, can be detrimental to democracy in several ways. In a democratic setup if a government is not able to deliver one can reasonably expect it to be voted out of power and replaced by a government which is expected to be more responsive to what the people want. But, if the State follows a policy of non-intervention in the economic domain and if what the people want requires some action in the economic domain then regardless of how they vote a change in the situation cannot be brought about. Inability of elected governments to bring about any meaningful and significant change can only undermine the people's belief in the efficacy of the democratic system. If the state of affairs cannot be changed regardless of how the electors vote, then one cannot expect participation in elections to remain unaffected. The futility of election outcomes gets aggravated if the States, in addition to their commitment to non-intervention in markets, also bind themselves in myriad ways through multilateral treaties to act or not to to act in certain ways, for the protection of the institutional structure dominated by the market mechanism. Basu (2001) [Article 11 of this Reader] points out that one concomitant of globalization and technological progress is that it has a natural corrosive effect on global democracy; as a consequence of this phenomenon, even if individual countries move in the direction of democracy the aggregate of global democracy is likely to decrease.

[14]See also Drèze and Sen (1987).

There is one aspect of becoming a party to a multilateral treaty which requires careful consideration from the perspective of democratic governance. If one takes the premise of sovereignty of people seriously then, when people elect their representatives they must be authorizing them to take decisions on their behalf only for a specified period and only in certain specified domains. The restriction to a specified period and to specified domains is crucial for democratic governance. It would, for instance, be completely illegitimate for the elected representatives to claim that they have the mandate to curtail basic rights or to indefinitely postpone the holding of elections. It is one thing to bind a nation through a peace treaty; but quite another through a treaty affecting livelihoods and rights of millions of people, and that too for an indefinite period involving transference of the decision-making powers of the people to organizations which the people have not elected and would not be able to elect in the future. The system of governance which is market-centred on the one hand, and dominated by rules and regulations of unelected international organizations on the other, is unlikely to be consistent with any meaningful conception of democratic governance.

12. EXPRESSIVE FUNCTION OF LAW

As values embodied in subsets of laws are of various types, some like efficiency being exclusively consequentialist in nature while some others like justice and liberty being consequentialist as well as procedural; similarly law as a whole apart from outcome-oriented purposes also has an expressive function.[15] A rule may be unacceptable because of what it expresses and not because of what it results in. For instance, if a law specifies as punishment a monetary fine for one group of people and imprisonment for another group of people for the same crime, most people would have no hesitation in terming the law as unjust. In this connection it is important to note that the existence of a rule which specifies unequal treatment for different sets of people does not necessarily imply existence of legal cases involving unequal treatment. This can happen for any number of reasons. Suppose for instance, the punishment of imprisonment is so harsh compared to the likely benefits of the activity proscribed by the legal rule in question that it proves to be an absolute deterrent;

[15] See Sunstein (1994) [Article 15 in this Reader] on this.

and consequently the legal rule is violated by no person belonging to the category for which imprisonment is the punishment for transgressing the provisions of the rule. Thus, all violators would be from the category of those for whom the punishment is levying of a fine. Thus, as far as the actual outcome is concerned all violators of the rule would have been treated equally. In this example it is evident that the absence of cases with unequal treatment would not make the rule in question any less unjust. For the purpose of determining which values are expressed by legal rules the textual analysis of a body of laws would have to look at not only individual rules, subsets of rules and the entire set of rules but also their interrelationships. For instance, each of the two legal rules dealing with transgressions of similar gravity taken singly may be fine; but together may be objectionable on the ground of disproportionate punishments for crimes of more or less similar magnitude.

13. STANDARDS, RULES AND, THE RULE OF LAW

In law in some contexts rules are used; and there are contexts in which standards are used. A rule specifies in advance whether a particular action is violative of law. In the case of standards, authority is delegated to a court to determine after the action has been performed to decide whether it is to be penalized. In the law and economics literature the question of when to go in for rules and when to opt for standards has been analyzed from efficiency perspective. Thus, the optimal form of law depends on the social costs involved. The actual mix of rules and standards might depend on the calculus of benefits and costs for the legislators concerned. For instance, they might go in for standards when the subject of the law is controversial, thus requiring courts to absorb the political costs of taking the wrong position. One might, therefore, expect uncontroversial laws like traffic regulations to appear as rules and controversial laws like affirmative action to appear as standards.[16]

Eric Posner (Article 14 of this Reader) argues that use of standards is not conducive to the rule of law. In a particular context it may turn out that use of standards involves lower social costs compared to use of rules; but he is of the opinion that one should still opt for rules over standards as such a choice is more in accordance with the political ideal of the rule of law. The rule of law requires that law should inflict

[16]See Kaplow (1992) and Posner (1997).

punishment only on people who engage in actions proscribed by that law, and not on people who engage in actions that the authorities conclude are undesirable after the fact. Because the rule of law implies a preference for identification of proscribed actions in advance, it implies a preference for rules over standards. He also argues that the use of standards, unlike the use of rules, has the potential of being misused by the State to bring about conformist behaviour without the recourse of explicit directives. Thus, according to Eric Posner, there can be a serious conflict between the goals of efficiency and the rule of law.

14. INDIVIDUAL VALUES, SOCIAL VALUES, AND INSTITUTIONS

We have seen above that there is a multiplicity of values which are relevant in the context of law. Although some law and economics scholars believe that all values embodied in law can be derived from the principle of wealth maximization,[17] not everyone shares this extreme viewpoint. In view of the conflict between basic rights, democracy, and the rule of law on the one hand, and efficiency on the other, under fairly general and plausible circumstances it seems reasonably clear that most of the fundamental societal values not only cannot be derived from the principle of wealth maximization but that they are incommensurable with efficiency. Sunstein (1994) puts it as follows: '... we value things in different ways; that is to say, we value things not only in terms of intensity, but in qualitatively distinct ways. It is not simply the case that some things are valued more; it is also the case that some things are valued differently from others'.

Sunstein, in fact, goes further and says that, in general, human goods are not commensurable. That is to say, there is no available metric along which various goods which are important to human beings can be aligned. In his view any effort to come up with a metric, like utility or dollars, while nominally designed to aid human reasoning actually makes it worse. He

[17]Richard Posner is one of the foremost exponents of this viewpoint. In his *Economics of Justice,* he says:

> Most of the conventional pieties—keeping promises, telling the truth, and the like—can also be derived from the wealth-maximization principle. Adherence to these virtues facilitates transactions and so promotes trade and hence wealth by reducing the costs of policing markets through self-protection, detailed contracts, litigation, and so on. Even altruism (benevolence) is an economizing principle, because it can be a substitute for costly market and legal processes.

applies the idea of incommensurability of goods to provide a rationale for the remedy of specific performance in case of breach of contract. Under specific performance the promisee is entitled to what was contracted. Earlier, we saw that expectation damages invariably induce the promisor to take socially correct decisions. Specific performance, however, unlike expectation damages, can lead to inefficient decisions. If the cost of performance is greater than the net gain to the promisee then under the wealth-maximization criterion breach is superior to performance. Under specific performance there would, however, be performance rather than breach. Sunstein argues that once it is recognized that the promisee is entitled not to something that is valued as much as the thing for which he or she contracted but is entitled to something that is valued in the same way as the thing for which he or she contracted, specific performance seems quite appropriate.

If one accepts the thesis of incommensurability of the fundamental societal values with efficiency then in view of the fact that efficiency conflicts with these basic values in an essential way it follows that advocacy of having only efficient rules in law or any other institution is tantamount to repudiation of all other values in the context of that institution. The viewpoint that only economic efficiency considerations are relevant and that all other values are either irrelevant or non-conflictive with efficiency in the context of legal and other social institutions is implicit in Coase's (1960) seminal paper 'The Problem of Social Cost', widely regarded as one of the two contributions responsible for the emergence of economic analysis of law.[18] Coase approaches the problem from a normative perspective. The following passage from the paper illustrates the point:

> To give another example, Professor George J. Stigler instances the contamination of a stream. If we assume that the harmful effect of the pollution is that it kills the fish, the question to be decided is: is the value of the fish lost greater or less than the value of the product which the contamination of the stream makes possible.

The point comes out even more clearly in the concluding paragraph of the paper:

> It would clearly be desirable if the only actions performed were those in which what was gained was worth more than what was lost. But in choosing between social arrangements within the context of which individual decisions are made, we have to bear in mind that a change in the existing system which will lead to an improvement

[18]The other contribution is Calabresi (1961).

in some decisions may well lead to a worsening of others. Furthermore we have to take into account the costs involved in operating the various social arrangements (whether it be the working of a market or of a government department), as well as the costs involved in moving to a new system. In devising and choosing between social arrangements we should have regard for the total effect. This, above all, is the change in approach which I am advocating.

In law and economics by and large legal rules are analyzed one at a time. The consequences of a particular rule cannot be entirely determined without specifying the institutional structure in which it is embedded. Depending on the context, a rule can have important unintended consequences. This point comes out very clearly in the context of rules and laws relating to child labor. Basu (2001) argues that an abrupt halt to child labor can lead to children falling victim to acute poverty and hunger. Humphries (2003) [Paper 12 of this Reader] attributes the boom in child labor in Britain during the late 18th and early 19th centuries to an unintended consequence of policies such as legislation weakening labor organization (the Combination Acts, the repeal of the Statute of Artificers) and the miserly treatment of the wives and children of soldiers.

The economic analysis of law, in addition to being solely preoccupied with efficiency, has some other serious limitations. The most important of these limitations is that individual values and preferences are taken to be independent of the social institutions under study. The articulation of individual preferences and values takes place through the medium of social institutions. The choice of social institution is quite important from the perspective of individual preferences and values as no institution can articulate all kinds of preferences and values. A particular institution may be able to articulate one kind of individual values and preferences extremely well; and may not be able to articulate another kind of individual preferences and values at all or only be able to articulate them poorly. Basu (2001) makes this point in relation to the use of market mechanism for articulating preferences which disapprove of child labor. He says that:

> ... punishments dispensed through informal social sanctions often turn out to be witch-hunts causing disproportionate pain to some and too little pain to others. Not surprisingly, when it comes to justice, most societies prefer to use a centralized, non-democratic system, namely, that of the courts and the judiciary. The free market is not the right instrument for passing moral judgements.

This of course means that in general different institutions are required for articulation of different kinds of individual preferences and values.

This characteristic has an important implication for actions undertaken by rational individuals. If individuals are deciding on their actions within the framework of responsive institutions then they can be expected to act in accordance with their values and preferences. On the other hand, if the institutions are by and large non-responsive with respect to certain preferences and values, rational individuals would find little point in undertaking actions in accordance with those preferences and values.

Which social values are realized under a particular institution depends partly on the institution and partly on the individual preferences and values. For a given configuration of individual values and preferences, which social values would be realized depends on the institution through which they are mediated. The same individual preferences and values in general would give rise to different social values under different institutions. Likewise, under a given institution, different configurations of individual preferences and values in general would result in very different social values.

As the actual character of a social institution partly depends on individual preferences and values, there can easily be a divergence between the social values embodied in the institution and the values for the attainment of which the institution in question is supposed to exist. From this it follows that the appropriateness of individual preferences and values is crucial for the attainment of social values for which the institutions are created. In the context of law the importance of this point cannot be overemphasized. The legal institutions perform quite differently when individuals by and large have internalized the values expressed through those institutions from when they have not done so.

Social institutions in turn have a profound influence on individuals in relation to formation of preferences and values. If a social institution is of great importance in the social order, the values that the institution embodies are bound to have significance for individual values and preferences. Thus we see that there is a symbiotic relationship between institutions on the one hand and individual values and preferences on the other. The nature of an institution is partly determined by individual preferences and values. Institutions on the other hand impact individual preferences and values in two different ways. Institutions by filtering in some preferences and values and filtering out the others determine which preferences and values would be articulated and which would not be. The preferences and values which are filtered out and consequently do not find articulation are bound to become insignificant sooner or later, if not disappear altogether. Second, the formation of individual values and preferences themselves is profoundly affected by the values embodied in the institutions, particularly those which are dominant.

In view of the fact that individual preferences and values and social values impact on each other, in the context of any institutional structure two very important questions arise: (i) Does the institutional structure admit of an equilibrium of individual and social values; and are these values consistent with a sustainable social structure? (ii) If there is an equilibrium then what is the extent of divergence under it between the realized social values and the values for the attainment of which the institutional structure exists in the first place? A comprehensive theory of law must contend with these questions.

In conclusion, it seems that an approach to studying law and other institutions of governance which recognizes that there is a multiplicity of values and that values have their domains of application, not necessarily disjoint, might be more fruitful than the law and economics approach, with its focus on a single normative criterion. It is possible, indeed likely, that most values have their domains of pre-eminence. Once the existence of a multiplicity of independent values is recognized, it is reasonable to suppose that legal institutions, which deal with many and varied aspects of social behaviour, would have embedded in them a multiplicity of values.

REFERENCES

Arrow, Kenneth J. (1963), *Social Choice and Individual Values*, 2nd edn, New York: Wiley.

Basu, Kaushik (2001), 'Compacts, Conventions, and Codes: Initiatives for Higher International Labor Standards', *Cornell International Law Journal*, 34, 487–500.

Brown, John Prather (1973),'Toward an Economic Theory of Liability', *Journal of Legal Studies*, 2, 323–350.

Brown, John Prather and William L. Holahan (1980), 'Taxes and Legal Rules for the Control of Externalities When There Are Strategic Responses', *Journal of Legal Studies*, 9, 165–178.

Calabresi, Guido (1961), 'Some Thoughts on Risk Distribution and the Law of Torts', *Yale Law Journal*, 70, 499–553.

——(1980), 'About Law and Economics: A Letter to Ronald Dworkin', *Hofstra Law Review*, 8, 553–562.

Coase, R.H. (1960), 'The Problem of Social Cost', *Journal of Law and Economics*, 3, 1–44.

Cooter, Robert D. (1985), 'Unity in Torts, Contracts and Property: The Model of Precaution', *California Law Review*, 73, 1–51.

Cooter, Robert D. and Thomas S. Ulen (2003), *Law and Economics*, 4th edn., New York: Addison-Wesley.
Demsetz, Harold (1972), 'When Does the Rule of Liability Matter?', *Journal of Legal Studies*, 1, 13–28.
Drèze, Jean and Amartya K. Sen (1987), *Hunger and Public Action*, Oxford: Clarendon Press.
Dworkin, R. (1977), *Taking Rights Seriously*, Cambridge (MA): Harvard University Press.
Endres, Alfred (1992), 'Strategic Behavior under Tort Law', *International Review of Law and Economics*, 12, 377–80.
Grady, Mark F. (1983), 'A New Positive Economic Theory of Negligence', *Yale Law Journal*, 92, 799–829.
——(1984), 'Proximate Cause and the Law of Negligence', *Iowa Law Review*, 69, 363–449.
——(1989), 'Untaken Precautions', *Journal of Legal Studies*, 18, 139–156.
Humphries, Jane (2003), 'Child Labor: Lessons from the Historical Experience of Today's Industrial Economies', *The World Bank Economic Review*, 17, 175–196.
Jain, Satish K. (2006), 'Efficiency of Liability Rules: A Reconsideration', *Journal of International Trade & Economic Development*, 15, 359–373.
—— (2009), 'Efficiency of Liability Rules with Multiple Victims', *Pacific Economic Review*, 14, 119–34.
Jain, Satish K. and Rajendra P. Kundu, (2006), 'Characterization of Efficient Simple Liability Rules with Multiple Tortfeasors', *International Review of Law and Economics*, 26, 410–427.
Jain, Satish K. and Ram Singh (2002), 'Efficient Liability Rules: Complete Characterization', *Journal of Economics (Zeitschrift für Nationalökonomie)*, 75, 105–124.
Kaldor, Nicholas (1939), 'Welfare Propositions of Economics and Interpersonal Comparisons of Utility', *Economic Journal*, 49, 549–52.
Kaplow, Louis (1992), 'Rules Versus Standards: An Economic Analysis', *Duke Law Journal*, 42, 557–629.
Kornhauser, Lewis A. and Richard L. Revesz, (1989), 'Sharing Damages Among Multiple Tortfeasors', *Yale Law Journal*, 98, 831–884.
Landes, William M. and Richard A. Posner (1980), 'Joint and Multiple Tortfeasors: An Economic Analysis', *Journal of Legal Studies*, 9, 517–556.
—— (1987), *The Economic Structure of Tort Law*, Cambridge (MA): Harvard University Press.
Miceli, Thomas J. (1997), *Economics of the Law: Torts, Contracts, Property, Litigation*, Oxford: Oxford University Press.
Patterson, Dennis (1999), *A Companion to Philosophy of Law and Legal Theory*, Oxford: Blackwell.
Polinsky, Mitchell A. (1989), *An Introduction to Law and Economics*, 2nd edn., Boston: Little, Brown and Company.

Posner, Eric A. (1997), Standards, Rules, and Social Norms, *Harvard Journal of Law and Public Policy*, 21, 101–117.
Posner, Richard A. (1981), *The Economics of Justice*, Cambridge (MA): Harvard University Press.
—— (1985), 'Wealth Maximization Revisited', *Notre Dame Journal of Law, Ethics and Public Policy*, 2, 85–105.
—— (2007), *Economic Analysis of Law*, (7th edn.), New York: Wolters Kluwer Law & Business.
Rubin, Paul H. (1977), 'Why is the Common Law Efficient? *Journal of Legal Studies*, 6, 51–63.
Scitovsky, Tibor (1941), 'A Note on Welfare Propositions in Economics', *Review of Economic Studies*, 9, 77–88.
Sen, Amartya K. (1970), *Collective Choice and Social Welfare*, San Francisco: Holden-Day.
—— (1999), 'Democracy as a Universal Value', *Journal of Democracy*, 10, 3–17.
Shavell, Steven (1980), 'Strict Liability versus Negligence', *Journal of Legal Studies*, 9, 1–25.
—— (1984), 'Liability for Harm versus Regulation of Safety', *Journal of Legal Studies*, 13, 357–374.
—— (1987), *Economic Analysis of Accident Law*, Cambridge (MA): Harvard University Press.
Sunstein, Cass R. (1994), 'Conflicting Values in Law', *Fordham Law Review*, 62, 1661–1673.

Perspectives on Efficiency of Common Law

2

Wealth Maximization Revisited†

*Richard A. Posner**

Some years ago, I published an article in which I argued that "wealth maximization" provides an ethically attractive norm for social and political choices, such as those made by courts asked to determine whether negligence or strict liability should be the rule for deciding whether an injurer must compensate his victim.[1] This article gave rise to a flurry of criticisms,[2] to which I replied[3]—without convincing many of the critics.[4] I am pleased to have this opportunity to reconsider my position. Perhaps as a result of my new perspective as a judge, I find myself slightly more sympathetic to some of the criticisms than I once was—but only slightly more.

†Originally published as "Wealth Maximization Revisited", 1985, *Notre Dame Journal of Law, Ethics and Public Policy*, Vol. 2, pp. 85–105.

*This is the revised text of a lecture given at the Thomas J. White Center on Law & Government at Notre Dame Law School on September 5, 1985. I am grateful to Gary Becker, Jules Coleman, Frank Easterbrook, Steven Shavell, George Stigler, David Strauss, and Cass Sunstein for helpful comments on a previous draft. The reader is asked to grant the usual indulgences in reading a paper originally intended for oral delivery.

[1]Posner, *Utilitarianism, Economics, and Legal Theory*, 8 J. Legal Stud. 103 (1979), which appears in slightly different form in R. Posner, *The Economics of Justice* Ch.3 (1981).

[2]*See*, e.g., Coleman, *Efficiency, Utility and Wealth Maximization,* 8 Hofstra L. Rev. 509 (1980); Dworkin, *Is Wealth a Value?,* 9 J. Legal Stud. 191 (1980); Kronman, *Wealth Maximization as a Normative Principle,* 9 J. Legal Stud. 227 (1980); Weinrib, *Utilitarianism Economics, and Legal Theory*, 30 U. Toronto L.J. 307 (1980).

[3]*See* R. Posner, *supra* note 1, ch. 4; Posner, *A Reply to Some Recent Criticisms of the Economic Theory of the Common Law*, 9 Hofstra L. Rev. 775, 786–94 (1981).

[4]*See*, e.g., N. Mercuro and T. Ryan, *Law, Economics and Public Policy* 130–37 (1984); Coleman, *The Normative Basis of Economic Analysis: A Critical Review of Richards Posner's* The Economics of Justice (Book Review), 34 Stan. L. Rev. 1105 (1982).

I. WHAT IS WEALTH MAXIMIZATION AND WHERE DOES IT COME FROM?

To most people who are not economists, the word "wealth" suggests money. But to an economist, it refers to weighting preferences for the things that people want, either by willingness to pay for a thing, if you do not own it, or by unwillingness to part with it voluntarily, if you do own it. So, if I am unwilling to part with my house for less than $100,000, and no one is willing to pay more than $90,000 for it, society's wealth is $10,000 greater than it would be if the house were taken from me and given to the highest bidder (I am not a bidder, because I am the owner). This would be so even if I were paid $100,000 for the house (which would require taxation, since no one will voluntarily pay $100,000 for it). I would be no wealthier than before, and the rest of the community would have $100,000 less, incompletely offset by a house worth only $90,000 to its new owner.

Now suppose that I want a car and would pay $10,000 for it, and the present owner would sell it for $5,000. Society's wealth will be increased if I am allowed to buy the car from him for any amount between $5,000 and $10,000 (ignore selling costs). Suppose the price is $7,500. After the transaction I will have $2,500 plus a car worth $10,000 to me. I will thus have total wealth (ignoring the house and any other wealth I have) of $12,500, and he $7,500, for a total of $20,000, whereas before the transaction our combined wealth was only $15,000.

Granted, both examples ignore a fundamental problem—how it is that I initially came to have the house, and he the car. I shall come back to that problem, but for now, I just want to explain what wealth means.

Wealth is not limited to market commodities such as houses and cars. As a matter of fact, the value of houses and cars is not always reducible to market values. The house I value at $100,000 might not be valued at more than $90,000 by anyone else because it has sentimental associations for me, and likewise with the car. In this case, the real value would exceed market value. Or, I might work for a lower salary than I could make, simply because I liked the work I did for that lower salary so much; that would mean that I derived part of my wealth from working and part from the pecuniary income that I earned by working.

These examples help to show that money, to an economist, is not wealth, but just a measure of one's entitlement to houses, cars, rewarding work, leisure, privacy, and countless other "things" that constitute a person's wealth; everyone's wealth added together constitutes the nation's wealth. The wealth of a nation is the present value of the flow of benefits, measured as suggested above, from the consumption of goods and services, tangible and intangible, by its people. Monetary measures of social income or wealth[5] such as Gross National Product or National Income are inadequate and inaccurate measures of a nation's wealth. When I used money as a component of wealth earlier, it was just a shorthand term for the things that money can buy.

The economist uses the concept of income or wealth in this broad sense all the time, but calls it "utility," meaning, however, something quite different from what utilitarian philosophers mean. To compound the confusion, the economist uses the word "wealth" to mean something different from the economic concept of "utility." To the economist, "utility" differs from "wealth" because utility is adjusted for people's preference for risk or (more commonly) aversion to risk, in the sense of the variance of possible outcomes of an uncertain event. If you were given gratis a fifty percent chance of winning ten dollars (and an equal chance of winning nothing), your "wealth" (in the narrow economic sense) would rise by five dollars, which is the expected utility of the chance to someone who is risk neutral. But if you were risk averse, the increment in your expected utility would be less than five dollars, so you would sell the ticket to someone less risk averse, or risk neutral, or risk preferring, if you could, and you would thereby increase your utility. If you were risk preferring, the chance would be worth more than five dollars to you. Thus "wealth," in my sense, is a synonym for expected utility. Bear in mind that wealth is a function of willingness to pay (or unwillingness to part with, but for present purposes, the difference is unimportant). If you will pay more for the fifty percent chance than its certain equivalent (because you are a risk preferrer), then it is worth more to you; its expected utility determines your willingness to pay, and hence describes the effect of the chance on your wealth. For example, if you would pay six dollars for the chance, the gift of it would increase your wealth by six dollars.

Wealth, in my sense, equates to utility in the economic sense but is distinct from the utilitarian concept of utility as happiness, however broadly (or narrowly) happiness is defined, though wealth and happiness are positively correlated. (Ask anyone whether he or she would turn

[5]"Income" is a flow concept, "wealth" the corresponding stock concept. The important thing to bear in mind is that income (and therefore wealth, which is the discounted present value of anticipated future income) refers to real rather than monetary phenomena—to housing or transportation services or leisure, not to wages or dividends.

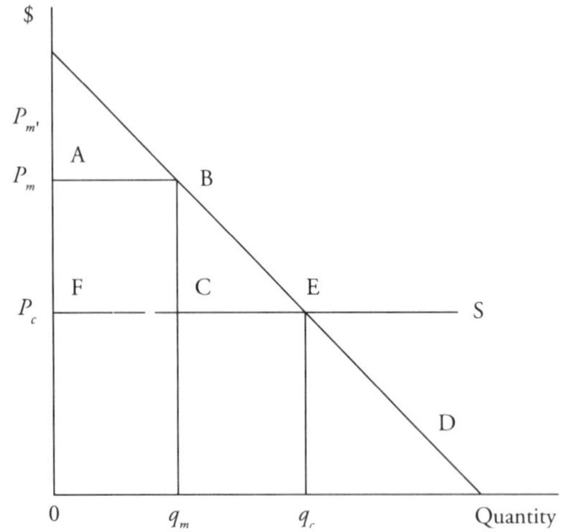

Figure 1

down an unconditional gift of money!) I might be made deliriously happy by being given a ticket to a Notre Dame football game, but if I am outbid by another football fan, it means that wealth maximization requires that I not get the ticket, even though the person who outbids me might derive less pleasure from the game than I would have derived. The refusal of modern economists to make "interpersonal comparisons of utility" means in effect that they use wealth rather than happiness as the criterion for an efficient allocation of resources.

People find it easier to picture wealth maximization in actual transactions than in potential transactions, but one of the most important uses of the concept is in connection with potential transactions. I refer to the analysis of the welfare loss (in my terminology, the wealth loss) caused by monopoly. In Figure 1, the monopolist, in order to increase his profits over the competitive (= zero) level, reduces his output to q_m, at which level the market-clearing price is p_m. Those customers who continue to buy the product at its new, monopoly price incur a wealth loss measured by the rectangle ABCF; but their loss is the monopolist's gain, so there is a wash. The net social loss from monopoly is the triangle BEC. This is the consumer surplus that is lost by those who are deflected to substitute products by the higher price, but that is not transformed into producer surplus (profit). In what sense is it a loss? At the competitive price and output, these consumers (all but the last, represented by the intersection of D and S, at point E) would have been willing to pay more for the product than they were charged. In other words, the product increased their wealth by more than the purchase price—as is still true of those consumers who continue to buy the product at its current price. The idea of consumer (and producer) surplus, a legacy of the great English economist Alfred Marshall, shows that wealth is not money. This is the crucial insight in making wealth maximization a standard of social welfare.

The welfare loss of monopoly is the least controversial, though no longer the only, ground on which economists denounce monopoly.[6] This denunciation illustrates the normative use of the concept of wealth maximization,[7] and my position in this paper amounts to nothing more than expanding the normative domain of the concept. If you think back to the house and car examples with which I began, you will realize that they were both cases where the objective was to maximize surplus value—the value that measures what people are willing to pay (or what they demand) over and above market price, the price paid by the marginal buyer (P'_m in Figure 1).

Anyone who is inclined to say that wealth is not a value in an ethical sense should ask himself whether he agrees that monopolies and cartels are bad because they lead to a reduction in the value of output. If he agrees with this traditional economic criticism, then he believes that wealth is a social, ethical value—whether he knows it or not. He also believes that interpersonal comparisons of wealth are possible—that is, that it is possible to compare the loss of surplus to the consumer with the gain to the monopolist. It is by such comparisons that one can determine whether a given transaction, policy or institution is wealth maximizing. Of course, the information costs may be formidable, but there is no objection in principle to measuring aggregate wealth.

II. CRITICISMS

The most basic criticism of an ethic of wealth maximization is one that I share: that you cannot deduce "ought" from "is"; you cannot prove, deductively or inductively, that social decisions ought to conform

[6] *See*, e.g., J. Hirshleifer, *Price Theory and Applications* 249–52 (1984).

[7] And makes quite extraordinary the assertion that wealth maximization requires monopoly because monopoly leads to higher prices. See N. Mercuro and T. Ryan, *supra* note 4, at 132; Kornhauser, *A Guide to the Perplexed Claims of Efficiency in the Law*, 8 Hofstra L. Rev. 591, 596–97 (1980); Coleman, *supra* note 2, at 523–24. This is known in the economic literature as the Earl of Lauderdale's fallacy. *See* G. Stigler, *The Theory of Price* 196–97 (third edition 1966).

to some ethical theory. The lack of provability imparts a pervasive uncertainty to ethical debates; it is not clear what it means to prevail in an ethical argument. Ethical arguments do not convince doubters but rather provide rationalizations for ethical positions taken on emotional grounds. Indeed, more ethical arguments have been won on the battlefield than in the lecture hall; and if the fascist powers had won World War II, the dominant ethical views in this society would probably be different today. Perhaps—speaking descriptively and in the long run—might is responsible for most opinions of what is right.

My goal is therefore quite modest. I do not seek to "convert" anyone to wealth maximization. I merely want to persuade you that it is a reasonable, though not a demonstrably or a universally correct, ethic (I shall explain later why my goal is so limited). But to do this I shall have to consider the principal arguments against its being even that.

A. Asking versus Offer Prices, and the Derivation of Property Rights

The first argument is that the idea of wealth maximization does not tell us whether to maximize in terms of asking or offering prices; in my example of a house, the asking price was \$100,000 but the offer price was only \$90,000. I reject this argument. The concept of wealth maximization tells us when to use asking and when to use offer prices, provided—an important qualification to which I shall return in a moment—that property rights have been assigned.

If the costs of voluntary transactions are low, the equilibrium prices, which provide the logical and natural means of measuring wealth, will be asking prices; for whenever an offer price is higher than an asking price, the offer will be accepted.[8] If the costs of voluntary transactions are prohibitive, however, then offer prices[9] may exceed asking prices indefinitely; and if, but only if, an involuntary transaction is possible at a cost less than the difference between offer and asking price, the offer price (that is, the hypothetical offer price) rather than the asking price will provide the correct guide for social choices designed to maximize wealth. Suppose millions of people would be willing to pay

[8]At the margin, of course, the offer and asking price will be the same; but there may be many intramarginal holders of the good or service transacted in the market, and for them the asking prices will exceed the offer prices and provide the correct measure of value. The house example illustrates this point.

[9]Hypothetical offer prices, that is, if transactions are prohibitively costly, no one will bother to make offers.

in the aggregate $1 billion for clean air, and the polluters would be willing to stop polluting the air for $100 million. But because there are so many polluters and pollutants, voluntary transactions are prohibitively costly. One way to look at this case would be to say that clean air is not really worth $900 million (benefits minus costs), because we have left out the transaction costs. These transaction costs, which exceed $900 million, are just like any other costs—like transportation costs, for example—and, when added in, show that the clean air really has no net value.

Transaction costs differ from transportation costs, however, because they sometimes can be circumvented by substituting a legal institution for the market as the method of allocating resources. In deciding whether this is possible in a particular case, we must have an idea of the value of an allocative change without regard to transaction costs, before we can decide whether that value exceeds the cost of the legal institution necessary to bring about the allocation.[10] If, in my example, the institution would cost less than $900 million, then society would be made wealthier by the legally coerced allocation of the rights in the air to the victims of the pollution. But $900 million may be an underestimate. Recall that asking prices can exceed offer prices. It might be that although the victims of air pollution would be willing to spend only $1 billion for cleaner air, once they had cleaner air they might demand $2 billion to give it up. This would be the relevant figure if the victims were deemed to own clear air, rather than if the polluters owned the right to dirty the air; and, precisely since asking and offer prices may differ,[11] and differ greatly, this assumption may affect the outcome of the hypothetical transaction—an important point to which I shall return in a moment. If the cost of abating pollution was $1.5 billion, the difference between deeming the victims the owners of the right and deeming the polluters the owners of the right would be crucial.

But the present point is simply that, given well-defined property rights, the question of whether wealth maximization concerns offer prices or asking prices is a pseudo-question. Wealth is maximized by creating a system which allows offer and asking prices to be compared, and offers to be accepted if, but only if, the offer price exceeds the asking price, and which imposes acceptance if, but only if, transaction costs

[10] Thus the social engineer is interested in the value of a transaction ex transaction costs in the same way that a transportation engineer is interested in the value of a transaction ex transportation costs.

[11] For empirical evidence, including evidence on air pollution, *see* Knetsch, *Legal Rules and the Basis for Evaluating Economic Losses,* 4 Int'l Rev. L. & Econ. 5 (1984).

make it impossible for the market to compare a (higher) offer price with a (lower) asking price, as in the pollution example.

Because asking and offer prices may differ, it is necessary to have a way of deciding who may charge an asking price and who must make offers; this is a question about property rights. For present purposes, a property right means the right not to be divested of the use, control, and enjoyment of a thing (tangible or intangible) at a price below one's asking price. Once property rights are assigned, it becomes clear who may charge asking prices and who must make offers. Wealth maximization can then proceed through the operation of the free market, and through market surrogates where the costs of market transactions are prohibitive and the costs of legal transactions tolerable.

It would, of course, be possible to take the assignment of property rights as given, and use wealth maximization to guide the shifting of the rights through trade and substitutes for trade. But I think one can go further and without circularity, can suggest how property rights should be assigned in the first place in order to maximize a society's wealth. And this is not so academic an endeavor as it may seem.

In my pollution example, there is no "natural" assignment of property rights over the use of the air; one could say that people have a right to breathe clean air, and polluters must buy that right, or equally that polluters have a right to emit pollutants as a byproduct of their activities, and people must buy that right (the "purchase" in either case would be an involuntary transaction, because market transactions are assumed to be unworkable). I do not know how to solve this particular problem; that is, I do not know whether in determining how much pollution is optimal we should use the asking or offer prices of clean air, which may of course differ, though presumably by little if we are talking about small changes in the cleanliness of air. If we are talking about whether the air shall be breathable or lethal, the difference between asking and offer prices could be enormous, since offer prices are limited by one's wealth, and asking prices may be infinite when the asker's life is at stake. However, cases of this kind—where wealth maximization provides no guidance to the initial assignment of property rights *and* asking and offer prices are likely to differ greatly—are rare; they reveal a limitation to an ethics of wealth maximization, but not a fatal limitation.

One can say a good deal about how property rights should be assigned in order to maximize wealth. For example, wealth maximization does not imply assigning property rights to whomever, regardless of his budget, gets the most pleasure out of the property in question, though he might have the highest asking price.[12] This approach appears to collapse wealth maximization into utility maximization in the sense used by utilitarian philosophers; worse, it actually dis-serves wealth maximization. If property rights were assigned on the basis of who would charge the highest asking prices, society would soon be impoverished. The method of assignment would destroy incentives to work and invest—unless rights could be sold free of any governmental power to take them away from their new owner; but that would depart from a system of assigning property rights so as to maximize utility in the utilitarian sense.

Bear in mind that wealth is a stock concept, not a flow concept; one's wealth is the present value of the stream of future income or other benefits generated by one's human and physical capital. The stream would be pitifully small if property rights were assigned and reassigned on the basis of who derived the most pleasure from having what property. People would cultivate the faculty of enjoyment rather than of hard work; little producer and consumer surplus would be created.

If you asked a random group of economists how to assign property rights in a new society with a literate population so as to maximize the prices (times quantities), explicit and implicit ("shadow"), asking and offer, in the society, they would almost certainly begin by giving each mentally competent adult the property rights to his own labor.[13] They would, in short, reject slavery, an inefficient institution under modern conditions. With unimportant exceptions, the costs of monitoring the output of a slave today would be much higher than the costs of monitoring a free man's output through contract. Although some slave owners would be quite wealthy, the society as a whole (which includes the persons who have been made slaves) would be poor. Society's wealth would be eaten up to a great extent by "agency costs." Arguably, this, rather than moral progress unrelated to material conditions, may be the main reason that slavery is no longer a common institution.

I recognize that some will count it a very great defect of my ethical system that it does not condemn slavery as always and everywhere bad. But partly, this is just a reaction to a word that has intensely pejorative

[12]Might, not would, because if he also got great pleasure out of other things, the money he could get for a given item of property might be very valuable to him because it would enable him to buy other pleasurable things.

[13]The qualification implies, of course, the persistence of institutions of quasi-slavery, as one might characterize (but for the pejorative overtones) the condition of children and mental incompetents.

connotations. Is it "slavery" to make a prison inmate work? Was indentured servitude, whereby immigrants to this country in the colonial period got their passage paid in exchange for becoming indentured servants for a period of years, "slavery," and therefore, bad? Was it an advance or retreat of civilization when victorious tribes began enslaving rather than killing the male population of the vanquished group? The answers are not so clear as to justify a blanket condemnation of all forms of involuntary servitude.

With natural resources, the initial assignment of property rights is not critical because presumably whoever gets the rights will sell or rent them to those who can get the most value out of them. The problem of the discrepancy between offer and asking prices will not be important here, because resources whose only use is "utilitarian" in the lay sense will tend to be valued at very near the market price. But this happy picture ignores important sources of friction. In particular, those who in the initial distribution receive no rights in natural resources will, in order to buy from those who do, have to borrow against inherently uncertain prospects. The same uncertainty makes it hard for the society to assign the property rights at the outset to those who can get the most value from them. Perhaps the best that can be done is, as in the nineteenth-century Homestead Acts, to parcel out the rights in an egalitarian fashion. This will give everyone some physical capital and therefore make it easier for the able and ambitious to rise.

An important application of this point suggests that the implications of wealth maximization are not entirely "illiberal," as those who deride it as capitalist ethics—which it is—may think. The maximization of wealth requires that people with productive potential have opportunities to develop that potential. This in turn requires means to identify such people and enable them to rent the tools they need to realize their potential. Because the potential of young children is not apparent unless they are given educational opportunities, and because it is difficult to borrow against one's future earnings (because the loan can be enforced only by making the borrower the lender's slave if he defaults—creating all the agency-cost problems of slavery), there is a solid argument based on wealth maximization for subsidizing education, especially (though not only) for the poor. The argument, however, need not imply government operation as distinct from financial support of the schools.

After rights are assigned, the free market can be relied on to reallocate them from time to time to those who value them the most as shown by willingness to pay an offer price equal to the current owner's asking price.

Problems of monopoly, the needs of public finance, the problem just discussed of financing investments in human capital, external benefits, and costs associated with such phenomena as charity (a source of external benefits) and crime (external costs), and concerns with political stability will require, however, some redistribution through the tax and government expenditure system. In short, a lightly regulated capitalism starting from conditions of broad equality will maximize a society's wealth. The history of this country, and, more generally, a comparison of capitalist and noncapitalist societies, illustrate the benefits of light regulation though it is no longer possible to describe our capitalism as lightly regulated.

B. The Instrumental Character of Wealth Maximization

I am reasonably satisfied that the objection based on the fact that wealth cannot even be measured unless property rights are first assigned can be met to the degree required in ethical discourse. I now move on to a second and more serious objection, which is that the ethic of wealth maximization rests on air. One does not value wealth for itself but for something else, and once we identify the something else, we can orient our social institutions toward accomplishing that end and cease pursuing the merely instrumental goal of maximizing wealth.

The values which provide the underlying ethical appeal of wealth maximization pull us in two seemingly opposite directions: toward utilitarianism and toward individualism. Wealth maximization promotes prosperity, and prosperity (not always but usually) engenders happiness. Wealth maximization also protects individual rights, and therefore promotes individualism. But, presumably, wealth maximization promotes each of these desiderata (particularly the second) to a lesser extent than a philosophy aimed directly at either one of them would do—a point that will now be illustrated and evaluated.

1. *Wealth and Happiness*

It is easy to think of examples where wealth maximization is at least superficially opposed to utilitarian goals—though, as the examples are rather extreme, maybe they should not trouble us much. But set aside that point and suppose as an example that a quantity of pituitary extract is being auctioned off. There are two bidders: one is a poor family whose child will be a dwarf unless he gets the extract; the other is a wealthy dilettante who wants to use the extract to grow a giant gerbil. The dilettante is the high bidder (let us assume away any imperfection in capital markets by supposing that even if the family could borrow against the child's future earnings, its offer price would still be lower than the dilettante's).

The result of wealth maximization in this case seems clearly contrary to the dictates of utilitarianism, besides being quite offensive. Yet these reactions may be superficial. We must consider, for example, who will get the pituitary extract if the dilettante is forbidden to buy it. More important, we must consider that, in the long run, there may be more and cheaper pituitary extract, and fewer dwarves, if the society does not try to allocate the product to those who will derive the greatest happiness from it. Or people may be sufficiently altruistic, even toward strangers, to support, as a component of the government's tax and expenditure system, a program for buying pituitary extract at market prices and giving it to children whose families are unable to afford it. Reliance on private charity may seem an obvious alternative to a public program but might not be efficient because of a free-rider problem. If I want fewer dwarves, I will benefit from your charitable contribution as much as you do, without having to make a contribution myself. The result will be a lower level of contributions than most people desire and, in the absence of free-rider problems, would make. This is an inefficient result which, in principle anyway, justifies government intervention even in a society dedicated to wealth maximization.

The real divergence between wealth maximization and utilitarianism occurs where utilitarianism is contrary to virtually everyone's moral intuitions. Suppose someone has such a well-developed sense of pleasure that he receives twice as much pleasure from a dollar than one who happens to be frugal and self-denying. Is that a reason for transferring a dollar from the second to the first person? A utilitarian would have to say it was a reason, although it might well be outweighed by the adverse effect on happiness in general if people's wealth were up for grabs in this way. Even worse, suppose a sadist got more pleasure from hurting people than his (involuntary) victims suffered pain; the sadist's conduct would be happiness-maximizing, and therefore good.

Utilitarianism makes the individual an input into the achievement of an aggregate quantity, the total happiness in society. This fact is the dark side of the most attractive feature of utilitarianism—its tolerance for different conceptions of the good. Somehow utilitarianism manages to be both radically individualistic and shockingly communitarian. It is so individualistic in its premises that it gives the same status to the sadist and the pleasure-loving scamp, on the one hand, as to the heroic physician or brilliant engineer on the other. At the same time, it is so aggregative that it invites us to consider the possibility of redistributing wealth and power from the productive and hard-working and self-restrained to people of unbridled appetites and vicious disposition.

What is missing from utilitarianism is any very direct concern with the productive side of human activity; all the focus is on the consuming, the appetitive. Perhaps this matters little in practice, because consumption is dependent on production, and the pleasure-loving will have few pleasures in a society that does not give its members incentives to produce. Indeed, the pleasure-loving might work particularly hard in order to get control of the resources that they need in order to maximize their pleasure and might support institutions that reward productive people. Nonetheless, it seems odd to give consumption moral precedence over production, to sacrifice the frugal for the pleasure-loving.

Wealth maximization reverses the order, and this is a mark in its favor. In a society dedicated to wealth maximization, the power to consume is limited by the ability to obtain claims on resources, and this ability depends on the production of goods or services that others value in trade. This is true even when the consumer is spending inherited money, as might have been the case with our wealthy dilettante buying pituitary extract for his gerbil. A person who accumulates more money than he spends during his lifetime is, in effect, deferring some of his spending until after his death, when it will be done by surrogates, his heirs. In deciding how much to accumulate and how much of that accumulation will go to his heirs rather than to charity, the testator will take into account the likelihood that his heirs will spend the money he leaves them in foolish or offensive ways. If, after taking this possibility (a form of "agency cost") into account, he nevertheless leaves them money, they become, in effect, his agents to spend it after his death. Any interference with their expenditures is an interference with his disposition of assets accumulated through his productive efforts.

Granted, he may not have accumulated his wealth by productive efforts; he may have stolen the money, or obtained it by monopolization, or inherited it from someone who had stolen it. These would be grounds for interfering with its expenditure in the next generation according to the testator's wishes. But if all illegitimate (i.e., unproductive) sources of wealth are assumed away as incompatible with wealth maximization, then in a society dedicated to wealth maximization, the right to consume will depend on productive activity.

To defend wealth maximization rigorously, it would of course be necessary to assign some ethical value to productivity. That would not be difficult but will not be attempted here. Although there is some well-merited skepticism about various aspects of modern life, very few people who live in wealthy societies would like to live in poor ones; and very many people who live in poor ones would, if allowed, move to wealthy ones. So there seems to be something good in a practical sense about wealthy societies, unless you think (as few economists do) that wealthy societies have become wealthy by exploiting poor ones. And if there is something good about wealthy societies, there must be something good about the people who make societies wealthy—and they are not the hedonists and the sybarites but the frugal and the hard-working. It is curious, but true, that to aim directly at maximizing happiness, by distributing and redistributing wealth to those who would get the most pleasure from it, is self-defeating because it results in a poor and unhappy society. Wealth maximization is a more effective instrument for attaining the goals of utilitarianism than utilitarianism itself. Stated otherwise, wealth maximization is the correct rule of decision in a system of rule utilitarianism.

Wealth maximization does not completely exclude governmental redistributions of wealth, as we saw in discussing the free-rider problem that depresses private charity. But it authorizes only those redistributions that conform to the altruistic feelings that most people harbor or that otherwise serve the interests of the productive people in the society. The free-wheeling redistributions of a utilitarian society are ruled out. This is also a mark in favor of wealth maximization.

A further criticism of wealth maximization that I will merely note and not try to answer is that, like utilitarianism, it assigns too much weight to individual preferences. Compare the sadist who assaults an involuntary victim and a sadist who obtains equivalent satisfaction from a mutually voluntary transaction with a masochist. The two sadists have similar standing in a system unflinchingly dedicated to maximizing happiness, provided that in the first case the sadist's pleasure exceeds his victim's suffering; but in a system of wealth maximization, the second sadist is a distinctly better man. The successful producer of an infantile television show who earns $500,000 a year would, in a system of wealth maximization, be counted as a better, more productive person than a laborer who earns $10,000. But the producer may not be more productive than a scientist who earns only $50,000, as the scientist may confer large external benefits on society, that is, benefits that he does not capture in a higher income for himself.

2. *Wealth and Individual Rights*

If wealth maximization has affinities with utilitarianism, it also has affinities with the individualist political philosophy that has been made respectable among professional philosophers in recent years through the work of Robert Nozick—though it has antecedents in the writings of Hobbes, Locke, Kant, Jefferson, and other classic expositors of Western liberalism. The premise of individualist political philosophy is that a person is defined by the possession of faculties such as reason and of rights thought appurtenant to the possession of such faculties. The conclusion is that the role of the state is to protect those rights, including the right to engage in voluntary exchange. In wanting to protect voluntary exchange, the individualist philosopher comes close to being a wealth maximizer. But he may also deduce rights that may be inconsistent with wealth maximization, as in Professor Epstein's suggestion that individualism implies that tort liability to strangers should be strict liability, even if negligence liability (or no liability) would be more efficient. In Epstein's view, if you run someone down, you must pay his damages because you have invaded his rights, even if you were faultless in the sense of being unable to avoid the accident at reasonable, perhaps at any, cost.[14]

A counterargument is possible, however.[15] If negligence is really cheaper than strict liability, then the sum of accident (first-party) and liability (third-party) insurance costs will be less under negligence than strict liability, and all drivers will prefer the former. Hence, negligence liability can be derived by a hypothetical voluntary transaction, which is a standard method of justifying institutions in an individualist philosophy. Stated differently, if a change (say from strict liability, assuming that is the regime initially deduced from individualist premises, to negligence liability) makes everyone better off by his own rights, it is hard to see it as trammeling anyone's individual rights. And if we are reasonably confident that the change would be adopted unanimously if we could somehow put it to a vote, this ought to come close enough to real (expressed) unanimity to satisfy the claims of individualism—as should also, I would contend, near unanimity, provided that the sacrifice by the opponents is a very small one in both an aggregate and an individual sense. That is, if ninety-five percent of drivers would have much lower insurance rates from a switch to a negligence standard, and none of the other five percent would pay more than a few dollars a year in additional premiums, it would be hard to condemn the change on individualist grounds without being accused of fanaticism.

[14]*See* Epstein, *A Theory of Strict Liability*, 2 J. Legal Stud. 151 (1973).

[15]For a slightly fuller treatment of this point, see R. Posner, *supra* note 1, at 94–99.

C. The Problem of Inalienable Rights

Some implications of individualism, however, are quite hard to reconcile with wealth maximization, and these deserve separate consideration. Almost everyone writing in the individualist tradition thinks slavery improper even if the slave became such through a voluntary transaction, as in contracts of indentured servitude, which, as I mentioned, were common in eighteenth-century America—though most individualists will make a narrow and partial exception for military service. Torture and lynching are other examples where the individualist will be inclined to say that the practice violates essential personhood even if it could be shown to maximize wealth, as it could be in the (far-fetched) example where a person is lynched in circumstances of absolute certainty that he is guilty and that the legal punishment would have been death if he had stood trial. In this case, the only effect of lynching is to reduce the costs of administering the legal system. A somewhat more plausible case is eliminating the privilege against self-incrimination, to make everyone (or nearly everyone) better off *ex ante*, by increasing the probability of convicting guilty people. The feeling against these practices runs very deep in our culture. It is bound up with a general aversion to cruelty that dates only from the humanitarian movement of the nineteenth century; yet Hobbes, who emphatically supported the privilege against self-incrimination,[16] was a man of the seventeenth century—and no softy.

Long after lynching, slavery, and torture were all thoroughly reprobated, it still would not have been thought unjust for the state to allow a man to starve who could not earn a subsistence income by his best efforts. Today it would be thought unjust, though not by all individualist philosophers in the sense in which I am using the term. There is for good or ill nothing in the ethic of wealth maximization which says that society has a duty to help the needy. It has a duty not to hurt them, to leave them alone; but it has no duty, and in a strict ethic of wealth maximization no right, to force the productive people to support the unproductive. Being needy does not establish a claim. A right implies a duty; and there is no basis in a system of wealth maximization for implying a duty to help someone you have not hurt. Charity is an important part of personal ethics, but except where the charitable impulse is impeded by free-rider problems, a political duty of charity cannot be deduced from the premises of wealth maximization. In this regard, wealth maximization is at one with individualist political

[16] *See*, T. Hobbes, *Leviathan*, pt. 2, Ch. 21 (London 1651).

philosophy, but both are out of phase with powerful currents of contemporary moral feeling; both, perhaps, neglect the role of luck in wealth and poverty and by doing so give excessive moral status to the condition of being a productive person.

All of the examples I have discussed are sufficiently troublesome to make me regard wealth maximization as an incomplete guide to social decision-making. But within the broad limits indicated by these examples, wealth maximization does provide a reasonable guide to social decision-making and, in particular, builds a bridge between utilitarian and individualist philosophies—and not an adventitious bridge, either. Wealth maximization shares with utilitarianism an emphasis on the moral value of individual preferences and desires, and with individualism a hostility to coercion.[17] It does not banish coercion entirely, because where market transaction costs are prohibitive, wealth maximization allows, and indeed requires, the state to use its powers to mimic the market—if this can be done at a cost lower than the gain in value brought about by the market-mimicking transaction. But the limited forms of coercion that are legitimate in a system of wealth maximization promote social welfare so broadly that they can be deemed to command almost universal consent. The institutions of criminal, property, tort, and contract law—indeed of common law in general—are of this character.

The strong hold that both utilitarianism and individualism have over American social thought suggests that a political philosophy which draws on both may command a broader support than either. The pluralistic and—let us face it—materialistic character of our civilization makes it inevitable that government will and should try to promote the greatest happiness of the greatest number, rather than decide what preferences are legitimate and whose preferences should count the most. But pushed to an extreme, utilitarianism creates a potential for wealth redistribution that is inconsistent with a commitment to individual autonomy (as illustrated by the claims of the 'utility monster' to have wealth redistributed to him because he is especially efficient at processing it into happiness, though only his own). Yet too rigid a commitment to individual autonomy would diminish the happiness of the society to an intolerable extent—a point with many potential illustrations from the writings of Kant and his followers, including Rawls, who to maximize

[17]The civilizing influence of capitalism—and what is wealth maximization but the ethics of capitalism?—is emphasized in Haskell, *Capitalism and the Origins of the Humanitarian Sensibility* (pts. 1 and 2), 90 Am. Hist. Rev. 339, 547 (1985).

the position of the least fortunate would be willing to impose enormous sacrifices on the rest of the society.[18]

Wealth maximization perhaps comes up short by not recognizing either inalienable (i.e., nonsalable) rights—a deficiency (if it is a deficiency) that it shares with utilitarianism—or claims to public assistance—a deficiency, in terms of contemporary intuitive morality, that it shares with individualism. In a system of wealth maximization, the needy (dramatically including the child in my pituitary-extract example) have no right to coerce even minimum assistance. Yet this characterization of wealth maximization is only approximately true. It would be more accurate to say that wealth maximization reflects the distributive preferences of the people who produce the wealth of the society. To the extent that such people are altruistic, but the full expression of their altruism is frustrated by free-rider problems, government is authorized (indeed, required) to undertake redistributive efforts. If altruistic feelings were not widespread, philosophers would not consider a political philosophy that made no room for the hard-hearted rather than hard-headed. To the wealth maximizer, altruism is neither good nor bad; but given that it exists, there is a legitimate if limited role for public wealth redistribution. If altruism did not exist, the absence of such redistribution would not be felt to be unjust.

It must also be emphasized that it is a *political* philosophy that I am expounding. You may be a bad person if you are selfish; but it may not be the proper role of the state to change your values and preferences.

III. APPLICATION TO LAW

Despite all I have said, or perhaps because of some of what I have said, I am sure that many of my readers will continue to regard wealth maximization as a dubious guide to social decision-making in general. But the case for using it to guide courts, in areas where the Constitution or legislation does not deprive them of initiative or discretion in the matter, is a powerful one—though with some limitations along the lines suggested above.

The legal profession long pretended that with unimportant exceptions, discretion—power—was something that bad judges seized, while good judges deduced the outcomes of their cases from rules laid

[18] *See*, e.g., J. Rawls, *A Theory of Justice* 152–54 (1971); Arrow, *Some Ordinalist-Utilitarian Notes on Rawls's Theory of Justice*, 70 J. Phil. 245, 251 (1973); Hodges, *Punishment*, 18 Phil. & Phenomenological Research 209 (1957–1959).

down by higher or prior courts, legislatures, and the framers of the Constitution. Today, however, it is generally recognized that even the best judges cannot decide difficult cases simply by deduction from premises found in authoritative sources of legal guidance (which is why the cases are called difficult)—that they have and must exercise substantial discretion. The question arises, in what frame of reference should that discretion be exercised? Pragmatic? Utilitarian? Christian? Darwinian? Rawlsian? Nozickian? I suggest that wealth maximization provides the most acceptable frame of reference. I shall not attempt to argue this position fully here but will content myself with the following rather summary points:

1. Wealth maximization combines, as I have said, elements of utilitarianism and individualism, and in so doing comes closer to being a consensus political philosophy (I do not suggest it is one) in our contentiously pluralistic society than any other overarching political principle. This point is concealed by the fact that the term 'wealth maximization' is not a term in common usage. It would be easy to show, however, that many invocations of fairness and justice, 'balancing' and due process and other familiar principles or methods of judicial decision-making are proxies for wealth maximization.[19]

2. The principal complaint likely to be leveled against wealth maximization as a guide to judicial action is its lack of a strong redistributive component; as we have seen, it validates some redistribution of wealth from rich to poor but much less than is desired by many reflective and influential students of social justice. Any possible collisions between wealth maximization and the strong modern feelings against slavery, lynching, and torture, however, are made moot by the constitutional prohibitions against these practices.[20]

Given the absence of anything approaching a consensus on the optimum distribution of wealth, however, it is very hard to see how courts could adopt a redistributive ethic to guide their decisions. For this and another reason—that courts do not have flexible instruments

[19]This is a major theme of my book, R. Posner, *Economic Analysis of Law* (Second edition 1977); the forthcoming third edition will be published in March, 1986.

[20]The Thirteenth Amendment forbids slavery; the due process clauses of the Fifth and Fourteenth Amendments lynching; the Fifth Amendment torture to obtain incriminating evidence; and the Eighth Amendment torture as a method of inflicting punishment on convicted criminals.

for redistribution compared to the (overtly) taxing, spending, and regulatory branches of government—a sensible division of labor has the courts focus on wealth maximization (making the pie as big as possible) while legislatures focus on redistributing some of that wealth (reslicing the pie).

My interest in wealth maximization grew from and remains centered upon its role, both actual and desirable, in guiding judicial decision-making in "common law" areas, broadly defined to include any field where judge-made law is important; where judicial discretion—lawful and legitimate judicial discretion—is important. By a happy coincidence, as I have said, many of the questions on which the unflinching embrace of the implications of wealth maximization might yield results contrary to widespread moral intuitions, such as lynching and torture, have been taken out of the area of judicial discretion by constitutional provisions. The domain in which wealth maximization is allowed to operate in the law is, not surprisingly, the domain in which the principle of wealth maximization—once it is correctly understood, and not confused with the ethics of Mammon or Midas—expresses fundamental values of our political culture.

3

Why Is the Common Law Efficient?†

*Paul H. Rubin**

Posner, in *Economic Analysis of Law,*[1] argues persuasively that the common law can be best understood as an attempt to achieve economic efficiency. He is less persuasive in his explanation of why this is so—his argument is essentially that judges may as well decide in terms of efficiency, since they have no other criteria to use. To an economist accustomed to invisible hand[2] explanations of efficiency in the marketplace, this justification seems weak.

Of related interest is the analysis by Landes,[3] Gould,[4] and Tullock[5] of the decision to litigate a dispute rather than settle. All have concluded that, in general, parties will settle out of court. But, for the common law to remain efficient, it must change as conditions change; changes in the common law require that some cases be litigated. Does the rationality of the common law rest on irrational behaviour of litigants?

In this paper I show that these issues—the presumed efficiency of the common law and the decision to use the courts to settle a dispute—are related. In particular, this relationship will occur because resorting to court settlement is more likely in cases where the legal rules relevant to the dispute are inefficient, and less likely where the rules are efficient. Thus, efficient rules may evolve from in-court settlement, thereby reducing the

†Originally published as "Why Is the Common Law Efficient?", 1977, *The Journal of Legal Studies*, Vol. 6, pp. 51–63.

*The author would like to thank Gordon Tullock, Carl Jordan, and an anonymous referee for comments on an earlier version of this paper.

[1]Richard A. Posner, Economic Analysis of Law (1972).

[2]For a general discussion of invisible hand explanations, see Robert Nozick, Anarchy, State and Utopia (1974).

[3]William M. Landes, An Economic Analysis of the Courts, 14 J. Law & Econ. 61 (1971).

[4]John P. Gould, The Economics of Legal Conflicts, 2 J. Leg. Studies 279 (1973).

[5]Gordon Tullock, The Logic of the Law (1971).

incentive for future litigation and increasing the probability that efficient rules will persist. In short, the efficient rule situation noted by Posner is due to an evolutionary mechanism whose direction proceeds from the utility maximizing decisions of disputants rather than from the wisdom of judges.

Section I of this paper contains an analysis of the framework which will be used to discuss pressures for efficiency. Section II contains the actual analysis, in which it is shown that efficiency occurs in situations where both parties to a dispute have an ongoing interest in cases, and that efficiency need not occur if one or both parties do not have such an ongoing interest. Section III contains some complications and extensions. The last section is a summary.

I. GENERAL FRAMEWORK

Throughout this paper, I use an example of accident liability to illustrate the arguments. The particular example does not matter, for, as Posner has shown, torts, property, and contract law can all be analyzed within the same framework.[6] Suppose there is a certain type of accident which costs X when it occurs. Parties of type B are the victims and parties of type A the defendants if the accident occurs. Liability may be placed on A or on B. If liability is placed on A, the optimal solution for A is to spend S_A on accident avoidance and allow N_A accidents to occur; conversely, if liability is placed on B, S_B will be spent on avoidance and N_B accidents will occur. Assume also that this is an either/or situation: the technology of avoidance in this case is such that there is no joint action which A and B could take to further reduce accident and prevention costs. For purposes of analysis, assume that it is efficient for liability to be placed on B; that is,

$$T_B = S_B + N_B X < S_A + N_A X = T_A \qquad (1)$$

where T_A and T_B represent total present value of accident costs plus prevention costs for parties A and B respectively. Equation (1) indicates that this total cost is less if B is liable than if A is liable.

Efficiency requires that A not be made liable for the accident; the most efficient solution is for B to spend S_B and for there to be N_B accidents. Whether B will spend S_B on avoidance or A will spend S_A depends on the current liability assignment—that is, on the decision which the parties expect the courts to reach if there is an accident and litigation occurs. Courts are somewhat bound by precedent. Thus, if precedents favor B, then S_A will be spent and total accident costs will be T_A; conversely if

[6]Richard A. Posner, *supra* note 1, at 98–102.

precedents favor *A*. (Because we have eliminated the possibility of joint action, one situation or the other will occur.)

Define *R* as the probability that *B* will win the suit if an accident occurs and the parties litigate. The value of *R* is defined by precedent: if $R > .5$, precedents favor *B* and *B* is likely to win if the case is litigated. If $R < .5$ precedents favor *A*. We assume throughout the paper that both parties agree on the value of *R*. The current liability assignment is then efficient if $R < .5$. It is assumed throughout that judges are likely but not certain to decide on the basis of precedent. As shown below, it is the possibility of changing current precedents which sometimes makes litigation worthwhile and which will in some circumstances lead to efficiency.

The Coase Theorem[7] indicates that placement of liability does not matter: if *A* were made liable, he would simply pay a bribe to *B* in order to induce *B* to avoid accidents; as indicated by (1), this would be the efficient solution. This will in fact occur if the costs of paying the bribe are sufficiently low; however, it is possible that the transactions costs will be greater than $(T_A - T_B)$: the saving from shifting liability to the efficient bearer. In this case, if he is liable, *A* will accept liability rather than paying *B*. Even if it is feasible for *A* to bribe *B*, there will be some transactions costs involved in paying the bribe. In Section II, it is assumed that paying a bribe is not feasible; in Section III the case of feasible bribery is examined.

II. ANALYSIS

Given the basic situation discussed above, there are some cases in which there will be pressure for the law to evolve towards efficiency. The crucial point is the interest which the parties have in decisions as precedents. Thus, some legal cases involve individuals with a one-time interest in the outcome, while other cases involve corporate bodies of some sort—government agencies, labor unions, firms, insurance companies. Such organizations would have an interest in legal cases as precedents as well as interests as litigants.[8] Insurance companies, for example, would be concerned with future liability cases as well as with a particular case. In analyzing the relation between efficiency and litigation, there are three basic situations which must be considered.

[7] R.H. Coase, The Problem of Social Cost, 3 J. Law & Econ. 1 (1960).

[8] Richard A. Posner, The Behavior of Administrative Agencies, 1 J. Leg. Studies 305 (1972), discusses the interest of agencies in settling cases for use as precedents.

In part A, the situation in which both parties have a substantial interest in the case as precedent will be considered. Part B discusses the situation in which only one party is interested in the case as precedent. Part C considers the situation where neither party is interested in the case as precedent.

A. Both Parties Interested in Precedent

If both parties to a certain type of legal dispute have a substantial interest in future cases of this sort, then precedents will evolve towards efficiency, the common law situation posited by Posner. If rules are inefficient, there will be an incentive for the party held liable to force litigation; if rules are efficient, there will be no such incentive. Thus, efficient rules will be maintained, and inefficient rules litigated until overturned.

Substantial interest in precedent refers to a situation in which the party is likely to be in many such cases in the future. In effect, such parties are concerned with the entire stream of costs, T_A or T_B, rather than with X, the damages from one particular accident. Start with an inefficient rule—A is held liable if accidents occur, so that A is now spending S_A on accident avoidance and $N_A X$ on damage payments for those accidents which still occur. An accident has just occurred; the parties must decide whether to settle or litigate.

If the case is litigated and B wins, he is paid X; if A wins, he does not pay X in this case, and, in addition, A saves T_A in the future, but B must begin to pay T_B. Court costs for each party are C. The value to A of a court settlement is

$$V_A = R(-X) + (1 - R)T_A - C \tag{2}$$

and to B:

$$V_B = R(X) + (1 - R)(-T_B) - C \tag{3}$$

The parties can settle out of court if

$$-V_A > V_B \tag{4}$$

which simply says that a settlement can be reached if the expected loss to A of going to court is greater than the expected gain to B. If this is so, there is room for negotiation. Conversely, if (4) is not satisfied, the parties will litigate. In this example, litigation will occur if

$$(1 - R)(T_A - T_B) > 2C \tag{5}$$

Here, $T_A - T_B$ is the cost of the inefficient legal rule. As this becomes larger, litigation is more likely. Conversely, as R becomes larger (that is, as the inefficient rule is more entrenched) litigation is less likely. As court costs are higher, litigation is less likely. Finally, if the current rule were efficient (that is, if T_B were greater than T_A), (5) would never be satisfied, so that there would be no litigation.

What will happen? If the parties go to court, B will probably win, since both parties agree that $R > .5$. However, whenever this stituation arises in the future A will again go to court. At some point, some court will find in favor of A; at this point, the law has been changed and is now efficient. From that time on, precedents will favor A in comparable cases. Since there is no deadweight loss to party B when he is forced to bear liability (i.e., no term comparable to $T_A - T_B$), B will not find it worthwhile to go to court when such an accident occurs; instead, B will spend S_B on avoiding such accidents and bear the cost $N_B X$ of those which do occur.

It is now possible to define precisely the meaning of substantial interest. A's interest in this sort of case is substantial precisely if T_A is large enough so that (5) is satisfied. As this problem has been defined, it is not relevant whether B has a substantial interest or not; however, as we will see in the next section, both parties must have a substantial interest if efficiency is to be guaranteed.

What if both parties are insurance companies with ongoing interests as either defendants or plaintiffs? Then both A and B become interested in $T_A - T_B$, the efficiency savings from future cases. It can easily be shown that, if both parties are equally likely to be on either side of such cases in the future, (5) is unchanged so that the pressure for efficiency will be maintained.

We have thus shown that if rules are inefficient, parties will use the courts until the rules are changed; conversely, if rules are efficient, the courts will not be used and the efficient rule will remain in force. An outside observer coming upon this legal rule would observe that the rule is efficient; but this efficiency occurs because of an evolutionary process, not because of any particular wisdom on the part of judges. If judges decide independently of efficiency, we would still find efficient rules. Intelligent judges may speed up the process of attaining efficiency; they do not drive the process.

B. Only One Party Interested in Precedent

If only one party to a dispute is interested in future cases of this sort, there will be pressure for precedents to evolve in favor of that party which does have a stake in future cases, whether or not this is the efficient solution. This is because a party with a stake in future decision will find it worthwhile to litigate as long as liability rests with him; conversely, a party with no stake in future decisions will not find litigation worthwhile.

Let us continue our example: an accident has happened to a certain *B*. As the law now stands *A* is likely to win the case—that is, $R < .5$, and both parties agree on the value of *R*. However, *B* has a stake in the result of this decision; *A* has no such stake. That is, this type of case is an ongoing case for *B*, but a one time case for *A*. If *B* goes to court and wins, then in the future he will save S_B per period. T_B is the present value of the stream of accident costs to *B* as long as he is liable. Thus, if the courts are used and *B* wins, he receives *X* from *A* as a result of this accident; in addition, he saves T_B in the future. On the other hand, if *A* wins, he does not pay *X*; *A* is, by assumption, not interested in future decision. The value to *A* of a court case is:

$$V_A = R(-X) - C \tag{6}$$

and the value to *B* is:

$$V_B = R(X) + R(T_B) - C \tag{7}$$

In this case, *A* will be willing to pay $R(X) + C$ to avoid a court settlement; *B* will be willing to accept $R(X) + R(T_B) - C$. Therefore, there will be no settlement if

$$R(T_B) > 2C \tag{8}$$

From (8), we see that, unless *R* is very small (that is, unless precedents are extremely clear and unfavorable to *B*), or unless court costs are large, *B* will find litigation worthwhile. Moreover, each time such an accident occurs, *B* will again go to court rather than settling. As such behavior continues, at some point some court may rule in *B*'s favor. At this point the rule favors *B*, and *B* will therefore cease taking precautions to avoid accidents. Rather, party *A* will begin spending S_A on accident avoidance. When such accidents again occur, the *A* who is involved will pay *X* to *B*, rather than litigate, since *A* has no future interest in the case.

This same argument could be turned around: if *A* has an ongoing interest in this type of case and *B* does not, then *A* will go to court until a favorable ruling is obtained; from this time on, precedents will favor *A*, and this rule will persist, since no *B* will find litigation worthwhile. Thus, when one party has an ongoing interest in a type of case there is a tendency for cases to be litigated until a precedent is established which favors this party. There is no tendency for efficiency in this situation.

This case appears to describe the evolution of nuisance law in the nineteenth century.[9] By the end of this century, those causing nuisances were largely factories, which would have ongoing interests in liability rulings; conversely, those suffering from nuisances were largely individuals with no such interest. (That is, factories were concerned with T_B, but individuals were indifferent to T_A.) The evidence indicates that nuisance law did in fact largely favor factories and firms, rather than individuals.

C. No Interest in Precedent

If neither party is interested in precedents, the current rule will persist, whether it is efficient or inefficient. That is, if neither party has an ongoing interest in cases of this sort, then neither will force use of the courts. All such cases will be settled on the basis of the current rule, whatever it might be. Since cases will not go to court, there will be no pressure to change this rule.

Again begin with the situation in which an accident has occurred. A certain party of type *B* has lost *X* and is considering suing the party *A* who is liable. Both parties agree that the probability of *B* winning is *R*. If there is no interest in precedent, then the exact value of *R* is irrelevant for our purposes. We assume risk neutrality since, as we shall indicate below, risk aversion would complicate the analysis without changing the results.

Clearly, if this is the entire problem, the parties should settle. To *A* the expected value of a court settlement is

$$V_A = -RX - C \tag{9}$$

and to *B* it is

$$V_B = RX - C. \tag{10}$$

The parties can settle out of court if (4) is satisfied; this becomes

$$RX + C > RX - C \tag{11}$$

which is obviously met. Thus rather than going to court, *A* can pay some amount *L* to *B*, where

$$RX - C < L < RX + C \tag{12}$$

[9]See Joel Franklin Brenner, Nuisance Law and the Industrial Revolution, 3 J. Leg. Studies 403 (1974). for a discussion which is consistent with this argument.

and this will be better than a court settlement for both parties. This is the essence of the arguments as to why most cases may be expected to be settled out of court. If the parties are risk averse, we replace terms in (9) and (10) with their utility equivalents. For risk averse individuals, the utility of a lottery is less than the utility of the expected value of the lottery; thus, in (4) the left side becomes relatively larger and the right side relatively smaller. Risk aversion makes out of court settlements relatively more likely.

In this situation, the courts will be used only if the parties disagree about the value of *R*. However, there is no reason to assume that such disagreement is related to the efficiency of current rules. Thus, as long as there is agreement about the probability of decisions, the legal rule will not change; and if there is disagreement and consequent pressure for rule change, there is no presumption that changes would be in the direction of increased efficiency. This situation is presumably that which exists when disputants are individuals with little ongoing interest in solutions. Furthermore, disputes would ordinarily be settled in accordance with current legal rules; it would be unusual for such cases to go to court, and there is no presumption that rules in such cases would be efficient. However, to the extent that the types of legal cases involving individuals are the same types of cases as those involving corporate bodies, this conclusion must be modified for, as we have seen, there is pressure for efficiency in the latter type of case, whereas individual disputants will accept the existing rule, whether it is efficient or not.[10]

III. SOME COMPLICATIONS

In this section I consider in turn: situations in which bribery is feasible; costs of out-of-court settlements; public good problems; situations in which different types of parties are interested in the same type of case; and some applications to statute law.

A. Bribery

Assume again that liability is currently inefficiently assigned—that, *A* is liable. As mentioned in Section I, it may be possible in this case for *A* to bribe *B* to take precautions, rather than taking precautions himself. As before, define T_A and T_B as the present value of the stream of costs if liability is placed, respectively, on *A* or *B*; from (1) we know that

$$T_B < T_A. \tag{13}$$

[10]See Section III, C.

Define T_N as the present value of costs to A of bribing B to take precautions. T_N would include normal aspects of transactions costs—costs of finding the relevant B, of actually making the payments, of monitoring B's behavior, etc. A will find it worthwhile to bribe B if

$$T_N < T_A - T_B \tag{14}$$

that is, if the cost of paying the bribe is less than the saving from taking efficient precautions. Even in this case, however, there is a deadweight loss—an efficiency loss caused by the actual cost of paying the bribe, T_N.

Even with the bribe, there will still be N_A accidents per period. One of these accidents has occurred. A is now liable to pay X to the injured B. As above, A must decide whether to pay or to litigate. If A settles out of court or loses the case in court, he must then spend $T_N + T_B$; he must continue to negotiate with parties B and pay the accident costs of these parties. If B loses, then he must pay T_B—that is, in the future A will not be liable if this type of accident occurs, so that B will spend S_B on avoiding such accidents. In addition, if B loses, he will not be paid X, damages in the accident which has already occurred. Thus, there is a $(1 - R)$ chance of B losing T_B. For A, the expected value of going to court becomes

$$V_A = R(-X) + (1 - R)(T_B + T_N) - C \tag{15}$$

and for B

$$V_B = R(X) + (1 - R)(-T_B) - C. \tag{16}$$

This occurs because, once A has won a case, the law is changed—precedents now favor A, rather than B. This is the essence of judge made common law.

The parties will again settle out of court if (4) is satisfied; but this now becomes

$$(1 - R)T_N < 2C. \tag{17}$$

They will go to court if (17) is reversed:

$$(1 - R)T_N > 2C \tag{18}$$

The parties will go to court if the expected present value of the costs to A of negotiating with B in the future to have B take precautions is greater than the total court costs. What has happened is that T_N, the present value of these negotiation costs, is a cost to A but not a gain to *B*. The stakes in the case are asymmetrical, so that there is less possibility of a settlement between the parties. Notice also that T_N is in this situation the present cost of the inefficient legal rule.

The situation described above is again that in which both parties have an ongoing interst in decisions. It is likely that this will be the only relevant situation for bribes; if *B* does not have such an interest, then it is likely that *B* will be unidentifiable in advance. In this case, it is likely that the cost of *A* of bribing *B* would be prohibitive, and the analysis used in Section II B would be relevant.

Notice also that there is no relationship between court costs and bribery (transactions) costs. The decision as to whether or not to bribe *B* is made before the accident occurs; the decision as to whether to go to court is made after an accident has happened. Our argument is that *A* is likely to go to court to save *future* transactions costs. Of course, as shown in (18), if court costs are high enough relative to the present value of transactions costs, the case will be settled; but this simply says that if court costs are greater than the costs of the inefficiency imbedded in the current rule it is not worth changing the rule.

B. Settlement Costs

Throughout, we have ignored the costs of settling the dispute out of court. This action will have some costs, and as these costs increase, the probability of going to court increases. Formally, such costs can be included in our analysis simply by redefining *C* everywhere as net court costs—the difference between court costs and settlement costs. The level of net court costs is itself an important parameter in our models. As can be seen from (5) and (18) the courts are more likely to be used in overturning inefficient rules as court costs are smaller. Gould[11] has argued that high court costs have the desirable effect of reducing inefficient litigation; but it must be pointed out that such costs also have the undesirable effect of. reducing efficient litigation—litigation aimed at overturning inefficient rules.

C. Different Types of Parties, Same Type of Case

In Section II we saw that when only one party has an ongoing interest in a type of case, precedents could be expected to evolve in favor of that party. Conversely, when both parties have an interest, precedents should evolve toward efficiency. However, it is possible that some cases

[11]John P. Gould, *supra* note 4, at 296.

of a certain type will involve only one party with an ongoing interest, while other cases of the same sort will involve two such parties. In this situation, there could easily arise a conflict—when only one party has an ongoing interest, the inefficient solution may be favored, while when both have such an interest the efficient solution will be favored.

It is possible that cases of this sort would be continually litigated. However, if this were to happen, parties would observe that precedents would not be binding, and this would reduce the incentive for litigation. A more likely solution is for parties to differentiate the cases, so that one sort of precedent would govern cases with one corporate body and a different set of precedents would govern cases with two corporate bodies. The law would then be inconsistent; but no litigant would have an incentive to capitalize on this inconsistency, and therefore it would continue to exist.[12] This explanation for legal inconsistency would seem to be a fruitful area of research for scholars trained in the law.

D. Public Good Problems

Once a decision is reached in a case, the decision is a public good.[13] It affects all parties of type A and B. Thus, a party of type A may decide not to litigate a case, even if such litigation would be efficient, in the hope that some other A may do the litigating and save the original A court costs. However, Equations (5) or (18) are not particularly stringent: In many cases, court costs are not prohibitively high. Nonetheless, we might expect some free rider problems. Our model would predict, for example, that large companies would be involved relatively more in litigation than would small companies.

E. Application to Statute Law

Statute law is often inefficient.[14] However, in some cases lobbying for passage of statute law can take the place of deciding to litigate in

[12]It might appear that the inconsistency would lead some disputants to litigate in the hope of capitalizing on the inconsistency. However, both parties would be aware of this possibility, and thus there would be no asymmetry. Our analysis rests on assuming that litigation occurs only when there is an asymmetry between parties.

[13]See Gordon Tullock, Public Decisions as Public Goods, 99 J. Pol. Econ. 913 (1971).

[14]Paul H. Rubin, On the Form of Special Interest Legislation, 21 Public Choice 79 (1975).

our model.[15] Thus, if some law were proposed benefitting one well defined small group at the expense of another well defined small group, and if the group which would lose would lose more than the gaining group would gain (i.e., if the law were inefficient), then the potential losers would be able to outspend the potential gainers, so that we would not expect the law to be passed. Thus, we would expect that inefficient statute laws would correspond to our analysis of the situation in which only one party has an interest in precedent; that is, such laws would be passed at the expense of large groups which would not be able to effectively lobby against their passage because of free rider problems.

IV. SUMMARY

We have shown that the efficiency of the common law, to the extent that it exists, can be explained by an evolutionary model—a model in which it is more likely that parties will litigate inefficient rules than efficient rules. If decisions are made randomly, there will be a movement in the direction of efficient laws. The same model provides an explanation for using the courts to settle some disputes, rather than relying on out of court settlements.

The evolutionary pressure comes from behavior of litigants, rather than judges. We therefore found it useful to study behavior of potential litigants, classified according to their interest in cases as precedents. We found that when neither party is interested in precedent, there is no incentive to litigate, and hence, no pressure on the law to change. When only one party is interested in precedent, that party will litigate until a favorable decision is obtained; the law in such cases will favor parties with such an ongoing interest. When both parties have an ongoing interest in a type of case, there will be pressure toward efficiency. When different types of parties have an interest in the same type of case, we would expect inconsistencies to exist in the law.

Finally, we would predict that the evolution toward efficiency, in those cases where there would be such an evolution, would be faster as current rules are more inefficient, as net courts costs (court costs less settlement costs) are lower, and as inefficient rules are less soundly entrenched.

[15]This point is due to Gordon Tullock.

ADDENDUM: COMMENT ON "THE COMMON LAW PROCESS AND THE SELECTION OF EFFICIENT RULES"

Professor George L. Priest in his comment[16] has provided a valuable extension of my results. However, this extension is purchased at some cost, and this cost is perhaps greater than Priest himself realizes. It appears that his relatively informal discussion in fact hides some of his assumptions. He is of necessity assuming something more than ". . . that transactions costs in the real world are positive."[17]

I assume throughout my paper that both parties agree on the probabilities of victory for each of them. Priest claims that he avoids this assumption, and that I make the assumption for "expositional convenience."[18] This is not so: the assumption is made for substantive, not expositional, reasons. One must make some assumption about probability estimates of the parties; it is my feeling that the assumption of equal probability assessments is more easily justified than Priest's implicit assumption of differing estimates. Specifically, rational informed individuals (or their attorneys) will have the same estimates about probabilities of any given judicial decision. To assume otherwise is tantamount to assuming ignorance by one or both parties, and as a methodological principle I prefer to avoid assuming any such ignorance wherever possible. Once ignorance is assumed, it is very easy to prove anything, and thus to derive tautological models. Priest's form of the ignorance assumptions—that each party is as likely as the other to misjudge probabilities of victory—is perhaps more innocuous than most such assumptions, but it is nonetheless an assumption I prefer to avoid.

(Priest does not explicitly make any assumption about probability estimates. However, it is a well known result that rational, risk neutral or risk averse individuals with symmetric stakes in a case will not go to law. Thus, cases will be litigated only if one of these assumptions is violated. I assume asymmetric stakes to motivate my litigants. Priest denies this assumption; therefore, he must be assuming different probability estimates. He claims to be concerned only with the number of cases which will be litigated under alternative rules and not with the motives for such litigation. But it is dangerous to make assumptions about aggregate behavior without considering the behavior of the individuals which make up the aggregate.)

[16]George L. Priest, The Common Law Process and the Selection of Efficient Rules, 6 J. Legal Studies 65 (1977).
[17]*Ibid.*
[18]*Id.* at 73, n. 18.

In this paper I desired to show how litigation would occur in a world with no ignorance, and how efficiency would be achieved in such a world. Specifically, I desired to show how rational behavior of litigants would lead to efficiency of legal decisions. I succeeded in this. Of course, to the extent that parties to disputes do in fact disagree about probabilities, Priest's mechanism would obtain, and his comment is to this extent a valuable extension of the model. However, I feel that the process described in this paper would be empirically more important in driving rules to efficiency than would Priest's process, for litigation will invariably occur if stakes are asymmetrical in my model, while Priest's mechanism is driven by random errors in perception by the parties.

I agree fully with Priest's point about judges. As stated in various places in my paper, the evolutionary model which I develop focuses attention on decisions of potential and actual litigants rather than on judges in driving the model.

Alternative Formulations of the Notion of Negligence

4

Toward an Economic Theory of Liability†

*John Prather Brown**

Recently there have appeared a number of important articles by both lawyers and economists analyzing the economic effects of liability rules.[1] This paper formalizes the analysis of these effects. When two parties, the injurer and the victim, can both take measures to reduce the likelihood of accidents, and the measures are costly for both, the standard theory of production with two inputs and one output yields the conditions for the socially optimal amount of each accident avoidance measure. The effects of decentralizing the problem and using only liability rules to solve it can then be analyzed in terms of a two-person noncooperative game. I first show that there is a complete symmetry within each of the following pairs of liability rules: no liability and strict liability; the negligence rule and strict liability with contributory negligence; and the negligence rule with contributory negligence and strict liability with what I call dual contributory negligence. An analysis of the legal standards for negligence follows. I show that there is an important ambiguity in the so-called

†Originally published as "Toward an Economic Theory of Liability", 1973, *The Journal of Legal Studies*, Vol. 2, pp. 323–49.

*The author would like to thank William Brock, Harry Kalven, Jr., J. Huston McCulloch, John L. Peterman, Lester Telser, John Ver Steeg, and the members of the Industrial Organization Workshop at the University of Chicago for helpful comments and criticism.

[1]See Guido Calabresi, The Costs of Accidents: A Legal and Economic Analysis (1970), and (with Jon T. Hirschoff), Toward a Test for Strict Liability in Torts, 81 Yale L.J. 1055 (1972); R.H. Coase, The Problem of Social Cost, 3 J. Law & Econ. 1 (1960); Harold Demsetz, When Does the Rule of Liability Matter?, 1 J. Leg. Studies 13 (1972); Roland N. McKean, Products Liability: Trends and Implications, in Symposium on Products Liability, 38 U. Chi. L. Rev. 3 (1970); Richard A. Posner, A Theory of Negligence, 1 J. Leg. Studies 29 (1972), and Strict Liability: A Comment, 2 J. Leg. Studies 205 (1973).

"Learned Hand Rule" for determining the level of avoidance effort below which a party is adjudged negligent. Two of the formulations of the rule lead to inefficient results.

Next the main results of the paper are presented. First, given the negligence rule with contributory negligence and what I call the Incremental Standard of care, the social optimum is shown to be the unique equilibrium for the noncooperative game. A corollary is that the same results hold when the negligence standard is replaced by strict liability with contributory negligence. When the Incremental Standard is replaced by the Limited Information Incremental Standard the identity between equilibrium and optimality is destroyed. In an appendix the Coase Theorem is restated in our framework and compared with our results.

I. THE MODEL

Consider a small device, a black box, which is attached to some otherwise useful object such as a railway crossing, an airplane, or a sidewalk. The only function of the device is to emit a bill for a large amount of money from time to time, so we shall call it a liability generator. That large amount of money is fixed at A.

On the liability generator are two controls, X and Y. Each of these controls is continuously variable. Increasing either or both increases the probability that the accident will be avoided, but at a decreasing rate. The probability that an accident is avoided in a given time interval is denoted $P(X, Y)$, so the probability that an accident occurs in that interval is $1 - P(X, Y)$.[2] Figure 1 shows the relationship between X, Y and $P(X, Y)$. Examples of what will be meant here by controls are built-in safety devices and careful driving in the railway crossing case, defect-free radar and careful flying in the airplane case, and shoveling snow and careful walking in the sidewalk case.

By this description of accident avoidance we have constructed an almost exact analogue of the neoclassical production function, familiar to economists, where there are two inputs, X and Y, producing one output, $P(X, Y)$, which in our case is the probability that an accident will be avoided.[3] Just as the inputs to production are costly and should

[2]The time interval is chosen small enough that the probability of more than one accident in the interval is negligible.

[3]I say an almost exact analogue because we must take explicit account of the possibility that the accident can be completely avoided and further amounts of accident avoidance contribute nothing. Formally, we assume (1)

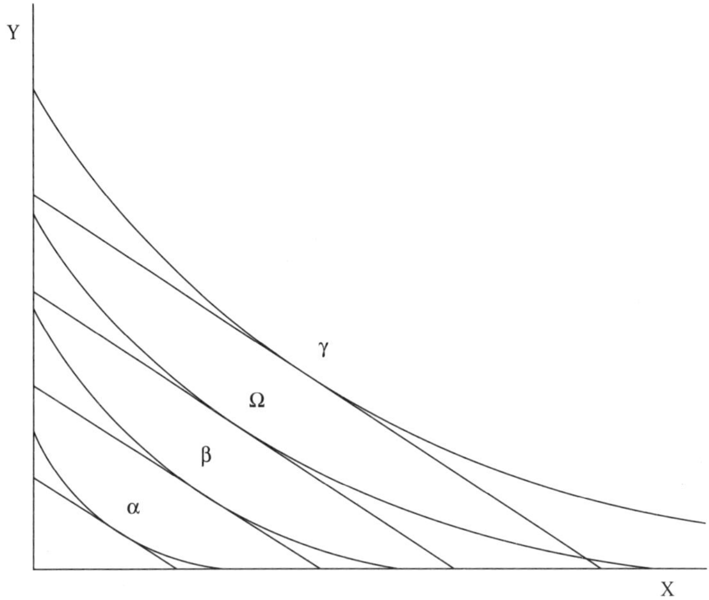

Figure 1

be economized on, so the accident avoidance controls X and Y are costly. Let the cost per unit of X be W_x and the cost per unit of Y be W_y. The total cost for a given level of X and Y is then $W_xX + W_yY$. The straight lines in Figure 1 are all of the combinations of X and Y having the same total cost. This completes the transformation of the accident avoidance problem into the standard production theory format. To find the least cost combination to X and Y which will yield a given probability of accident avoidance one need only find the point on the equiprobability curve just tangent to a cost line. Examples are drawn in Figure 1 at α, β, γ and Ω.

Which combination of avoidance measures X and Y and the resulting probability of accident $P(X, Y)$ is the most preferred? To answer that

---

that $P(X, Y)$ is continuous and twice differentiable in X and Y, (2) that the marginal products of both inputs are non-negative, and (3) marginal products do not increase. The possibility of complete avoidance admits the possibility that marginal products and their rate of change are zero. Our final assumption about $P(X, Y)$ is (4) that $P_{xy}(X, Y) \equiv \dfrac{\partial P^2(X, Y)}{\partial X \partial Y} < 0$. We shall discuss this assumption later in the analysis.

question we consider the case where both X and Y are under the control of the same party. In the simple case first before us, all quantities are measured in terms of money, so it makes no difference who makes the decision. The outcome we shall call the social optimum, and we shall use it to evaluate outcomes when X and Y are controlled by different people, which is of course the most interesting problem.

The social optimum we shall define as that combination of avoidance measures which minimizes the sum of the costs of the controls and the expected cost of the accident. With the apparatus that we have developed it is now a simple matter to write down the problem and to characterize the solution. Formally, the socially optimal values of X and Y are those that minimize social cost, $C_S(X, Y)$. Thus,

$$\min_{X,\,Y} C_S(X, Y) = W_x X + W_y Y + A[1 - P(X, Y)]. \tag{1}$$

The first two terms are the costs of the two controls, for example the costs of the crossing gates and of slower, more cautious driving in the railway crossing case. The last term is the expected cost of the accident and is the product of the cost of the accident and the probability that it will occur.

For the social cost to be at a minimum it must be true that the marginal cost of each input be equal to the expected value of its marginal product. That is

$$W_x = A P_x(X, Y) \qquad \text{and} \tag{2}$$

$$W_y = A P_y(X, Y) \tag{3}$$

where $P_x(X, Y)$ denotes the marginal product of X and $P_y(X, Y)$ denotes the marginal product of Y. The optimal solution can be found by solving equations (2) and (3) simultaneously for X and Y. Call the values which minimize social cost X_Ω and X_Ω. Then it is true for all values of X and Y that

$$C_S(X_\Omega, Y_\Omega) \leq C_S(X, Y) \qquad \text{for all } X \text{ and } Y. \tag{4}$$

I have chosen to have two controls to concentrate on the necessity in most accident contexts of having more than one party take costly measures to avoid accidents. Formally, it is a trivial extension to have more than two parties, but the legal implications of explicitly recognizing that there are more than two parties with responsibilities to avoid accidents should be explored carefully. The occasional cases where only one party can avoid the accident are special cases of this analysis where the equiprobability curves of Figure 1 would be either horizontal or vertical straight lines.

The optimal values are those that would be chosen if both X and Y were under common control. The problem that interests us here is where X and Y are controlled by different people.

Before proceeding further it will be helpful to deal with two misleading concepts, one used by lawyers and the other used by economists. The first is the notion that liability ought to be placed on whoever caused the accident. In the scheme we have described, who caused the accident, the victim or the injurer? They both did. The problem is exactly analogous to the futile arguments among economists in the nineteenth century about whether capital or labor causes production. They both do. We must go on to further considerations to decide how the fruits of production should be divided; similarly we have to decide who should bear the liability for accidents when they are jointly caused. The only role for discussions of causation is to exonerate a party completely by proving that he is a stranger to the accident.

A similar issue arises with the notion of "least cost avoider." A number of writers, among them Calabresi and Demsetz, have recommended placing liability on the best cost avoider. For example, Demsetz states: "It is difficult to suggest any criterion for deciding liability other than placing it on the party able to avoid the costly interaction most easily."[4] Looking back at Figure 1, how can we identify the best cost avoider? One possible meaning would be to compare the cost of the victim's completely avoiding the accident (*i.e.*, setting $P(0, Y) = 0$, with the cost of the injurer's completely avoiding the accident $P(X, 0) = 0$. The party with the lowest cost would be the cheapest cost avoider. Another possible interpretation of the phrase "least cost avoider" is that it is a local notion depending on (X, Y), that is, on what the parties in fact chose to do. This leaves unanswered how liability should be assigned in order to induce the parties to take the optimal amount of avoidance action. The notion of least cost avoider is thus likely to confuse rather than to clarify matters.

II. DECENTRALIZATION USING A LIABILITY RULE

When the two avoidance mechanisms are in the hands of different people, for example the manufacturer and the driver when the liability generator is attached to an automobile, or the manufacturer and patient in the case of a drug, the question arises as to how the bill shall be paid when an accident takes place. The question is answered by the court. Since this paper is

[4]Harold Demsetz, *supra* note 1, at 28.

concerned with how injurer and victims can be expected to respond under different liability rules I have chosen to provide only the simplest abstraction of the court and its functioning. For our purposes the only function of the legal system is the impeccable administration of whatever liability rule is in force. In order to concentrate on what is our major concern, the parties' behavior, we ignore the distinction between judge and jury, the problems of proof and burden of proof, the uncertainty of the outcome, the mistakes that the court can make, and the expense of operating the legal system.

To fix ideas for the rest of the discussion, let X be controlled by Xavier the Injurer, and Y by Yvonne the Victim. The rule that determines which party must pay the bill emitted by the liability generator is called a liability rule. The liability rule will in general be a function of the level of avoidance chosen by each party and will be expressed as the fraction of the bill, A, owed by each party. Let $L_x(X, Y)$ and $L_y(X, Y)$ be the liabilities of Xavier and Yvonne, respectively. Then

$$L_x(X,Y) \geq 0, L_y(X,Y) \geq 0 \qquad \text{for all } X,Y \tag{5}$$

$$L_x(X,Y) + L_y(X,Y) = 1 \qquad \text{for all } X,Y. \tag{6}$$

The amount that must be paid by Xavier when an accident takes place is $A\, L_x(X, Y)$ and the amount to be paid by Yvonne is $A\, L_y(X, Y)$.

A number of different liability rules have been discussed in the recent literature.[5] They are simple to put into the framework we propose but for some of them we require one further notion, that of a legal standard of negligence. Let (X^*, Y^*) be the legal standard of negligence. If X is less than X^* then the injurer will be found legally negligent. Similarly, if Y is less than Y^*, the victim will be found negligent. Now we are ready to describe the liability rules.

1. *No liability*. The victim is liable under all circumstances.

$$L_x(X,Y) = 0 \quad L_y(X,Y) = 1 \qquad \text{for all } X,Y. \tag{7}$$

2. *Strict liability*. The injurer is liable under all circumstances.

$$L_x(X,Y) = 1 \quad L_y(X,Y) = 0 \qquad \text{for all } X,Y. \tag{8}$$

3. *The negligence rule*. The victim is liable unless the injurer is found negligent.

$$L_x(X,Y) = \begin{cases} 0 \\ 1 \end{cases} L_y(X,Y) = \begin{cases} 1 & \text{if } X \geq X^* \\ 0 & \text{if } X < X^* \end{cases}. \tag{9}$$

[5]See Calabresi, Calabresi and Hirschoff, and Posner works cited in note 1 *supra*.

4. *Strict liability with contributory negligence.* The injurer is liable unless the victim is found negligent.

$$L_x(X,Y)=\begin{cases}1\\0\end{cases}\; L_y(X,Y)=\begin{cases}0 & \text{if } Y \geq Y^*\\1 & \text{if } Y < Y^*\end{cases}. \tag{10}$$

5. *The negligence rule with contributory negligence.* The injurer is liable if he is negligent *and* the victim is not. The victim is liable otherwise.

$$L_x(X,Y)=\begin{cases}1\\0\end{cases}\; L_y(X,Y)=\begin{cases}0 & \text{if } X < X^* \text{ and } Y \geq Y^*\\1 & \text{otherwise}\end{cases}. \tag{11}$$

The negligence rule with contributory negligence has been the dominant rule in tort law since *Brown v. Kendall*.[6] In that landmark case the defendant (the injurer) took up a stick to separate fighting dogs belonging to the plaintiff (the victim) and the defendant. In the course of beating the dogs the defendant accidentally hit the plaintiff in the eye, injuring him severely. Chief Justice Shaw laid down the rule: "... if both plaintiff and defendant at the time of the blow were using ordinary care, or if at that time the defendant was using ordinary care, and the plaintiff was not, or if at that time, both the defendant and the plaintiff were not using ordinary care, then the plaintiff could not recover."[7]

Notice that there is complete symmetry in our model between no liability and strict liability on the one hand and between the negligence rule on the one hand and strict liability with contributory negligence on the other. The strict liability rule that would be symmetrical to the negligence rule with contributory negligence has been mentioned only by Calabresi and Hirschoff in the recent literature. It might be called:

6. *Strict liability with dual contributory negligence.* The victim is liable if he is negligent *and* the injurer is not. The injurer is liable otherwise.

$$L_x(X, Y)=\begin{cases}0\\1\end{cases}\; L_y(X, Y)=\begin{cases}1 & \text{if } Y < Y^* \text{ and } X \geq X^*\\0 & \text{otherwise}\end{cases} \tag{12}$$

The six liability rules are displayed graphically in Figure 2.

There are two further liability rules that are somewhat outside the tradition encompassed in the six rules presented here in that the standard of care for one party is the level of care exercised by the other party. They are relative negligence and comparative negligence.

[6] 60 Mass. (6 Cush.) 292 (1850).

[7] *Id.* at 296.

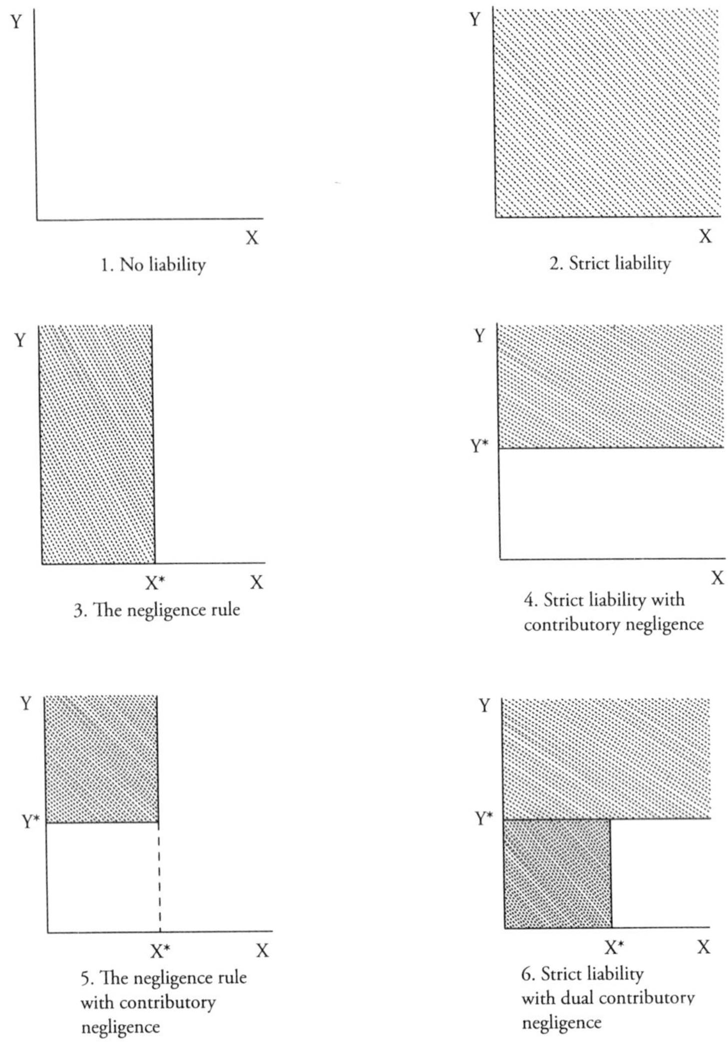

Figure 2 (Injurer liable in shaded area)

7. *Relative negligence.* The injurer is liable if the increment to accident avoidance per dollar of avoidance by him is greater than that per dollar of avoidance by the victim, *i.e.*, if a dollar spent by the injurer could have bought more avoidance than a dollar spent by the victim.

In our notation the liability rule for the injurer is

$$L_x(X, Y) = \begin{cases} 1 & \text{if } \dfrac{P_x(X, Y)}{W_x} > \dfrac{P_y(X, Y)}{W_y} \\ 0 & \text{otherwise} \end{cases} \tag{13}$$

$L_y(X, Y)$ is, as usual, the complement of $L_x(X, Y)$, that is,

$$L_y(X, Y) = 1 - L_x(X, Y) \tag{14}$$

Graphically, there is a very simple interpretation of the relative negligence rule. The slope of the equiprobability lines (isoquants) is $-\dfrac{P_x(X, Y)}{P_y(X, Y)}$ and the slope of the equal cost lines is $-\dfrac{W_x}{W_y}$. Therefore the injurer is negligent at (X, Y) if the equiprobability line is steeper than the equal cost line at (X, Y). Notice that at any (X, Y) either the injurer or the victim is relatively negligent. In case of ties we have arbitrarily assumed that the victim is liable. The negligence boundary is the locus of least cost combinations for different probabilities. See Figure 3.

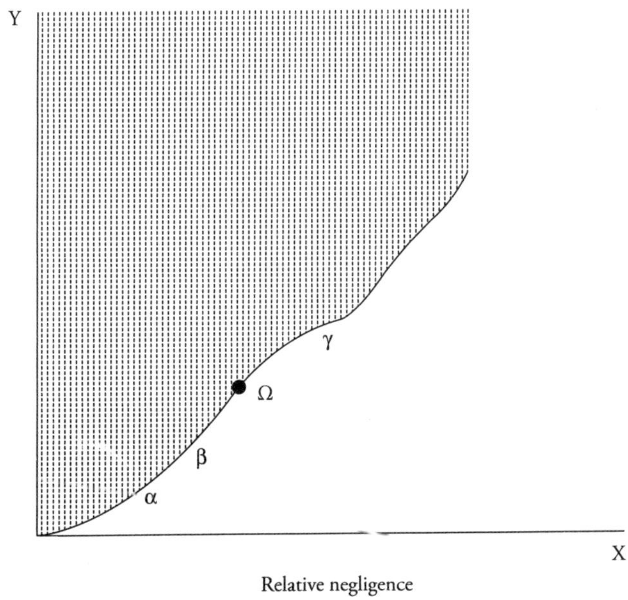

Figure 3 (Injurer liable in shaded area)

8. *Comparative negligence.* The doctrine of comparative negligence apportions the liability according to the relative liability of the two parties. This doctrine is established in admiralty law, but otherwise it is not recognized in any state except where it is established by statute, *e.g.*, in Wisconsin, Georgia, and Mississippi.[8] It is not clear whether negligence is defined as a marginal concept or an average one. If a marginal negligence concept is used, then, if n_x is the negligence of the injurer and n_y the negligence of the victim,

$$n_x = \frac{P_x(X, Y)}{W_x} \quad \text{and} \quad n_y = \frac{P_y(X, Y)}{W_y} \tag{15}$$

Negligence is the incremental reduction in accident probability per dollar spent, and the liability of the injurer is his negligence divided by the negligence of both parties:

$$L_x(X, Y) = \frac{n_x}{n_x + n_y} \tag{16}$$

The liability of the victim is $1 - L_x(X, Y)$.

III. THE LEGAL STANDARD OF NEGLIGENCE

We noted above that some of the liability rules require a legal determination of negligence by one party or the other. Call the legal standard of negligence for the injurer X^* and for the victim Y^*. In legal discussions this is often called the standard of care. If X is found to be less than X^* then the injurer will be judged negligent. Similarly, if Y is found to be less than Y^* the victim will be judged negligent.

The negligence standard most often cited in legal discussions of the problem is the so-called Learned Hand Rule,[9] which can be paraphrased as follows. The duty of a party is a function of three variables: (1) the probability of an accident; (2) the gravity of the accident; and (3) the burden of adequate precaution. Liability depends on whether the product of the first two is greater than the third. In our notation, the probability of an accident is $1 - P(X, Y)$, the gravity of the accident is A, and the burden of precaution is $W_x X$ for the injurer and $W_y Y$ for the victim. Thus, the Learned Hand Rule compares $A(1 - P(X, Y))$ with $W_x X$ for the injurer and with $W_y Y$ for the victim.

[8] See Charles O. Gregory and Harry Klaven, Jr., Cases and Materials on Torts 250–54 (2d ed. 1969).

[9] United States v. Carroll Towing Co., 159 F.2d 169 (2d Cir. 1947).

The Learned Hand Rule is ambiguous in important ways, as we shall show. In fact there are three closely related standards of negligence that can be derived from Judge Hand's formulation. The first we shall call the Literal Learned Hand Standard, or the Literal Standard for short. If we take literally the standard as given by Judge Hand, the injurer would be found negligent if

$$W_x X < A(1 - P(X, Y)) \tag{17}$$

and the victim would be found negligent if

$$W_y Y < A(1 - P(X, Y)) \tag{18}$$

This standard compares the total cost to a party with the expected cost of the accident.

There is one question for which the Literal Standard unambiguously gives the correct answer, but it is typically the wrong question, and might well suggest the wrong answer to the right question. Consider Figure 4. As drawn, the expected benefits are greater than the costs to the injurer for every level of X. The question that the Literal Standard

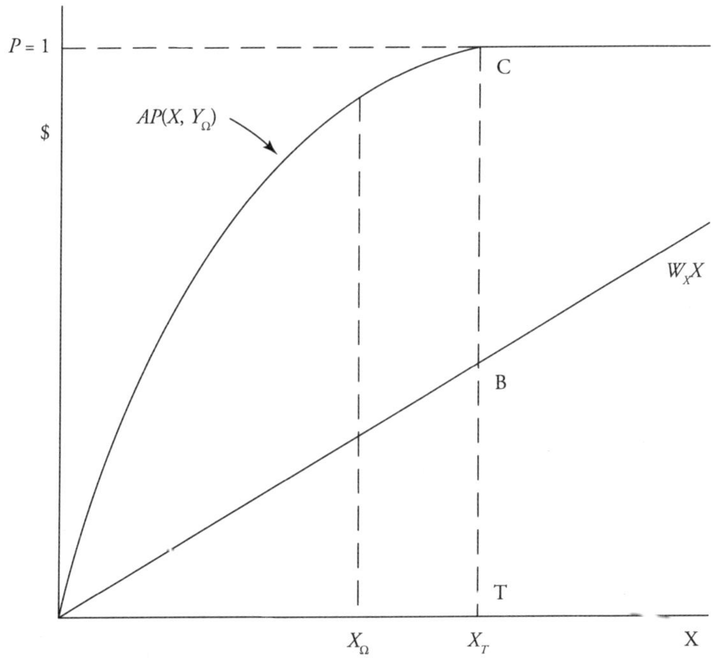

Figure 4

answers correctly is this: Is it better to provide complete protection, $X = T$, rather than no protection at all, $X = 0$? Then we need only compare the product of the probability of an accident and the gravity of the accident, *TC*, with the burden of adequate precaution, *TB*. In the case described in the figure, because *TC* is greater than *TB*, it is better to provide complete protection than no protection at all. Should it be the duty of the injurer to provide complete protection in this case? Clearly the answer is no. Although it is better to provide full protection than none at all, the optimal amount of protection from an overall point of view is Ω, where the marginal cost of protection is equal to the marginal expected benefit from the protection. By moving from X_T to X_Ω costs would decrease more than benefits. Clearly, we need a better negligence standard.[10]

The second standard derivable from Judge Hand's formulation is the Incremental Standard. Here we assume that the judicial system can ferret out complete information about the underlying technology of accident prevention so that negligence for one party is determined on the *assumption that the other party is already acting in an optimal manner.* Thus, the negligence standard for the injurer, X^*, is that value of X such that

$$W_x = A\, P_x(X^*, Y_\Omega) \tag{19}$$

and for the victim is Y^*, that value of Y such that:

$$W_y = A\, P_y(X_\Omega, Y^*) \tag{20}$$

Under the Incremental Standard the negligence standard is identical to the conditions for social cost minimization independently for both the injurer and the victim. Thus $X^* = X_\Omega$ and $Y^* = Y_\Omega$. Solving for the Incremental Standard is equivalent to identifying the social cost minimizing solution. The court uses the Incremental Standard to find the social optimum and defines any avoidance less than optimal as negligent. Below we shall investigate the effect of using the Incremental Standard with the various liability rules.

The third standard we shall call the Limited Information Incremental Standard. Rather than assuming that the court knows the entire technology of accident prevention as we did in the full information

[10]Calabresi and Hirschoff seem to have been misled by a literal reading of the Learned Hand rule. They say, for example (*supra* note 1, at 1057), "If the cost to the defendant of avoiding the accident would have been less than the cost of the accident, discounted by the probability of its occurrence, the defendant's failure to avoid the accident is termed negligence." This is the Learned Hand Literal Standard, in our terminology.

standard, we assume here that the court is able to investigate only the effects on the probability of an accident of small changes in the immediate neighborhood of the (X, Y) pair actually chosen by the two parties. In mathematical terms this means that the court is only able to determine the partial derivatives of $P(X, Y)$ at (X, Y). In effect, if the court uses the Limited Information Incremental Standard it is saying that an avoidance level is negligent if it is less than that which would be optimal *given what the other party has in fact done*. The injurer will be held negligent at some point (X, Y) if that X is less than would be required to minimize social cost, treating Y as fixed. Thus the lowest value of X for which the injurer will not be judged negligent is the minimum with respect to X of

$$C_S(X, Y) = W_x X + W_y Y + A(1 - P(X, Y))$$

The necessary marginal conditions for a minimum imply that the injurer will be found negligent at (X, Y) if

$$W_x < A\,P_x(X, Y) \tag{21}$$

and the victim will be found negligent at (X, Y) if

$$W_y < A\,P_y(X, Y). \tag{22}$$

To emphasize that the level of X that just allows the injurer to avoid being found negligent, X^*, depends on the avoidance actions taken by the victim, we shall use the functional notation $X^*(Y)$. Similarly, since the level of Y that just allows the victim to avoid being found negligent depends on the actions taken by the injurer, we write $Y^*(X)$.

The Incremental Standards are a good approximation, I think, of the way that courts actually proceed. The attorney for the plaintiff will try to find some act which, if the defendant had taken it, would have significantly reduced the probability of the accident at low cost. But that is precisely the statement that the increment in the expected loss was greater than the cost of avoidance, which is the definition of the Incremental Standards of negligence. The defendant will try to respond that the expected benefits of the proposed act were, in fact, less than the costs of undertaking it. When the court is asked to decide between the two points of view it is being asked to compare the incremental expected benefits with the incremental costs. Thus it is not peculiar that the outcome of large, important cases often seems to turn on the value of small changes in the behavior of one party or the other.

IV. A NONCOOPERATIVE GAME PLAYED ACCORDING TO LIABILITY RULES

What are the equilibrium values of X and Y when they are chosen by different people independently? How will Xavier and Yvonne behave when their only communication with each other will be in court after an accident occurs? All other transactions are assumed to be so costly that they do not take place.

We shall assume that the goal of Xavier is to choose X to minimize his expected private costs, that is:

$$\min_{X} C_x(X, Y) = W_x X + A\, L_x\, (X, Y)(1 - P(X, Y)) \tag{23}$$

and Yvonne minimizes her private costs:

$$\min_{Y} C_y(X, Y) = W_y Y + A\, L_y\, (X, Y)(1 - P(X, Y)). \tag{24}$$

These are simply the sum of the cost of their own preventive efforts and their expected liability when an accident occurs.

Both parties are assumed to know A, W_x, W_y, and $P(X, Y)$ as well as the liability rule in force and that the other party is interested only in private costs. Our problem is to try to find equilibria for the games and determine whether they are unique. An equilibrium for a game is a pair of values (X, Y) chosen by the two players such that, given the choice by the opponent, neither party has an incentive to change his own choice.

Before analyzing the various rules it will be useful to describe two response functions for each party. They are called response functions because, like the response functions in Cournot's analysis of duopoly, they show what response a party would choose, given the choice of the opponent.

The first response function we call $X^f(Y)$. The superscript f denotes full cost. It is defined as the injurer's preferred value of X given Y, assuming that the injurer must pay in full for any damages. That is, $X^f(Y)$ is that X for which $W_x X + A(1 - P(X,Y))$ is at a minimum. Alternatively, $X^f(Y)$ is the value of X which minimizes social cost when Y is fixed, since the only difference between private and social costs is the constant $W_y Y$, since Y is considered fixed. It is a necessary condition of minimization that at each value of $X^f(Y)$

$$W_x = A\, P_x(X^f, Y). \tag{25}$$

We take the total differential of this condition

$$A\, P_{xx} dX^f + A\, P_{xy} dY = 0 \tag{26}$$

and solve it for $\dfrac{dX^f}{dY}$

$$\frac{dX^f}{dY} = -\frac{P_{xy}}{P_{xx}}. \tag{27}$$

This gives us the change in the optimal X for a change in Y. Convexity implies that $P_{xy} < 0$. Therefore if $P_{xy} < 0$ as we assume, then

$$\frac{dX^f}{dY} < 0 \tag{28}$$

that is, a decrease in Y will call forth an increase in X.

Throughout the rest of our analysis we shall employ one slightly restrictive assumption about the technology of accident avoidance, namely that $P_{xy} < 0$. The technical effect of the assumption is to insure that the full cost response functions X^f and Y^f are both downward sloping. If they were upward sloping there could be a second intersection on one axis or the other and hence a second equilibrium. Assuming $P_{xy} < 0$ is equivalent to assuming that a decrease in accident avoidance by one party ought to call forth an increase in accident avoidance by the other. For example, if cars drive faster on one residential street than on another we would expect mothers to take greater care that their children do not stray onto the first street than onto the second, or as trains approach a crossing more rapidly we would expect cars to approach more slowly. Only in the bizarre case where the technology of accident prevention were such that the appropriate response to faster trains would be *less* caution on the part of drivers would the assumption of $P_{xy} < 0$ be inappropriate.

Correspondingly, there is, of course, the response function for the victim, $Y^f(X)$, which is the victim's preferred value of Y given X, assuming that the victim must pay in full for any damages. Therefore $Y^f(X)$ is the value of X which minimizes $W_yY + A[1 - P(X,Y)]$. Figure 5 shows $X^f(Y)$ and $Y^f(X)$.

The second response function we shall consider gives the party's preferred strategy, given the opponent's strategy, for the actual expected private costs, $C_x(X, Y)$ or $C_y(X, Y)$, which depend on the liability rule in force. This response function is denoted $X^e(Y)$ for the injurer and $Y^e(X)$ for the victim. The superscript e signifies equilibrium. $X^e(Y)$ is that value of X for each Y that minimizes $C_x(X, Y)$. For example, if the liability rule is the negligence rule with contributory negligence and the negligence standard is the Incremental Standard,

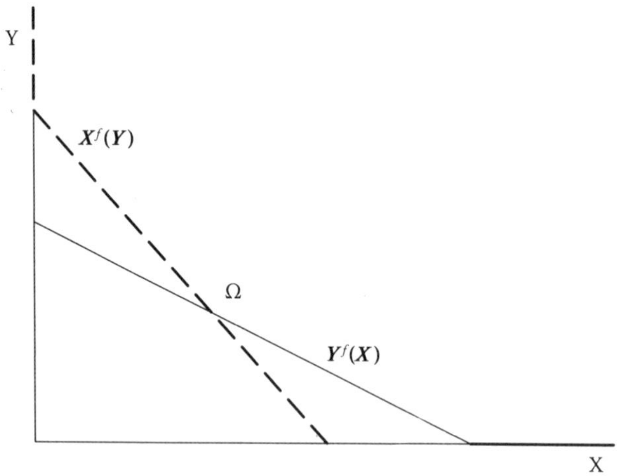

Figure 5

$$C_x(X, Y) = \begin{cases} W_x X + A[1 - P(X, Y)] & \text{if } X < X_\Omega \text{ and } Y \geqslant Y_\Omega \\ W_x X & \text{otherwise} \end{cases} \quad (29)$$

In the same case $Y^e(X)$ is that value of Y which minimizes the victim's expected private costs, which are

$$C_y(X, Y) = \begin{cases} W_y Y & \text{if } X < X_\Omega \text{ and } Y \geqslant Y_\Omega \\ W_y Y + A[1 - P(X, Y)] & \text{otherwise} \end{cases}$$

$X^e(Y)$ and $Y^e(X)$ are plotted in Figure 6. The shaded area is the area where the injurer is liable.

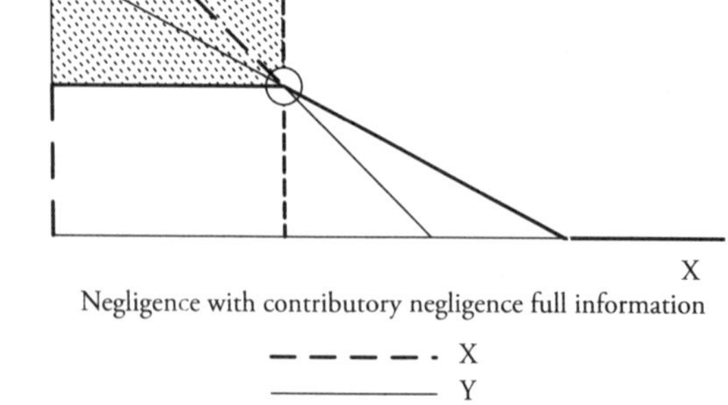

Figure 6

V. EQUILIBRIUM UNDER THE VARIOUS LIABILITY RULES

1. No Liability

First consider the rule of no liability. All bills emitted by the liability generator are to be paid by the victim, Yvonne, without regard to any measures either she or the injurer took. Then the costs paid by the injurer are only the costs of his own avoidance measures, so his problem is to

$$\min_{X} C_x(X, Y) = W_x X \tag{30}$$

It is obvious that he will choose $X = 0$; there are no benefits to him from avoiding accidents. In other words $X^e(Y) = 0$ for all Y.
For the victim the task is to

$$\min_{Y} C_y(0, Y) = W_y Y + A(1 - P(0, Y)) \tag{31}$$

that is, minimize the sum of his avoidance costs and expected losses given that the injurer will do nothing. This sum will be at a minimum when:

$$W_y = A\,P_y(0, Y) \tag{32}$$

that is, at $Y^f(0)$. The equilibrium values of the game are $X = 0$ and $Y = Y^f(0)$, rather than the social optimum $(X_\Omega\ Y_\Omega)$. It is obvious that the equilibrium is unique. See Figure 7a.

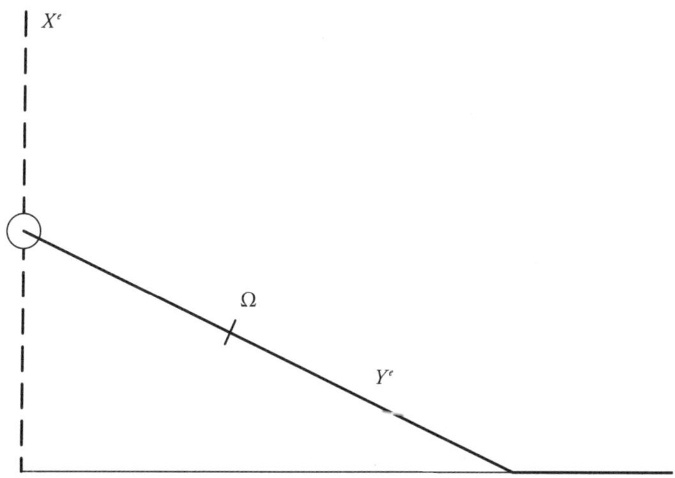

No liability

Figure 7a

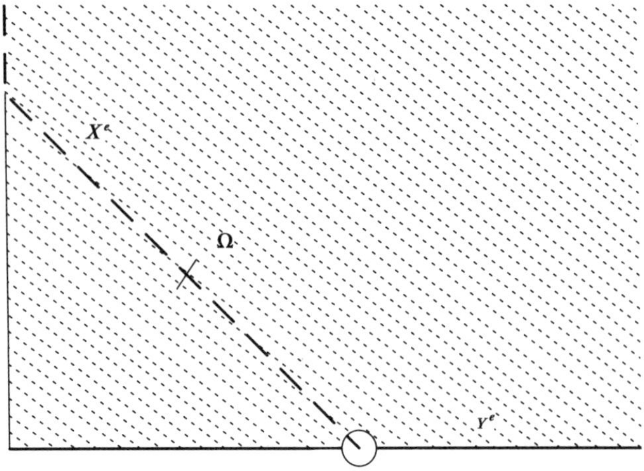

Figure 7b

2. Strict Liability

Next consider the rule of strict liability. The injurer is responsible for all accidents. The argument is identical to that for the rule of no liability except that the roles of injurer and victim, *X* and *Y*, are reversed. The victim will have no incentive to take any precautions: the injurer will choose the best level of precaution given that the victim takes none. The equilibrium is $(X^f(0), 0)$.Again, it is obvious that the equilibrium is unique. See Figure 7b.

The situation changes radically when we move on to liability rules that apply negligence standards to one or both parties.

3. Negligence Rule with Contributory Negligence, Incremental Standard

We can now state the first of the major results of the paper.

Theorem 1: If the social optimum (X_Ω, Y_Ω) is a unique minimum of the social cost function $C_S(X, Y)$, the liability rule in force is the Negligence Rule with Contributory Negligence, the negligence standard is the Incremental Standard, and $P_{xy} < 0$, then the social optimum is a unique noncooperative equilibrium.

Proof of Theorem 1: First we show that (X_Ω, Y_Ω) is a non-cooperative equilibrium. For the injurer we have to show that his costs, given Y_Ω, are less at X_Ω than at any other value of *X*. That is, we have to show that

$$C_x(X_\Omega, Y_\Omega) \leqslant C_x(X, Y_\Omega) \qquad \text{for all } X. \tag{33}$$

Recall that

$$C_x(X, Y_\Omega) = \begin{cases} W_x X + A[1 - P(X, Y_\Omega)] & \text{if } X < X_\Omega \\ W_x X & \text{if } X \geqslant X_\Omega \end{cases} \tag{34}$$

This cost function is plotted in Figure 8a. It is clear that it is a minimum at X_Ω.

In analogous fashion we must show that given the injurer's choice of X_Ω, the victim can do no better than Y_Ω. See Figure 8b. That is, we must show that

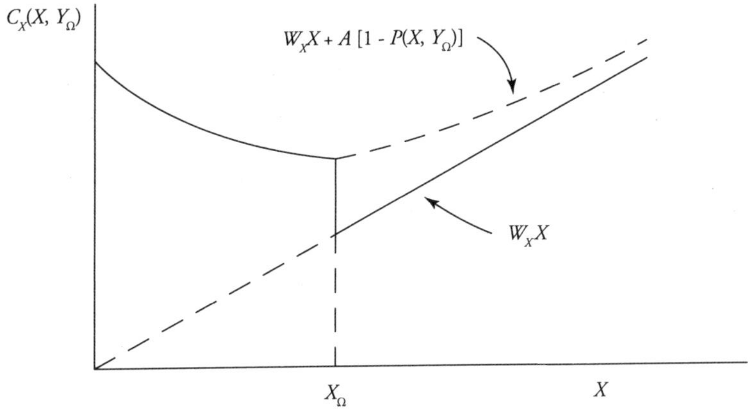

Injurer's costs when victim has chosen Y_Ω

Figure 8a

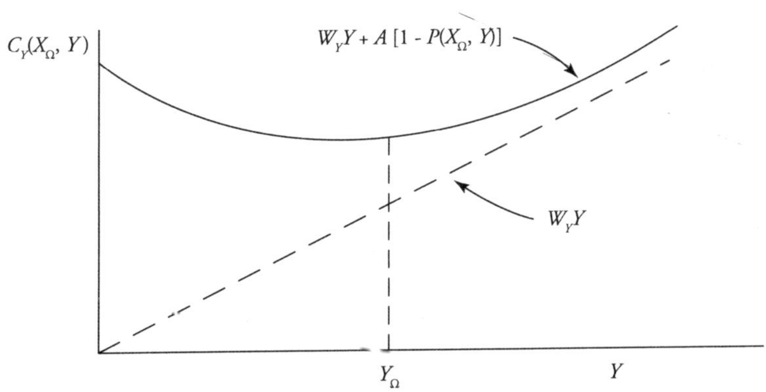

Victim's costs when injurer has chosen X_Ω

Figure 8b

$$C_y(X_\Omega, Y_\Omega) \leq C_y(X_\Omega, Y) \qquad \text{for all } Y. \tag{35}$$

This we do by writing out $C_y\ (X_\Omega, Y)$

$$C_y(X, Y) = W_y Y + A[1 - P(X_\Omega, Y) \tag{36}$$

and minimizing it. The condition for its being a minimum is

$$W_y = A\, P_y(X_\Omega, Y) \tag{37}$$

which is identically a condition for the minimization of social cost at (X_Ω, Y_Ω). Therefore $C_y(X_\Omega, Y)$ is minimized at Y_Ω, which completes the proof that (X_Ω, Y_Ω) is a non-cooperative equilibrium. What has been shown is that $X^e(Y_\Omega) = X_\Omega$ and $Y^e(X_\Omega) = Y_\Omega$.

To show that (X_Ω, Y_Ω) is a unique equilibrium we show that X^e and Y^e intersect only once, at (X_Ω, Y_Ω) . See Figure 9a. A party will never choose a point where he is liable other than on the full cost equilibrium, X^f or Y^f. Also a party will never choose any point where he is not liable other than the one which requires him to do the least. Therefore, each party's equilibrium will be either on the full cost equilibrium X^f or Y^f or the lowest cost point where he is not liable. Thus in the figure X^e crosses the shaded area on X^f and then drops to zero as soon as the injurer is not liable. Similarly, Y^e stays at the lowest part of the shaded area, where the victim is not liable, and then crosses the unshaded area, where she is liable, on Y^f. The only intersection of X^e and Y^e is at (X_Ω, Y_Ω) ; hence (X_Ω, Y_Ω) is a unique non-cooperative equilibrium, because both parties are in equilibrium there and only there.

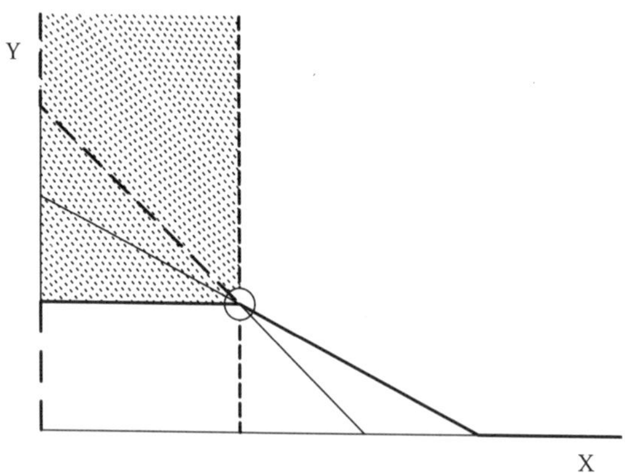

Negligence with contributory negligence full information

Figure 9a

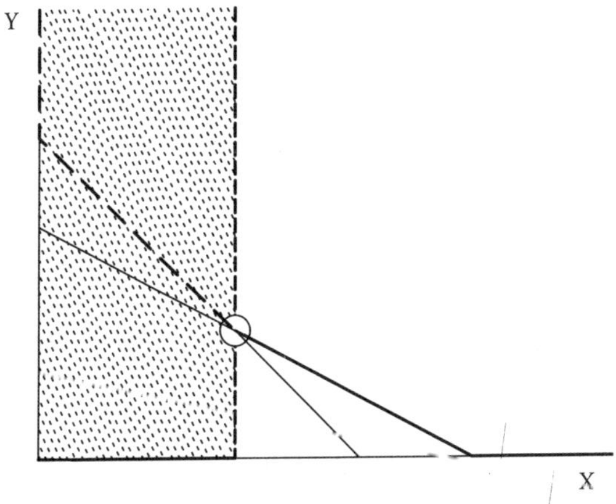

Negligence rule full information

Figure 9b

4. The Negligence Rule, Incremental Standard

Corollary 1: The results of Theorem 1 hold if the liability rule is changed from the negligence rule with contributory negligence to the negligence rule.

Proof: The equilibrium reaction functions $X^e(Y)$ and $Y^e(X)$ are plotted in Figure 9b for the case of the negligence rule and the Incremental Standard. The changes in the functions resulting from the change in liability rule are inconsequential from the point of view of the proof of the theorem. The reaction functions still only intersect at the social optimum, (X_Ω, Y_Ω).

5. Strict Liability with Contributory Negligence and with Dual Contributory Negligence

Corollary 2: The results of Theorem 1 hold if the liability rule is changed to either strict liability with contributory negligence or strict liability with dual contributory negligence.

Proof: To obtain the results for strict liability with contributory negligence we merely exchange the roles of X and Y in the proof of Corollary 1. To obtain the results for strict liability with dual contributory negligence we exchange X and Y in the argument of the theorem.

One can summarize the results on decentralized games with liability rules so far as follows: with either no liability or strict liability rules in effect the incentives on the party without liability are perverse so the resulting equilibrium will not be the optimal one. For all four remaining rules, which are based on negligence of one or both parties, given the

Incremental Standard the game will have a unique equilibrium and that equilibrium is the social optimum. Within the framework of our analysis there is no preferred choice among any of the four rules.

Perhaps it would be useful to point out here what the analysis does not say. It does not say that there is no basis for choice among the four rules; only that the factors that we have chosen to analyze do not lead us to choose any one of the negligence rules. If the cost of using the courts to transfer liability is very high, then the negligence rule with contributory negligence becomes more attractive because it transfers liability least often. Within the scope of our analysis any of the negligence rules is preferable to either the no liability rule or strict liability. That preference could, of course, be overthrown by factors outside the analysis. One could construct an argument for no liability (as in the case of "no-fault" insurance schemes) by showing that the costs of administering the negligence system far outweigh the losses caused by the incorrect incentives which are inherent in no-fault schemes. Also our analysis assumes a completely informed court system that does not have difficulty in producing accurate evidence. There are no evidentiary problems and who has the burden of proof is irrelevant.

VI. THE LIMITED INFORMATION INCREMENTAL STANDARD

Now we turn to the case where the court no longer knows what the social optimum is and only judges each party's behaviour on the basis of small changes from where the parties actually were when the accident occurred. That is, we shall assume that the courts use the Limited Information Incremental Standard as the standard of care. The boundary between the injurer being negligent and not, $X^*(Y)$, is no longer a vertical line at X_Ω but rather is identical with $X^f(Y)$ passing through (X_Ω, X_Ω). Similarly, $Y^*(X) = Y^f(X)$.

1. The Negligence Rule with Contributory Negligence

Theorem 2: The results of Theorem 1 are destroyed when the Incremental Standard of negligence is replaced by the Limited Information Incremental Standard. The social optimum is not an equilibrium; in fact there is no equilibrium.

Proof: First we shall show that the social optimum, (X_Ω, Y_Ω), is not an equilibrium. To do so we need only consider the cost function of the injurer when the victim is at the social optimum $C_x(X, Y_\Omega)$.

$$C_x(X, Y_\Omega) = W_x X \tag{38}$$

That is, at no value of X is the injurer liable when $Y = Y_\Omega$; therefore the injurer will have no incentive to provide any accident avoidance measures at all. His costs will be at a minimum if $X = 0$. Therefore (X_Ω, Y_Ω) is not an equilibrium.

X^e and Y^e are plotted in Figure 10a for the case of the Limited Information Incremental Standard. The argument for the shape of the curves is the same as in Theorem 1 and does not need to be repeated. What appears to be an intersection at $(0, Y^f(0))$ is not. $X^e(Y^f(0))$ is not zero. (Only for $Y^f(0) - \epsilon$, where ϵ is arbitrarily small, is X^e zero.) Hence there is no equilibrium and the parties will cycle about as shown in Figure 10a.

Corollary 1: When the liability rule is changed from the negligence rule with contributory negligence to the negligence rule, the social optimum is again not an equilibrium.

Proof: Refer to Figure 10b. The logic of the proof is to confirm that X^e and Y^e are as drawn.

Corollary 2: Symmetrical results hold for strict liability with contributory negligence when the standard of care is the Limited Information Incremental Standard.

Proof: Merely exchange the roles of X and Y in Corollary 1.

Corollary 3: Symmetrical results hold for strict liability with dual contributory negligence when the standard of care is the Limited Information Incremental Standard.

Proof: Exchange the roles of X and Y in Theorem 2.

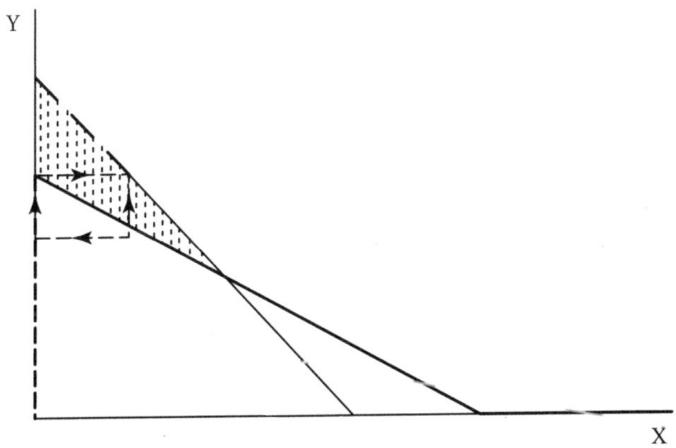

Negligence with contributory negligence limited information

Figure 10a

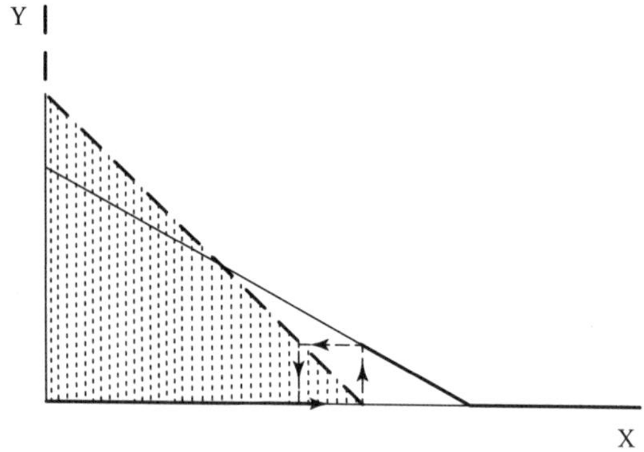

Negligence rule limited information

Figure 10b

2. Relative Negligence

Theorem 3: If the liability rule in force is the relative negligence rule, then the social optimum is a unique noncooperative equilibrium.

Proof: X^e and Y^e are plotted in Figure 11. The shaded area is the area where the injurer is liable. In the unshaded area, the victim is liable. As

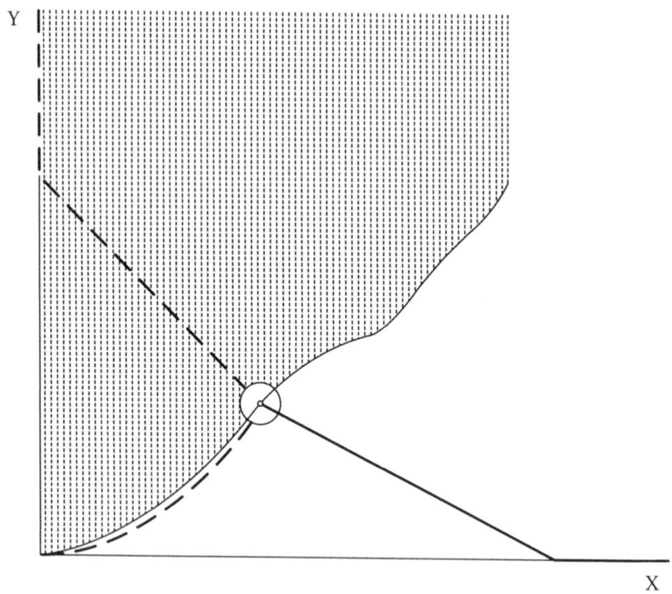

Relative negligence

Figure 11

before, the injurer will choose the least costly place where he is not liable unless X^f lies to the left, *i.e.*, is less expensive. Then he will choose X^f. Similarly, the victim will choose a strategy of the least costly place where she is not liable unless Y^f lies below that point, in which case she will choose Y^f. X^e and Y^e intersect at (X_Ω, X_Ω). The two equilibria are adjacent from zero to (X_Ω, X_Ω). In that range, the injurer's strategy will be to follow exactly the relative negligence boundary (the expansion path in conventional economic production theory parlance) because by our convention the victim is liable exactly on the boundary. The victim's strategy here is, in principle, undefined. There does not exist an optimal strategy in this area, only a limit to the strategy. What she wants to do is to get as close to the boundary as possible without touching it. For any given strategy not on the boundary one can in principle get closer to the boundary, *e.g.*, half as far, but this technical difficulty is not critical since (X_Ω, Y_Ω) is a well-defined equilibrium in any case.

3. Comparative Negligence

Rather than analyze completely the comparative negligence rule, I shall simply show that the social optimum is *not* an equilibrium under the comparative negligence rule. At (X_Ω, Y_Ω), $L_x(X,Y) = \frac{1}{2}$ since both parties are equally "negligent." Let Y be fixed at Y_Ω. The injurer will choose X_Ω only if his expected cost is at a minimum there. Now

$$C_x(X_\Omega, Y_\Omega) = W_x X + \frac{1}{2} A[1 - P(X,Y)] \tag{39}$$

which will be the minimum over X only if

$$W_x = \frac{1}{2} A\, P_x(X_\Omega, Y_\Omega) \tag{40}$$

But by the definition of (X_Ω, Y_Ω) ,

$$W_x = A\, P_x(X_\Omega, Y_\Omega) \tag{41}$$

so (X_Ω, Y_Ω) cannot be an equilibrium.[11]

[11]This argument is not strictly true. We have left out the effect of changing X on the liability rule. It is possible, for particular values of the first and second derivatives, that the neglected effect will exactly cancel out the difference we point to in the text. Though it is possible, in general we cannot expect it to happen.

CONCLUSIONS

In this paper economic analysis has been used to subject a variety of liability rules and standards of care to scrutiny in an abstract setting. It is my contention, which I hope the paper supports, that economic analysis is a useful method of organizing legal questions. It brings out similarities among apparently different legal doctrines, and it allows one to bring a large body of analysis to bear.

The paper first described accident avoidance by two parties in such a way that we could exploit the analogy with the economic theory of production. We used the model thus developed to characterize eight different liability rules discussed in the legal literature, and three variants of the Learned Hand formulation of the standard of care. The literal variant of Judge Hand's formulation we rejected immediately because it was not an incremental standard. Then we analyzed each of the liability rules, using (where appropriate) both of the remaining standards of care, the Incremental Standard and the Limited Information Incremental Standard. The analysis consisted of considering the victim and the injurer as noncommunicating parties in a game played according to liability rules. We identified the noncooperative equilibrium point as the solution for the game and in each case compared it with the social optimum.

To summarize the results, equilibrium for the simple no-liability rule as well as for the simple strict-liability rule did not coincide with the social optimum, nor did equilibrium for the comparative-negligence rule. When the standard of care was the Incremental Standard the social optimum was identical with the equilibrium for the relative-negligence rule, as well as with the equilibrium for all four of the common law negligence-based rules. The standard of care is critical, for, when it was changed to the Limited Information Incremental Standard, the identity between equilibrium and optimality was destroyed.

APPENDIX

The Case of Free Transactions: The Coase Theorem

In the body of the paper I analyzed the polar case where the only transactions that occurred between parties took place in court after an accident occurred. The parties played a game according to whatever liability rules were in force at the time. Here I explore briefly the opposite case, where transactions between parties may be freely arranged at any time. This problem has been examined by many authors since Ronald Coase's important article,[12] although Coase was not entirely or even primarily interested in the case of costless transactions. On the contrary, he was mainly interested in the costless-transaction case as a convenient expository device, a polar case. The Coase Theorem, a phrase coined and used by later writers, states roughly that regardless of the initial assignment of rights, if rights can be traded costlessly, the resulting allocation of rights will be efficient. Furthermore, if the income effects resulting from the transfer of rights can be neglected, the allocation of rights after bargaining will be independent of the initial assignment of those rights.

The questions that we shall ask here are, what transactions will take place between the parties, and what will the final amounts of X and Y be after all transactions have taken place? To set the stage let us define the initial property rights as follows: Xavier, the injurer, has complete control over the amount of X chosen as well as the liability for any bills that the liability rules assess him for. Similarly, Yvonne the victim has complete control over Y and responsibility for any bills that are assessed to her.

In the first situation we shall analyze, where the liability rule in force is no liability, all bills emitted by the liability generator must be paid by Yvonne. We have shown that the equilibrium amounts of X and Y in the absence of transactions will be $X = 0$ and $Y = Y^f(0)$. The expected cost to her is $C_y(0, Y^f(0))$, which is the same as the social cost since Xavier pays nothing.

Free bargaining assures that Yvonne will continue to pay Xavier to increase X until the marginal value of X to Xavier and to Yvonne are equal. The marginal value of X to Xavier is simply W_x; the marginal value to Yvonne is $A\,P_x(X, Y)$. This condition is exactly that in equation (3), and the cost-minimizing choice of Y by Yvonne assures us of (4). These two together are the conditions of the social optimum. The cost to Yvonne of attaining (X_Ω, Y_Ω) is

$$W_y Y_\Omega + A\,(1 - P(X_\Omega, Y_\Omega)) + \text{Payment to } X. \qquad \text{(A1)}$$

The payment is undetermined except that it is bounded from below by $W_x X_\Omega$, the minimum amount that Xavier would accept in order to provide X_Ω, and from above

[12]R.H. Coase, *supra* note 1.

by $C_S(0, Y^f(0)) - C_S(X_\Omega, Y_\Omega)$, the maximum that Yvonne would be willing to pay. If X is provided competitively, then the competitive price of X would be W_x and the payment to the injurer would be exactly $W_x X_\Omega$. In any event, the socially optimal amount of X and Y will be chosen and the net social cost will be $C_S(X_\Omega, Y_\Omega)$.

The result for the second liability rule, the rule of strict liability, is exactly the same, as is the argument leading to the result, except that the roles of the injurer and victim are reversed. The amount of X and Y chosen this time by Xavier will be X_Ω and X_Ω, and the net social cost will be $C_S(X_\Omega, Y_\Omega)$. The only difference between the results of the first and second liability rules is a transfer of income. In the first case, when there is no liability, the victim, Yvonne, pays the whole social cost plus a net payment to Xavier. In the case of strict liability, Yvonne not only pays nothing but receives some net payment from Xavier which depends on relative bargaining strength, while Xavier must pay the whole social cost.

I turn now to the case of costless transactions when more complicated liability rules, such as the negligence rule, are in force. Consider the negligence rule. What transactions will take place when they are free?

In the absence of transactions X_Ω and X_Ω will be chosen, as we have shown above. Thus the victim, Yvonne, can be assured that the injurer will set X at X_Ω without her having to pay a bribe. The benefit of having the injurer increase X above X_Ω would be less than the minimum cost of the increase, W_x. Similarly, Xavier would have no reason to bribe Yvonne to increase Y, because he is not liable. Therefore, under the negligence rule no transactions will take place and the level of avoidance measures chosen by the injurer and the victim will be X_Ω and X_Ω. The cost to the injurer will be $W_x X_\Omega$, and the expected cost to the victim will be $W_y Y_\Omega + A(1 - P(X_\Omega, Y_\Omega))$. The results for the rest of the liability rules can easily be shown to be similar to those of the negligence rule.

5

A New Positive Economic Theory of Negligence†

*Mark F. Grady**

Within the last generation, economic analysis has produced a wealth of insights into common law principles and especially into the common law of tort.[1] Two distinct traditions have emerged within the economic approach to tort law. The normative tradition attempts to evaluate the economic desirability of liability rules with a view toward reforming them.[2] In contrast, the positive tradition uses economic concepts to

†Originally published as "A New Positive Economic Theory of Negligence", 1983, *The Yale Law Journal*, Vol. 92, pp. 799–829.
*I wish to acknowledge the encouragement and assistance of Wesley J. Liebeler, James E. Krier, and George L. Priest in writing this Article. I am also grateful to the participants of the several workshops at which I presented it: the Chicago Law and Economics Workshop, particularly Richard Posner, Richard Epstein, and William Landes; the Yale Law and Economics Workshop, particularly George Priest, Guido Calabresi, Alvin Klevorick, and Henry Hansmann; the Iowa Economics Workshop, particularly Donald McCloskey and John Kennan. Thanks are also due to those others who provided helpful comments on earlier drafts, particularly Harold Demsetz, Ronald Allen, Michael Green, Dorsey Ellis, Steven Burton, Gary Schwartz, and Steven Shavell. I received financial assistance for this work from the Yale Civil Liability Program, the Iowa faculty fellowship program, and the U.L.C.A. graduate economics fellowship program.
[1]The history of the law and economics movement is discussed in Landes & Posner, *The Positive Economic Theory of Tort Law,* 15 GA. L. REV. 851, 852–56 (1981); G. Priest, The Rise of Law and Economics (Oct. 28, 1982) (unpublished manuscript on file with Civil Liability Program, Yale Law School).
[2]The leading normative theorist and the co-founder of the economic approach to tort is Guido Calabresi, whose fully developed theory is laid out in G. Calabresi, The Costs of Accidents: A Legal and Economic Analysis (1970). The earliest statement of his theory is in Calabresi, *Some Thoughts on Risk Distribution and the Law of Torts,* 70 Yale L.J. 499 (1961). Other important articles by Calabresi on the normative

explain common law liability rules with a view toward gaining a better understanding of the rules themselves and of their social consequences.[3] The hypothesis that the positive economic theory of tort seeks to confirm or refute is that tort rules are designed to minimize social cost—the sum

---

economic theory of tort are Calabresi, *Concerning Cause and the Law of Torts: An Essay for Harry Kalven, Jr.*, 43 U. Chi. L. Rev. 69 (1975) [hereinafter cited as Calabresi, *Concerning Cause and the Law of Torts*]; Calabresi, *Fault, Accidents and the Wonderful World of Blum and Kalven*, 75 Yale L.J. 216 (1975); Calabresi, *Does the Fault System Optimally Control Primary Accident Costs?*, 33 Law & Contemp. Probs. 429 (1968); Calabresi, *Transaction Costs, Resource Allocation and Liability Rules—A Comment*, 11 J.L. & Econ. 67 (1968); Calabresi, *The Decision for Accidents: An Approach to Nonfault Allocation of Costs*, 78 Harv. L. Rev. 713 (1965); Calabresi & Hirschoff, *Toward a Test for Strict Liability in Torts*, 81 Yale L.J. 1055 (1972); Calabresi & Melamed, *Property Rules, Liability Rules, and Inalienability: One View of the Cathedral*, 85 Harv. L. Rev. 1089 (1972).

The other co-founder of the economic approach to tort is Ronald Coase, whose leading work in this area is Coase, *The Problem of Social Cost*, 3 J.L. & Econ. 1 (1960). Some parts of Coase's analysis are normative, *see id.* at 36–38, and other parts are positive, *see id.* at 19–28. Coase's theory has been reconsidered and extended in Cooter, *The Cost of Coase*, 11 J. Legal Stud. 1 (1982); Demsetz, *When Does the Rule of Liability Matter?*, 1 J. Legal Stud. 13 (1972). The most recent important contribution to the normative economic theory of tort is Rizzo & Arnold, *Causal Apportionment in the Law of Torts: An Economic Theory*, 80 Colum. L. Rev. 1399 (1980).

[3]The leading work in the positive economic theory of tort is Posner, *A Theory of Negligence*, 1 J. Legal Stud. 29 (1972). Other important contributions by Richard Posner and William Landes are Landes & Posner, *Causation in Tort Law: An Economic Approach*, 12 J. Legal Stud. 109 (1983) [hereinafter cited as Landes & Posner, *Causation*]; Landes & Posner, *supra* note 1; Landes & Posner, *An Economic Theory of Intentional Torts*, 1 Int'l L. & Econ. Rev. 127 (1981); Landes & Posner, *Joint and Multiple Tortfeasors: An Economic Analysis*, 9 J. Legal Stud. 517 (1980) [hereinafter cited as Landes & Posner, *Joint and Multiple Tortfeasors*]; Landes & Posner, *Salvors, Finders, Good Samaritans, and Other Rescuers: An Economic Analysis of Law and Altruism*, 7 J. Legal Stud. 83 (1978). Additional significant contributions by Posner alone are R. Posner, Economic Analysis of Law 119–61 (2d ed. 1977); Posner, *Privacy, Secrecy, and Reputation*, 28 Buffalo L. Rev. 1 (1979); Posner, *The Right of Privacy*, 12 Ga. L. Rev. 393 (1978); Posner, *Strict Liability: A Comment*, 2 J. Legal Stud. 205 (1973). Important contributions to the positive economic theory of tort by scholars other than Landes and Posner include Brown, *Toward an Economic Theory of Liability*, 2 J. Legal Stud. 323 (1973); Diamond, *Accident Law and Resource Allocation*, 5 Bell J. Econ. & Mgmt. Sci. 366 (1974); Diamond & Mirlees, *On the Assignment of Liability: The Uniform Case*, 6 Bell J. Econ. & Mgmt. Sci. 487 (1975); Green, *On the Optimal Structure of Liability Laws*, 7 Bell J. Econ. & Mgmt. Sci. 553 (1976); Shavell, *An Analysis of Causation and the Scope of Liability in the Law of Torts*, 9 J. Legal Stud. 463 (1980) [hereinafter cited as Shavell, *Causation and the Scope of Liability*]; Shavell, *Strict*

of precaution costs expended in attempting to prevent accidents and injury costs resulting when such accidents occur.[4]

Positive theory must have means to ascertain which liability rules minimize social cost and whether the actual liability rules that courts employ do so. Thus, each positive tort theory contains two parts. First, there is a formal part that posits particular rules and ascertains their social consequences using the tools of economic theory. Second, there is an empirical part that assesses whether the rules posited in the formal model correspond to decision rules that courts actually use. Any particular positive theory of tort can thus be challenged on two levels: that its formal liability rules would not minimize social cost or that its formal liability rules do not correspond to the ones that courts use.

This Article seeks to provide an alternative to the conventional theory of negligence law, set forth by John Prather Brown,[5] William Landes, and Richard Posner.[6] First, it discusses the formal negligence rules specified by this theory. Next, it argues that these rules do not lead to minimum social cost under conditions of uncertainty. As an alternative, it proposes a new formal rule that appears more surely to lead to minimum social cost under uncertainty. Finally, it shows that this new negligence rule is more consistent with the actual decision rules used by courts than the formal rules posited by the conventional theory.

Liability Versus Negligence, 9 J. Legal Stud. 1 (1980); Wittman, *Optimal Pricing of Sequential Inputs: Last Clear Chance, Mitigation of Damages, and Related Doctrines in the Law*, 10 J. Legal Stud. 65 (1981).

[4]This condition is somewhat different from the Kaldor-Hicks welfare test, which states that a transfer from *A* to *B* is efficient when *B*'s gain in utility is more than sufficient to compensate *A* for his loss. In its weakest form, the test states that such a transfer is efficient even if *B* does not actually compensate *A*. For a discussion of the test, see W. Baumol, *Economic Theory and Operations Analysis* 528–31 (4th ed. 1977). For a provocative discussion of different standards of efficiency, see Coleman, *Efficiency, Exchange,* and *Auction: Philosophic Aspects of the Economic Approach to Law*, 68 Calif. L. Rev. 221 (1980). On the related controversy surrounding the hypothesis that tort law is attempting to maximize wealth, see Dworkin, *Is Wealth a Value?*, 9 J. Legal Stud. 191 (1980); Kronman, *Wealth Maximization as a Normative Principle*, 9 J. Legal Stud. 227 (1980).

[5]Brown, *supra* note 3. This theory replaced some of Richard Posner's earlier theory, which he developed in Posner, *A Theory of Negligence, supra* note 3. Posner and Landes have now adopted the Brown theory of breach of duty in preference to Posner's original theory on this subject. *See* Landes & Posner, *supra* note 1, at 865 n. 41.

[6]Landes and Posner have significantly extended the Brown theory in Landes & Posner, *Causation, supra* note 3; Landes & Posner, *supra* note 1; Landes & Posner, *Joint and Multiple Tortfeasors, supra* note 3.

I. THE CONVENTIONAL POSITIVE THEORY OF NEGLIGENCE

A negligence rule performs two tasks.[7] First, it determines when an injurer—usually the defendant[8]—has not taken enough precaution. This task is performed by the "breach of duty" element of negligence. Second, a negligence rule decides when an injurer's insufficient precaution makes him liable for the victim's loss. This is the "causation" element of negligence. Only when the injurer's breach of duty was the legal cause of the victim's loss will the injurer be liable for it under the rule of negligence. There are two corresponding parts to the positive economic theory of negligence: one about breach of duty and another about legal causation.

A. Defining Breach of Duty

The conventional theory of negligence defines breach of duty by comparing an individual's actual level of precaution with the level that minimizes social costs.[9] I will call the social cost-minimizing precaution level P^* and the conventional method of defining breach of duty the P^*-comparison approach. Under the conventional theory, whenever an injurer has imposed loss on a victim and the injurer's actual precaution was less than the P^* level, the injurer has committed a breach of duty.

Figure 1 is a geometrical depiction of the negligence problem. It shows, from an injurer's perspective, the marginal costs and benefits (measured along the y-axis) associated with different levels of precaution (measured along the x-axis).

The curve labeled R denotes the marginal reduction in expected harm at different levels of precaution.[10] The height of the R-curve at a

[7] *See* Shavell, *Causation and the Scope of Liability, supra* note 3, at 463–64.

[8] In some proximate cause situations, there will be more than one injurer, one of whom may not be a defendant. *See* Pittsburg Reduction Co. v. Horton, 87 Ark. 576, 113 S.W. 647 (1908). Also where contributory or comparative negligence is involved the plaintiff is simultaneously the victim and one of his own injurers. *See* Landes & Posner, *Joint and Multiple Tortfeasors, supra* note 3, at 518; Wittman, *supra* note 3. This Article does not analyze problems of victim fault or of proximate cause.

[9] Brown, *supra* note 3, at 328; Landes & Posner, *supra* note 1, at 873–74; Landes & Posner, *Joint and Multiple Tortfeasors, supra* note 3, at 521–22.

[10] In Figure 1, R decreases as P increases. Thus, additional units of precaution decrease expected harm by decreasing amounts. This assumption is consistent with the traditional economic assumption of diminishing marginal returns.

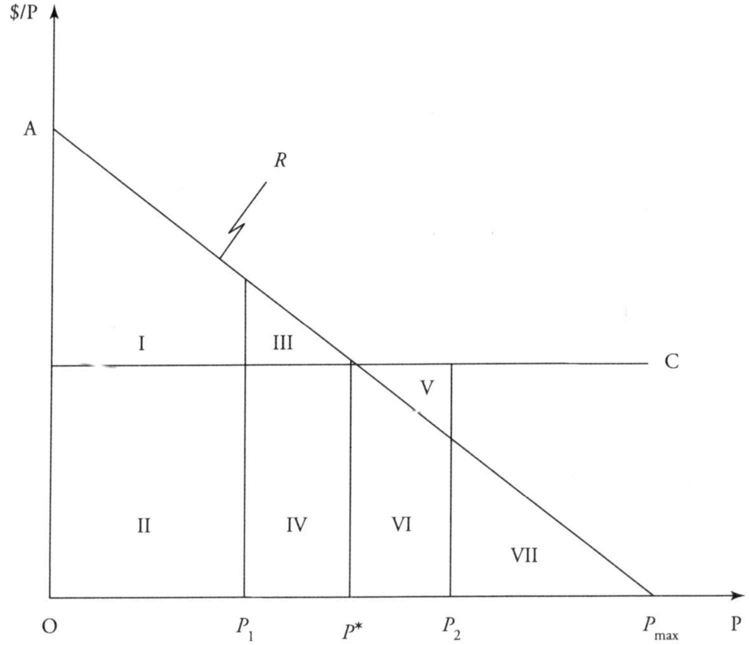

Figure 1

particular precaution level is the reduction in expected harm that would result from a one-unit increase in precaution. The area under the *R*-curve between one precaution level and another is the reduction in expected accident costs caused by the increase in precaution over the interval. For example, if precaution is increased from P_1 to P^*, expected harm decreases by an amount equal to the sum of areas III and IV. The area defined by points O, A, and P_{max} represents the total harm that would be expected if no precaution were taken.[11]

The curve labeled *C* represents the marginal cost of precaution. In Figure 1, this curve is flat, reflecting a constant marginal cost for all levels

[11]For the total area under the *R*-curve to correspond to the total expected harm that would exist if the injurer took zero precaution one must assume that total expected harm at P_{max} is zero. This assumption will aid the exposition, but will not limit the generality of the analysis that follows.

An *R*-curve is defined only with respect to some amount of information. This level of information is assumed to be given (or exogenous) when the *R*-curve is drawn. The amount of information that courts use in estimating expected harm is "reasonable foresight." The Figure 1 *R*-curve is thus assumed to be drawn based on reasonable foresight. The theory of what amount of information constitutes reasonable foresight of precaution.[12] The area under the C-curve between one precaution level and another is the increase in the total cost of precaution that results from the increase in precaution over the interval. Thus, if precaution is increased from P_1 to P^*, the cost of precaution increases by an amount equal to area IV.

The optimal level of precaution, P^*, which minimizes the sum of expected harm and precaution cost,[13] is the precaution level at which the R- and the C-curves intersect. When actual precaution is less than P^*, society would benefit from additional precaution; conversely, when actual is greater than P^*, society would benefit from less precaution. Precaution level P_1 is not optimal because an increase in precaution to P^* would decrease expected harm by an amount equal to the sum of areas III and IV, but would increase precaution cost only by an amount equal to area IV. Thus, the net social saving from this increase in precaution is equal to area III, which is the amount by which social cost at P_1 exceeds social cost at P^*. Because social cost is lower at P^*, social cost cannot be at a minimum when the injurer is operating at P_1. Similarly, precaution level P_2 is not optimal; using analogous reasoning one can easily determine that decreasing precaution to P^* would result in a net social saving equal to the area V.

B. Determining Legal Causation

Under the P^*-comparison approach, an individual who has taken due care—has selected P^*—is not liable for any harm that he has imposed on another. Victims will still be harmed by the injurer's activity. Their expected losses will equal the areas of VI and VII, but the injurer will

---

is beyond the scope of this Article. The area superscribed by the R-curve can be called the "reasonably foreseeable risk"; it is the amount and type of expected harm that reasonable foresight would predict.

Although Shavell does not use the R-curve construct, he has a theory about how courts determine the relevant expected harm. *See* Shavell, *Causation and the Scope of Liability, supra* note 3, at 485–89.

[12] The analysis in this Article is not dependent upon the assumption of constant marginal costs. To avoid corner solutions, however, the C- and R-curves must intersect, and the C-curve cannot fall at a faster rate than the R-curve.

[13] The model here is simplified by assuming that the level of activity is independent of the level of precautionary behavior, that is, that reductions in the level of production are not an available precaution strategy, and hence not potential costs of precaution. For an example of a model in which reducing the level of activity is one possible precautionary strategy, see Shavell, *Causation and the Scope of Liability, supra* note 3, at 465 (taking into account "benefits parties derive from engaging in their activities").

not be liable for these "unavoidable accidents."[14] Only under a rule of strict liability—not under a rule of negligence—would an injurer who has taken P^* be liable for such losses.[15]

A question about legal causation arises only when an injurer has committed a breach of duty by taking less precaution than P^*.[16] Courts using the P^*-comparison approach to breach of duty could resolve this legal causation problem in either of two possible ways. One way would be to hold the negligent individual[17] strictly liable for all harm that results. Under this rule, which I will call the full liability rule, an injurer operating at P_1 is liable for the entire amount of expected harm that remains at P_1—the areas III, IV, VI, and VII.[18] Alternatively, a court might impose liability on an injurer only if the accident would have been prevented had the individual exercised due care.[19] Under this latter rule, which I will call the P^*-cutoff rule, an injurer operating at P_1 would be liable only for an amount equal to the areas III and IV.

[14]*See* Brown v. Kendall, 60 Mass. (6 Cush.) 292, 297 (1850).

[15]In traditional strict liability, there is liability for the entire amount under the *R*-curve. *See, e.g.*, Smith v. Lockheed Propulsion Co., 247 Cal. App. 2d 774, 56 Cal. Rptr. 128 (1967); Siegler v. Kuhlman, 81 Wash. 2d 448, 502 P.2d 1181, *cert. denied*, 411 U.S. 983 (1973). So, if strict liability attaches to concussion harm from rocket testing, there would be liability for all concussion harm under the *R*-curve regardless of how much precaution was taken. The rocket tester, however, would not be strictly liable for non-concussion harm (if strict liability does not attach to it).

[16]In legal analysis the problem of causation is not always posterior to the problem of breach of duty. Courts will sometimes assume a breach of duty, for the sake of analysis, in order to dispose of a case on easy causation grounds. See, e.g., *McDowall v. Great Western Ry.*, [1903] 2 K.B. 331, 338 (C.A.) (Vaughan William, L.J.); *infra* pp. 827–28 (discussing *Nussbaum v. Lacopo*, 27 N.Y. 2d 311, 265 N.E.2d 762, 317 N.Y.S.2d 347 (1970)); *infra* note 67 (discussing *McDowall*). For present purposes, it is convenient to analyze the two negligence issues, breach of duty and cause in fact, as if breach of duty were always the prior question.

[17]For purposes of this Article, a negligent individual is one who commits a breach of duty.

[18]This full liability negligence rule is the one used in Shavell, *Causation and the Scope* of *Liability, supra* note 3 at 489 ("once one recognizes that under the negligence rule there is an important element of strict liability (for a variety of reasons a party attempting to exercise due care may be found negligent), all the results concerning the scope of liability under strict liability become relevant under the negligence rule"). Landes and Posner also used the full liability model of negligence in Landes & Posner, *Joint and Multiple Tortfeasors, supra* note 3, at 521–22; Landes & Posner, *supra* note 1, at 874, 882.

[19]This is the approach that Landes and Posner seem to take in their most recent article. *See* Landes & Posner, *Causation, supra* note 3, at 115–18.

The two rules embody very different notions of legal causation. The causal concept implicit in the P^*-cutoff rule is but-for causation. Under this rule, courts conduct an evaluation[20] of whether an accident that has occurred could have been prevented if the injurer had exercised due care.[21] In contrast, under the full liability rule the relevant concept is that of a "causal link": Courts attempt to ascertain, on an actuarial basis, whether the harm that the victim suffered resulted from the injurer's activity and was of the kind that more precaution by the injurer would have reduced or prevented.[22] Thus, the full liability rule has a less restrictive notion of causation than does the P^*-cutoff rule.

[20]Unlike breach of duty, which is largely an *ex ante* standard, cause in fact is an *ex post* determination.

[21]*See* New York Cent. R.R. v. Grimstad, 264 F. 334 (2d Cir. 1920). This is the most rigorous formulation of cause in fact. When it is not certain whether this test is met, a problem of evidence and presumptions arises that is beyond the scope of this Article. It can be said, however, that the greater the breach of duty, the more probable it is that the untaken precaution would have prevented the harm. Thus, less independent evidence of cause in fact will be required when the untaken precaution is of a character that "greatly multiplies the chances of accident." Reynolds v. Texas & P. Ry., 37 La. Ann. 694 (1885). In other words, less independent evidence of cause in fact is needed when the defendant was at P_1 than when he was at a precaution level infinitesimally less than P^* (and the breach of duty is shown in both cases with the failure to take P^*). Because the plaintiff can offer several different untaken precautions as alternative theories of the breach of duty, there can be several cause in fact issues in a given case, that is, whether untaken precaution *x* would have prevented the harm, whether untaken precaution *y* would have prevented the harm, and so forth. *See, e.g.*, Allied Chem. Corp. v. Hess Tankship Co., 661 F.2d 1044, 1052–54 (5th Cir. 1981); Stacy v. Knickerbocker Ice Co., 84 Wis. 614, 616–17, 54 N.W. 1091, 1091–92 (1893).

The courts have relaxed the requirement of but-for causation in the special situation of concurrent sufficient causation where two causal chains for which two different people are responsible each would have been sufficient to cause the plaintiff's harm. *See, e.g.*, Corey v. Havener, 182 Mass. 250, 65 N.E. 69 (1902); Kingston v. Chicago & N.W. Ry., 191 Wis. 610, 211 N.W. 913 (1927). This is a relatively rare but interesting situation. Shavell has given an account of the economic policy underlying the special rule for cases of this type. Shavell, *Causation and the Scope of Liability, supra* note 3, at 494–95. The special situation of concurrent sufficient causation is beyond the scope of this Article. The peculiar problems of successive causation of the type involved in Maddux v. Donaldson, 362 Mich. 425, 108 N.W.2d 33 (1961), are also beyond the scope of this article.

For an excellent discussion of the general problem of cause in fact, see Weinrib, A *Step Forward in Factual Causation*, 38 Mod. L. Rev. 518 (1975).

[22]Calabresi originally developed the concept of causal link in Calabresi, *Concerning Cause and the Law of Torts, supra* note 2, at 71 ("There is a causal link between an act or activity

Despite these differences, both rules will induce injurers to exercise the level of precaution that minimizes social cost under conditions of perfect certainty. Under either rule, injurers will have an incentive to operate at P^*.

Consider the full liability rule first. An individual will never exercise precaution greater than P^*. Operating at P^*, he will be found to have exercised due care and thus be shielded from liability. Precaution beyond P^* will increase the injurer's precaution costs, but will not reduce his expected liability (which, by definition, will already be zero).[23] Similarly, an injurer will not choose to operate below P^*. Suppose for example that he chose P_1 as his level of precaution. He would then face an expected liability equal to the sum of areas III, IV, VI, and VII. By expending an amount equal to area IV in additional precaution, that is, by moving to P^*, he can reduce his expected liability to zero, thus saving an amount equal to the sum of areas III, VI, and VII. This argument is a general one, as it does not depend on the distance between P^* and P_1.[24]

Now, consider the P^*-cutoff rule. Once again, an individual will never operate beyond P^* because he will be shielded from liability by picking P^*. Neither will an individual pick P_1, because at that level he would face an expected liability equal to the sum of areas III and IV. (An injurer subject to the P^*-cutoff rule who is operating at P_1 will not face liability for areas VI and VII because the but-for cause requirement will shield him from liability for accidents that would have occurred even

---

and an injury when we conclude on the basis of the available evidence that the recurrence of that act or activity will increase the chances that the injury will also occur").

[23]Following the conventional theory, *see* Landes & Posner, *supra* note 1, at 867–68, I assume that individuals are risk-neutral. I also assume that litigation and settlement costs are so low that all plaintiffs with meritorious negligence cases are compensated for the full amount of their damages, so that injurers expect to be liable for all legally recoverable harm. Proponents of the conventional theory have made the same assumption. *See Id.* at 882.

[24]There is, however, an important qualification regarding this exposition. Each individual's *R*-curve is a function of the precaution taken by other individuals. To facilitate the exposition of the central argument of this Article, this interdependency is ignored. As a formal matter, the interdependency is not significant for the problems analyzed here when: (1) the injurer knows that other individuals will exercise the levels of precaution that would be optimal given optimal precaution by the injurer himself; or (2) these other individuals either make their precaution choices before the injurer does or do not have the opportunity of noticing the increased risk created by the injurer's suboptimal precaution. In terms of the example used below, *see infra* pp. 807–08, the people living beneath the dam are assumed to be taking precaution consistent with the dam owner being at P^*, and they are assumed to be unable to notice the increased risk that results when the dam owner takes less precaution than P^*.

if he had exercised due care.) By moving from P_1 to P^* he can decrease his expected liability by an amount equal to the sum of areas III and IV. These savings can be accomplished by expending an amount equal to area IV in additional precaution. Thus, the exercise of due care will lead to a private saving equal to area III.

The major claim of the conventional positive theory of negligence law is that the P^*-comparison approach will lead to the minimization of social cost. The preceding discussion shows that under conditions of perfect certainty, this result is independent of whether the scope of liability is limited by a restrictive but-for causation requirement or a broad causal link requirement.

II. A CRITIQUE OF THE CONVENTIONAL VIEW

The two rules for defining the scope of liability have different consequences for a negligent individual, but both create an incentive for individuals to exercise due care under conditions of perfect certainty. This result, while correct, is somewhat counterintuitive. In a model in which behavior is shaped by expected costs, one would imagine that the choice between liability rules having different economic consequences should affect the conduct of a potential injurer. The absence of these effects suggests an underlying rigidity in the specification of the model. For this reason, it is important to focus on whether the behavioral results that flow from the model depend on unduly restrictive assumptions.

My critique of the conventional theory stems from the examination of the effects of the assumption that injurers can always identify with perfect certainty the precaution level that courts will determine to be P^*.[25]

[25]Brown assumes that both courts and injurers make no errors in identifying P^*. As to courts, he writes, "For our purposes the only function of the legal system is the impeccable administration of whatever liability rule is in force. In order to concentrate on what is our major concern, the parties' behavior, we ignore . . . the mistakes that a court can make . . . ." Brown, *supra* note 3, at 327. That injurers also do not make errors in estimating P^* is implicit in Brown's assumption that they know their own *R*-curves and *C*-curves perfectly. He writes, "Both parties [injurer and victim] are assumed to know *A* [the magnitude of harm that will result if precaution is not taken], W_x [the injurer's *C*-curve], W_y [the victim's *C*-curve], and *P(X, Y)* [the *R*-curve that depends on the levels of injurer and victim precaution]." *Id.* at 335. Shavell also expressly assumes that courts make no errors in locating P^*: "[S]ince we assume the courts have perfect information about accidents, they make no 'mistakes'. They correctly calculate the level of due care; they 'observe' with complete accuracy the level of care actually exercised by injurers, and so on" Shavell, *Causation and the Scope of Liability, supra* note 3, at 485. Implicit in Shavell's

Probably the best way for an injurer to assess whether he is at P^* would be for him to consider whether there are any further precautions—beyond those currently planned or taken—that would reduce expected harm by a greater amount than the cost that they would impose. This is also the most plausible way by which a court could determine whether an injurer was taking less precaution than P^*. If the injurer was operating at some level below P^*, such as P_1, either the court or injurer could determine this to be the case by finding some further precaution beyond P_1 that

---

analysis of causation is also the idea that injurers do not make mistakes estimating P^*, because they are assumed to know with certainty whether they are taking due care. He writes, "When deciding whether to exercise due care (clearly, he will not wish to exercise more than due care), the injurer will have to consider the consequences of exercising less than due care, of acting in a negligent way." *Id.* at 486. *But see id.* at 489 ("for a variety of reasons a party attempting to exercise due care may be found negligent"). The general premise of Shavell's causal analysis is that the injurer can know the due care level with certainty and can also correctly predict the expected liability from exercising less than due care, though both of these assumptions are more implicit than explicit.

Landes and Posner's assumptions on whether courts and injurers can make mistakes are no longer clear. In Landes & Posner, *Joint and Multiple Tortfeasors, supra* note 3, at 521, they make no express assumption about whether either courts or injurers make mistakes in locating P^*, though it seems implicit in their analysis as it develops that neither courts nor injurers make errors very frequently, if they do at all. In Landes & Posner, *supra* note 1, at 879, they expressly assume that both injurers and courts can make mistakes, but they do not explicitly analyze the consequences of either assumption. In their most recent article, *Causation in Tort Law: An Economic Approach,* apparently anticipating the reasoning of this Article on the tendency of the full liability rule to induce overprecaution, see *infra* pp. 811–12, they write that their own analysis

> may appear to overlook an easier route, not involving administrative costs, to the conclusion that there should be no liability in this class of cases [where there is no cause in fact]: if the defendant is liable for accidents he could not prevent, he will use excessive care. This reasoning is incorrect, however—at least under certain conditions concerning the nature and implementation of the liability standard. If the standard is negligence, if negligence has no stochastic element, if the negligence standard is applied on an individual rather than average basis, and if the standard is applied correctly in every case, then liability of however broad a scope will have only one effect, and that is to induce the defendant to take due care and thereby avoid liability. In these circumstances, to impose liability for accidents that could not have been prevented (or whose probability could not have been lowered) by due care is no different from imposing punitive damages for negligent behavior. However severe, the sanction will not induce any inefficient behavior; it will induce the taking of care, which will avoid the sanction completely.

Landes & Posner, *Causation, supra* note 3, at 117. They then add that these assumptions are "excessively restrictive," *id.,* but they do not say what the proper assumptions are. It is therefore difficult to assess whether they are assuming that injurers and courts make errors. It would appear, however, that they are assuming that at least courts which, they say, apply the standard "correctly in every case," do not make errors.

would have cost less than the amount by which it would have reduced expected harm. In contrast, if the injurer is at P^*, no further precaution can be found that will yield a net benefit.

The incentives to make this analysis accurately are very different before an accident than after an accident. For example, most dams will never produce any overflow harm, whether the walls are 110 feet high (P_1) or 120 feet high (P^*). Before the accident, the value of information to the potential injurer that P^* is 120 feet—not 110 feet—will approach the area III, under the P^*-cutoff rule, or the areas III, VI, and VII under the full liability rule. If the expected liability from operating at 110 feet is \$100,000, the value of this information to the injurer before the accident is some fraction of this amount: It is slightly less than \$100,000 minus the cost of the additional precaution that would insulate the injurer from liability. Now, let us suppose, the unlikely occurs and the dam does overflow, and damages totalling \$1,000,000 result. The value of the information to the victim that a further precaution would have been cost-beneficial will now approach \$1,000,000 and the value of the contrary information will have an equal value to the injurer. Therefore, it would not be surprising that at trial the information that the court will receive about the costs and benefits of 120-foot walls versus 110-foot walls will be far more perfect than the information that the dam owner would have found it economical to collect before the accident. It would thus seem reasonable to assume that the courts after a trial will be able to assess whether actual precaution was less than P^* far more accurately than will an injurer before an accident.[26] For the sake of analysis, let us assume that courts do not make mistakes in estimating P^*, but that injurers do. Although this is a strong assumption, it is somewhat realistic in that the

[26]It is true, of course, that if an accident causing a harm of \$100 occurred the plaintiff and defendant would have little incentive to introduce much evidence at trial. But for the vast majority of activities, the probability that an accident—any accident—will occur is quite small over the time period in which the set of precautions in question is a sunk cost. Thus, it is reasonable to assume that once an accident takes place, the harm that is caused will be greater than the expected harm, given that expected harm is equal to the sum of the products of actual harms and the probabilities that accidents causing such harms will occur.

There is, however, a group of activities for which this proposition will not hold. An injurer who is involved in very large numbers of accidents (for example, an auto manufacturer) will often estimate expected harm before an accident with practically the same accuracy as a court after an accident. Many injurers of this type, however, seem to be regulated by principles of products liability rather than by principles of negligence.

prior reasoning would indicate that injurer estimates of P^* before an accident would be significantly less accurate than court estimates after an accident. Also, this assumption that courts do not make mistakes is the same as that made by the conventional theory.[27]

Although injurers are estimating P^* based on imperfect information, there is no reason to suppose that their information is biased in favor of either overprecaution or underprecaution. Therefore, I assume that when they estimate P^* they are just as likely to guess high as low. If we call injurer estimates of P^* their $\hat{p}$'s, it follows from the last assumption that the $\hat{p}$-distribution is a symmetric distribution whose mean is P^*.

Finally, I assume that injurers make small errors in estimating P^*. Thus, an injurer is not uncertain that zero precaution is less than P^*, nor is he uncertain that P_{max} is greater than P^*. He is only uncertain whether his estimate is greater or less than P^* when his estimate is between P_1 and P_2 (a small band around P^*).[28]

Once an injurer has estimated P^*—has selected his $\hat{p}$—the important social question becomes whether he will actually take the level of precaution that he has estimated. The injurer is not bound to take his $\hat{p}$ under either of the two rules. Whether the injurer actually will take the level of precaution that he has estimated to be P^* depends on the penalties he faces when his actual choice is not equal to P^*. Every liability rule creates two kinds of penalties: a penalty for taking more precaution than P^* and one for taking less precaution than P^*. In deciding whether actually to operate at $\hat{p}$ when he is not certain whether $\hat{p}$ is greater or less than P^*, the injurer must consider and compare the magnitudes of these penalties. At an extreme, if the penalty for taking less precaution than P^* is one million dollars and the penalty for taking greater precaution than P^* is one cent, an injurer would never actually operate at $\hat{p}$, his estimate of P^*, if he is at all uncertain where a court would locate P^*. Instead, the injurer would add a substantial "insurance factor" to his $\hat{p}$ estimate to minimize the probability that the level of precaution that he ultimately takes is lower than P^*.

Although the point has never been stressed by the conventional positive economic theory, which concludes that both liability rules will produce the optimal result,[29] the full liability and P^*-cutoff rules assign very different

[27] *See supra* note 25.

[28] These limits are important to the analysis here because the *R*-curve may not be a straight line. If the *R*-curve is convex throughout its range from zero to P_{max}, however, it will approximate a straight line within a small band around P^*. The narrower the band of error, of course, the more the *R*-curve will approximate a straight line within it.

[29] *See supra* pp. 805–07.

penalties for injurer errors, and they induce very different injurer behavior under conditions of uncertainty. In fact, neither rule produces the optimal behavior under these conditions. The full liability rule will frequently induce injurers to take more precaution than P^*, and the P^*-cutoff rule will frequently induce injurers to take less precaution than P^*.

A. The Full Liability Rule

Suppose that an injurer has estimated $\hat{p}$ at a value that is infinitesimally less than P^*. If the injurer takes his $\hat{p}$ estimate as his actual precaution level, the court would find that he has committed a breach of duty. His expected liability under the full liability rule would be infinitesimally greater than the sum of areas VI and VII. If instead an injurer takes a precaution level that is infinitesimally greater than P^*, the loss that he would suffer is of a different magnitude and nature. It would be merely the infinitesimally small cost of precaution that the injurer could have saved without being subjected to additional liability for accidents. This "sword of Damocles" effect suggests that given a choice between one unit of overprecaution and one unit of underprecaution, the injurer will choose the overprecaution.[30]

To establish this point more rigorously, consider Figure 2, which depicts the penalties that an injurer subject to the full liability rule faces when he overinvests and underinvests in precaution. In this Figure, the height of the penalty curve above the x-axis indicates the magnitude of the penalty that the injurer will incur at given levels of precaution. By definition, at P^* the value of the penalty function is zero because at this level the injurer minimizes the sum of his precaution costs and expected liability. If the injurer takes infinitesimally less precaution than P^*, the penalty that the injurer incurs is the value b indicated on the y-axis of Figure 2. This value equals the sum of the areas VI and VII on Figure 1. By moving from a precaution level infinitesimally less than P^* to P^* itself, which would cost the injurer only an infinitesimal amount in additional precaution, the injurer saves the areas VI and VII in expected liability; thus, the penalty function is discontinuous.

The value b on Figure 2 is a fixed component of the penalty, which attaches whenever an injurer operates at a precaution level less than P^*. In addition, the penalty for underinvesting also has a variable component. At P_1, an injurer faces an expected liability equal to the sum of the areas III, IV, VI, and VII. Relative to operating at P^*, however, he saves an

[30] In fact, the actual result is even more striking. *See infra* pp. 811–12.

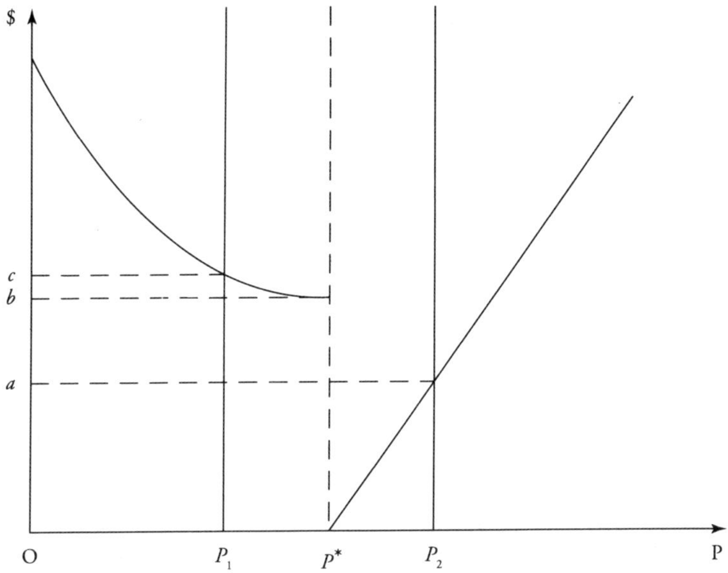

Figure 2

amount of precaution cost equal to the area IV by being at P_1. Thus, the penalty for being at P_1 is the sum of areas III, VI, and VII. The area III is the variable component of the penalty function; this component shrinks to zero as the injurer moves from P_1 to P^*. In Figure 2, *c* is equal to the penalty at P_1; the difference between *b* and *c* equals the area III on Figure 1.[31]

The value of the full liability penalty function for precaution levels greater than P^* is simply the amount under the *C*-curve between P^* and the precaution level in question. The penalty that the injurer incurs from being at P_2 is the areas V and VI on Figure 1, because the areas V and VI are needless expense. Because courts correctly locate P^*, operating at P^* itself avoids liability just as well as operating at P_2. On Figure 2, the value of the areas V and VI is denominated a. Within the range that is relevant to this analysis, *a* is always less than *c*; P_2 imposes a lesser penalty on the injurer than does P_1. Thus, within this relevant range, the full liability rule always imposes a larger penalty for underprecaution than for overprecaution; in fact, the penalty for

[31]The full liability penalty function is decreasing in slope (is convex) at levels of precaution less than P^*. This is so because area III has a triangular shape. On the other hand, the full liability penalty function has a constant slope at levels of precaution greater than P^* because the areas V and VI, when combined, have a rectangular shape.

operating at P_2 is smaller than the penalty for operating at a level only infinitesimally less than P^*.[32]

An uncertain injurer is therefore not indifferent between the two kinds of error. To attempt to avoid the "sword of Damocles" effect of underprecaution, an injurer subject to the full liability rule will add an insurance factor to his $\hat{p}$ estimate. Thus, the distribution of actual precaution choices (which I will call the $\overline{P}$-distribution) will be dislocated to the right of the $\hat{p}$ distribution by an amount equal to the insurance factor.[33] The most likely actual precaution choice (the mean of the full liability $\overline{P}$-distribution) will not be P^* itself but will be some precaution level greater than P^*.

B. The P^*-Cutoff Rule

The results under the P^*-cutoff rule are less striking but equally important. If an injurer chooses an actual precaution level infinitesimally lower than P^*, the injurer will face liability only over an infinitesimally small range. On the other hand, if an injurer chooses an actual precaution level infinitesimally greater than P^*, the injurer will not face any liability, and his loss will be an infinitesimally small amount of overprecaution. Thus, the P^*-cutoff rule produces no "sword of Damocles" effect. Nonetheless, the analysis of the relative penalties for underprecaution and overprecaution is important

[32]The value *b* on Figure 2 is greater than the value *a* because the areas VI and VII on Figure 1—the fixed component of the penalty from underprecaution—are greater than the areas V and VI, which together constitute the penalty from the greatest possible error of overprecaution (P_2). *See supra* p. 809. Within the relevant range, *see id.*, these conditions make the penalty from any injurer error of underprecaution, no matter how small, greater than the penalty from the maximum possible overprecaution. Given any significant doubt, the injurer strongly prefers P_2 to some much smaller level of underprecaution.

[33]It is assumed that all injurers add the same insurance factor. If not, the full liability $\overline{P}$-distribution still will be dislocated to the right of the $\hat{p}$-distribution and will also have a somewhat different variance (or shape) than the $\hat{p}$-distribution. Even with different insurance factors for different injurers, the full liability $\overline{P}$-distribution will still be less desirable than a $\overline{P}$-distribution exactly coincident to the $\hat{p}$-distribution, so long as each injurer's insurance factor is positive. The assumption that each injurer's insurance factor is the same seems to follow both from the assumption that all injurers are risk neutral, which is a standard assumption in the conventional theory, see *supra* note 23, and from the absence of an a priori reason to assume that people engaging in the same activity (building the same-sized dam) would entertain very different judgements about the probability that their estimates of P^* would be wrong. Indeed, the estimates of P^* made by different injurers will be subject to similar costs and rewards.

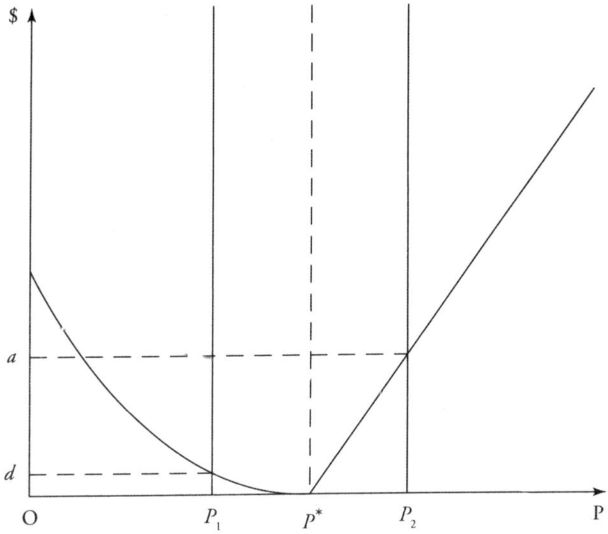

Figure 3

because it reveals that under the P^*-cutoff rule an uncertain injurer will choose one unit of underprecaution over one unit of overprecaution—the exact opposite of the behavior induced by the full liability rule.[34]

In Figure 1, suppose that the injurer has taken precaution level P_1. At that level, he faces liability for areas III and IV; in order to avoid this liability he would have to incur an amount equal to area IV in additional precaution costs. Hence, the penalty for being at P_1 instead of at P^* is area III. On the other hand, if the injurer took an equal amount of overprecaution—precaution level P_2—the penalty for not being at P^* would be the sum of areas V and VI, which is the amount spent in useless additional precaution. Because areas III and V are equal, an injurer given the choice between operating at P_1 or P_2 will pick P_1 and thereby save an amount equal to area VI. More generally, one can say that an uncertain injurer faced with the P^*-cutoff rule will prefer a given amount of underprecaution over an equal amount of overprecaution.

Figure 3, which depicts the penalty function for the P^*-cutoff rule, illustrates two noteworthy results. First, there is no discontinuity in the

[34]The result under the P^*-cutoff rule is less striking than that under the full liability rule, where *any* overprecaution in the relevant ranges is more desirable than *any* underprecaution. *See supra* note 32.

The P^*-cutoff penalty function decreases in slope at levels below P^* and has constant slope at levels above P^*. *See supra* note 31.

value of the penalty function at P^*, as there was for the full liability rule. Second, consistent with the prior reasoning, the magnitude of the penalty for underprecaution (the height of the penalty function at any precaution level) is always less than that for an equal amount of overprecaution. In Figure 3, the value *d*—the penalty from being at P_1—is equal to the area III on Figure 1. The value *a*, once again, is equal to the areas V and VI in Figure 1.

Under the P^*-cutoff rule, an individual estimating P^* under conditions of uncertainty will have the same $\hat{p}$ distribution as he would under the full liability rule. This time, though, when he is making his decision about what precaution level to take, he does not add an insurance factor to his $\hat{p}$ estimate; instead, being aware that underprecaution imposes a lower penalty than overprecaution, he subtracts a "low ball" factor. In doing so, the injurer assumes that he is better off by underinvesting more than half of the time and overinvesting less than half of the time; therefore, he takes a level of precaution less than his estimate of P^*. The distribution of actual precaution choices produced by these unequal penalties, $\overline{P}$, will be dislocated to the left of the $\hat{p}$-distribution. The mean of actual precaution choices will be less than P^*, even though the mean of injurer estimates is exactly P^*.

III. THE NEW THEORY

The preceding critique of the conventional positive theory of negligence demonstrates that the major claim of that theory—that the P^*-comparison test promotes minimum social cost—does not hold under the very realistic assumption that injurers will not always be able correctly to identify P^*. It is important to emphasize that in making the critique, I did not assume that injurers are incapable of ascertaining P^*. I merely assumed that in attempting to find P^* injurers will sometimes make mistakes. I conceded, however, that these mistakes would be random and symmetrically distributed around P^*. These specifications are not radically different from those of the conventional model,[35] a fact that makes the critique all the more striking. First, random errors by injurers do not produce random variations in the level of precaution, but systematic variations. Second, the two rules that have so far coexisted in the conventional theory with little attention having been paid to their difference[36] lead to dramatically different results. As an alternative to

[35] *See supra* note 25.

[36] *See supra* pp. 809–13. In their most recent article, Landes and Posner seem to argue that their formulation of the P^*-cutoff rule was always implicit in "the economist's"

both rules, I propose a new formal theory, which I will call the cost–benefit approach. This theory retains the concept of legal causation of the P^*-cutoff rule, but defines breach of duty in a manner altogether different from the P^*-comparison approach. Under conditions of uncertainty, the new theory leads to results that are more socially desirable than those produced by its conventional counterparts.

A. The Cost–Benefit Approach

Under the P^*-comparison approach, courts determine breach of duty by comparing an injurer's actual level of precaution to P^*. If actual precaution is less than P^* there is a breach of duty; if actual precaution is at least equal to P^*, there is no breach of duty. Suppose, instead, that courts listen to allegations of untaken precautions—for example, the failure to build a 120-foot wall on a dam, the failure to place a fence around a swimming pool, or the failure to station a lifeguard on a beachfront—and find an injurer negligent whenever the costs of at least one specific untaken precaution are less than the reduction in expected harm that would have resulted from that precaution. They would then impose liability if the specific act of negligence used to prove the breach of duty was the cause in fact of the harm the victims suffered—that is, when but for the failure to take the particular precaution constituting the defendant's breach of duty the plaintiff's harm would not have occurred.

---

theory of negligence, even in its full liability form. They analyze Weeks v. McNulty, 101 Tenn. 495, 48 S.W. 809 (1898), in which the court found that, although the defendant committed a breach of duty by failing to install fire escapes, he was not liable because fire escapes would not have prevented the decedent's death. Landes & Posner, *Causation, supra* note 3, at 116–17. This case seems scarcely explainable if courts are adopting the full liability rule. Nonetheless, Landes & Posner argue that "the economist" would have been right all along to think of *McNulty* as a case in which there was no negligence. As they reason:

> Now there may seem an element of paradox in asserting that McNulty was not really negligent, when the premise of the court's decision was that he had been negligent per se but should be excused for want of a causal relationship between negligence and injury. But this just shows that the courts do in two steps what the economist, via the refined version of the Hand formula, does in one. The court first asks whether there is negligence in a rather crude sense, a failure to do something which in the general run of cases would be socially cost justified and then, under the rubric of causation, inquires whether the taking of additional care would have been socially cost justified in the particular circumstances of the case, given other factors that may have made additional care fruitless. *Id.* at 116. This account of why the differences between the P^*-cutoff rule and the full liability rule were not noticed seems to be an over-simplification.

Although one might at first imagine that this cost–benefit approach is really the same as the P^*-comparison approach, there are some significant differences between them. The most important difference between the two approaches is that under the cost–benefit approach the maximum level of untaken precaution that can be used to show breach of duty is not fixed, but depends on the injurer's actual level of precaution. For example, if the injurer is taking precaution level P_1, the plaintiff can point to any precaution level smaller than P_2 and successfully argue that the injurer's failure to have taken that precaution level was a breach of duty. This result follows easily from Figure 1. Because P_1 and P_2 are equidistant from P^*, area III is equal to area V and area IV is equal to the sum of areas V and VI. It follows that areas IV, V, and VI (the additional costs of taking P_2) are exactly equal to areas IV, III, and VI (the additional benefits from taking P_2). For any precaution level smaller than P_2, the additional benefits outweigh the additional costs. On the other hand, if the injurer's actual precaution is not P_1, but instead a level infinitesimally smaller than P^*, the maximum untaken precaution that the plaintiff could use to prove breach of duty would be an amount infinitesimally greater than P^*.[37]

Thus, as the injurer takes less precaution, he creates more opportunities for the victim to show a breach of duty. In this sense, the cost–benefit approach permits alternative proofs of breach of duty, and the levels of untaken precaution available for the victim's proof increase as the injurer's actual precaution decreases. In contrast, under the P^*-comparison standard the maximum untaken precaution that the victim can use to prove breach of duty is P^*, regardless of whether the injurer is at P_1 or a

[37] The cost–benefit approach is a theory about specific negligence cases. Res ipsa loquitur cases, which are beyond the scope of the conventional theory, are also beyond the scope of this Article. There is no clear line of demarcation between res ipsa and specific negligence cases, because the difference between them depends on the degree to which the plaintiff proves negligence using particular untaken precautions. The clearest case of specific negligence is where the plaintiff offers a highly defined untaken precaution as proof of the breach of duty (the failure to build the dam wall 120 feet high). The clearest case of res ipsa loquitur (or general negligence as it was once called) is where the plaintiff offers no particular untaken precaution to prove the breach of duty (the dam was within the exclusive control of the defendant, dams do not ordinarily overflow in the absence of negligence, and so forth). The middle case is where the plaintiff alleges negligence in very general terms (the failure to operate and maintain the dam using due care). Depending on whether the proof uncovers a particular untaken precaution that might constitute a breach of duty, this middle kind of case is properly seen either as a res ipsa case or as a specific negligence case, or as one that went to the jury on alternative theories.

precaution level infinitesimally less than P^*, and negligence can never be premised on the failure to take a precaution level greater than P^*.

This new cost–benefit approach shares an important feature with the conventional approach. If an injurer is operating at least at level P^*, he cannot be found negligent under either approach. From the geometry of Figure 1, it is clear that the cost of any precaution beyond P^* will always be higher than the corresponding reduction in expected harm.

Why would the victim ever want to prove the breach of duty with an untaken precaution beyond P^*? If the injurer had been operating at a level slightly over P_1, why not prove that the breach of duty was the failure to take P^*? It should be easier to prove that the failure to take P^* was a breach of duty than it would be to show that the injurer was negligent because he failed to operate at P_2. The benefits of taking P^* instead of a little more precaution than P_1 exceed the additional costs by a significant amount (area III). In contrast, the benefits of taking P_2 are only infinitesimally greater than the increase in costs. Why go to the limit?

By merely proving that the injurer was negligent by failing to operate at P^*, the plaintiff might fail to prove legal causation. Suppose on Figure 1 that P_1 is a 110-foot wall for a dam, P^* is a 120-foot wall, and P_2 is a 130-foot wall. Suppose also that the plaintiff's property floods and that this flood could have been prevented only by a wall at least 125 feet high. If the victim establishes breach of duty with the dam owner's failure to build a 120-foot wall (P^*), the victim will fail on the cause in fact issue. The court will say, "It may be true as you say that the defendant was negligent in failing to build the wall up to 120 feet, but you have not shown that a 120-foot wall would have prevented the harm that actually occurred, and therefore you have failed to prove that the defendant's negligence was the cause in fact of that harm."[38] To avoid losing the case on the cause in fact issue, the plaintiff must carry a heavier burden on

[38]As the court said in City of Piqua v. Morris, 98 Ohio St. 42, 54, 120 N.E. 300, 303 (1918), which was a dam overflow case:

> An apt illustration which has been suggested is that if a river levee had been maintained at the height of 10 feet and the custodians of the levee had been warned that flood waters might require a levee 16 feet in height, and they neglected to so increase the height of the levee, and an unprecedented flood should ensue, during which it should appear that a levee 26 feet in height would not have held the flood waters, the parties responsible for the levee would not be liable for negligence in failing to maintain a 16-foot levee, when a 26-foot levee would have been unavailing.

In other words, the plaintiff must pick an untaken precaution level sufficiently high so that it would have prevented the particular harm that he sustained. And, he must prove that this same untaken precaution was a breach of duty, given the defendant's actual level of precaution.

the breach of duty issue.[39] In particular, the plaintiff must show that the failure to build the wall up to some height higher than 125 feet was a breach of duty. Only this more ambitious proof of the breach of duty issue will satisfy the cause in fact requirement.

The "zone" of liability created by the cost–benefit rule, that is, by joining the cost–benefit approach to breach of duty with the but-for cause in fact requirement, is different than that of the two rules of the conventional theory. Under the cost–benefit rule, an injurer operating at P_1 faces expected liability in the areas III, IV, and VI. By contrast, under the P^*-cutoff rule, he would face liability only in areas III and IV; under the full liability rule, the areas of expected liability are III, IV, VI, and VII.

B. Evaluating the Cost–Benefit Approach

Under conditions of certainty, the cost–benefit rule, like the P^*-cutoff and full liability rules, leads to the socially optimal level of precaution. An individual would not operate above P^* under the cost–benefit rule, because doing so would not reduce his expected liability, but would result in additional precaution costs. Consider, however, the possibility that he might operate at P_1, a level below P^*. There, his expected liability would be the sum of areas III, IV, and VI. By expending an amount equal to area IV in additional precaution, the injurer can escape all liability. Thus, he will never intentionally operate at P_1. A similar exercise will rule out all other values less than P^*.

Now, consider the case of uncertainty. Uncertainty acquires a slightly different meaning under the cost–benefit approach to breach of duty, because this approach assumes that courts are not in the express business of locating P^*. Instead, under the cost–benefit approach courts are judging whether at particular actual levels of precaution, the costs of further precautions are greater or less than the benefits. If courts make no mistakes—the same assumption as before—they will locate the least-cost precaution level that will preclude the victim from showing a breach of duty at P^*. Therefore, although courts do not expressly locate P^*, they behave as if they did. The injurer, as before, can make mistakes. In searching for the least-cost precaution level that will preclude the showing of a breach of duty, P^*, he can incorrectly estimate the *R*-curve or the *C*-curve. For example, the injurer's pre-accident notions of expected harm may be different from the

[39]This tension between the breach of duty and cause-in-fact issues is apparent in Stacy v. Knickerbocker Ice Co., 84 Wis. 614, 54 N.W. 1091 (1893).

estimates that he would have made if he had access to post-trial information. Similarly, he may decide not to build a higher dam, under the impression that the additional cost is greater than the additional benefit, and then find out at trial that new technology available before the dam was built would have made a higher wall cheaper than he had originally thought.

Under uncertainty, the cost–benefit rule has more desirable properties than the conventional rules because it does not create incentives for underprecaution or overprecaution. An injurer operating at P_1 under the cost–benefit approach faces expected liability in areas III, IV, and VI in Figure 1. If, instead, he operated at P^*, he would pay an amount equal to area IV in additional precaution, but face no liability. Thus, the penalty from operating at underprecaution P_1 is equal to the sum of areas III and VI. On the other hand, the penalty from operating at P_2 instead of P^* is equal to the areas V and VI, just as it is under the two other rules. Under all three rules, P^* will avoid liability just as P_2 will, so the areas V and VI always represent an expense for needless precaution. What is different about the cost–benefit rule is that it alone makes the penalties from overprecaution and underprecaution equal. When P_1 and P_2 are equal but opposite errors, the sum of the areas III and VI (the penalty for underprecaution) exactly equals the sum of the areas V and VI (the penalty for overprecaution), since areas III and V are congruent triangles.

Another way to see the advantages of the cost–benefit rule is illustrated by Figure 4. There, because the penalty for underprecaution is exactly the same as the penalty for equal overprecaution, both parts of the cost–benefit rule penalty function have equal (but opposite) slopes.[40] Also, unlike the full-liability penalty function, the cost–benefit penalty function has no discontinuity at P^*. These equal penalties for the two kinds of error have a highly desirable implication for the way that an injurer will approach the question of whether to take the precaution level that he has estimated to be P^*. Indeed, once the injurer has made his $\hat{p}$ estimate, he has no incentive under the cost–benefit rule either to add an insurance factor or to subtract a low ball factor. He is indifferent between opposite but equal errors. Therefore, he will estimate his $\hat{p}$ and take precisely the amount of his estimate, without biasing his actual precaution choice in either direction.

[40]The slopes of the two wings on the cost–benefit rule penalty function are both constant because underprecaution and overprecaution each produce penalties in rectangular (not triangular) areas. Therefore, the penalty for any given increment of error is always the same.

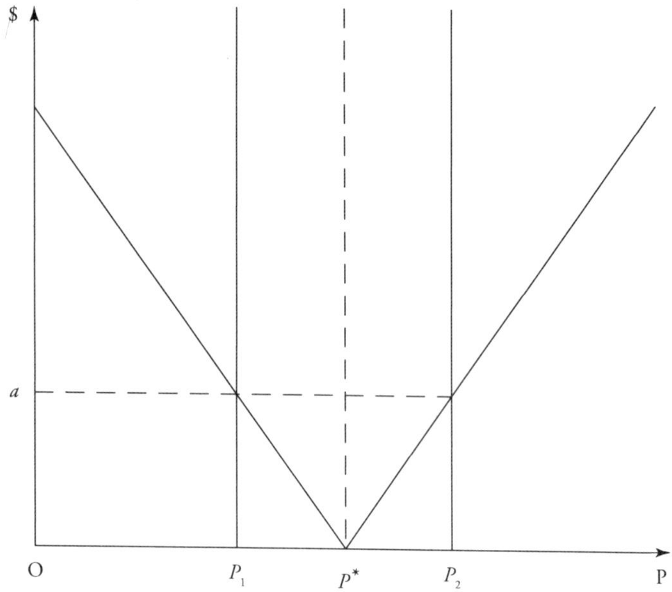

Figure 4

The social consequences of the three alternative negligence rules can be seen on Figure 5. Each rule operates against the same $\hat{p}$-distribution—the same set of injurer estimates of P^*. This $\hat{p}$-distribution is the middle one, because under the prior assumption injurers are just as likely to estimate P^* high or low, whatever the liability rule. Under the P^*-cutoff rule, injurers' actual precaution choices will be dislocated toward lower levels of precaution, because each injurer is subtracting a low ball factor from his estimate of P^*, taking an amount of precaution equal to his estimate less the low ball factor. Under the full liability rule, the $\hat{p}$-distribution also will not be actually realized because injurers are adding an insurance factor to their estimates of P^*, taking an amount of precaution that equals their $\hat{p}$ estimates plus the insurance factor. Hence, each of these two rules produces an actual distribution of precaution, $\overline{P}$, that is dislocated from the $\hat{p}$-distribution. In contrast, the distribution of actual precaution choices induced by the cost–benefit rule is exactly the same as the $\hat{p}$-distribution. The dislocated $\overline{P}$-distribution produced by the full liability rule might be socially preferable to the alternatives if society lost more from errors of underprecaution than from equal errors of overprecaution. Similarly, the $\overline{P}$ distribution of the P^*-cutoff rule might be preferable if society preferred underprecaution to overprecaution.

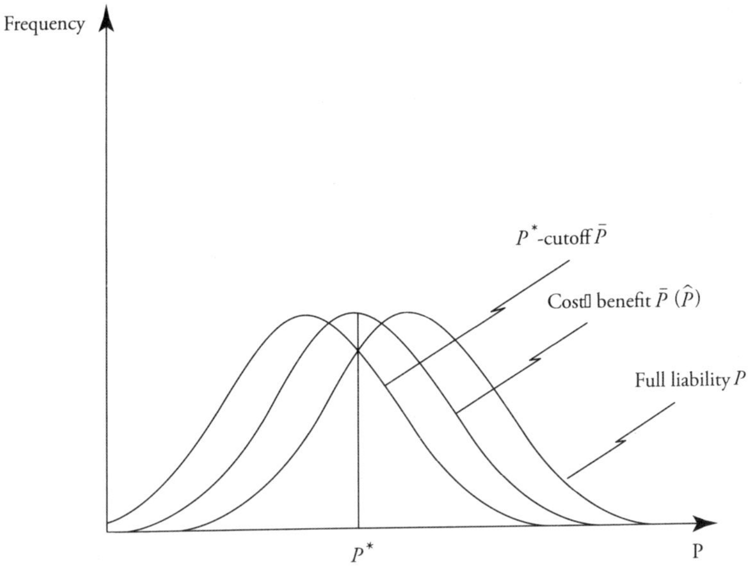

Figure 5

Society, however, loses the same amount from underprecaution as from equal overprecaution.[41] When the injurer is at P_1, society foregoes an amount equal to the area III, which represents a possible surplus that society has lost. Similarly, when the injurer is at P_2, society loses the area V, which represents a deficit that society has incurred. Within a range of error around P^* where the *C*- and *R*-curves can be assumed to be linear, these two areas are equal.[42] Thus, society is indifferent between errors of underprecaution and equal errors of overprecaution. In addition, because the area of triangles similar to III and V is proportional to the square of the departure from P^*, the social loss function is proportional to the sum of the squares of the departures of actual precaution levels from P^*. For example, one injurer error that is double another injurer error costs society four times as much. As Figure 5 indicates, for any given $\hat{p}$-distribution of the type previously assumed, society is better off if the $\overline{P}$-distribution generated by a legal rule is the same as the $\hat{p}$-distribution than if it is shifted away from the $\hat{p}$-distribution. The $\hat{p}$-distribution crowds more precaution choices close

[41]Thus, the private terms of trade between the two types of errors under the cost–benefit approach are the same as the social terms of trade.
[42]*See supra* note 28.

to P^*, the region in which society loses least, than the alternative distributions depicted in Figure 5. Society loses least under the cost–benefit rule because the $\overline{P}$-distribution generated by that rule is equal to the $\hat{p}$-distribution Society does not prefer the full liability $\overline{P}$-distribution because it is dislocated to the right of the $\hat{p}$-distribution. By the same token, society does not prefer the P*-cutoff $\overline{P}$-distribution because it is dislocated to the left of the $\hat{p}$-distribution. Hence, the cost–benefit rule has better formal properties than the rules of the coventional theory.

IV. THE NEW THEORY AND THE COURTS

The preceding discussion shows that the cost–benefit approach can provide a desirable alternative to the formal economic model that underlies the conventional positive theory of negligence. This part shows that the cost–benefit approach is also a more practical one for courts to implement, and that it is more consistent with the way courts actually decide specific negligence cases than either of the two other rules. Thus, from an empirical standpoint, it provides a better basis for positive analysis.

A. The Informational Requirements of the Competing Approaches

In determining whether a party has acted negligently and should be liable, courts consider certain types of information. The next section shows that the evidence generally before the courts concerns the costs and expected benefits of specific untaken precautions. This information is sufficient to determine the issue of negligence under the cost–benefit rule. As we have seen, under that rule a party is held liable if the cost of an untaken precaution that would have prevented the accident is smaller than the reduction in expected harm that would have resulted from taking that precaution. Under the cost–benefit approach, this condition is necessary and sufficient for a finding of liability.[43] It can be called the "cost–benefit condition."

Under the P^*-cutoff rule the corresponding liability conditions are far more complex. In Figure 1, consider the case of an injurer who has built a 111-foot wall (one foot more than P_1). The property downstream is flooded, and the property owner can prove that the overflow would have been prevented by constructing a 130-foot wall (P_2), but cannot show that

[43]This condition will hold provided that proximate cause, duty, and defenses arising from the plaintiff's conduct are not a problem. All of these matters are beyond the scope of this Article.

the overflow would have been prevented by building a 120-foot wall (P^*). From the geometry of Figure 1, it follows that the plaintiff will prevail under the cost–benefit rule. Under the P^*-cutoff rule, however, the court would find for defendant. Thus, the cost–benefit condition is not sufficient for a finding of liability under the P^*-cutoff rule. If courts actually apply the P^*-cutoff rule, then after the plaintiff satisfies the cost–benefit condition they must allow the defendant to raise the defense that the accident would have occurred even if the level of precaution had been P^*. This defense appears to be missing in negligence law. If it were available, one would expect that it would be a routine feature of negligence litigation, because when the defendant has taken less precaution than P^* there will always be precautions beyond P^* that satisfy the cost–benefit condition.

I know of only one case in which a defendant tried to make an argument similar to the missing defense, and in that case the court rejected the argument. In *Haft v. Lone Palm Hotel*,[44] a statute provided that swimming pool managers should either post a sign saying that there was no lifeguard or else provide a lifeguard. Because posting a sign would have precluded liability under the statute, this precaution level has at least a plausible claim for being considered P^*, particularly since it is improbable that any precaution as great as providing a lifeguard could be considered to minimize social costs in a motel swimming pool during the off-season time when the accident occurred.[45] On the cause-in-fact issue, the plaintiff was able to show with much greater force that a lifeguard, rather than a mere warning sign, would have prevented the drowning of her husband and son. The defendant, following a tack very similar to the missing defense, argued that because posting the sign would have precluded the showing of a breach, liability should be tested not by whether a lifeguard would have prevented the deaths—as plaintiff wanted—but by whether a sign would have prevented the deaths. The California Supreme Court rejected the argument. This case, which presented an alternative statutory duty, would seem to provide the most favorable setting for the missing defense to be accepted. In this case, unlike most that would arise in the absence of a statute, it was obvious that if the defendant had taken a precaution level less than the one that the plaintiff had actually used to prove the breach of duty, the plaintiff would have been foreclosed from showing the breach

[44]3 Cal. 3d 756, 478 P.2d 465, 91 Cal. Rptr. 745 (1970).

[45]Of course, P^* will frequently not be a single precaution. In almost all cases, P^* will be a set of precautions that would be optimal with respect to a particular expected harm or "reasonably foreseeable risk." *See supra* note 10. With respect to the risk that

of duty that she did show. When the *Haft* court rejected the defendant's argument, it rejected the missing defense in a setting most conducive to the defense's success. If this defense existed, the case reports would be filled with its refinements and successes because injurers would frequently wish to rely on it. Instead, the defense that has just been described truly is missing and seems rejected.

Another way that courts could cut off liability at P^* would be to impose some ceiling on the victim's selection of untaken precautions. This ceiling would have to be more restrictive than the cost–benefit condition. One possible ceiling would be custom. Under this restriction, only customary precautions could be alleged to be the breach of duty, even in situations where it appears that the costs of uncustomary precautions were less than their benefits. Yet, courts have long held that in most areas of negligence liability the mere compliance with custom is no defense to the injurer whose breach of duty is predicated on cost–benefit considerations.[46]

If courts adopted the full liability rule we would not observe them asking whether the defendant's breach of duty was the but-for cause of the plaintiff's harm. They would be asking instead whether the kind of precaution that the plaintiff failed to take (higher walls) was causally linked to the plaintiff's harm. In other words, if the plaintiff proved that the failure to raise the wall from 110 feet to 112 feet was a breach of duty, the defendant would be liable for the harm done by a 135-foot flood, even though the cost of the additional precaution that would have prevented the accident is greater than the corresponding reduction in expected harm. Thus, the cost–benefit condition cannot be a necessary

---

people may drown in a motel swimming pool during the off-season, the optimal set of precautions would probably include posting a sign that no lifeguard was on duty, having lifesaving equipment nearby, cleaning up any grease that might get onto the pool deck, and so forth. The argument made in the text that it is unlikely that posting a lifeguard at the pool "is P^*" is shorthand for saying that it is unlikely that this precaution is within the set of various precautions (and associated levels of each) that together constitute the P^* set of precautions.

[46]E.g., Texas and P. Ry. v. Behymer, 189 U.S. 468, 470 (1903); Wabash Ry. v. McDaniels, 107 U.S. 454, 460–61 (1882); Bahamas Agricultural Indus., Ltd. v. Riley Stoker Corp., 526 F.2d 1174, 1178 (6th Cir. 1975); Princemont Constr. Corp. v. Smith, 433 F.2d 1217, 1220 (D.C. Cir. 1970) (per curiam); The T.J. Hooper, 60 F.2d 737, 740 (2d Cir.), *cert, denied*, 287 U.S. 662 (1932); Klein v. Mr. Transmission, Inc., 294 Ala. 437, 441–42, 318 So. 2d 676, 679–80 (1975); Roberie v. Sinclair Refining Co., 252 So. 2d 488, 493 (La. Ct. App. 1971); Thompson v. Ohio Fuel Gas Co., 9 Ohio St. 2d 116, 117–19, 224 N.E.2d 131, 134–5 (1967).

condition for a finding of liability under the full liability rule. Under this rule, a plaintiff could make an alternative argument and prevail. That argument would contain the following elements: (1) a showing that the reduction in expected harm from any given untaken precaution, no matter how small, exceeds its cost; and (2) a showing that the harm sustained resulted from the defendant's activity.[47] Under the full liability

---

The one exception to this principle is medical and possibly other forms of malpractice. In most jurisdictions, the victim injured by a doctor must demonstrate that the untaken precaution used to establish the doctor's breach of duty was customary among doctors. Tant v. Women's Clinic, 382 So. 2d 1120, 1121 (Ala. 1980); Walton v. Jones, 286 N.W.2d 710, 714 (Minn. 1979); see King, *In Search of a Standard of Care for the Medical Prefession: The "Accepted Practice" Formula*, 28 Vand. L. Rev. 1213, 1234–35 (1975); McCoid, *The Care Required of Medical Practitioners*, 12 Vand. L. Rev. 549, 605–06 (1959). But see Helling v. Carey, 83 Wash. 2d 514, 519 P.2d 981 (1974) (finding breach of duty of physician based on uncustomary precaution). For discussions of other types of malpractice, see Kenney v. Oak Builders, *Inc.*, 224 So. 2d 161, 168 (La. Ct. App. 1969) (architects); Lambert v. Soltis, 422 Pa. 304, 307–10, 221 A.2d 173, 175–77 (1966) (dentists); Elizondo v. Tavarez, 596 S.W.2d 667, 672–73 (Tex. Civ. App. 1980) (nurses).

The precautions customary among doctors have a good claim for being considered P^*, because most doctors would have every expectation that their patients would wish to pay for all precautions whose costs are less than their benefits and, if their patients are risk neutral, for no more. There is a good reason for the law to subject doctors to the P^*-cutoff rule, as opposed to the cost–benefit rule. By virtue of his special kind of relationship with his patient, who is the possible victim of his negligence, the doctor faces a penalty function very different from that of most injurers. For the doctor the penalty from being at P_1 is the sum of the areas III and IV, not just the area III, because if the doctor is ever found at P_1 he will have the unhappy awareness that his patient would have been willing to pay the area IV for him to have taken P^* instead. (In this scenario, the C-curve includes a competitive rate of return for the doctor on the medical procedures that he sells.) On the other hand, if the doctor takes P_2, he can recover the area VI in fee even from a perfectly informed patient. Therefore, the doctor's penalty from being at P_2 is at most the area V. For the doctor, then, and possibly for other injurers with similar special relationships to their victims, even the P^*-cutoff rule imposes a higher penalty for underprecaution than for equal overprecaution. If courts applied the cost–benefit rule to this peculiar situation, they would further imbalance the penalties for the two types of errors, because the penalty for operating at P_1 would become the areas III, IV, and VI. It is presumably for this reason that the courts apply a standard more similar to the P^*-cutoff rule to this special situation. The conventional theory does not make this distinction, but maintains instead that the P^*-comparison approach is the general rule of breach of duty.

[47]In other words, using the formulation given at *supra* note 11, the sole causal issue would be whether the harm sustained arose from a reasonably foreseeable risk.

rule, the plaintiff does not have to show that the untaken precaution used to satisfy the breach of duty requirement also satisfies the cause in fact requirement by being one that would have prevented the particular harm that the plaintiff sustained.

In summary, to justify the P^*-cut-off rule, its proponents need to show that courts apply the defense that shields a negligent defendant from liability for untaken precautions beyond P^*, even if such untaken precautions satisfy the cost–benefit condition. To justify the full liability rule they need to show that the cost–benefit comparison need not involve the actual untaken precaution that would have prevented the accident. In contrast to both these cases, a proponent of the cost–benefit approach need show only that courts compare the costs and benefits of particular untaken precautions to determine breach of duty and predicate cause in fact on the ability of the untaken precaution constituting the breach of duty to have prevented the harm that the plaintiff sustained.

B. Cost–Benefit Comparisons and the Case Law

In a recent article, William Landes and Richard Posner examine a set of cases with the view of defending the P^*-comparison approach.[48] These cases can be divided into two groups: cases on negligence reprinted in the Gregory, Kalven, and Epstein torts casebook,[49] thought by Landes and Posner to be neutral with respect to their theory; and their own personal selections, which may have been chosen to validate the P^*-comparison theory.[50] For the sake of brevity, the analysis here focuses on Landes and Posner's own selection of injurer negligence cases,[51] because those cases are the ones that one would expect would support the conventional theory most strongly. But even this latter group of cases provides better support for the hypothesis that courts are using the cost–benefit approach.

It should be noted that Landes and Posner performed this case analysis before they clarified their theory of legal causation. In the article in which the case analysis appears, there is no explicit formal

[48] Landes and Posner, *supra* note 1, at 892–903.

[49] C. Gregory, H. Kalven & R. Epstein, Cases and Materials on Torts 102–30 (3d ed. 1977); *see* Landes & Posner, supra note 1, at 899–903.

[50] *See* Landes & Posner, *supra* note 1, at 899.

[51] I do not consider Liming v. Illinois Cent. R.R., 81 Iowa 246, 47 N.W. 66 (1890), which is a contributory negligence case, and therefore beyond the scope of this Article.

theory of how the cause in fact doctrine limits liability; the formal model relates solely to the breach of duty doctrine, which they model using the P^*-comparison approach.[52] Their more recent clarification of their causation theory explicitly adds the concept of but-for causation to their formal model of the negligence rule.[53] Hence, Landes and Posner seem now committed to the P^*-cut-off rule and not to the full liability rule. In any event, as the following discussion indicates, the cases that they selected to validate their theory clearly do not support the hypothesis that courts are using the full liability rule.[54] Therefore, the relevant question becomes whether these cases better support the hypothesis that courts are using the P^*-cutoff rule or the hypothesis that courts are using the cost–benefit rule.

In *Hendricks v. Peabody Coal Co.*,[55] the first case from the Landes and Posner selection, the plaintiff, who was a minor, was seriously injured while swimming in the defendant's abandoned strip mine. Consistent with the cost–benefit approach to the breach of duty issue, the court was clear that of the various untaken precautions that the plaintiff had demonstrated, the one constituting the defendant's breach of duty was the defendant's failure to build a "six-foot high steel chain-link fence with steel posts set in concrete surrounding the entire pit."[56] The court noted that this steel fence would have cost between $12,000 and $14,000, but concluded that "[t]his cost was slight compared to the risk to the children involved."[57] The court seemed convinced that this precaution, if it had been taken, would have virtually eliminated the relevant expected harm, so a conclusion that the cost was less than the "risk" was tantamount to a conclusion that the additional cost was less than the reduction in expected harm.

It would be unreasonable to infer from the *Hendricks* court's opinion a specific finding that the six-foot steel fence set in concrete was necessarily within the set of social-cost-minimizing precautions. The court also laid emphasis on the defendant's failure either to post signs warning of the danger or to police the area effectively. Presumably, some combination

[52]Landes & Posner, *supra* note 1, at 874, 882.

[53]Landes & Posner, *Causation, supra* note 3, at 115–18.

[54]In none of the cases is the analysis consistent with the "causal link" theory of causation. See *supra* p. 824.

[55]115 Ill. App. 2d 35, 253 N.E.2d 56 (1969); *see* Landes & Posner, *supra* note 1, at 892–93.

[56]115 Ill. App. 2d at 39, 253 N.E.2d at 58.

[57]*Id.* at 45, 253 N.E.2d at 61.

of signs and very effective policing would have precluded the plaintiff from showing that the absence of the fence was a breach of duty. What combination of precaution technologies would minimize social cost is something that cases like *Hendricks* do not decide. All *Hendricks* decided was that, given the defendant's actual level of precaution, the costs of building a fence would have been less than the reduction in expected harm from doing so and that a fence would have prevented the particular injury that occurred. This limited finding of fact would conclude the liability issue if the court were following the cost–benefit approach; if the court were following the P^*-comparison approach, however, the analysis would be far more complicated, since the court would have to determine what combination of these three—and possibly other—precaution technologies would truly minimize social cost.

Adams v. Bullock,[58] the second case that Landes and Posner discuss, is also one in which the court seems to have been using the cost–benefit approach. Here the court narrowed the possibilities of what untaken precautions might support liability by using cause in fact analysis. The plaintiff was a boy who was shocked when the wire that he was swinging while walking on a bridge came into contact with the defendant's trolley wires. The court noted that "[g]uards [for wires] . . . are of little value."[59] What the court meant was that if the defendant had placed the guards "here and there" on the wires, it is doubtful that it would have prevented the particular harm that the plaintiff sustained.[60] The only untaken precaution that would have satisfied the cause in fact requirement was placing the trolley wires underground. If they had been underground, the plaintiff's harm would have been prevented, because his swinging wire would surely not have come into contact with them. The court was not satisfied "upon the facts exhibited in this record" that the cost of placing the wires underground was justified by the benefits.[61] There is

[58]227 N.Y. 208, 125 N.E. 93 (1919); see Landes & Posner, *supra* note 1, at 893–94.
[59]227 N.Y. at 211, 125 N.E. at 94.
[60]A similar, but harder, cause in fact issue is presented when the defendant has failed to place fire escapes on a building. Granting this omission to be a breach of duty, courts have denied recovery because of a failure to demonstrate cause in fact. *See, e.g.*, Rosser v. Atlantic Trust & Sec. Co., 168 Va. 389, 191 S.E. 651 (1937); Berry v. Farmers' Exch., 286 P. 46 (Wash. 1930). To prove cause in fact, the plaintiff has to demonstrate that if a fire escape had been built, it would have been positioned in a way to have allowed the plaintiff (or the plaintiff's deceased) to have escaped.
[61]227 N.Y. at 211, 125 N.E. at 94.

no suggestion in this case that liability depends on any condition more restrictive than the cost–benefit condition, as would be the case if the court were using the P^*-cutoff rule.

In the next case that Landes and Posner discuss, *Nussbaum v. Lacopo*,[62] the plaintiff, who had bought a house next to a golf course, was struck by a ball that the defendant had hit.[63] The court analyzed two untaken precautions, again in the alternative: The defendant's failure to take more care in making his shot to prevent the golf ball from hooking, and the defendant's failure to shout "Fore!" once he knew it had hooked. The court decided that the first untaken precaution did not constitute a breach of duty. The court noted that "[g]olfers are notorious in the tedious preparation they give to a shot."[64] So, it was unlikely that the cost to the defendant of further precaution in striking the ball would have been less than the reduction in expected harm, especially when the defendant could see that there was a natural barrier of foliage between the tee and the plaintiff's property. In any event, as the court also noted, "Plaintiff made no effort to show that defendant failed to use due care in striking the ball."[65] In the court's mind, this resolved the issue on the first untaken precaution in favor of the defendant.

What consumes most of the court's analysis and what the court obviously regarded as the most serious breach of duty issue of the case arose on the second untaken precaution, namely, the defendant's failure to have shouted "Fore!" once he knew that he had hooked the ball. Landes and Posner do not mention this issue in their analysis. Of course, normally the burden of shouting "Fore!" after a seriously hooked shot is less than the reduction in expected harm. The court, however, refused to send the case to the jury, stating: "Living so close to a golf course, plaintiff would necessarily hear numerous warning shouts

[62] 27 N.Y. 2d 311, 265 N.E.2d 762, 317 N.Y.S.2d 347 (1970); see Landes & Posner, *supra* note 1, at 894–95.

[63] Actually there were two defendants, the golfer and the golf course. The untaken precaution alleged against the golf course was its failure to design the course in a way that would reduce the expected harm to those in and around the plaintiff's home. The court resolved this issue with assumption-of-the-risk analysis, saying the evidence was that golf balls only occasionally landed on the plaintiff's property and that "[t]hese invasions are the annoyances which must be accepted by one who seeks to reside in the serenity and semi-isolation of such pastoral setting." 27 N.Y.2d at 317, 265 N.E.2d at 765, 317 N.Y.S.2d at 353.

[64] *Id.* at 319, 265 N.E.2d at 767, 317 N.Y.S.2d at 353.

[65] *Id.* at 318, 265 N.E.2d at 766–67, 317 N.Y.S.2d at 353.

each day. As the warning would ordinarily be directed to other golfers, plaintiff could be expected to ignore them."[66] In other words, even if the failure to have taken the precaution of shouting "Fore!" was a breach of duty, it could not have been the cause in fact of the plaintiff's harm because this precaution would not have prevented the plaintiff's harm, even if it had been taken. Thus, the court's refusal to send the case to the jury was premised on a "cause in fact" reason, not a "breach of duty" reason.[67] Because the cost–benefit rule has the same cause in fact requirement as the P^*-cutoff rule, this case is no more consistent with the P^*-comparison approach than it is with the cost–benefit approach,

[66] *Id.* at 318, 265 N.E.2d at 766, 317 N.Y.S.2d at 353.

[67] Landes and Posner make the same error relative to McDowall v. Great W. Ry., [1903] 2 K.B. 331 (C.A.) (Vaughan Williams, L.J.), *rev'g* [1902] 1 K.B. 618, a Gregory, Kalven and Epstein case, which was also finally decided by the Court of Appeal on cause in fact or proximate cause grounds, not on breach of duty grounds as Landes and Posner write. *See* Landes & Posner, *supra* note 1, at 901–2. In this case, a group of boys broke into one of the defendant's boxcars and sent it rolling down a hill where it crashed into the plaintiff. The defendant's actual level of precaution was high in that the defendant had (1) locked the boxcar, (2) left it braked, and (3) left it coupled to other railcars. The untaken precaution that the plaintiff alleged to be the breach of duty was the defendant's failure to have set the boxcar behind a "catchpoint" as the defendant easily could have done. Because the defendant's actual level of precaution was high, it is doubtful that setting the boxcar behind the catchpoint would have reduced expected harm by any significant amount. The jury found in a special verdict, however, that it was a breach of duty to have failed to set the boxcar behind the catchpoint, and the King's Bench Division entered judgment on the verdict for the plaintiff. The Court of Appeal reversed, and it is this reversal that Landes and Posner are trying to explain. They say that the Court of Appeal found that the evidence of the defendant's breach of duty was insufficient to support the verdict, and that this finding was justified because after all the actual precautions had been taken the marginal reduction in expected harm was "probably negative," suggesting that it would have been inefficient to make even a negligible expenditure to move the car behind the catchpoint. Landes & Posner, *supra* note 1, at 907. Landes and Posner's analysis implies that the defendant had taken precaution up to the point where the last units of precaution were actually increasing expected harm. This conclusion seems unlikely. Surely, braking the boxcar, if that was the last unit of precaution, would not have increased expected harm. Rather, the Court of Appeal seems to have decided the case on cause in fact, not breach of duty, grounds. As the court noted in a key passage:

> The truth of the matter is that, if it had been placed there [behind the catchpoint], all these boys would have had to do was to open or close, as the case might be, this catch-point and let the van go by, which would have been a very much simpler operation than that they went through when they got into the van, of uncoupling and unbraking the van.

except, of course, that this case does not suggest the existence of the "missing defense" or any other condition of liability more restrictive than the cost–benefit condition.

In these injurer negligence cases that Landes and Posner marshal in support of their P^*-comparison theory, the issue that the courts considered was not whether actual precaution was less than the P^*-level but whether the cost of at least one specific untaken precaution was less than the benefit. Indeed, at points in their analysis, Landes and Posner write as if they are really trying to validate the cost–benefit approach, not their P^*-comparison theory. For example, in their discussion of *Blyth v. Proprietors of the Birmingham Waterworks*,[68] Landes and Posner write:

> The court was not interested in whether the total costs of burying the main to a depth at which it would not have burst even in the unusually severe frost of 1855 were less than the expected accident costs. It was interested in whether, given that the mains had been buried to a depth that would prevent their freezing in any ordinary frost, the incremental expense of protecting against an unusually severe frost would have been justified by the incremental reduction in accident costs brought about by such an expense.[69]

Evaluating the costs and benefits of a particular untaken precaution seems more consistent with the cost–benefit approach than with the P^*-comparison approach. It is true, however, that a court can attempt to locate P^* by searching for untaken precautions that would have been cost–beneficial. Indeed, if an injurer operates at P^*, no untaken precaution could possibly have that property. What Landes and Posner neglect, however, is that untaken precautions beyond P^* can have greater benefits than costs when the injurer is taking less precaution than P^*. Landes and Posner seem to embrace the cost–benefit condition as the test of liability when they do their case

2 K.B. at 336–37. This means that the court found that there was no cause in fact because the untaken precaution said to constitute the breach of duty would not, under the circumstances, have prevented the particular accident that occurred. In a later passage, the court makes this point even more clearly: "[I]n my judgement, there is nothing to justify the finding that the not placing the van to the east of the catch-point was an effective cause of the accident which occurred." *Id.* at 337. The other decisional language in the opinion bears on whether the intervention of the boys should have been reasonably foreseeable to the defendant, which is proximate cause analysis outside the scope of this Article.

[68] 11 Ex. 781, 156 Eng. Rep. 1047 (1856); *see* Landes & Posner, *supra* note 1, at 895–96.

[69] Landes & Posner, *supra* note 1, at 896; *see also id.* at 896–7 (discussing additional costs and benefits of untaken precautions).

analysis, but they neglect the point that this condition, if it is not further restricted, leads to a liability beyond P^* that is inconsistent with their theory.

CONCLUSION

This Article identifies an alternative to the conventional approach of comparing an injurer's level of precaution with the level that would minimize social costs. The proposed alternative, to compare the costs and benefits of an untaken precaution that was a "but for" cause of the accident, is preferable for two reasons. First, as a formal economic model, it appears more likely to promote the minimization of social costs. More importantly, it is more consistent with the actual practice of the courts. Thus, from the standpoint of the two criteria that are relevant to the evaluation of the positive economic theory of tort, the proposed approach performs better than the conventional theory that it seeks to replace.

6

Efficiency of Liability Rules

A Reconsideration[†]

*Satish K. Jain**

An important question that one can ask regarding any institution is whether its structure is such that when rational individuals act within its framework they are induced to act in ways so that the social outcome which results as a consequence of the totality of actions undertaken by the individuals is efficient. It is evident that, from the perspective of governance, particularly of governance with focus on the objective of economic development, the importance of efficient institutions, institutions with the characteristic of invariably yielding efficient outcomes from the interplay of actions undertaken by purposive individuals, cannot be overemphasized. In recent decades a large part of contemporary law has been analysed to determine whether the relevant legal rules and procedures have this characteristic of always giving rise to efficient outcomes.

A central question in the economic analysis of tort law is how to apportion accident loss between victim and tortfeasor so that both parties involved in the harmful interaction are induced to take socially optimal levels of care. There is an extensive literature on the efficiency of liability rules, the rules for apportioning losses between victims and injurers. Considerations relating to efficiency of liability rules have occupied an important place in the law and economics literature right from its inception. The pioneering contribution by Calabresi (1961)

†Originally published as "Efficiency of Liability Rules: A Reconsideration", 2006, *Journal of International Trade & Economic Development*, Vol. 15, pp. 359–73.
*The author wishes to thank Sugato Dasgupta, Rajendra Kundu, Taposik Banerjee, Papiya Ghosh, Anirban Mitra and two referees for helpful comments.

analysed the effect of liability rules on parties' behaviour. In his seminal contribution, Coase (1960) looked at liability rules from the point of view of their implications for social costs. The rule of negligence was analysed by Posner (1972) from the perspective of economic efficiency. The first formal analysis of liability rules was done by Brown (1973). His main results demonstrated the efficiency of the rule of negligence and the rule of strict liability with the defence of contributory negligence; and the inefficiency of strict liability and no liability. Formal treatment of some of the most important results of the vast literature on liability rules is contained in Landes and Posner (1987) and Shavell (1987). A complete characterization of efficient liability rules is contained in Jain and Singh (2002).

In the literature, dealing with the question of efficiency of liability rules, the problem has generally been considered within the framework of accidents resulting from interaction of two risk-neutral parties, the victim and the injurer. The social goal is taken to be the minimization of total social costs, which are defined to be the sum of costs of care taken by the two parties and expected accident loss. The probability of accident and the amount of loss in case of occurrence of accident are assumed to depend on the levels of care taken by the two parties. A liability rule determines the proportions in which the two parties are to bear the loss in case of occurrence of accident, on the basis of whether and by what proportions the parties involved in the interaction were negligent. A liability rule is efficient iff it invariably induces both parties to behave in ways which result in socially optimal outcomes, i.e., outcomes under which total social costs are minimized. The central result regarding the efficiency question that has emerged is that a liability rule is efficient if and only if it satisfies the condition of negligence liability. The condition of negligence liability requires that, in a two-party interaction, if one party is non-negligent and the other party is negligent then the entire loss, in case of occurrence of accident, must be borne by the negligent party. From the necessity and sufficiency of negligence liability for efficiency it follows that the rules of negligence, negligence with the defence of contributory negligence and strict liability with the defence of contributory negligence, among the commonly used liability rules, are efficient; the rules of strict liability and no liability are not.

In the mainstream of law and economics, the notion of negligence is defined with respect to the legally specified due care level. If an individual's care level is found to be less than the legally specified level then the individual is adjudged to have been negligent. On the other hand, if the care level is equal to or greater than the legally specified care level, the individual is adjudged to have been non-negligent. The efficiency of liability rules, with few exceptions, has been discussed using this mainstream notion of negligence; coupled with the assumption that the courts specify the due care levels appropriately from the perspective of minimization of total social costs.

While in the law and economics literature it is common to conceptualize the notion of negligence as described above, it is by no means uncontroversial. In opposition to the mainstream view, it has been argued that the courts do not determine negligence as visualized in the law and economics literature. Rather, whether a party is adjudged to be negligent or not depends on whether the opposite party is able to show the existence of some cost-justified precaution which was not taken. That is to say, a party is deemed to be negligent if and only if it can be shown that the party could have averted some harm by taking care which would have cost less than the loss due to harm.[1] This paper is concerned with deriving the implications of this way of defining negligence for the efficiency of liability rules.

The main result of the paper shows that if negligence is determined on the basis of cost-justified untaken precautions then there is no liability rule which is efficient. Thus, the results on the efficiency of liability rules crucially depend on what constitutes negligence. If it turns out that the courts indeed determine negligence on the basis of cost-justified untaken precautions, and not on the basis of shortfall of actual care from some legally specified standard, there would be far-reaching implications for both positive and normative analysis of tort law.

The paper is divided into three sections. The first section sets out the framework of analysis and formalizes the notion of negligence determined on the basis of cost-justified untaken precautions. The next section contains the statement and the proof of the general impossibility theorem. The final section contains some concluding remarks on the implications of the general impossibility theorem from positive and normative perspectives.

DEFINITIONS AND ASSUMPTIONS

We consider accidents resulting from interaction of two parties, assumed to be strangers to each other, in which, to begin with, the entire loss falls on one party, to be called the victim (plaintiff). The other party will be referred to as the injurer (defendant). We denote by $a \geq 0$ the index of the level of care taken by the victim; and by $b \geq 0$ the index of the level of care taken by the injurer.

Let

$$A = \{a \mid a \geq 0 \text{ is the index of some feasible level of care that can be taken by the victim}\}, \text{ and}$$

$$B = \{b \mid b \geq 0 \text{ is the index of some feasible level of care that can be taken by the injurer}\}$$

We assume:

$$0 \in A \wedge 0 \in B. \tag{A1}$$

We denote by $c(a)$ the cost to the victim of care level a and by $d(b)$ the cost to the injurer of care level b.

Let $C = \{c(a) \mid a \in A\}$, and $D = \{d(b) \mid b \in B\}$.

We assume:

$$c(0) = 0 \wedge d(0) = 0. \tag{A2}$$

We also assume that c and d are strictly increasing functions of a and b respectively. (A3)

In view of Assumptions (A2) and (A3) it follows that:

$$(\forall c \in C)(c \geq 0) \wedge (\forall d \in D)(d \geq 0)$$

A consequence of Assumption (A3) is that c and d themselves can be taken as indices of levels of care of the two parties.

Let π denote the probability of occurrence of accident and $H \geq 0$ the loss in case of occurrence of accident. Both π and H will be assumed to be functions of c and d; $\pi = \pi(c, d)$, $H = H(c, d)$. Let $L = \pi H$. L is thus the expected loss due to accident.

We assume:

$$(\forall c, c' \in C)(\forall d, d' \in D)[[c > c' \rightarrow L(c, d) \leq L(c', d)] \wedge [d > d' \rightarrow L(c, d) \leq L(c, d')]] \tag{A4}$$

In other words, it is assumed that a larger expenditure on care by either party, given the expenditure on care by the other party, results in lesser or equal expected accident loss.

Total social costs (TSC) are defined to be the sum of cost of care by the victim, cost of care by the injurer, and the expected loss due to accident; $TSC = c + d + L(c, d)$. Let $M = \{(c', d') \in C \times D \mid c' + d' + L(c', d')$ is minimum of $\{c + d + L(c, d) \mid c \in C \wedge d \in D\}\}$. Thus, M is the set of all costs of care configurations (c', d') which are total social cost minimizing. It will be assumed that:

C, D and L are such that M is non-empty. (A5)

Corresponding to each $(c, d) \in C \times D$, we define:

$$C^u(c, d) = \{c^u \in C \mid c^u > c \wedge L(c, d) - L(c^u, d) > c^u - c\}$$

$$D^u(c, d) = \{d^u \in D \mid d^u > d \wedge L(c, d) - L(c, d^u) > d^u - d\}$$

Thus, $C^u(c, d)$ is the set of all cost-justified untaken precautions at (c, d) which the victim could have taken; and $D^u(c, d)$ is the set of all cost-justified untaken precautions at (c, d) which the injurer could have taken.

We define:

$$\begin{aligned} \hat{c}(c, d) &= \sup C^u(c, d) && \text{if } C^u(c, d) \neq \emptyset \\ &= c && \text{if } C^u(c, d) = \emptyset \end{aligned}$$

and

$$\begin{aligned} \hat{d}(c, d) &= \sup D^u(c, d) && \text{if } D^u(c, d) \neq \emptyset \\ &= d && \text{if } D^u(c, d) = \emptyset \end{aligned}$$

Let I denote the closed unit interval $[0, 1]$.[2] Given C, D, π, and H, we define functions p and q as follows:

$$\begin{aligned} p : C \times D \mapsto I \text{ by} : p(c, d) &= \frac{c}{\hat{c}(c, d)} && \text{if } \hat{c}(c, d) \neq 0 \\ &= 1 && \text{if } \hat{c}(c, d) = 0 \end{aligned}$$

$$\begin{aligned} q : C \times D \mapsto I \text{ by} : q(c, d) &= \frac{d}{\hat{d}(c, d)} && \text{if } \hat{d}(c, d) \neq 0 \\ &= 1 && \text{if } \hat{d}(c, d) = 0 \end{aligned}$$

p and q would be interpreted as proportions of non-negligence of the victim and the injurer respectively. $(1 - p)$ and $(1 - q)$ consequently would denote the proportions of negligence of the victim and the injurer respectively.[3]

A liability rule is a rule which specifies the proportions in which the two parties are to bear the loss in case of occurrence of accident as a function of proportions of non-negligence of the two parties. Formally, a liability rule is a function f from I^2 to I^2, $f : I^2 \mapsto I^2$, such that: $f(p, q) = (x, y)$, where $x + y = 1$.

Let C, D, π, and H be given. If accident takes place and loss of $H(c, d)$ materializes, then $x[p(c, d), q(c, d)]H(c, d)$ will be borne by the victim and $y[p(c, d), q(c, d)]H(c, d)$ by the injurer. As, to begin with, in case of occurrence of accident, the entire loss falls upon the victim, $y[p(c, d), q(c, d)]H(c, d)$ represents the liability payment by the injurer to the victim. The expected costs of the victim and the injurer, to be denoted by EC_1 and EC_2 respectively, therefore, are $[c + x[p(c, d), q(c, d)]L(c, d)]$ and $[d + y[p(c, d), q(c, d)]L(c, d)]$ respectively. Both parties are assumed to prefer smaller expected costs to larger expected costs and be indifferent between alternatives with equal expected costs.

Let f be a liability rule. An application of f consists of specification of C, D, π and H satisfying Assumptions (A1) – (A5). The class of all applications satisfying Assumptions (A1) – (A5) will be denoted by $\mathcal{A}$.

f is defined to be efficient for a given application $< C, D, \pi, H >$ satisfying Assumptions (A1) – (A5) iff $(\forall(\bar{c}, \bar{d}) \in C \times D)[(\bar{c}, \bar{d})$ is a Nash equilibrium $\rightarrow (\bar{c}, \bar{d}) \in M]$ and $(\exists(\bar{c}, \bar{d}) \in C \times D)[(\bar{c}, \bar{d})$ is a Nash equilibrium].[4] In other words, a liability rule is efficient for a given application $< C, D, \pi, H >$ satisfying Assumptions (A1) – (A5) iff (i) every pure-strategy Nash equilibrium is total social cost minimizing, and (ii) there exists at least one pure-strategy Nash equilibrium. f is defined to be efficient with respect to a class of applications iff it is efficient for every application belonging to the class.

The following example illustrates some of the above ideas.

Example 1

Let liability rule f be the negligence rule defined by: $(\forall p \in [0,1](\forall q \in [0, 1)) [f(p, q) = (0, 1)] \wedge (\forall p \in [0, 1])[f(p, 1) = (1, 0)]$.

Consider an application of f such that:

$C = D = \{0, 1, 2\}$

For $(c, d) \in C \times D$, let $L(c, d)$ be as given in the following array:

		d 0	1	2
	0	10.0	7.0	5.5
c	1	7.0	4.0	2.5
	2	5.5	2.5	1.0

Here (2, 2) is the unique TSC-minimizing configuration of costs of care. For $(c, d) \in C \times D$, we have $C^u(c, d)$ as given in the following array:

		d 0	1	2
	0	{1,2}	{1,2}	{1,2}
c	1	{2}	{2}	{2}
	2	∅	∅	∅

And the following array gives $D^u(c, d)$ for $(c, d) \in C \times D$:

		d 0	1	2
	0	{1,2}	{2}	∅
c	1	{1,2}	{2}	∅
	2	{1,2}	{2}	∅

Therefore, we obtain:

$$(\forall(c,d) \in C \times D)[\hat{c}(c,d) = 2 \wedge \hat{d}\,(c,d) = 2].$$

The following array gives, for $(c,d) \in C \times D, EC(c,d) = (EC_1(c,d), EC_2(c,d))$:

		d 0	1	2
	0	(0,10)	(0,8)	(5.5,2)
c	1	(1,7)	(1,5)	(3.5,2)
	2	(2,5.5)	(2,3.5)	(3,2)

Therefore (2, 2) is the only pure-strategy Nash equilibrium. Thus, f is efficient for this application.

Now, we define a condition on liability rules.

Condition of Negligence Liability (NL): A liability rule f satisfies the condition of negligence liability iff $[[\forall p \in [0,1)][f(p,1) = (1,0)] \wedge [\forall q \in [0,1)][f(1,q) = (0,1)]]$. In other words, a liability rule satisfies the condition of negligence liability iff its structure is such that: (i) whenever the injurer is non-negligent and the victim is negligent, the entire loss in case of accident is borne by the victim; and (ii) whenever the victim is non-negligent and the injurer is negligent, the entire loss in case of an accident is borne by the injurer.

NEGLIGENCE AS COST-JUSTIFIED UNTAKEN PRECAUTION AND EFFICIENT LIABILITY RULES: THE GENERAL IMPOSSIBILITY THEOREM

Proposition 1: *If a liability rule f is efficient for every application belonging to $\mathcal{A}$ then it satisfies the condition of negligence liability.*

Proof: Let f be any liability rule violating condition NL. As condition NL is violated, we must have:

$$[\exists p \in [0,1)][f(p,1) \neq (1,0)] \vee [\exists q \in [0,1)][f(1,q) \neq (0,1)]$$

Suppose $[\exists q \in [0,1)][f(1,q) \neq (0,1)]$ holds.

Suppose for $q_0 \in [0,1)$ we have:

$$f(1,q_0) = (x_{q0}\, 0, y_{q0}), \quad y_{q0} \neq 1$$

Let t be a positive number. As $y_{q0} \in [0,1)$, we have $y_{q0}\, t < t$. Choose a positive number r such that $y_{q0} t < r < t$.

As $q_0 \neq 1, (1-q_0) \neq 0$. Let $d_0 = \frac{r}{1-q_0}$. Let $0 < \epsilon$ and $0 < c_0$.

Now let C and D be specified as follows:

$C = \{0, c_0\}, \qquad D = \{0, q_0 d_0, d_0\}$.

For $(c,d) \in C \times D$, Let (c,d) be as given in the following array:

		d	
	0	$q_0 d_0$	d_0
c 0	$t + q_0 d_0 + c_0 + \epsilon$	$t + c_0 + \epsilon$	$c_0 + \epsilon$
c c_0	$t + q_0 d_0$	t	0

It should be noted that the above specification of C, D and L is consistent with Assumptions (A1) – (A5). Furthermore, the specification of L is done in such a way that no inconsistency would arise even if $q_0 = 0$.

As $\epsilon > 0$ and $t > r = (1-q_0)d_0$, it follows that (c_0, d_0) is the unique total social cost minimizing configuration.

The following array gives $C^u(c,d)$ for $(c,d) \in C \times D$:

		d	
	0	$q_0 d_0$	d_0
c 0	$\{c_0\}$	$\{c_0\}$	$\{c_0\}$
c c_0	$\emptyset$	$\emptyset$	$\emptyset$

And the following array $D^u(c,d)$ for $(c,d) \in C \times D$:

		d	
	0	$q_0 d_0$	d_0
c 0	$\{d_0\}$	$\{d_0\}$	$\emptyset$
c c_0	$\{d_0\}$	$\{d_0\}$	$\emptyset$

Therefore, we obtain:

$$(\forall(c,d)\in C\times D)[\hat{c}(c,d)=c_0 \wedge \hat{d}(c,d)=d_0]$$

Now, expected costs of the injurer at $(c_0, q_0 d_0)$

$$= EC_2(c_0, q_0 d_0) = q_0 d_0 + y_{q0} L(c_0, q_0 d_0) = q_0 d_0 + y_{q0} t$$

$$EC_2(c_0, d_0) = d_0$$

$$EC_2(c_0, d_0) - EC_2(c_0, q_0 d_0) = d_0 - q_0 d_0 - y_{q0} t = (r - y_{q0} t) > 0$$

This establishes that (c_0, d_0) is not a Nash equilibrium. Thus, f is not efficient for the application under consideration. Consequently, it is not the case that f is efficient for every application belonging to $\mathcal{A}$. In case $[\exists p \in [0,1)][f(p,1) \neq (1,0)]$ holds, an analogous argument shows that it is not the case that f is an efficient liability rule for every application belonging to $\mathcal{A}$.

Thus, it follows that if f is efficient for every application belonging to $\mathcal{A}$ then it must satisfy condition NL; establishing the proposition.

Proposition 2: *If a liability rule f is efficient for every application belonging to $\mathcal{A}$ then it violates the condition of negligence liability.*

Proof: Let f be any liability rule satisfying condition NL.

Let $f(1,1) = (x^*, y^*)$.
First suppose that $x^* > 0$.
Let t be a positive integer such that: $\frac{1}{t} < x^*$.[5]

Choose positive numbers $c_0, d_0, \theta_1, \theta_2, L_0, \epsilon_1, \epsilon_2, \epsilon_3, \epsilon_4, \epsilon_5$ such that:

(i) $\epsilon_3 < \epsilon_2$

(ii) $\epsilon_4 < \epsilon_1$

(iii) $\epsilon_1 < \epsilon_4 + \epsilon_5$

(iv) $\epsilon_2 < \epsilon_3 + \epsilon_5$

(v) $\epsilon_3 + \epsilon_4 + \epsilon_5 < \epsilon_1 + \epsilon_2$

(vi) $\epsilon_1 - \epsilon_4 < \theta_1$

(vii) $\epsilon_2 - \epsilon_3 < \theta_2$

(viii) $L_0 > t\epsilon$, where ϵ is any number greater than $\max\{\epsilon_1, \epsilon_2, \epsilon_3, \epsilon_4, \epsilon_5\}$.[6]

Now consider the following application belonging to $\mathcal{A}$:

$$C = \{0, c_0, c_0 + \epsilon_1\}, \qquad D = \{0, d_0, d_0 + \epsilon_2\}$$

For $(c, d) \in C \times D$, let $L(c, d)$ be as given in the following array:

		d: 0	d_0	$d_0 + \epsilon_2$
c	0	$c_0 + d_0 + \theta_1 + \theta_2 + L_0$	$c_0 + \theta_1 + L_0$	$c_0 + \theta_1 + L_0 - \epsilon_3$
	c_0	$d_0 + \theta_2 + L_0$	L_0	$L_0 - \epsilon_3$
	$c_0 + \epsilon_1$	$d_0 + \theta_2 + L_0 - \epsilon_4$	$L_0 - \epsilon_4$	$L_0 - \epsilon_3 - \epsilon_4 - \epsilon_5$

(c_0, d_0) is the unique total social cost minimizing configuration.

We obtain $C^u(c, d), (c, d) \in C \times D$, as given in the following array:

		d: 0	d_0	$d_0 + \epsilon_2$
c	0	$\{c_0, c_0 + \epsilon_1\}$	$\{c_0, c_0 + \epsilon_1\}$	$\{c_0, c_0 + \epsilon_1\}$
	c_0	$\emptyset$	$\emptyset$	$\{c_0 + \epsilon_1\}$
	$c_0 + \epsilon_1$	$\emptyset$	$\emptyset$	$\emptyset$

And $D^u(c, d), (c, d) \in C \times D$, as given in the following array:

		d: 0	d_0	$d_0 + \epsilon_2$
c	0	$\{d_0, d_0 + \epsilon_2\}$	$\emptyset$	$\emptyset$
	c_0	$\{d_0, d_0 + \epsilon_2\}$	$\emptyset$	$\emptyset$
	$c_0 + \epsilon_1$	$\{d_0, d_0 + \epsilon_2\}$	$\{d_0 + \epsilon_2\}$	$\emptyset$

Therefore, we obtain $\hat{c}(c, d), (c, d) \in C \times D$, as given in the following array:

		d: 0	d_0	$d_0 + \epsilon_2$
c	0	$c_0 + \epsilon_1$	$c_0 + \epsilon_1$	$c_0 + \epsilon_1$
	c_0	c_0	c_0	$c_0 + \epsilon_1$
	$c_0 + \epsilon_1$	$c_0 + \epsilon_1$	$c_0 + \epsilon_1$	$c_0 + \epsilon_1$

And $\hat{d}(c, d), (c, d) \in C \times D$, as given in the following array:

		d		
		0	d_0	$d_0+\epsilon_2$
	0	$d_0+\epsilon_2$	d_0	$d_0+\epsilon_2$
c	c_0	$d_0+\epsilon_2$	d_0	$d_0+\epsilon_2$
	$c_0+\epsilon_1$	$d_0+\epsilon_2$	$d_0+\epsilon_2$	$d_0+\epsilon_2$

Now, expected costs of the victim at (c_0, d_0)

$$= EC_1(c_0, d_0) = c_0 + x^* L(c_0, d_0) = c_0 + x^* L_0$$

$$EC_1(c_0+\epsilon_1, d_0) = c_0+\epsilon_1 + x\left(1, \frac{d_0}{d_0+\epsilon_2}\right) L(c_0+\epsilon_1, d_0) = c_0+\epsilon_1$$

as $x\left(1, \frac{d_0}{d_0+\epsilon_2}\right) = 0$ by condition NL.

$$EC_1(c_0, d_0) - EC_1(c_0+\epsilon_1, d_0) = c_0 + x^* L_0 - c_0 - \epsilon_1 = x^* L_0 - \epsilon_1$$

Now,

$$x^* > \frac{1}{t} \wedge L_0 > t\epsilon \wedge t > 0 \wedge \epsilon > 0 \rightarrow x^* L_0 > \epsilon$$

$$\rightarrow x^* L_0 > \epsilon_1$$

$$\rightarrow x^* L_0 - \epsilon_1 > 0.$$

Therefore it follows that (c_0, d_0) is not a Nash equilibrium. Thus, f is not efficient for the application under consideration. Consequently, it is not the case that f is an efficient liability rule for every application belonging to $\mathcal{A}$. By an analogous argument it can be shown that if $y^* > 0$ then it is not the case that f is an efficient rule for every application belonging to $\mathcal{A}$.

As we must have $(x^* > 0 \vee y^* > 0)$, it follows that it is not the case that f is efficient for every application belonging to $\mathcal{A}$.

This establishes that if f is efficient for every application belonging to $\mathcal{A}$ then it must violate condition NL.

Theorem 1: *There is no liability rule which is efficient for every application belonging to A.*

Proof: Follows immediately from Propositions 1 and 2.

An implication of the above general impossibility theorem is that it is not the case that the negligence rule is efficient for every application belonging to $\mathcal{A}$. The following example shows the inefficiency of the negligence rule for a particular application.

EXAMPLE 2

Consider the following application of the negligence rule:

$C = D = \{0, 1, 5\}$.

For $(c, d) \in C \times D$, let $L(c, d)$ be as given in the following array:

		d = 0	1	5
c	0	18	14	12
	1	14	10	8
	5	12	8	3

Here (1, 1) is the unique TSC-minimizing configuration of costs of care.

For $(c, d) \in C \times D$, we have $C^u(c, d)$ as given in the following array:

		d = 0	1	5
c	0	{1, 5}	{1, 5}	{1, 5}
	1	∅	∅	{5}
	5	∅	∅	∅

And the following array gives $D^u(c, d)$ for $(c, d) \in C \times D$:

		d = 0	1	5
c	0	{1, 5}	∅	∅
	1	{1, 5}	∅	∅
	5	{1, 5}	{5}	∅

Therefore, the following array gives $\hat{c}(c, d)$ for $(c, d) \in C \times D$:

		d = 0	1	5
c	0	5	5	5
	1	1	1	5
	5	5	5	5

And the following array $\hat{d}(c, d)$ for $(c, d) \in C \times D$:

		d		
		0	1	5
	0	5	5	5
c	1	5	1	5
	5	5	5	5

The following array gives, for $(c, d) \in C \times D, EC\ (c, d) = (EC_1(c, d), EC_2(c, d))$:

		d		
		0	1	5
	0	(0, 18)	(14, 1)	(12, 5)
c	1	(1, 14)	(11, 1)	(9, 5)
	5	(5, 12)	(5, 9)	(8, 5)

Therefore (5, 5) is the only pure-strategy Nash equilibrium. Thus, the negligence rule is inefficient for this application.

CONCLUDING REMARKS

The economic analysis of common law carried out in the last four and a half decades, starting from the pioneering contributions of Calabresi and Coase, has shown that common law is by and large efficient. This has resulted in economic efficiency being perceived as an idea capable of providing a unified positive theory of law. In this connection it is rather important to note that, in order for an idea to constitute an explanation for an institution it is not sufficient to demonstrate that the institution in question embodies the idea; it also needs to be shown that there is no other institution that can be an embodiment of the idea. Merely showing that the institution embodies the idea, at best, can constitute a partial explanation for the institution. For a complete theory one would need a set of ideas which can completely characterize the institution for which a theory is to be provided. Thus, viewing of economic efficiency as a unifying explanation for law is, strictly speaking, not warranted on the basis of the findings of economic analysis; from the findings one can only claim a partial explanatory role for efficiency. The significance of the results of this paper lies in the fact that if the courts in fact determine negligence on the basis of existence of some cost-justified untaken precaution then even the status of economic efficiency as that of providing a partial explanatory role in the context of legal institutions would become questionable.

In the contemporary discourse on rules and institutions, the desirability of having efficient rules and institutions is taken for granted. If, in reality, the courts decide question of negligence on the basis of shortfall of actual care from the due care level then most liability rules used in practice are efficient; and consequently do not need to be replaced by other rules if the sole consideration in the selecting of the rules is economic efficiency. On the other hand, if the courts in fact decide the question of negligence on the basis of the existence of some cost-justified untaken precaution, then exclusive or even predominant preoccupation with efficiency would suggest need for reform. To bring in efficiency one would either have to have a procedure for determining negligence which is more conducive from the efficiency perspective, or alternatively design rules different from liability rules, which in conjunction with negligence as failure to take cost-justified untaken precautions would achieve efficient outcomes.

If one wants to accommodate efficiency considerations within the framework of negligence as failure to take cost-justified precautions to the extent possible, one possible way to proceed would be first to define a quasi-ordering over the set of all liability rules $\mathcal{L}$ and then consider the maximal elements of $\mathcal{L}$ with respect to the quasi-ordering as follows. Let f be a liability rule and let $\mathcal{A}^i_f \subseteq \mathcal{A}$ denote the set of applications for which f is inefficient. Define a binary relation R over the set of all liability rules by: $[(\forall f, g \in \mathcal{L})[fRg \leftrightarrow \mathcal{A}^i_j \subseteq \mathcal{A}^i_g]]$. It is clear that R is reflexive and transitive, i.e., is a quasi-ordering. Let $\mathcal{L}_m$ denote the set of maximal elements of $\mathcal{L}$ with respect to R. If one wants to retain the framework of negligence as failure to take cost-justified precautions and has no requirement other than efficiency, then at first glance it would seem that the choice of a liability rule must be made from $\mathcal{L}_m$ only.

NOTES

1. This view has been most consistently, and cogently, articulated by Grady (1983, 1984, 1989).
2. In addition to denoting the set $\{x \mid 0 \leq x \leq 1\}$ by $[0, 1]$, we denote by $[0, 1)$ the set $\{x \mid 0 \leq x < 1\}$.
3. To define proportions of negligence and non-negligence the way they have been defined here seems to be an appropriate way to do so in a framework where negligence is determined on the basis of existence of some cost-justified untaken precaution. It should, however, be noted that there are other plausible ways of defining proportions of negligence and non-negligence. For the impossibility result of this paper, the particular way in which proportions of negligence and non-negligence have been defined here, is not crucial.

4. Throughout this paper we consider only pure-strategy Nash equilibria.
5. It should be noted that as $x^* \in (0, 1]$, it follows that $t > 1$.
6. This can always be done. $\epsilon_1 = \epsilon_2 = 4, \epsilon_3 = \epsilon_4 = 2, \epsilon_5 = 3, \theta_1 = \theta_2 = 3, \epsilon = 5$, provides a simple example.

REFERENCES

Brown, J.P. (1973) Toward an economic theory of liability, *Journal of Legal Studies*, 2, pp. 323–350.

Calabresi, G. (1961) Some thoughts on risk distribution and the law of torts, *Yale Law Journal*, 70, pp. 499–553.

Coase, R.H. (1960) The problem of social cost, *Journal of Law and Economics*, 3, pp. 1–44.

Grady, M.F. (1983) A new positive theory of negligence, *Yale Law Journal*, 92, pp. 799–829.

Grady, M.F. (1984) Proximate cause and the law of negligence, *Iowa Law Review*, 69, pp. 363–449.

Grady, M.F. (1989) Untaken precautions, *Journal of Legal Studies*, 18, pp. 139–156.

Jain, S.K. and R. Singh (2002) Efficient liability rules: complete characterization, *Journal of Economics (Zeitschrift für Nationalökonomie)*, 75, pp. 105–24.

Kahan, M. (1989) Causation and incentives to take care under the negligence rule, *Journal of Legal Studies*, 18, pp. 427–447.

Landes, W.M. and R.A Posner, (1987) *The Economic Structure of Tort Law* (Cambridge, MA: Harvard University Press).

Miceli, T.J. (1996) Cause in fact, proximate cause, and the hand rule: extending Grady's positive economic theory of negligence, *International Review of Law and Economics*, 16, pp. 473–482.

Posner, R.A. (1972) A theory of negligence, *Journal of Legal Studies*, 1, pp. 28–96.

Shavell, S. (1987) *Economic Analysis of Accident Law* (Cambridge, MA: Harvard University Press).

Liability Rules: Efficiency and Some Strategic Aspects

7

When Does the Rule of Liability Matter?[†]

Harold Demsetz[*]

The active interface between law and economics has been limited largely to antitrust and regulation, but recent work, primarily in economics, has revealed a much wider area of common interest. The new development, which deals with the definition and structure of property rights, has implications for central areas of the law, such as real property, torts, and contracts, although it originated in an economic analysis of the divergence between private and social cost. While still in its embryonic stage, the analysis has proceeded far enough for it to be called to the attention of a wider audience.

The questions with which we shall be concerned are whether and under what conditions a legal decision about liability affects the uses to which resources will be put and the distribution of wealth between owners of resources. If ranchers are held liable for the damage done by their cattle to corn fields, how will the outputs of meat and corn be affected? If drivers or pedestrians, alternatively, are held liable for automobile-pedestrian accidents, how will the accident rate be affected? What implications for extortion (an extreme form of wealth redistribution) are found in the decision about who is liable for damages?

[†]Originally published as "When Does the Rule of Liability Matter?", 1972, *The Journal of Legal Studies*, Vol. 1, pp. 13–28.
[*]The author wishes to thank the Charles R. Walgreen Foundation for financial aid through its grant to the University of Chicago, and, also, the Lily Endowment through its grant to the University of California.

I.

Recent developments in this area began with an article by Professor R.H. Coase.[1] Coase's work presented a penetrating criticism of the conventional treatment by economists of divergences between private and social cost. The social cost of furthering an economic activity is the resulting reduction in the value of production that is obtainable from other activities. Such reductions occur because the resources required to further an activity are scarce and must be diverted from other possible uses. According to the view that Coase challenged, social cost, being the sum total of the costs incurred to carry on any activity, might very well differ from private cost. For example, the social cost of running steam locomotives properly includes the fire damage done to surrounding farm crops by sparks from the locomotive. If the railroad is not required to pay for these damages, perhaps through a tax per train, then, according to the conventional analysis, the railroad would not take account of crop damage costs in deciding how many trains to run. In the absence of a specific public policy to intervene, the rate at which an activity is carried forth, which is determined solely by private cost, would diverge from the optimum rate, which is determined by social cost. In the present example, the private cost of running additional trains, being less than the social cost because crop damage is not taken into account, would encourage the railroad to run too many trains per day. The conventional economic analysis called for the levy of a tax per train, equivalent to the damages, in order to bring social cost and private cost into equality.

Coase demonstrated that the imposition of such a tax could, in some circumstances, aggravate the difficulty, but two other aspects of his work are of more concern to us. Coase (1) showed that powerful market forces exist that tend to bring private and social cost into equality without the use of a tax, and (2) discussed the conditions under which the legal position toward liability for damages would and would not alter the allocation of resources. Coase discusses an interaction between two productive activities, ranching and farming, in the context of a competitive regime in which the cost of transacting (or negotiating) is assumed to be zero.[2] His analysis concludes that social cost and private cost will be brought into equality through market negotiations—and this regardless of which party is assigned the responsibility for bearing the cost that results from the proximity of ranching and farming.

[1]R.H. Coase, The Problem of Social Cost, 3 *J. Law & Econ.* 1 (1960).

[2]*Id.* at 2–8

The law, reasoning that crops *stand in the way* of a neighbor's cattle, can leave the farmer to bear the cost of crop damage; alternatively, reasoning that cattle *stray errantly* across farm fields, the law can assign liability for crop damages to ranchers. Coase's work demonstrates that either legal position will result in the same resource allocation—*i.e.*, in the same quantities of corn and meat—and, also, that negotiations between the parties to the damage will, with either legal position, eliminate any divergence between private and social cost. If the law favors ranchers by leaving farmers to bear the cost of crop damage, then there exist incentives for farmers to pay ranchers to reduce the sizes of the herds, or to take other measures that will reduce the amount of damage. A summary arithmetic example reveals how such market transactions lead to Coase's results.

Suppose that the net return to an owner of ranchland would be increased by $50 if herd size were increased by one head of cattle but that the additional head of cattle would impose corn damage on the owner of neighboring farmland that reduced his net return by $60. If the law did *not* require the rancher to compensate the farmer, the farmer would offer to pay the rancher a sum up to $60, the damage he would suffer if the rancher increased his herd by one head. The rancher would accept the offer since any amount above $50 would be more than ample compensation for the reduction in net returns associated with the smaller herd size.

Negotiations would continue until the net return to the rancher of a head of cattle exceeded the reduction in net return to the farmer associated with the damage done by that head of cattle. Such negotiations would bring the total value of corn and beef produced to a maximum since herd size would be reduced only when the consequent increase in the net value of corn output ($60 in the above example) exceeded the decrease in the net value of beef output ($50 in the example) required to reduce crop damage.

If the rule of liability were the reverse, requiring the owner of ranchland to compensate the farmer for the crop damage, the same equilibrium would be reached. Since the rancher earns a net return of only $50 and must pay damages of $60 if he raises an additional head of cattle, he would find it in his interest not to increase the size of his herd. Moreover, he would reduce the size of his herd as long as the net return forgone was smaller than the resulting increase in the net return to farming since this would be the liability to him if he did not reduce herd size by another unit. He would be led to settle upon the same herd size, with the same consequence for crop size, as he would have chosen in the absence of liability. The mix of output is not changed[3] because negotiations between the parties eliminate all divergence between private and social cost.

The resulting equality between social and private cost is important enough to warrant a few more words. The conventional analysis of the farmer–rancher interaction would have concluded that in the absence of liability for damage (or of an appropriate tax per head of cattle) the social cost of increasing herd size would have exceeded the rancher's private cost by the $60 damage done to the neighboring farmer's crops. The rancher, if he were neither held liable nor taxed, would have no reason to take account of this damage and would therefore be led to raise too many cattle and impose too much damage on farm crops. It is the supposed existence of this gap between private and social cost that seems to call for a tax per head of cattle or for an assignment of liability to the rancher. Coase's reasoning shows this logic to be in error. Even in the absence of a tax or liability for damage, the harmful effects of his activities on surrounding crops would be brought to bear on the private calculations of the owner of ranchland, for he must reckon as a true (but implicit) cost of increasing herd size the payment from the farmer that he must forgo if he refuses to agree to the farmer's request for a reduction in herd size. Market negotiations bring the full cost of his decision to bear on him through the offers made by the farmer and thereby eliminate any difference between private and social cost. This, as Coase recognized, would not be true if the cost of negotiating could not be assumed to be negligible. We shall return to this problem later.

It is not generally appreciated that Coase's reasoning has legal applications that extend beyond problems of the divergence between social and private cost as these typically are conceived. What is at issue in the farmer–rancher case is which party has a particular property right. In the one case the farmer has the right to allow or prohibit cattle grazing on certain specified lands, while in the other case it is the rancher who has the right. Private property takes the form of a bundle of rights, of which different components may be held by different persons. In the absence of significant negotiating cost, the use to which these property rights is put is independent of the identities of the owners since each owner will be given market incentives to use his property right in the most valuable way. Just what is the most valuable way depends on market conditions and not owner identities.

---

[3]I ignore other possibilities such as building a fence. These are discussed by Coase (*id.* at 3). Consideration of them changes the exposition but not the results.

One further assumption is required for the mix of output to remain unchanged. Any redistribution of wealth resulting from a change in the rule of liability is assumed to

The analysis can be extended to many types of property right problems. One that is of current interest to lawyers is the continuing litigation about the legal status of the reserve clause in organized baseball. An important defense of the reserve clause has been the assertion that it prevents wealthy baseball clubs from acquiring too large a share of the good players. By applying the above analysis to this problem it is possible to refute the assertion, especially since the cost of negotiations would seem to be negligible in this case. For what is at issue is whether the identity of the owner of a player's baseball services will alter the location of his playing activities. An application of Coase's analysis to this problem suggests that the reserve clause should have no effect on the identity of the team for which a player plays.

When signing initially with a major league organization, a player owns his baseball talent in the sense that he has the right to offer his services for sale to any ball club. But once he signs with a major league club, he can no longer negotiate with other clubs for the sale of his services, although he retains the right to refuse to play. The reserve clause, which is written into every major league contract, requires major league clubs who wish to acquire the services of a player who is already under contract to purchase his contract from the club currently owning it. Thus, once a player signs with a major league organization, part of the bundle of property rights to his services are transferred from the player to the club with which he signs. The right to play on various teams passes via the reserve clause from the player to the club owning his contract, and this club can reserve the player for its own use even though other teams might be willing to pay the player more than he is receiving.

The question considered here is *not* whether there exists a correlation between the wealth of a club and the quality of its players. The relevant question is whether the distribution of players among teams would change were the reserve clause to be declared illegal. Would wealthier clubs acquire more good players if the right to negotiate with other teams always resided with the player?[4]

---

have no consequences for the demands for the products produced. Owners of farmland and ranchland should be vegetarians in equal proportions, for otherwise a redistribution of wealth between these two groups would alter the market demands for corn and beef and thereby indirectly alter the mix of output produced. The wealth redistribution problem will be discussed later when we turn to the subject of extortion.

[4]The reserve clause and other aspects of organized baseball are discussed in Simon Rottenberg, The Baseball Player's Labor Market, 64 J. Pol. Econ. 242 (1956). The reasoning employed by Rottenberg is similar but not identical to the above argument.

In the absence of the reserve clause, a player would change clubs only if he found it in his interest to do so. With the reserve clause, a player will change clubs only if the club that owns his contract finds it in its interest. It appears that a different pattern of player migration between clubs might exist with the reserve clause than without it. But the appearance is deceptive. No matter who owns the right to sell the contract for the services of a baseball player, the distribution of players among teams will remain the same.

To see why this is so, assume that a player *not* subject to the reserve clause receives a $15,000 per annum wage from club A for which he currently plays. Club B offers him $16,000 to play for them. If this amount exceeds the value of the player to club A, the club will not find it in its interest to make a counteroffer large enough to retain the player's services and he will join club B. However, if his services are worth more than $16,000 to club A, the club will find it in its interest to make a counteroffer large enough to retain his services. With no reserve clause the player plays for the club that most highly values[5] his services.

Let us now suppose that the reserve clause is effective and, as before, that the player is currently paid $15,000 by club A. Club B now offers club A $1,000 per annum (or its present value equivalent) for the player's contract, so that if the negotiations succeed club B will pay $16,000 for the player's services of which $15,000 is paid to the player under the terms of the purchased contract and $1,000 is paid to club A. If $1,000 per annum exceeds the player's net value to club A after it pays his $15,000 annual salary, then it will be in club A's interest to sell his contract to club B, but if the player is worth more to club A than $16,000 (equal to the $1,000 offer from club B plus the player's $15,000 salary), it will refuse to sell his contract.

The condition under which the player is transferred to club B when he is subject to the reserve clause is precisely the condition under which he will elect to transfer to club B when he is not subject to the reserve clause. He transfers to club B if club B finds his services more valuable than does club A whether or not the reserve clause is in effect. The reserve clause, therefore, cannot be expected to result in a different distribution of players among teams than would prevail in its absence.

The reader may object, suggesting that nonpecuniary considerations might make the distribution of players different depending on the

---

Rottenberg's argument is based partly on the premise, not used here, that it takes two fairly well matched teams to produce a good game.

[5]Nonpecuniary aspects of his employment are discussed later, but it should be noted that the argument for retention of the reserve clause is not based on nonpecuniary job amenities.

legal status of the reserve clause. But this objection also would be in error. Suppose that the player, presently owned by a California club, has developed a preference for working in California. If there were no reserve clause, his preference would lead him to ask at least $1,000 more to play ball with a Chicago club than he earns playing for a California club; and, in the absence of a reserve clause, a Chicago club would need to bid $1,000 more than a California club to obtain his services. But this is also true with the reserve clause. Under reserve clause arrangements, suppose that the Chicago club offers the California club only $500 more than the player's net value to the California club. The California club, indeed, will be tempted to sell the player's contract to Chicago. It appears that the $500 increment, which would be too small to move the player were there no reserve clause, is large enough to move him if there is a reserve clause. This is incorrect because the player, when working under the reserve clause arrangement, would be willing to offer a sum of up to $1,000 (the value of the nonpecuniary amenities to him of California) to the California club to induce it to refuse to sell his contract to Chicago. Any amount above $500 would be sufficient to make the California club reject Chicago's offer since Chicago is offering only $500 more than the player is worth to the California club. (The player can "offer" such an amount by accepting a pay reduction.) With or without the reserve clause, then, the player will locate where the value he places on amenities plus the value of his baseball talent is greatest.

II.

The significance of Coase's work quickly led to critical responses by Wellisz,[6] Calabresi,[7] and others, although Calabresi withdrew his criticism in a later paper.[8] The criticism centered around two allegations—that the Coase theorem neglects long-run considerations that negate it and that the spirit of the work endorses the use of resources for the undesirable purpose of "extortion". The long-run issue is discussed here and the "extortion" problem in Part III. In Part IV, I discuss the problems introduced when the assumption of negligible transaction cost is dropped.

[6]Stanis law Wellisz, On External Diseconomies and the Government Assisted Invisible Hand, 31 Economica (N.S.) 345 (1964).

[7]Guido Calabresi, The Decision for Accidents: An Approach to Nonfault Allocation of Costs, 78 Harv. L. Rev. 713 (1965).

[8]Guido Calabresi, Transaction Costs, Resource Allocation and Liability Rules—A Comment, 11 J. Law & Econ. 67 (1968).

The question of long-run considerations has been raised because it would seem that different liability rules would alter the profitability of remaining inside or outside each industry. It is alleged that if farmers are left to bear the cost that arises from proximity to cattle, the rate of return to farming will fall and resources will therefore leave the farming industry. Alternatively, if ranchers are left to bear the cost, the resulting reduction in rate of return to ranching will lead to the exit of resources from that industry. Hence, even if transaction cost is zero, the market will allocate resources differently in the long run depending upon which rule of liability is chosen.

But short-run versus long-run considerations should have no bearing on the Coase theorem, which is based on the proposition that an implicit cost (the forgone payment from the farmer) is just as much a cost as is an explicit cost (the liability damage), and this proposition surely must hold in the long run as well as in the short run. One way of demonstrating this is by allowing the two activities to be merged under a common owner. A detailed example of this is given by G. Warren Nutter.[9] If there is no special cost to operating a multiproduct firm, the costly interaction between farming and ranching will be fully brought to the owner's attention in his operation of a farming–ranching enterprise. The mix of output that he produces will be that which maximizes his earnings. The rule of liability that is chosen can have no effect on his decisions because the owner of such a firm must bear the interaction cost whichever legal rule is adopted. The cost interdependence is a technical-economic interdependence, not a legal one. Since such merged operations are possible, the rule of liability is rendered irrelevant to the choice of output mix. But a refutation of the criticism that is based on the use of the joint product enterprise gives rise to the (incorrect) suspicion that the basic problem has been begged, since the rule of liability that is chosen cannot in this case alter the wealth of the owner of a farming-ranching enterprise. The spirit of the argument can be preserved, while the suspicion is allayed, by assuming that the advantages offered by specialization of ownership are so great that it is uneconomic to merge the two activities into a single ranching–farming firm.

If owners of farmland bear the cost of crop damage, what must be the cost conditions that are associated with an equilibrium allocation of land to farming, ranching, and other uses? For such damage to arise there must be a sufficient scarcity of land to force farms and ranches into proximity. Marginal farm acreage (acreage that just "breaks even") must earn revenue

[9] G. Warren Nutter, The Coase Theorem on Social Cost: A Footnote, 11. *J. Law & Econ.* 503 (1968).

sufficient to cover all cost, including the cost of crop damage done by straying cattle. Suppose the proximity of ranching and farming reduces the net return to the owner of farmland by $100 as compared with what could be earned were there no neighboring ranch. If ranching continues on the neighboring acres, it must be true that the net return to the owner of the ranchland exceeds $100, for otherwise the farmer would have been able to purchase the removal of cattle from neighboring land by offering $100 to the neighboring ranchers. The reduction in net return to farming brought about because of crop damage is thus implicitly taken into account by the owner of the ranchland when he refuses the offer of the owner of the neighboring farmland. The money offered by the farmer is refused by the rancher precisely because the continued use of the land for grazing brings in additional net revenue in excess of $100.

Land that is submarginal as farm or ranchland (land that cannot be profitably farmed or ranched) is unable to earn revenue sufficient to cover the explicit $100 damage cost if it is put to the plough or the $100 implicit cost if it is employed in ranching. Were this land to be employed in farming, its owner would suffer losses attributable in part to the damage done to his crops by straying cattle, whereas if it were employed in ranching its owner would suffer the implicit loss of forgoing a $100 payment from the neighboring farmer (the owners of farmland bearing the cost of crop damage). Submarginal land by definition can be neither farmed nor ranched profitably.

Now let the rule of liability be changed so that ranchers become liable for crop damage. If there is to be a long-run effect, it must be true that the cost interrelationships change in a manner that causes either the conversion of ranchland to farmland or submarginal land to farmland. But neither conversion can be made profitable by the change in liability.

Acreage that was marginally profitable in ranching must remain ranchland because it had been earning net revenues in excess of the $100 damages done by cattle to surrounding farmland. If a producing ranch were to be switched from ranching to farming to avoid the new liability its owner would forgo revenues (in excess of $100) that exceeded the resulting reduction in liability ($100). The owner of what was marginal ranchland, therefore, will continue to employ his land in ranching under the new liability rule.

The land that previously was submarginal must remain submarginal. The changed liability rule will not attract this land into farming. Submarginal lands under the original rule of liability earned insufficient revenues in farming to cover the $100 cost of crop damage. Under the new rule of liability, neighboring ranchers will succeed in negotiating with the owners of this land to keep it out of farming. Operating ranches, under the old rule of liability, had been yielding net revenues in excess of $100; therefore it will be possible and profitable for ranchers, in order to avoid the $100 crop damage that otherwise would result, to offer an amount to the owners of submarginal land that is sufficient to keep the land out of farming.

There is a temptation at this point in the argument to believe that an error has been made. Suppose that the farmer suffers damages equal to $100 and the rancher enjoys a net return equal to $110. If the rancher is not liable he will choose to continue ranching and to refuse a payment from a neighboring farmer of $100 to stop ranching. But if the rule of liability is reversed, he will continue ranching only if his $110 net return is sufficient to cover the cost imposed on the farmer ($100) *plus* the payment required to keep submarginal land (which can be assumed to border on another boundary of the ranch) out of farming. There has been no error in the argument, but there is an error in introducing the second neighbor halfway through the analysis. With the rancher not liable, he would have elected to remain in ranching only if the net return to ranching exceeded the payments to leave ranching offered to him by *both* his neighbors. If the rancher finds it remunerative to remain in ranching in the face of both these offers he must earn a sufficient net return from ranching, after the rule of liability is changed and he is held liable, to be able to pay damages to his neighboring farmer *and* to pay the owner of neighboring submarginal land to keep that land out of production.

The change in the rule of liability does not lead to a conversion of ranchland or submarginal land to farming. The use of land that maximized returns before the change in liability rule continues to maximize returns after the new rule is adopted, and the mix of output is unaffected by the choice of liability rule even when long-run considerations are analyzed. To understand the effect of altering the rule of liability it is important to recognize that the owner of a resource who finds it in his interest to employ that resource in a particular way when he bears the cost of an interaction will be paid to employ that resource *in the same way* when the rule of liability is reversed. What can happen, and in this case does happen, when the rule of liability is changed is that present owners of land having a comparative advantage in ranching suffer a *windfall* loss in the value of their land while owners of farmland enjoy a *windfall* gain. But this redistribution of wealth cannot alter the uses of these lands.

III.

The problem of "extortion" is part of the larger problem of wealth redistribution that may accompany a change in the rule of liability. Our concern here is with situations in which such a redistribution takes place. However, it should be noted that, when there is no restriction on contracting, a change in the rule of liability need not be accompanied by wealth redistribution. If owners of firms are made liable for industrial accidents, for example, then the equilibrium wage will move downward to reflect the shifting of this explicit cost from workers to employers. Employers no longer will need to cover the cost of industrial accidents in the wages they pay since this cost will be paid by them in the form of industrial accident insurance or self-insurance required by the new rule of liability. The general effect of shifting accident liability directly to firms will be merely to change the classification, not the amount, of remuneration. What under no employer liability were simply wages become under employer liability wages plus accident benefits. No redistribution of wealth accompanies the change in liability. Workers who, when they had to bear the cost of accidents directly, received $X in wages will, under the new rule of liability, receive part of the $X in the form of accident compensation and the remainder in wages, but there will be no change in their total income after taking account of expected accident costs under the two systems.

This holds strictly only if workers and employers are allowed to enter into voluntary contractual arrangements for reshifting the explicit cost back to workers, a matter that need not be discussed in detail here. If such agreements are disallowed by the law—*i.e.*, if the costs of making such agreements is prohibitively high because of their illegality—then some wealth may be redistributed from those workers who would have found it advantageous to self-insure to workers who find it advantageous to buy insurance; such a law would force workers, in the wage reductions they must accept, to purchase insurance for industrial accidents from their employers.

The problem of "extortion" arises when a change in liability gives rise to a redistribution in wealth. In the farmer–rancher case, the relative values of nearby farm and ranchlands will be changed when the rule of liability is altered. Under one rule of liability, with farmers required to bear the cost of crop damage, farmers will need to pay ranchers to reduce herd size; under the other rule ranchers will have to pay farmers for damages or for any alteration in the quantity of corn grown nearby. The change in the direction of payments must affect the rents that can be collected by owners of these lands and thus the market values of these lands.

In these cases the owner of the specialized resource, ranchland or farmland, that is not required to bear the cost of the interaction may threaten to increase the intensity of the interaction in an attempt to get his neighbor to pay him a larger sum than would ordinarily be required to obtain his cooperation in adjusting the intensity of the interaction downward. The owner of ranchland, if he is not liable for crop damage done by straying cattle, might, in the absence of a neighboring farmer, raise only 1,000 head of cattle. With proximity between farming and ranching, a neighboring owner of farmland might be willing to pay the rancher the sum required to finance a 200-head reduction in herd size. However, if the owner of ranchland *threatens* to raise 1,500 head, he may be able to secure more than this sum from the farmer because of the additional crop damage that would be caused by the larger herd size. With or without this "extortion" threat, the size of the herd will be reduced to 800 because that is the size, by assumption, that maximizes the total value of both activities. Given the interrelationship between the two activities, that is the herd size that will maximize the return to the farmer and, indirectly, the sum available for possible transfer to the rancher. What is at issue is the sharing of this maximum return.

To the extent that there exist alternative farm sites, the ability of the owner of ranchland to make such a threat credible is compromised. Competition among such owners will reduce the payment that farmers make to ranchers to that sum which is just sufficient to offset the revenue forgone by ranchers when herd size is reduced. No rancher could succeed in a threat to increase herd size above normal numbers because other ranchers would be willing to compete to zero the price that farmers are asked to pay to avoid abnormally large herd sizes. Abnormally large herd size, in itself, will generate losses to owners of ranchland and, for this reason, competition among such owners will reduce the price that owners of farmland must pay to avoid such excessive herd sizes to zero.

But if a ranchland owner has a locational monopoly, in the sense that there are no alternative sites available to farmers, then the rancher may succeed in acquiring a larger sum from his neighboring farmer in order to avoid abnormally large herd sizes. The acquisition of a larger sum by the owner of ranchland generally will require him to incur some cost to make his threat credible, perhaps by actually beginning to increase herd size beyond normal levels. If the cost of making this threat credible is low relative to the sum available for transfer from the owner of farmland, the rancher will be in a good position to accomplish the transfer. The sum available for transfer will be the amount by which the value of the neighboring land when used as farmland exceeds its value in the next best use. If the rancher were to demand a larger payment from his neighbor, the neighboring land would be switched to some other use.

The temptation to label such threats extortion or blackmail must be resisted by economists for these are legal and not economic distinctions. The rancher merely attempts to maximize profits. If his agreements with neighboring farmers are marketed in competition with other ranchers, profit maximization constrained by competition implies that an agreement to reduce herd size can be purchased for a smaller payment than if effective competition in such agreements is absent. The appropriate economic label for this problem is nothing more nor less than monopoly. It takes on the cast of such legal classifications as extortion only because the context seems to be one where the monopoly return is received by threatening to produce something that is not wanted—excessively large herds. The conventional monopoly problem involves a reduction or a threat to reduce the output of a desired good. In the unconventional monopoly problem presented here, there is a threat to increase herd size beyond desirable levels. But this difference is superficial. The conventional monopoly problem can be viewed as one in which the monopolist produces more scarcity than is desired, and the unconventional monopoly problem discussed here can be considered one in which the monopolist threatens to produce too small a reduction in crop damage. Any additional sum that the rancher succeeds in transferring to himself from the farmer is correctly identified as a monopoly return.

The temptation to resolve this monopoly problem merely by reversing the rule of liability must be resisted. Should the liability rule be reversed and the owner of ranchland now be held liable for damage done by his cattle to surrounding crops, the specific monopoly problem that we have been discussing would be resolved. But if the farmer enjoys a locational monopoly such that the rancher has nowhere else to locate, the shoe will now be on the other foot. The farmer can threaten to increase the number of bushels of corn planted, and hence the damage for which the rancher will be liable, unless the rancher pays the farmer a sum greater than would be required under competitive conditions. The potential for monopoly and the wealth redistribution implied by monopoly is present in principle whether or not the owner of ranchland is held liable for damages. Both the symmetry of the problem and its disappearance under competitive conditions refute the allegation that Coase's analysis implicitly endorses the use of resources in undesirable activities.

Should the law treat such classes of monopoly problem as "extortion" or "blackmail"? It may not be useful for the law to take this step because the threat is made credible by increasing the output of an economic good—cattle if the rancher is not liable, corn if he is. Because it is difficult to sort desirable from undesirable increases in herd or crop size, there is a real danger of penalizing desirable increases in herd or crop size by mistake if such wealth transfers are treated as extortion. Activities to which anti-extortion laws normally apply typically involve the use of violence or the threat to take some action that falls within a general class of actions considered socially undesirable. The application of anti-extortion legal measures in such cases is less likely to penalize socially desirable actions by mistake. In other cases, it may be possible for the courts to limit the amount of payments to levels that are reasonable compensations for costs incurred (or profits forgone), although it is not clear how easily such determinations can be made by courts. Alternatively, it is possible to attempt to eliminate the source of the problem—monopoly—but the wisdom of relying on antitrust in this context is a matter on which the author is unprepared to speak.

IV.

The costly interaction between farming and ranching is not properly attributed to the actions of either party individually, being "caused", instead, by resource scarcity, the scarcity of land and fencing materials. If transaction cost is negligible, it would seem that the choice of liability rule cannot depend on who "causes" the damage since both jointly do, or on how resource allocation will be altered, since no such alteration will take place, but largely on judicial or legislative preferences with regard to wealth distribution.

Once significant transacting or negotiating cost is admitted into the analysis, the choice of liability rule will have effects on resource allocation, and it no longer follows that wealth distribution is the main or even an important consideration in choosing the liability rule. The assumption of negligible transacting cost can be only a beginning to understanding the economic consequences of the legal arrangements that underlie the operations of the economy, but little more can be done here than to illustrate the nature of the considerations.[10]

[10]Other considerations that arise when the cost of transacting is positive are discussed in Harold Demsetz, Some Aspects of Property Rights, 9 J. Law & Econ. 61 (1966).

The most obvious effect of introducing significant transacting cost is that negotiations will not be consummated in those situations where the expected benefits from exchange are less than the expected cost of exchanging. Exchange opportunities will be exploited only up to the point where the marginal gain from trade equals the marginal cost of trade. Of course, there is nothing necessarily inefficient in halting exchange at this point. If this were all that could be said on the subject, there would be little more to do than call the reader's attention to the similar analytical roles of transport cost in international trade and transacting cost in exchange generally. But there is more to say.

Significant transacting cost implies that the rule of liability generally will have allocative effects (as Coase recognizes). Consider the problem of liability for automobile-pedestrian accidents. To the extent that "accident" has any economic meaning it must mean that circumstances are such that voluntary negotiations between the driver and the pedestrian are prohibitively costly in many driving situations. The parties to an accident, either because of the speed with which the accident occurs or because of a failure to notice the presence of a competing claimant for the right-of-way, cannot conclude an agreement over the use of the right-of-way at costs that are low enough, *ex ante,* to make the effort worthwhile.

Partly as a consequence of the costliness of such negotiations, rules of the road are developed. Speed limits, traffic signals, and legal constraints on passing are substituted for the development of saleable private rights. In a specific case it may be possible to assign private rights to use the road in a way that makes the exchange of these rights feasible, but, in general, if these rules make economic sense it is precisely because the cost of transacting is expected to be too high in most cases to warrant the development of saleable private rights to the use of roads.

The practicality of such rules is not an argument for or against government action, but a rationale for the substitution of rules for negotiation. The use of rules to eliminate costly negotiations can be found in the management of privately owned parking lots and toll roads as well as in those that are publicly owned.

Such rules notwithstanding, accidents do take place. Assuming that the cost of transacting is too high to make negotiated agreements practical in such cases, we can compare the effect on resource allocation of the rule of liability that is chosen. If drivers are held liable in automobile-pedestrian accidents, the incentives for pedestrians to be careful about how and where they cross streets will be reduced. The incentives for drivers to be careful will be increased. Indeed, if each pedestrian could be guaranteed *full* compensation for all financial, physical, and psychological costs suffered in an accident, then pedestrians would become indifferent between being struck by an auto and not being struck. Drivers, however, would actively seek to avoid accidents since they would always be liable, whereas if it were possible to have a system of complete and full pedestrian liability it would be the drivers who became indifferent between accidents and no accidents and it would be the pedestrians who actively sought to avoid accidents.

In a regime in which transacting cost was zero, either system of liability would generate the same accident-avoiding behavior, as the Coase analysis suggests. With driver liability, drivers would themselves avoid accidents or, if such avoidance could be purchased at lower cost from pedestrians, drivers would pay pedestrians to avoid accidents. Under a scheme of pedestrian liability it would be the pedestrians who took direct action to avoid accidents or indirect action by paying drivers to avoid accidents. Under either rule of liability those accidents are avoided for which the accident cost exceeds the least cost method of avoiding accidents, where the least cost is the lesser of either the driver or pedestrian cost of avoiding accidents. Both rules of liability, assuming zero transacting cost, yield the same accident rate and the same accident-avoiding behavior. The effect of switching from one rule of liability to another is limited to wealth redistribution.

In a situation in which transacting cost is prohibitively high, driver liability leads to the avoidance only of those accidents for which the cost of avoidance to the *driver* is less than the expected accident cost, and pedestrian liability leads to the avoidance of only those accidents for which the cost of avoidance to the *pedestrian* is less than the expected accident cost. In general, the accident rate that results will differ under these two systems since the cost of avoiding accidents will not be the same for drivers and pedestrians. Both systems will lead to higher accident rates than would be true if transacting costs were zero. The effect of positive transacting cost is to raise the cost of avoiding accidents through the foreclosure of the use of possibly cheaper cost-avoidance techniques when these can be employed only by the other party to the accident. A similar conclusion can be reached for all liability problems when transacting cost is prohibitive and when the law cannot particularize the rule of liability to take account of who is the least-cost damage avoider in every instance.

One liability rule may be superior to another if transacting costs are more than negligible precisely because the difficulty of avoiding costly interactions is not generally the same for the interacting parties. It may be less costly for pedestrians to avoid accidents or for farmers to relocate their crops than it is for drivers to avoid accidents or ranchers to reduce the number of cattle they raise. If information about this were known, it would be possible for the legal system to improve the allocation of resources by placing liability on that party who in the usual situation could be expected to avoid the costly interaction most cheaply.

The use of words such as "blame", "responsible", and "fault" must be treated with care by the economist because they have no useful meanings in an economic analysis of these problems other than as synonyms for the party who could have most easily avoided the costly interaction. Whether the interaction problem involves crop damage, accidents, soot, or water pollution, the qualitative relationship between the interacting parties is symmetrical. It is the *joint* use of a resource, be it geographic location, air, or water that leads to these interactions. It is the demand for scarce resources that leads to conflicting interests.

The legal system does produce rules for determining *prima facie* "fault," but in this context "fault" means only according to some acceptable and applicable legal precedent. In an accident involving a rear-end collision, the court generally will place the burden for proving the absence of negligence on the party driving the following car. If a car strikes a person running across a fenced expressway at night the burden of proving the absence of negligence is likely to be placed on the pedestrian. In treating such cases differently, the law bases its decisions on acceptable and appropriate precedents, but the acceptability of these precedents should not be confused with the morality of the interacting parties. A deeper analysis of these precedents may reveal that they generally make sense from the economic viewpoint of placing the liability on that party who can, at least cost, reduce the probability of a costly interaction happening. Less care need be taken by the driver of the following car in a rear-end collision than would need to be taken by the lead driver to avoid the accident, and less care is needed by a pedestrian to refrain from running across an expressway than is needed by a driver to avoid striking the pedestrian. Nor need the acceptability of such precedents be based on restitution since, as these precedents become known, their long-run effect is to deter accidents at least cost. If courts are to ignore wealth, religion, or family in deciding such conflicts, if persons before the courts are to be treated with regard only to the cause of action and available proof, then, as a normative proposition, it is difficult to suggest any criterion for deciding liability other than placing it on the party able to avoid the costly interaction most easily.

8

Efficient Liability Rules

Complete Characterization[†]

*Satish K. Jain and Ram Singh**

1. INTRODUCTION

Some of the most important results of the law and economics literature relate to the question of efficiency of liability rules. Calabresi (1961, 1965, 1970) in his pioneering contributions analyzed the effect of liability rules on parties' behavior. While Calabresi's work emphasized various versions of strict liability, in Posner (1972) the focus was on the negligence rule.[1] The first formal analysis of liability rules was put forward by Brown (1973). He showed that the rule of strict liability with the defense of contributory negligence and the negligence rule induce both victims and injurers to take optimal levels of care. Formal analysis of liability rules was also carried out in Diamond (1974a,1974b). Shavell (1987), Landes and Posner (1987), Posner (1992), and Cooter and Ulen (1999) present systematic and detailed treatment of liability rules. In a recent contribution, Feldman and Frost (1998) provided an exhaustive analysis of liability rules when care is alternative and discrete. The main conclusion emerged that while various negligence rules and the rule of strict liability with the defense of contributory negligence are efficient, the rules of no liability and strict liability are not. The purpose of this paper is to provide a complete characterization of efficient liability rules by obtaining a necessary and sufficient condition for efficiency of any liability rule.

[†]Originally published as "Efficient Liability Rules: Complete Characterization", 2002, *Journal of Economics*, Vol. 75, pp. 105–24.
*The authors wish to thank the referees for helpful comments.
[1]See also Calabresi and Hirschoff (1972), Posner (1973), and Calabresi (1975).

In the literature pertaining to efficiency of liability rules,[2] the problem has been considered generally within the framework of accidents resulting from interaction of two parties, assumed to be strangers to each other. It is assumed that, in case of occurrence of an accident, the entire loss falls, to begin with, on one party, to be called the victim or plaintiff, the other party being the injurer or defendant. The probability of an accident and the amount of loss in case an accident occurs are assumed to depend on the levels of care taken by the two parties. Both parties are assumed to be risk-neutral and the social goal is taken to be the minimization of total social costs, which are the sum of the costs of care taken by the two parties and the expected accident loss. In the literature, it is generally assumed that costs of care and expected accident loss functions are such that there is a unique configuration of care levels of the two parties at which total social costs attain their minimum. Depending on the liability rule, there could be legally binding due care levels for both parties, for only the defendant, for only the victim, or for neither party. It is assumed that in case there are legally binding due care levels for both parties, the configuration of the legally binding due care levels is identical with the unique total social cost minimizing configuration of care levels; that in case there is legally binding due care level for the defendant only, it is identical with the care level of the defendant which figures in the unique total social cost minimizing configuration of care levels; and that in case there is legally binding due care level for the victim only, it is identical with the care level of the victim which figures in the unique total social cost minimizing configuration of care levels.

This assumption is crucial for the results on the efficiency of liability rules. In the context of liability rules, there are two conceptually distinct ways in which the notions of negligence and nonnegligence figure. In the first instance one can ask whether the behavior of the parties is appropriate from the point of view of the objective of minimizing total social costs. This is a meaningful question and can be asked regardless of the legal position with respect to parties' liabilities in case of occurrence of accident. The technical notion of negligence or nonnegligence characterizes the parties' behavior in terms relevant from the efficiency point of view. The legal notions of negligence and nonnegligence, on the other hand, are relevant for determining the actual behavior of the

[2]The literature on liability rules has been discussed in detail in Landes and Posner (1987), Shavell (1987), Posner (1992), Feldman and Frost (1998), and Cooter and Ulen (1999), among others.

parties. It is the conjuncture of these two notions of negligence and nonnegligence which is decisive for the efficiency question.

A liability rule determines the proportions in which the two parties are to bear the loss in case of an accident as a function of whether and by how much the parties' levels of care were below the due care levels. A liability rule is efficient if it induces both parties to take the total social cost minimizing care levels. In the presence of the assumption that there is a unique configuration of care levels which is total social cost minimizing, the question of efficiency of a liability rule reduces to the question of whether the configuration of total social cost minimizing care levels of the two parties constitutes a unique Nash equilibrium or not.

In this paper, while retaining most of the assumptions of the standard framework within which the question of efficiency of liability rules has been discussed in the literature, the problem is considered in a somewhat more general context. No assumptions are made on the costs of care and expected loss functions, apart from postulating that they are such that the minimum of total social costs exists; and that a higher level of care never results in greater expected losses. The possibility that there could be more than one configuration of care levels at which total social costs are minimized is not ruled out. In the context of this more general framework, in order to show that a liability rule is efficient, one has to show (i) that all Nash equilibria are total social cost minimizing, and (ii) that at least one Nash equilibrium exists.[3]

The main theorem of the paper shows that a necessary and sufficient condition for efficiency of any liability rule is to satisfy the condition of negligence liability. The condition of negligence liability requires that (i) if the victim is nonnegligent and the injurer is negligent then the entire loss, in case of occurrence of accident, must be borne by the injurer, and (ii) if the injurer is nonnegligent and the victim is negligent then the entire loss, in case of occurrence of accident, must be borne by the victim. Thus the common feature of negligence rules and the strict liability rule with the defense of contributory negligence turns out to be the characteristic the presence or otherwise of which completely settles the efficiency question for any liability rule. All standard results on efficiency of liability rules immediately follow from this general characterization.

It is remarkable that the standard assumptions on costs of care and expected loss functions turn out to be completely irrelevant for the

[3]Throughout this paper we consider only pure-strategy Nash equilibria.

question of the efficiency of liability rules. In particular, the question whether or not there is a unique configuration of care levels at which total social costs attain their minimum turns out to be irrelevant for the efficiency of liability rules. We show that the characterization of efficient liability rules does not change even if it is assumed that there is a unique configuration of care levels at which total social costs attain their minimum.

2. DEFINITIONS AND ASSUMPTIONS

We consider accidents resulting from interaction of two parties, assumed to be strangers to each other, in which, to begin with, the entire loss falls on one party to be called the victim (plaintiff).[4] The other party would be referred to as the injurer (defendant). We denote by $c \geq 0$ the cost of care taken by the victim and by $d \geq 0$ the cost of care taken by the injurer. Costs of care would be assumed to be strictly increasing functions of indices of care, i.e., care levels; consequently, costs of care themselves can be taken to be indices of care. Let $C = \{c \mid c$ is the cost of some feasible level of care which can be taken by the victim$\}$ and $D = \{d \mid d$ is the cost of some feasible level of care which can be taken by the injurer$\}$. Both C and D would be assumed to be nonempty; and in particular it would be assumed that $0 \in C$ and $0 \in D$.

Let π denote the probability of occurrence of accident and $H \geq 0$ the loss in case of occurrence of accident. Both π and H will be assumed to be functions of c and d; $\pi = \pi(c, d)$, $H = H(c, d)$. Let $L = \pi H$. L is thus a function of c and d, $L = L(c, d)$; and denotes the expected loss due to accident. $L \geq 0$ as $H \geq 0$. We assume:

$$(\forall c, c' \in C)(\forall d, d' \in D)[[c > c' \rightarrow L(c, d) \leq L(c', d)] \text{ and } [d > d' \rightarrow L(c, d) \leq L(c, d')]]. \quad \text{(A1)}$$

That is to say, it is assumed that a larger expenditure on care by either party, given the expenditure on care by the other party, results in lesser or equal expected accident loss. The decrease can take place because of decrease in the probability of occurrence of accident or because of decrease in loss in case of occurrence of accident or both. Total social costs (TSC) are defined to be the sum of cost of care by the

[4]Throughout this paper it would be assumed that the activity levels of both the parties are fixed. Shavell (1980) has shown that no liability rule exists which is efficient if both activity and care levels determine the expected losses from accidents.

victim, cost of care by the injurer, and the expected loss due to accident; $\text{TSC} = c + d + L(c, d)$. Total social costs are thus a function of c and d. Let $M = \{(c', d') \mid c' + d' + L(c', d')$ is minimum of $\{c + d + L(c, d) \mid c \in C$ and $d \in D\}\}$. Thus M is the set of all costs of care configurations (c', d') which are total social cost minimizing. It will be assumed that:

C, D, and L are such that M is nonempty. (A2)

Let I denote the closed unit interval $[0,1]$[5]. Given C, D, L and $(c^*, d^*) \in M$, we define functions p and q as follows:

$$
\begin{aligned}
p: C &\mapsto I && \text{by:}\\
p(c) &= 1 && \text{if } c \geq c^*,\\
p(c) &= \frac{c}{c^*} && \text{if } c < c^* \text{ and } c^* > 0;\\
q: D &\mapsto I && \text{by:}\\
q(d) &= 1 && \text{if } d \geq d^*,\\
q(d) &= \frac{d}{d^*} && \text{if } d < d^* \text{ and } d^* > 0.
\end{aligned}
$$

Liability rules can be divided into four mutually exclusive and exhaustive subclasses: (i) the rules with legally binding due care levels for both the victim and the injurer, (ii) the rules with legally binding due care level for only the injurer, (iii) the rules with legally binding due care level for only the victim, and (iv) the rules with legally binding due care levels for neither party. The rule of negligence with the defense of contributory negligence, the rule of negligence, the rule of strict liability with the defense of contributory negligence, and the rule of strict liability provide examples of these four categories of liability rules. If the liability rule belongs to subclass (i), c^* and d^* used in the definitions of functions p and q will be taken to be identical with the legally binding due care levels for the plaintiff and the defendant, respectively. If the liability rule belongs to subclass (ii), d^* used in the definition of function q will be taken to be identical with the legally binding due care level for the defendant. c^* used in the definition of function p can be any element of $\{c \in C \mid (c, d^*) \in M\}$. $\{c \in C \mid (c, d^*) \in M\}$

[5]In addition to denoting the set $\{x \mid 0 \leq x \leq 1\}$ by $[0,1]$, we use the following standard notation to denote: by $[0, 1)$ the set $\{x \mid 0 \leq x < 1\}$, by $(0, 1]$ the set $\{x \mid 0 < x \leq 1\}$, and by $(0,1)$ the set $\{x \mid 0 < x < 1\}$.

may contain more than one element, in which case one can have $(c^*, d^*), (c^{**}, d^*) \in M, (c^*, d^*) \neq (c^{**}, d^*)$. If the liability rule belongs to subclass (iii), c^* used in the definition of function p will be taken to be identical with the legally binding due care level for the plaintiff. d^* used in the definition of function q can be any element of $\{d \in D \mid (c^*, d) \in M\}$. As $\{d \in D \mid (c^*, d) \in M\}$ may contain more than one element, one can have $(c^*, d^*), (c^*, d^{**}) \in M$, $(c^*, d^*) \neq (c^*, d^{**})$. If the liability rule belongs to subclass (iv), then any element of M can be used for the purpose of defining functions p and q. Thus in all cases c^* would denote the legally binding due care level for the plaintiff whenever the idea of legally binding due care level for the plaintiff is applicable; and d^* would denote the legally binding due care level for the defendant whenever the idea of legally binding due care level for the defendant is applicable.[6]

$p(c) = 1\,[q(d) = 1]$ would be interpreted as meaning that the victim [the injurer] is taking at least the due care and $p(c) < 1\,[q(d) < 1]$ as meaning that the victim [the injurer] is taking less than the due care. If $p(c) = 1[q(d) = 1]$, the victim [the injurer] would be called nonnegligent; and if $p(c) < 1\,[q(d) < 1]$, the victim [the injurer] would be called negligent. $1 - p(c)\,[1 - q(d)]$ is the proportion by which the victim's care [the injurer's care] falls short of the due care, i.e., the proportion of negligence; and $p(c)[q(d)]$ is the proportion of the victim's [the injurer's] nonnegligence.

A liability rule is a rule specifying the proportions in which the two parties are to bear the loss in case of occurrence of an accident as a function of proportions of two parties' nonnegligence. Formally, a liability rule is a function f from I^2 to I^2, $f\colon I^2 \mapsto I^2$, such that: $f(p, q) = (x, y) = [x(p, q), y(p, q)]$, where $x + y = 1$. Let C, D, L and $(c^*, d^*) \in M$ be given. If accident takes place and loss of $H(c, d)$ materializes, then $x[p(c), q(d)]\ H(c, d)$ will be borne by the victim and $y[p(c),\ q(d)]\ H(c, d)$ will be borne by the injurer. As, to begin with, in case of an accident, the entire loss falls upon the victim, $y[p(c), q(d)]\, H(c, d)$ represents the liability payment by the injurer to the victim. The victim's expected costs are therefore: $c + L(c, d) - y[p(c), q(d)]L(c, d) = c + x[p(c), q(d)]L(c, d)$. The injurer's expected costs are: $d + y[p(c), q(d)]\, L(c,\ d)$. Both parties are assumed to prefer

[6]It is implicitly assumed that the legally binding due care levels are always set appropriately from the point of view of minimizing total social costs. This standard assumption is crucial for the results on the efficiency of liability rules.

smaller expected costs to larger expected costs and be indifferent between alternatives with equal expected costs.

Remark 1: Let f be a liability rule. Then, for any proportions of nonnegligence (p, q) by the two parties, f assigns the proportions (x, y) in which the loss is to be borne by the parties in case of an accident. Application of the liability rule consists of specification of C, D, L, and $(c^*, d^*) \in M$. Once C, D, L, and $(c^*, d^*) \in M$ have been specified, for any configuration of costs of care (c, d) by the two parties, proportions of nonnegligence p and q are uniquely determined. The liability rule then uniquely determines the liability proportions (x, y) corresponding to (p, q).

As application of a liability rule consists of specification of C, D, L and $(c^*, d^*) \in M$, it follows that any change in any of these would result in a different application. In particular, even if C, D, and L remain unchanged, a different choice of $(c^*, d^*) \in M$ would result in a different application.

Remark 2: In the terminology of this paper:
The rule of negligence is defined by:

$$(q < 1 \rightarrow x = 0) \quad \text{and} \quad (q = 1 \rightarrow x = 1).$$

The rule of negligence with the defense of contributory negligence is defined by:

$$(p < 1 \rightarrow x = 1) \quad \text{and} \quad (p = 1 \text{ and } q < 1 \rightarrow x = 0)$$
$$\text{and} \quad (p = 1 \text{ and } q = 1 \rightarrow x = 1).$$

The rule of strict liability is defined by:

$$x = 0, \qquad \text{for all } p, q \in [0, 1].$$

The rule of strict liability with the defense of contributory negligence is defined by:

$$(p < 1 \rightarrow x = 1) \quad \text{and} \quad (p = 1 \rightarrow x = 0).$$

The rule of no liability is defined by:

$$x = 1, \qquad \text{for all } p, q \in [0, 1].$$

Let f be a liability rule. f is defined to be efficient for given C, D, L and $(c^*, d^*) \in M$ satisfying (A1) and (A2) iff $(\forall(\bar{c}, \bar{d}) \in C \times D)[(\bar{c}, \bar{d})$ is a Nash equilibrium $\rightarrow (\bar{c}, \bar{d}) \in M]$ and $(\exists(\bar{c}, \bar{d}) \in C \times D)[(\bar{c}, \bar{d})$ is a Nash equilibrium]. Liability rule f is efficient in general iff for every possible choice of C, D, L, and $(c^*, d^*) \in M$ satisfying (A1) and (A2),

f is efficient. In other words, a liability rule is efficient for given C, D, L, and $(c^*, d^*) \in M$ satisfying (A1) and (A2) iff (i) every Nash equilibrium is total social cost minimizing, and (ii) there exists at least one Nash equilibrium. A liability rule is efficient in general iff it is efficient for every possible choice of C, D, L and $(c^*, d^*) \in M$ satisfying (A1) and (A2).

Remark 3: It should be noted that if (A2) is not satisfied then no liability rule can be efficient.

When one considers the class of all liability rules, with respect to Nash equilibria, all possibilities are open as the following examples show:

Example 1: Consider the liability rule which requires equal sharing of losses regardless of the proportions of nonnegligence of the two parties, i.e., the rule given by:

$$(\forall p, q \in [0,1])\left[f(p,q) = \left(\frac{1}{2}, \frac{1}{2}\right)\right].$$

Let

$$C = \{0,1\},\ D = \{0,1\},$$
$$L(0,0) = 5,\ L(0,1) = 3.2,\ L(1,0) = 3.2,\ L(1,1) = 0.$$

(1, 1) is the unique total social cost minimizing configuration of care levels.

Let $(c^*, d^*) = (1,1)$. Here both $(0,0)$ and $(1,1)$ are Nash equilibria. While (1, 1) is total social cost minimizing, $(0,0)$ is not, and thus the rule is inefficient for the given application.

Example 2: Consider the rule of no liability, i.e., the rule given by:

$$(\forall p, q \in [0,1])\,[f(p,q) = (1,0)].$$

Let

$$C = \{0,1\},\ D = \{0,1\},$$
$$L(0,0) = 5,\ L(0,1) = 3,\ L(1,0) = 3.5\ \ L(1,1) = 0.$$

(1, 1) is the unique total social cost minimizing configuration of care levels.

Let $(c^*, d^*) = (1,1)$. Here there is only one Nash equilibrium, namely, (1, 0), which is not total social cost minimizing. The rule is therefore inefficient for the given application.

Example 3: Consider the following rather perverse rule:

$$\left[p<1 \text{ and } q<1 \rightarrow f(p,q)=\left(\frac{1}{2},\frac{1}{2}\right)\right] \text{ and}$$

$$\left[p<1 \rightarrow f(p,1)=\left(\frac{3}{17},\frac{14}{17}\right)\right] \text{ and}$$

$$\left[q<1 \rightarrow f(1,q)=\left(\frac{2}{17},\frac{15}{17}\right)\right] \text{ and } \left[f(1,1)=\left(\frac{2}{7},\frac{5}{7}\right)\right].$$

Let

$$C=\{0,1\},\ D=\{0,1\},$$
$$L(0,0)=10,\ L(0,1)=8.5,\ L(1,0)=8.5,\ L(1,1)=7.$$

(1, 1) is the unique total social cost minimizing configuration of care levels.

Let $(c^*, d^*)=(1,1)$. It can be easily checked that there is no $(c,d)\in C\times D$ which is a Nash equilibrium. The rule is therefore inefficient for the given application.

Example 4: Consider the rule of negligence given by:

$$[[q<1 \rightarrow f(p,q)=(0,1)] \text{ and } [q=1 \rightarrow f(p,1)=(1,0)]], \text{ for all } p\in[0,1].$$

Let

$$C=\{0,1\},\ D=\{0,1\},$$
$$L(0,0)=5,\ L(0,1)=3,\ L(1,0)=3.5,\ L(1,1)=0.$$

(1, 1) is the unique total social cost minimizing configuration of care levels.

Let $(c^*, d^*)=(1,1)$. Here there is only one Nash equilibrium, namely, (1, 1), which is total social cost minimizing. Thus for the given application the rule is efficient.

3. CHARACTERIZATION OF EFFICIENT LIABILITY RULES

Condition of Negligence Liability (NL): A liability rule f satisfies the condition of negligence liability iff $[\forall p\in[0,1)]\ [f(p,1)=(1,0)]$ and $[\forall q\in[0,1)][f(1,q)=(0,1)]$.

In other words, a liability rule satisfies the condition of negligence liability iff its structure is such that (i) whenever the injurer is nonnegligent and the victim is negligent, the entire loss in case of an accident is borne by the victim, and (ii) whenever the victim is nonnegligent and the injurer is negligent, the entire loss in case of an accident is borne by the injurer.

Proposition 1: If a liability rule satisfies condition NL then for any arbitrary choice of C, D, L, and $(c^*, d^*) \in M$ satisfying (A1) and (A2), (c^*, d^*) is a Nash equilibrium.

Proof: Let liability rule f satisfy condition NL. Take any C, D, L, and $(c^*, d^*) \in M$ satisfying (A1) and (A2).

Consider any $c \geq c^*$.

As total social costs are minimized at (c^*, d^*), total social costs at (c, d^*) must be at least as large as total social costs at (c^*, d^*), i.e.,

$$c + d^* + L(c, d^*) \geq c^* + d^* + L(c^*, d^*). \tag{1.1}$$

Therefore,

$$c + L(c, d^*) \geq c^* + L(c^*, d^*). \tag{1.2}$$

Denote $f(1, 1)$ by (x_1, y_1). As $x_1 \geq 0$, (1.2) implies:

$$x_1 c + x_1 L(c, d^*) \geq x_1 c^* + x_1 L(c^*, d^*). \tag{1.3}$$

As $1 - x_1 \geq 0$ and $c \geq c^*$, it follows that:

$$(1 - x_1)c \geq (1 - x_1)c^* \tag{1.4}$$

(1.3) and (1.4) imply:

$$c + x_1 L(c, d^*) \geq c^* + x_1 L(c^*, d^*). \tag{1.5}$$

Now, expected costs of the victim at $(c, d^*) = c + x[p(c), q(d^*)] L(c, d^*) = c + x_1 L(c, d^*)$, as $c \geq c^*$. Expected costs of the victim at $(c^*, d^*) = c^* + x[p(c^*), q(d^*)]\, L(c^*, d^*) = c^* + x_1 L(c^*, d^*)$.

Thus inequality (1.5) says that:

$$\begin{aligned} c \geq c^* \rightarrow & \text{ expected costs of the victim at } (c, d^*) \\ & \geq \text{expected costs of the victim at } (c^*, d^*). \end{aligned} \tag{1.6}$$

Next consider any $c < c^*$.

As total social costs at (c, d^*) are at least as large as total social costs at (c^*, d^*), we obtain:

$$c + d^* + L(c, d^*) \geq c^* + d^* + L(c^*, d^*), \tag{1.7}$$

which in turn implies:

$$c + L(c, d^*) \geq c^* + L(c^*, d^*). \tag{1.8}$$

As $0 \leq x_1 \leq 1$ and $L(c^*, d^*) \geq 0$, from (1.8) it follows that:

$$c + L(c, d^*) \geq c^* + x_1 L(c^*, d^*). \tag{1.9}$$

Expected costs of the victim at $(c, d^*) = c + x[p(c), q(d^*)]\, L(c, d^*) = c + L(c, d^*)$, by condition NL, as $c < c^*$. Expected costs of the victim at $(c^*, d^*) = c^* + x[p(c^*), q(d^*)]\, L(c^*, d^*) = c^* + x_1 L(c^*, d^*)$.

Therefore inequality (1.9) says that:

$c < c^* \rightarrow$ expected costs of the victim at (c, d^*)
$\geq$ expected costs of the victim at (c^*, d^*). (1.10)

(1.6) and (1.10) establish that:

$(\forall c \in C)$ [expected costs of the victim at (c, d^*)
$\geq$ expected costs of the victim at (c^*, d^*)]. (1.11)

By an analogous argument one can show that:

$(\forall d \in D)$ [expected costs of the injurer at (c^*, d)
$\geq$ expected costs of the injurer at (c^*, d^*)]. (1.12)

(1.11) and (1.12) establish that (c^*, d^*) is a Nash equilibrium. □

An intuitive explanation of Proposition 1 is as follows. Suppose the injurer is using d^*. Consider a change by the victim from c^* to some $c > c^*$. Now, the reduction in expected loss $L(c^*, d^*) - L(c, d^*)$ cannot exceed the increase in cost of care $c - c^*$, otherwise (c^*, d^*) could not have been a TSC-minimizing configuration. Thus, a change from c^* to $c > c^*$ cannot be advantageous for the victim. Next consider a change from c^* to some $c < c^*$. The increase in expected loss $L(c, d^*) - L(c^*, d^*)$ must be at least as large as the decrease in cost of care $c^* - c$, otherwise (c^*, d^*) could not have been TSC-minimizing. By condition NL, the entire increase in expected loss must be borne by the victim. Consequently a shift from c^* to $c < c^*$ can never be advantageous. Thus, given the choice of d^* by the injurer, c^* is best for the victim. By an analogous argument one shows that, given the choice of c^* by the victim, d^* is best for the injurer.

Proposition 2: If a liability rule satisfies condition NL then for every possible choice of C, D, L, and $(c^*, d^*) \in M$ satisfying (A1) and (A2):

$$(\forall (\bar{c}, \bar{d}) \in C \times D)[(\bar{c}, \bar{d}) \text{ is a Nash equilibrium} \rightarrow (\bar{c}, \bar{d}) \in M].$$

Proof: Let liability rule f satisfy condition NL. Take any C, D, L, and $(c^*, d^*) \in M$ satisfying (A1) and (A2).

Let $(\bar{c}, \bar{d})$ be a Nash equilibrium. $(\bar{c}, \bar{d})$ being a Nash equilibrium implies:

$$(\forall c \in C)[\bar{c} + x[p(\bar{c}), q(\bar{d})]L(\bar{c}, \bar{d}) \leq c + x[p(c), q(\bar{d})]L(c, \bar{d})] \quad (2.1)$$

and

$$(\forall d \in D)[\bar{d} + y[p(\bar{c}), q(\bar{d})]L(\bar{c}, \bar{d}) \leq d + y[p(\bar{c}), q(d)]L(\bar{c}, d)]. \quad (2.2)$$

$$(2.1) \rightarrow \bar{c} + x[p(\bar{c}), q(\bar{d})]\, L(\bar{c}, \bar{d}) \leq c^* + x[p(c^*), q(\bar{d})]L(c^*, \bar{d}). \quad (2.3)$$

$$(2.2) \rightarrow \bar{d} + y[p(\bar{c}), q(\bar{d})]\, L(\bar{c}, \bar{d}) \leq d^* + y[p(\bar{c}), q(d^*)]\, L(\bar{c}, d^*). \quad (2.4)$$

Adding (2.3) and (2.4) we obtain:

$$\bar{c} + \bar{d} + L(\bar{c}, \bar{d}) \leq c^* + d^* + x[p(c^*), q(\bar{d})]L(c^*, \bar{d}) + y[p(\bar{c}), q(d^*)]L(\bar{c}, d^*), \quad (2.5)$$

as $x[p(\bar{c}), q(\bar{d})] + y[p(\bar{c}), q(\bar{d})] = 1$.

Designate $f(1, 1)$ by (x_1, y_1).

If $\bar{c} \geq c^*$ and $\bar{d} \geq d^*$, then $x[p(c^*), q(\bar{d})] = x_1$ and $y[p(\bar{c}), q(d^*)] = y_1$. And, (2.5) reduces to:

$$\bar{c} + \bar{d} + L(\bar{c}, \bar{d}) \leq c^* + d^* + x_1 L(c^*, \bar{d}) + y_1 L(\bar{c}, d^*). \quad (2.6)$$

As $\bar{c} \geq c^*$ and $\bar{d} \geq d^*$, we have: $L(c^*, \bar{d}) \leq L(c^*, d^*)$ and $L(\bar{c}, d^*) \leq L(c^*, d^*)$. Therefore:

$$x_1 L(c^*, \bar{d}) \leq x_1 L(c^*, d^*), \quad (2.7)$$

and

$$y_1 L(\bar{c}, d^*) \leq y_1 L(c^*, d^*), \quad (2.8)$$

From (2.6) – (2.8), we conclude:

$$\bar{c} + \bar{d} + L(\bar{c}, \bar{d}) \leq c^* + d^* + L(c^*, d^*).$$

As $(c^*, d^*) \in M$, we conclude that $\bar{c} + \bar{d} + L(\bar{c}, \bar{d}) = c^* + d^* + L(c^*, d^*)$ must be the case, and consequently $(\bar{c}, \bar{d}) \in M$.

Thus we have shown that:

$(\bar{c}, \bar{d})$ is a Nash equilibrium

$$\text{and } \bar{c} \geq c^* \text{ and } \bar{d} \geq d^* \rightarrow (\bar{c}, \bar{d}) \in M. \tag{2.9}$$

Next suppose that $\bar{c} \geq c^*$ and $\bar{d} < d^*$. Then $x[p(c^*), q(\bar{d})] = 0$ by condition NL, and $y[p(\bar{c}), q(d^*)] = y_1$.

(2.5), therefore, reduces to:

$$\bar{c} + \bar{d} + L(\bar{c}, \bar{d}) \leq c^* + d^* + y_1 L(\bar{c}, d^*).$$

As $0 \leq y_1 \leq 1$, we obtain:

$$\bar{c} + \bar{d} + L(\bar{c}, \bar{d}) \leq c^* + d^* + L(\bar{c}, d^*).$$

As $\bar{c} \geq c^*$, we have $L(\bar{c}, d^*) \leq L(c^*, d^*)$. Consequently: $\bar{c} + \bar{d} + L(\bar{c}, \bar{d}) \leq c^* + d^* + L(c^*, d^*)$. This establishes that:

$$(\bar{c}, \bar{d}) \text{ is a Nash equilibrium and } \bar{c} \geq c^* \text{ and } \bar{d} < d^* \rightarrow (\bar{c}, \bar{d}) \in M. \tag{2.10}$$

By an analogous argument, one can show that:

$$(\bar{c}, \bar{d}) \text{ is a Nash equilibrium and } \bar{c} < c^* \text{ and } \bar{d} \geq d^* \rightarrow (\bar{c}, \bar{d}) \in M. \tag{2.11}$$

Finally consider the case when $\bar{c} < c^*$ and $\bar{d} < d^*$. By condition NL we obtain $x[p(c^*), q(\bar{d})] = 0$ and $y[p(\bar{c}), q(d^*)] = 0$. (2.5) then reduces to:

$\bar{c} + \bar{d} + L(\bar{c}, \bar{d}) \leq c^* + d^*$, which implies:

$\bar{c} + \bar{d} + L(\bar{c}, \bar{d}) \leq c^* + d^* + L(c^*, d^*)$, establishing that:

$$(\bar{c}, \bar{d}) \text{ is a Nash equilibrium and } \bar{c} < c^* \text{ and } \bar{d} < d^* \rightarrow (\bar{c}, \bar{d}) \in M. \tag{2.12}$$

(2.9) – (2.12) establish the proposition. □

Less formally, the argument establishing Proposition 2 can be put somewhat more simply. First we note that as $x[p(c^*), q(\bar{d})]\, L(c^*, \bar{d}) = 0$ if $\bar{d} < d^*$, by condition NL, and $= x_1 L(c^*, \bar{d}) \leq x_1 L(c^*, d^*)$ if $\bar{d} \geq d^*$; it follows that, regardless of the value of $\bar{d}$, $x[p(c^*), q(\bar{d})]L(c^*, \bar{d})$ cannot exceed $x_1 L(c^*, d^*)$. Now, as $(\bar{c}, \bar{d})$ is a Nash equilibrium, it follows that: $c^* + x[p(c^*), q(\bar{d})]L(c^*, \bar{d}) \geq \bar{c} + x[p(\bar{c}), q(\bar{d})]L(\bar{c}, \bar{d})$. Which in turn implies that: $c^* + x_1 L(c^*, d^*) \geq \bar{c} + x[p(\bar{c}), q(\bar{d})]L(\bar{c}, \bar{d})$. Thus, a consequence of condition NL and the hypothesis that $(\bar{c}, \bar{d})$ is a Nash equilibrium is that the expected costs of the victim at (c^*, d^*) must be at least as large as expected costs at $(\bar{c}, \bar{d})$. By an analogous argument it follows that the expected costs of the injurer at (c^*, d^*) must be at least as large as expected costs at $(\bar{c}, \bar{d})$. As total social costs are the sum of expected costs of the two parties, it immediately follows that $(\bar{c}, \bar{d})$ is TSC-minimizing.

Proposition 3: If a liability rule is efficient for every possible choice of C, D, L, and $(c^*, d^*) \in M$ satisfying (A1) and (A2), then it satisfies condition NL.

Proof: The proposition to be proved is logically equivalent to:

If a liability rule violates condition NL then it is not the case that it is efficient for every possible choice of C, D, L, and $(c^*, d^*) \in M$ satisfying (A1) and (A2). That is, if a liability rule violates condition NL then for some choice of C, D, L, and $(c^*, d^*) \in M$ satisfying (A1) and (A2) it is inefficient.

Let f be a liability rule. Suppose f violates condition NL. Then:

$$[\exists p \in [0,1)][f(p,1) \neq (1,0)] \quad \text{or} \quad [\exists q \in [0,1)][f(1,q) \neq (0,1)].$$

Suppose $[\exists q \in [0,1)][f(1,q) \neq (0,1)]$ holds. Suppose for $q \in [0,1)$ we have: $f(1,q) = (x_q, y_q)$, $x_q + y_q = 1$, $y_q \neq 1$.

Let t be a positive number. As $y_q \in [0,1)$, we have $y_q t < t$. Choose a positive number r such that $y_q t < r < t$. As $q \neq 1$, $1 - q \neq 0$. Let $d_0 = r/(1-q)$.

Now, let C, D, L and $(c^*, d^*) \in M$ be specified as follows:

$$C = \{0, c_0\}, c_0 > 0, \ D = \{0, qd_0, d_0\},$$

$$L(0,0) = t + qd_0 + c_0 + \epsilon,$$

$$L(0, qd_0) = t + c_0 + \epsilon, L(0, d_0) = c_0 + \epsilon,$$

$$L(c_0, 0) = t + qd_0, \ L(c_0, qd_0) = t, \ L(c_0, d_0) = 0,$$

where $\epsilon > 0$.

As $\epsilon > 0$ and $t > r = (1-q)d_0$, it follows that (c_0, d_0) is the unique total social cost minimizing configuration.

Let $(c_0, d_0) = (c^*, d^*)$.

It should be noted that the above specification of C, D, L and $(c^*, d^*) \in M$ is consistent with (A1) and (A2). Furthermore, the specification of L is done in such a way that no inconsistency would arise even if $q = 0$.

Now, given that the victim employs c_0; if the injurer employs strategy qd_0 his expected costs are $qd_0 + y_q t$, and if he employs strategy d_0 his expected costs are d_0. As $(1-q)d_0 > y_q t$ by construction, it follows that $d_0 > qd_0 + y_q t$. Therefore the unique total social cost minimizing configuration (c_0, d_0) is not a Nash equilibrium. This establishes that

f is not an efficient liability rule for every possible choice of C, D, L and $(c^*, d^*) \in M$ satisfying (A1) and (A2). The proof is completed by noting that, in case $[\exists p \in [0,1)][f(p,1) \neq (1,0)]$ holds, an analogous argument shows that it is not the case that f is an efficient liability rule for every possible choice of C, D, L, and $(c^*, d^*) \in M$ satisfying (A1) and (A2). □

The argument of Proposition 3 can be put less formally but more concisely as follows. Suppose the liability rule f is such that when one party is fully nonnegligent (say the victim) and the other party (the injurer) is partly or wholly negligent, the liability assignments are such that the injurer is not required to bear the entire loss, i.e., for some $q < 1$, $f(1,q) = (x_q, y_q)$, where $y_q < 1$. Consider an application of f, i.e., specification of C, D, L and $(c^*, d^*) \in M$, consistent with (A1) and (A2), such that: (i) TSC-minimizing configuration is unique, (ii) both c^* and d^* are positive; and if both parties take optimal care then the expected loss is zero, and (iii) qd^* is an element of D. Given that the victim is using c^*; if we consider a shift by the injurer from d^* to qd^* then the increase in expected loss $L(c^*, qd^*) - L(c^*, d^*) = L(c^*, qd^*)$, must be greater than the reduction in cost of care $(1-q)d^*$. As $y_q < 1$, the injurer bears only a part of the increase in expected loss. On the other hand, the entire decrease in the cost of care accrues to the injurer. Therefore, it follows that one can always find an application such that, in addition to (i) – (iii), $L(c^*, qd^*) > (1-q)d^* > y_q L(c^*, qd^*)$. This establishes the existence of an application for which the unique TSC-minimizing configuration is not a Nash equilibrium; and consequently the existence of an application for which the rule is inefficient.

Theorem 1: A liability rule is efficient for every possible choice of C, D, L, and $(c^*, d^*) \in M$ satisfying (A1) and (A2) iff it satisfies the condition of negligence liability.

Proof: If liability rule f satisfies the condition of negligence liability then by Propositions 1 and 2 it is efficient for every possible choice of C, D, L, and $(c^*, d^*) \in M$ satisfying (A1) and (A2). Proposition 3 establishes that if f is efficient for every possible choice of C, D, L, and $(c^*, d^*) \in M$ satisfying (A1) and (A2) then it satisfies the condition of negligence liability. □

The following important corollary follows immediately from Theorem1.

Corollary 1: (i) The rules of negligence, negligence with the defense of contributory negligence, comparative negligence, and strict liability with the defense of contributory negligence are efficient for every possible choice of C, D, L, and $(c^*, d^*) \in M$ satisfying (A1) and (A2).

(ii) The rules of no liability and strict liability are not efficient for every possible choice of C, D, L, and $(c^*, d^*) \in M$ satisfying (A1) and (A2).

In the law and economics literature relating to liability rules it is generally assumed that costs of care and expected loss functions are such that there is a unique (c, d) configuration at which total social costs are minimized, i.e.,

M consists of a single element. (A3)

The next theorem establishes that the characterization of efficient liability rules remains unchanged even if (A3) is assumed, in addition to (A1) and (A2).

Theorem 2: A liability rule is efficient for every possible choice of C, D, L, and $(c^*, d^*) \in M$ satisfying (A1) – (A3) iff it satisfies the condition of negligence liability.

Proof: Sufficiency of NL follows from Theorem 1. The necessity of NL follows from the proof of Proposition 3 in view of the fact that C, D, L, and (c^*, d^*) considered there, in addition to being consistent with (A1) and (A2), also satisfy (A3). □

4. CONCLUDING REMARKS

Theorem 1 establishes that (i) if a liability rule f satisfies NL then it is efficient for every application satisfying (A1) and (A2), i.e., for every configuration of C, D, L and $(c^*, d^*) \in M$ satisfying (A1) and (A2); and that (ii) if f violates NL then f is inefficient for some application satisfying (A1) and (A2). Now suppose that the class of admissible applications is a subclass of the class of applications satisfying (A1) and (A2). If f satisfies NL then (i) immediately implies efficiency of f for every admissible application. However, if f violates NL then (ii) does not imply the existence of an admissible application for which f is inefficient. The point can be illustrated by considering the liability rule defined by: $f(p, q) = \left(\frac{1}{2}, \frac{1}{2}\right)$, for all $p, q \in [0, 1]$, which is not efficient for every application satisfying (A1) and (A2). If the class of admissible applications consists of only the applications given by: $C = \{0, w\}, 0 < w,\ D = \{0, w\}, L(0, 0) = 10w,\ L(0, w) = 5w, L(w, 0) = 5w, L(w, w) = 0, (c^*, d^*) = (w, w)$; then the rule is efficient for every admissible application.

From these considerations it follows that Theorem 2 is independent of Theorem 1. If in a theoretical or empirical context, in addition to (A1)

and (A2) or in addition to (A1) – (A3), further restrictions turn out to be appropriate then it is possible that some condition weaker than NL might turn out to be necessary and sufficient for efficiency.

REFERENCES

Barnes, D.W. and L.A. Stout (1992): *The Economic Analysis of Tort Law*. St. Paul: West Publishing Company.

Brown, J.P. (1973): "Toward an Economic Theory of Liability." *Journal of Legal Studies* 2: 323–350.

Calabresi, G. (1961): "Some Thoughts on Risk Distribution and the Law of Torts." *Yale Law Journal* 70: 499–553.

Calabresi, G. (1965): "The Decision for Accidents: An Approach to Non-Fault Allocation of Costs." *Harvard Law Review* 78: 713–745.

Calabresi, G. (1970): *The Costs of Accidents: A Legal and Economic Analysis*. New Haven: Yale University Press.

Calabresi, G. (1975): "Optimal Deterrence and Accidents." *Yale Law Journal* 84: 656–671.

Calabresi, G. and J.T. Hirschoff (1972): "Toward a Test for Strict Liability in Torts." *Yale Law Journal* 81: 1054–1085.

Calabresi, G. and A. Klevorick (1985): "Four Tests for Liability in Torts." *Journal of Legal Studies* 14: 585–627.

Cooter, R.D. (1985): "Unity in Torts, Contracts and Property: The Model of Precaution." *California Law Review* 73: 1–51.

Cooter, R.D. (1991): "Economic Theories of Legal Liability," *Journal of Economic Perspectives* 5: 11–30.

Cooter, R.D, and T.S Ulen (1999): *Law and Economics*, 3rd ed. New York: Addison-Wesley.

Diamond, P.A. (1974a): "Accident Law and Resource Allocation." *Bell Journal of Economics* 5: 366–405.

Diamond, P.A. (1974b): "Single Activity Accidents." *Journal of Legal Studies* 3: 107–64.

Diamond, P.A. and J.A. Mirrlees (1975): "On the Assignment of Liability: The Uniform Case." *Bell Journal of Economics* 6: 487–516.

Eisenberg, M.A. (1988): *The Nature of the Common Law*, Cambridge, Mass.: Harvard University Press.

Englard, I. (1980): "The System Builders: A Critical Appraisal of Modern Tort Theory," *Journal of Legal Studies* 9: 27–69.

Englard, I. (1991): "Law and Economics in American Tort Cases: A Critical Assessment of the Theory's Impact on Courts," *University of Toronto Law Journal* 41: 359–430.

Feldman, A.M. and J.M. Frost (1998): "A Simple Model of Efficient Tort Liability Rules," *International Review of Law and Economics* 18: 201–215.

Landes, W.M. and R.A. Posner (1981): "The Positive Economic Theory of Tort Law," *Georgia Law Review* 15: 851–924.

Landes, W.M. and R.A Posner (1987): *The Economic Structure of Tort Law*. Cambridge, Mass.: Harvard University Press.

Levmore, S. (1994): *Foundations of Tort Law*. Oxford: Oxford University Press.

Miceli, T.J. (1997): *Economics of the Law: Torts, Contracts, Property, Litigation*. Oxford: Oxford University Press.

Polinsky, A.M. (1980): "Strict Liability versus Negligence in a Market Setting," *American Economic Review* 70: 363–367.

Polinsky, A.M. (1989): *An Introduction to Law and Economics*. 2nd ed. Boston: Little, Brown and Company.

Posner, R.A. (1972): "A Theory of Negligence." *Journal of Legal Studies* 1: 28–96.

Posner, R.A. (1973) : "Strict Liability: A Comment." *Journal of Legal Studies* 2: 205–221.

Posner, R.A. (1992) : *Economic Analysis of Law*. 4th ed. Boston: Little, Brown and Company.

Shavell, S. (1980): "Strict Liability versus Negligence," *Journal of Legal Studies* 9: 1–25.

Shavell, S. (1987): *Economic Analysis of Accident Law*. Cambridge, Mass.: Harvard University Press.

9

Taxes and Legal Rules for the Control of Externalities When There are Strategic Responses†

John Prather Brown and William L. Holahan

Tort rules of liability allow accident victims to go to court to try to collect damages from the harming party, unless there is a superseding contract between the parties or there is criminal intent. Since both accidents and accident prevention are costly, the rule which applies has important consequences. This body of law has only recently been the object of economic analysis and it has been found to have interesting and subtle properties.[1]

This paper analyzes the economics of accidents when there is a single legal rule which governs cases where there are transaction costs *ex ante* as well as where there are not and cases where parties negotiate strategically and where they do not. We analyze situations where participants contract completely (i.e., there are no transaction

†Originally published as "Taxes and Legal Rules for the Control of Externalities When There Are Strategic Responses", 1980, *The Journal of Legal Studies*, Vol. 9, pp. 165–78.

[1]John Prather Brown, Toward an Economic Theory of Liability, 2 J. Legal Stud. 323 (1973); Peter A. Diamond, Single Activity Accidents, 3 J. Legal Stud. 107 (1974); *id*, Accident Law and Resource Allocation, 5 Bell J. Econ. & Management Sci. 366 (1974); Jerry Green, On the Optimal Structure of Liability Laws, 7 Bell J. Econ. 553 (1976); and A. Mitchell Polinsky, Controlling Externalities and Protecting Entitlements: Property Right, Liability Rule, and Tax-Subsidy Approaches, 8 J. Legal Stud. 1 (1979). It has also been studied by lawyers from an economics perspective: Guido Calabresi, The Cost of Accidents (1970); and Richard A. Posner, Economic Analysis of Law (2 ed. 1977).

costs), where participants play a Cournot–Nash game, and where they behave strategically according to the game of Stackelberg. Where there are large numbers of participants both as potential plaintiffs and as potential defendants, then the Cournot–Nash equilibrium resulting from nonstrategic behavior is a very plausible model. However, there are many tort contexts that are one-on-many or one-on-a-few or one-on-one in character where strategic behavior by the one is plausible and worthy of study. The set of possible strategies is, of course, immense. Here we shall study the Stackelberg strategy in the hopes that it is illustrative and provocative. The Stackelberg formulation has the advantage of familiarity and simplicity and it captures the central notion of strategic behavior.

Economists since Pigou[2] have suggested substitutes for traditional tort law. Pigou suggested taxes to raise marginal private costs to the level of marginal social costs so that private parties will have incentives to cut back the offending activity to the appropriate level.[3] Alternatively, Coase[4] pointed out that in many cases bargaining between the relevant parties can lead to an efficient outcome regardless of the initial allocation of responsibility for damages: under those circumstances, a Pigovian tax would have a perverse effect—the harm-generating activity would be underproduced.

In this paper we extend a model by Brown[5] to show the formal equivalence between Pigovian taxes and certain liability rules. We use the model to find the Cournot–Nash and the Stackelberg equilibria under these rules. It will be shown that the traditional common law rule is strategy-proof—there are no rewards to being a Stackelberg leader—and the Pigovian tax is not. Finally, we show that the efficient Cournot–Nash equilibrium under the Pigovian tax is not robust with respect to reductions of transaction costs, but the efficient Cournot–Nash and Stackelberg equilibrium under the common law rule is robust with respect to reductions in transaction costs.

In the first part of the paper we present the model and characterize the social-cost-minimizing combination of precautions. In the second part we show the formal equivalence of the ancient rule of an eye for an eye

[2]A. C. Pigou, The Economics of Welfare (4th ed. 1932).

[3]See William J. Baurmol, On Taxation and the Control of Externalities, 62 Am. Econ. Rev. 307 (1972), for an up-to-date statement and defense of the Pigovian tradition, as well as an extensive bibliography.

[4]R. H. Coase, The Problem of Social Cost, 3 J. Law & Econ. 1 (1960).

[5]Brown, *supra* note 1.

and the Pigovian tax. We then analyze the rule and tax and show that the Cournot–Nash equilibrium is social-cost minimizing, that the rule is not strategy-proof (i.e., that there exist distinct Stackelberg equilibria and these Stackelberg equilibria are not efficient), and that the efficient Cournot–Nash equilibrium is not robust with respect to lower transaction costs. In the third part we analyze the traditional common law rule of negligence with a contributory negligence defense. There the Cournot–Nash equilibrium is efficient; the rule is strategy-proof in that the Stackelberg equilibria are identically the Cournot–Nash equilibrium, and the equilibrium is robust with respect to lower transaction costs. The fourth part analyzes a combination of the Pigovian tax and the common law rule taken together. The addition of the Pigovian tax does not change the efficiency of the Cournot–Nash equilibrium, but it removes the protection against strategic behavior by the plaintiff and destroys the robustness of the equilibrium with respect to lower transaction costs. Part five analyzes the rules of strict liability and no fault. The Cournot–Nash equilibrium in each of these symmetric rules is not efficient, is (perversely) strategy-proof, but fortunately is not robust with respect to lower transaction costs. In Part six we show that a rule which uses a Pigovian tax to indemnify victims is formally identical to the rule of strict liability. Part seven contains our conclusions.

I. THE MODEL

The model that we shall use is one where two precautions, x and y, are inputs in the production of a single output, $P(X, Y)$, which is the probability that accident costs A will be avoided in a given interval of time.[6] The total expected cost to society of any pair of precautions is the

[6]Brown, *supra* note 1, introduced this probability production function to analyze the efficiency of liability rules. Our assumptions about the production function are

(a) $P_x > 0$, (b) $P_y > 0$, (c) $P_{xx} < 0$, (d) $P_{yy} < 0$, and (e) $0 > P_{xy} > \dfrac{(P_y)^2 P_{xx} + (P_x)^2 P_{yy}}{2P_xP_y}$

Assumptions (a) through (d) are quite standard and imply that the marginal products of the inputs are positive and declining. Assumption (e) is not standard but is appropriate for our problem. See Diamond, Accident Law and Resource Allocation, *supra* note 1, at 371. Assumption (e) means that the two precautions are weak substitutes. If the second inequality of (e) is violated, we have concave isoquants, which will lead to corner solutions. Corner solutions are degenerate cases of the interior solutions in which it is socially efficient for only one person to exercise caution. We have shown elsewhere (John Prather Brown & William L. Holahan, Taxes and Legal Rules in the Control of Externalities (April 1977) (Working Paper No. 145, Cornell Univ., Dep't of Economics)) that these corner solutions retain the efficiency of the common law rules derived above.

sum of the precaution costs and the expected cost of the accident. The expected social cost, C^S, can be written

$$C^S(X,Y) = \alpha X + \beta Y + A[1 - P(X,Y)], \tag{1}$$

where

X, Y is the level of precaution taken by the defendant, plaintiff;
α, β is the per unit precaution costs of the defendant, plaintiff;
$P(X, Y)$ is the probability of avoiding the accident, $P_x(X, Y) > 0$.[7]

Both parties are assumed to know A, α, β, and $P(X, Y)$, as well as the liability rule in force, and that the other party is interested only in private costs.

For social cost to be a minimum it must be true that the marginal cost of each input be equal to the expected value of its marginal product. That is

$$\alpha = A\,P_x(X, Y), \tag{2}$$

$$\beta = A\,P_y(X, Y). \tag{3}$$

The point where (2) and (3) are solved simultaneously minimizes expected social cost and is denoted Ω or (X^Ω, Y^Ω).

II. THE EQUIVALENCE OF AN EYE FOR AN EYE AND THE PIGOVIAN TAX

Under the eye-for-an-eye rule if a plaintiff is harmed in the amount of A, the defendant must pay A also.[8] Under this rule the private costs to the parties are the cost to the defendant,

$$C^x(X, Y) = \alpha X + A[1 - P(X, Y)], \tag{4}$$

which is the defendant's precaution costs plus his payment to the treasury if an accident occurs, and the cost to the plaintiff,

$$C^y(X, Y) = \beta Y + A[1 - P(X,Y)], \tag{5}$$

[7]Subscripts indicate differentiation with respect to the subscript. We are somewhat imprecise in our use of plaintiff and defendant here. Of course, one becomes a plaintiff or a defendant only after a lawsuit is filed following an accident, but we are considering precaution choices made before any accident occurs. More properly we should say potential plaintiff and potential victim, but it is much more convenient to drop the adjective, potential, since it leads to no ambiguity.

[8]This rule dates at least from the code of Hammurabi, a Babylonian king of the eighteenth century B.C., and continues to this day in some societies. Under the literal eye-for-an-eye rule the defendant's A is destroyed by the state. We shall assume that the defendant's payment is not destroyed but taken by the state and deposited in the treasury. What appears as a cost from the defendant's point of view is a transfer from society's point of view. Apparently this variant of the rule is almost as ancient as the rule itself.

which is the plaintiff's precaution costs plus the expected cost of the accident. The plaintiff is not reimbursed by either the defendant or the treasury.

Following Pigou, suppose that a tax is imposed on the defendant's activity which exactly reflects the expected damages resulting from the defendant's choices of precaution, $A[1-P(X, Y)]$.[9] If so, the private cost to the defendant, including the tax, is, again, (4). Because the plaintiff is not indemnified under the Pigovian tax, his private cost is, similarly, (5). Hence from a formal point of view the Pigovian tax and the eye-for-an-eye rule of liability are equivalent. To analyze the Stackelberg strategies we must first obtain the Cournot–Nash reaction functions which are the loci of private-cost-minimizing responses to given choices by the other party. The response function of the defendant, $R^x(Y)$, is defined by the first-order conditions for minimization of (4)

$$\alpha = A\, P_x[R^x(Y), Y]. \tag{6}$$

Similarly, using (5), the reaction function of the plaintiff $R^y(X)$ is defined by:

$$\beta = A\, P_y[X, R^y(X)]. \tag{7}$$

The Cournot–Nash equilibrium, denoted by ϵ, takes place at the intersection of the two reaction functions which are drawn in Figure 1.[10] The equilibrium ϵ is at the minimum point of C^s, (X^Ω, Y^Ω). Therefore $\epsilon = \Omega$.

Now we turn to the two possible Stackelberg equilibria: one when the defendant is a leader and one when the plaintiff is a leader. In order to find the Stackelberg equilibrium where the defendant is a leader, S_x, we need to know the reaction function of the plaintiff $R^y(X)$, and we need to know the best isocost curve of the defendant[11] along $R^y(X)$ as drawn in Figure 1. The defendant as Stackelberg leader will choose the point S_x on the follower's reaction function that minimizes his own costs. Comparing

[9]Note that the tax is placed on the defendant's choice of precaution. Another interpretation of the same formal structure would be to tax the defendant the amount A if and when an accident occurs. The difference between the two interpretations is carefully discussed in Donald Wittman, Prior Regulation versus Post Liability: The Choice between Input and Output Monitoring, 6 J. Legal Stud. 193 (1977).

[10]The efficiency of ϵ was demonstrated at length by Brown, *supra* note 1, at 335. That discussion serves as a point of departure for the analysis of strategic behavior which is the subject of this paper. See Brown & Holahan, *supra* note 6, for a discussion of the stability and uniqueness of the equilibrium.

[11]Only the defendant's best achievable isocost curve along $R^y(X)$ is drawn in Figure 1. Obviously there is an entire family of defendant isocost curves not drawn. They are

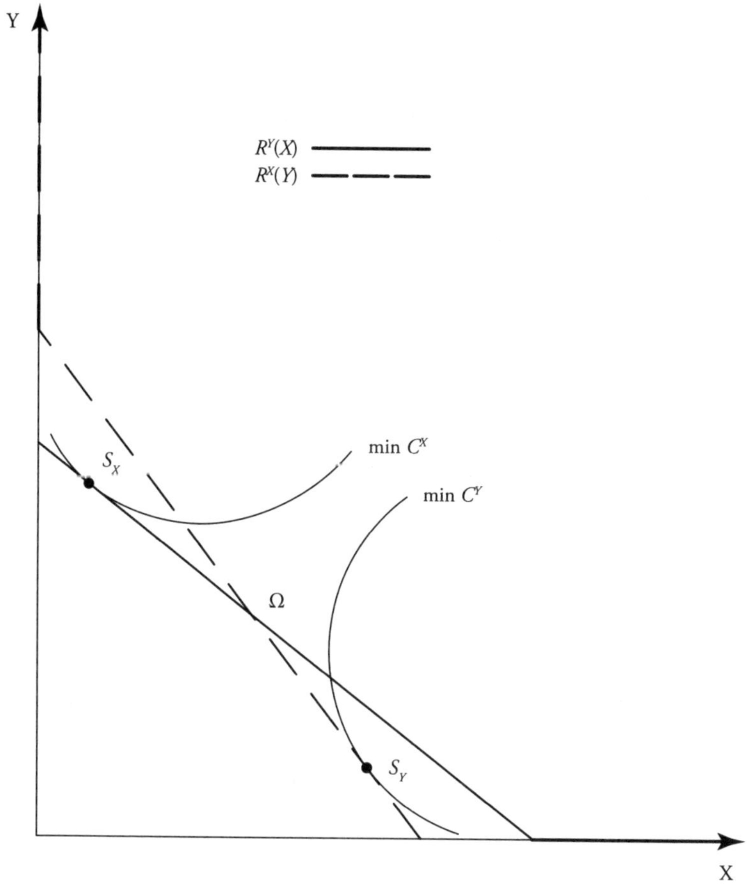

Figure 1

S_x with the Cournot equilibrium at Ω, the private costs to the leader are lower, the private costs to the follower are higher, the costs to society are higher, and the expected number of accidents will be higher.[12] Similarly if the plaintiff is a Stackelberg leader and the defendant is a follower the equilibrium is at S_y in Figure 1. Therefore, neither the eye-for-an-eye rule nor the Pigovian tax on externalities are strategy-proof rules; there are gains to be had from being a Stackelberg leader.

---

convex downward with costs declining upward and to the left. The argument that leads to that shape is in Brown & Holahan, *supra* note 6, at app. C.

[12]It has been shown elsewhere that the expected number of accidents will be higher at S_x than at Ω. See Brown & Holahan, *supra* note 6, at app. D.

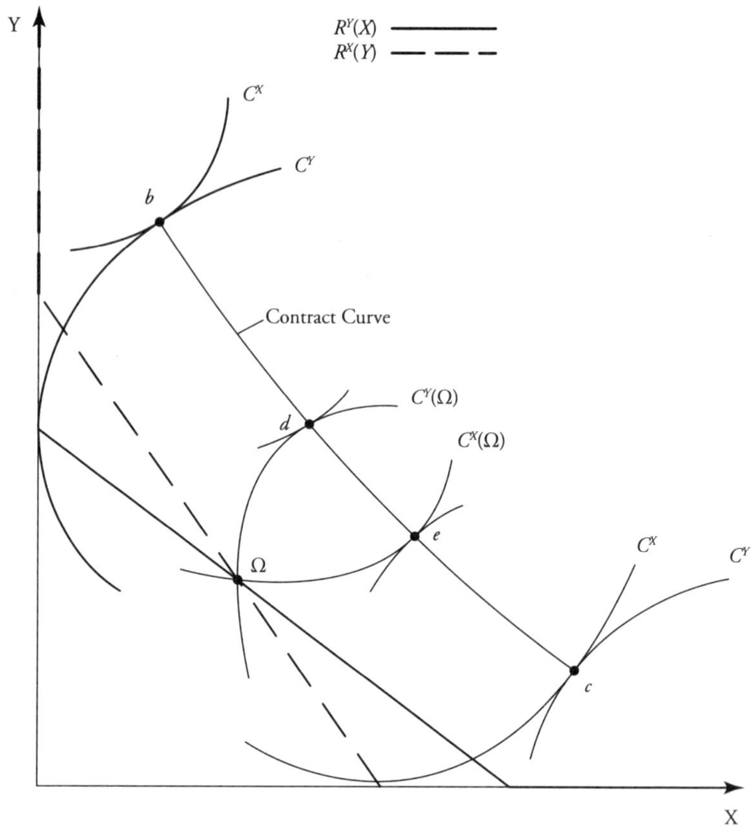

Figure 2

Let us now assume the parties to be in initial equilibrium at $\epsilon = \Omega$ as in Figure 2 and let there be costless transactions between parties. At Ω the isocost lines of the parties intersect at a right angle so there will be gains from trade if both parties increase precautions. The parties will agree to leave Ω and go to some point on the contract curve *d - e* which reduces private costs for both parties even though it increases social costs. The addition of the tax distorts private incentives. The result merely sharpens the earlier claim of Coase's[13] "even if the tax is exactly adjusted to equal the damage . . . the tax would not necessarily bring about optimal conditions."

Ω need not be the starting point of the trading. As Stackelberg leader the defendant might choose to start bargaining at S_x, but he could do even

[13]See Coase, *supra* note 4.

better if he started the bargaining with a threat to take no precautions whatsoever. Then if the follower were also a weak bargainer, he could be pushed as far as *b* in Figure 2. To get to *b* the leader defendant would threaten to take no precautions and then agree to take the amount consistent with *b*. One can draw a range of bargaining equilibria, like a contract curve, from *b* to *c*, where *c* is a point symmetric to point *b*, where the plaintiff is a Stackelberg leader who is also a tough bargainer.

Because the initial position from which trading commences is so unclear, the possibility of bargaining greatly increases the range of possible strategic behavior, increases the gains from strategic behavior, and increases the social cost of the eventual outcome. Rather than go further into the complexities of this analysis we shall step back and simply point out that neither the Cournot equilibrium nor the Stackelberg equilibria are robust with respect to reductions in transaction costs.

III. THE TRADITIONAL COMMON LAW RULE

The common law of tort allows someone who is harmed by someone else to sue for damages. The suit will be successful only if the defendant was found negligent in the amount of care he chose to take and if the plaintiff was not found negligent in his own care. This rule of negligence with a contributory negligence defense we shall call the traditional common law rule.[14]

We shall assume that the standard of care that defines negligence is the social cost-minimizing combination of precautions, X^{Ω} and Y^{Ω}.[15] The defendant will be found liable if he has not met his standard of care, $X < X^{\Omega}$, and the plaintiff has met his standard of care $Y > Y^{\Omega}$. Therefore, the defendant's private costs are

$$C^{x}(X,Y)=\begin{cases}\alpha X + A[1-P(X,Y)], & \text{if } X < X^{\Omega} \text{ and } Y \geq Y^{\Omega} \\ \alpha X & \text{otherwise}\end{cases} \tag{8}$$

[14]In the United States this rule dates to a famous 1850 decision in Massachusetts, Brown v. Kendall, 60 Mass. (6 Cush.) 292 (1850).

[15]Brown, *supra* note 1, at 333, argues at length that this interpretation of the standard of care is equivalent to Judge Learned Hand's famous decision in U.S. v. Carroll Towing Co., 159 F.2d 169 (2d Cir. 1947). There Hand explained that the standard of care depends on the product of the gravity of the accident and its probability, on the one hand, and on the burden of adequate precaution, on the other. Diamond's paper, Accident Law and Resource Allocation, see *supra* note 1, deals with the impact of different standards of care on the resulting equilibrium.

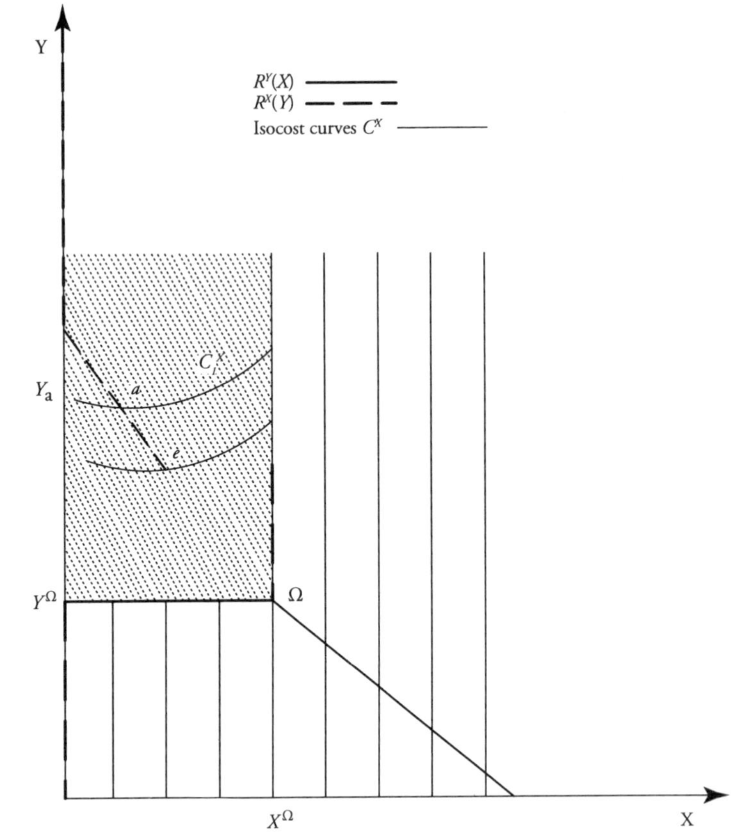

(Defendant liable in shaded area)

Figure 3 Reaction Functions under Common Law Rule

and the private costs to the plaintiff are

$$C^y(X,Y) = \begin{cases} \beta Y & \text{if } X < X^\Omega \text{ and } Y \geq Y^\Omega \\ \beta Y + A[1 - P(X,Y)] & \text{otherwise.} \end{cases} \quad (9)$$

All cases (*X*, *Y* pairs) where the defendant is liable are shaded in Figure 3.

The reaction functions[16] of the defendant will have the shapes drawn in Figure 3. The Cournot–Nash equilibrium is where the two reaction functions intersect—at Ω. Therefore, the traditional common law rule is

[16]See Brown, *supra* note 1, for the derivation.

efficient: $\epsilon = \Omega$. We can now use the reaction functions to find the two Stackelberg equilibria.

When the defendant is the leader, he will choose a point on the reaction function of the plaintiff, $R^y(X)$, where his own costs are at a minimum. The cost curves of the defendant have quite a different character depending on whether or not the defendant is liable for damages. If he is liable, his costs are

$$C^x(X, Y) = \alpha X + A[1 - P(X, Y)]$$

and his isocost curves are as drawn in the shaded area of Figure 3, convex downward with the minima tracing his full-cost reaction function. His costs decline upward and to the left. When the defendant is not liable, his costs are simply

$$C^x(X, Y) = \alpha X$$

and his isocost curves are simply vertical lines with his costs declining as he lowers his precaution. The least-cost point for the defendant on the horizontal sections of the plaintiff's reaction function is at Ω. On the rest of the plaintiff's reaction function, the defendant's costs depend only on his own level of precaution, so the best point on that segment of the reaction function is again Ω. Therefore, the place on the plaintiff's reaction function where the defendant's private costs are lowest is at Ω; the Stackelberg equilibrium S_x is at Ω. But that is also the Cournot equilibrium. Therefore, we have shown that the defendant gains nothing from strategic behavior of the Stackelberg variety; more loosely, it does not pay for the defendant to be a bully under the traditional common law rule.

Now let us turn to the case of the potential plaintiff as Stackelberg leader. Here we need the reaction function of the defendant and the isocost curves of the plaintiff as in Figure 4. The uppermost segment of the defendant's reaction function is in the shaded area where the plaintiff is not liable. There the plaintiff's isocost curves are horizontal. Therefore, on that segment of the defendant's reaction function, the lower the better for the plaintiff. On the vertical segment from *d* to Ω where the defendant meets the standard of care, the plaintiff is everywhere liable for the costs of the accident. There the relevant isocost curves are the convex curves, and the minimum is at Ω. Similarly, the plaintiff is liable on *bc*, the lowest segment of the defendant's reaction function. Along *bc* the plaintiff minimizes costs at *b*. As between *b*, the top of the lowest segment, and Ω, the less costly is Ω because costs decline to the right. Finally, the plaintiff's

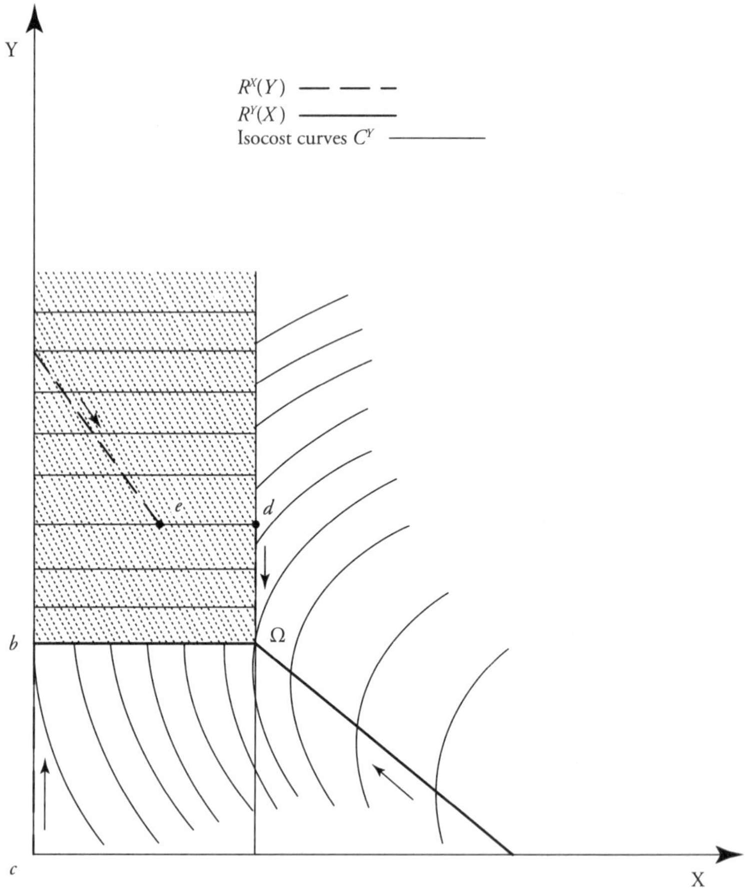

Figure 4

costs are lower at Ω than at *e*.[17] Therefore, the point on the defendant's reaction function that has the lowest cost is again Ω. Once again, the Stackelberg equilibrium is the Cournot–Nash equilibrium.

The results we have presented are obtained when the costs of direct transactions between the parties are effectively infinite. It is easily shown that the traditional common law rule is robust with respect to lowering transaction costs. In the absence of any transactions each party knows, from the preceding analysis, that the other party will go to Ω. Any move from Ω will increase social costs so whoever might

[17]To see this, note that $C^s(e) = C^x(e) + C^y(e)$ and $C^s(\Omega) = C^x(\Omega) + C^y(\Omega)$. But since $C^s(\Omega) < C^s(e)$ and $C^x(e) = C^x(d) = C^x(\Omega)$, it follows that $C^y(e) > C^y(\Omega)$.

benefit from such a move will not be able to compensate the loser for the move.

IV. A TAX ON EXTERNALITIES AND THE COMMON LAW RULE TOGETHER

Since taxes are not imposed nor administered by courts,[18] it is quite conceivable that the courts would not consider payment of the tax a defense against a negligence claim when the injured plaintiff sues for damages under the traditional common law rules. If liable under this tax-cum-liability rule, as in the shaded area of Figure 5, the defendant is billed for damages and taxed an amount equal to expected damages so his expected costs are

$$C^x(X, Y) = \alpha X + 2A[1 - P(X, Y)]. \qquad (10)$$

If the defendant is not liable his costs are given by (4). Regardless of the liability of the defendant, the plaintiff's private costs are given by (5). The reaction functions $R^x(Y)$ and $R^y(X)$ are as shown in Figure 5.[19] The Cournot–Nash equilibrium is at Ω.

The addition of the Pigovian tax to the traditional common law rules does not cause the Cournot–Nash equilibrium to move away from Ω. However, it does destroy the strategic properties of the rule. The rule is still strategy-proof when the defendant is leader since he is still best off at Ω. But when the plaintiff is a leader, the rule is no longer strategy-proof. Everywhere to the right of X^Ω the defendant's reaction function and the plaintiff's isocost curves are the same as under the pure Pigovian rule shown in Figure 1. Therefore, there is a distinct Stackelberg equilibrium at S_y as drawn in Figure 5. Thus the addition of a Pigovian tax leaves the traditional common law rule only partially strategy-proof. Furthermore, when transaction costs are lowered to zero there is incentive to bargain away from Ω and S_y. The relevant isocost curves are drawn in Figure 5. Trade will lead to a point on the contract

[18]Taxing powers are not administered by the common law courts.

[19]The derivation is similar to the derivation of the defendant's reaction function under the traditional common law rule. When the plaintiff does not meet the standard of care ($Y < Y^\Omega$), the defendant cannot be liable so his reaction function is the full cost reaction function below Y^Ω. Above Y^Ω he has the choice of meeting the standard or taking on liability and saving precaution costs. The only difference is that due to higher defendant private costs here the vertical segment of the reaction function will be longer and the other segment will be above the full-cost reaction function.

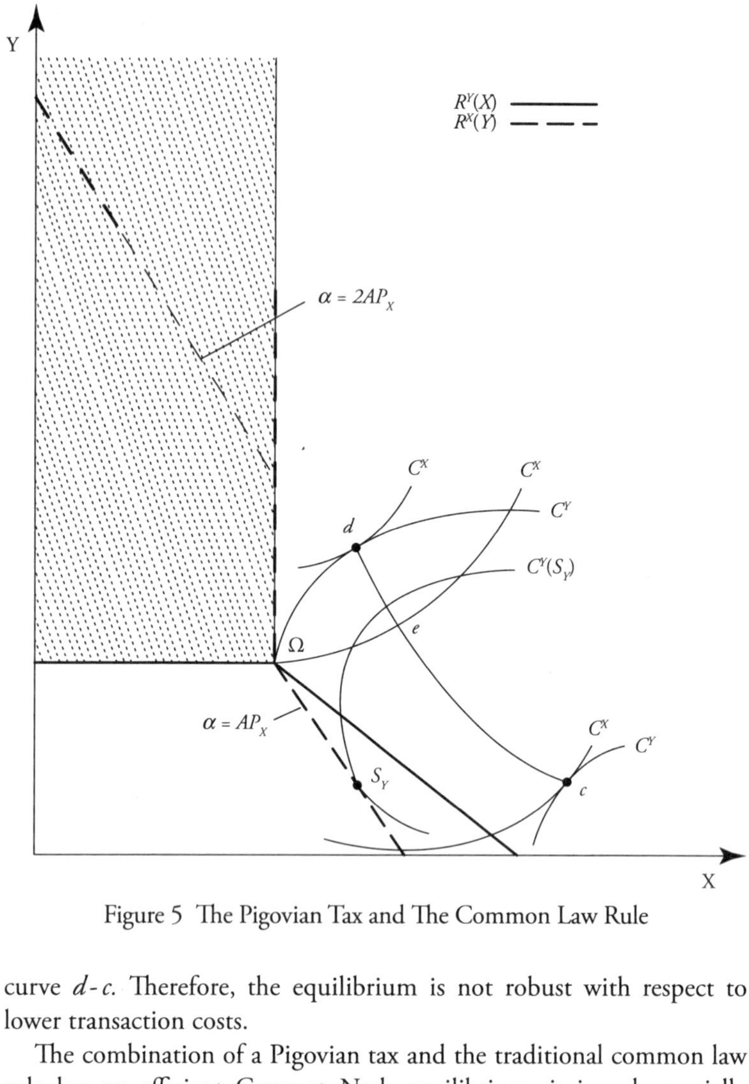

Figure 5 The Pigovian Tax and The Common Law Rule

curve *d-c*. Therefore, the equilibrium is not robust with respect to lower transaction costs.

The combination of a Pigovian tax and the traditional common law rule has an efficient Cournot–Nash equilibrium, it is only partially strategy-proof, and it is not robust with respect to lower transaction costs.

V. STRICT LIABILITY AND NO-FAULT RULES

In the last twenty years there has been a shift away from the traditional common law rule toward either strict liability or no-fault rules. Under strict liability, the plaintiff can collect damages from the defendant without regard to fault.[20] Under no fault, the injured plaintiff cannot collect damages from the defendant, regardless of circumstances.[21]

The plaintiff gains nothing by being a Stackelberg leader under strict liability because in any case his costs are zero and they cannot go lower. Similarly, there is no room for the defendant to be a Stackelberg leader, because no matter what he does he will have no effect on the precaution level chosen by the plaintiff. Therefore, neither party can gain by becoming a Stackelberg leader. The same is true under the rule of no fault because of the complete symmetry between the rule of strict liability and the no-fault rule. When transaction costs are zero under strict liability or no-fault, transactions will occur that will lead away from the inefficient Cournot–Nash or Stackelberg equilibrium to the social-cost-minimizing point Ω.[22]

VI. A TAX ON EXTERNALITIES WITH COMPENSATION OF VICTIMS

Another variant of the tax on externalities is to use the proceeds of the tax to pay victims for damages suffered.[23] The analysis of this variant is quite simple. The private costs facing both parties and hence the analytic conclusions are identical to those under the rule of strict liability.

VII. CONCLUSION

The results of this analysis can be presented conveniently in Table 1. To summarize, Pigovian taxes can be looked upon and analyzed as liability rules. The traditional common law rule and the Pigovian tax (as long as the proceeds are not used to indemnify the victim) are both efficient rules, separately or together. However, only the traditional common law rule is strategy-proof. Furthermore, the equilibrium

[20]This is indeed an oversimplification. Many of the so-called strict liability rules in fact have many elements of the traditional rule. However, it is useful for analytical purposes to consider the pure polar case of strict liability that is, as the name implies, strict.

[21]This too is simplified. None of the present state no-fault schemes are pure; they are full of limits and qualifications and lead to plenty of lawsuits.

[22]See Brown *supra* note 1.

[23]Effectively, accident costs are socialized. This is approximately the situation at present in New Zealand. The government takes responsibility for both parts of the accident problem: control of externalities and compensation of victims.

Table 1

Rule	Tax Equivalent	Efficient Rule ($\epsilon = \Omega$)	Strategy-Proof	Robust
Eye for an eye	Pure Pigovian	Yes	No	No
Traditional common law rule	None	Yes	Yes	Yes
Common law and Pigovian tax	None	Yes	Partially	No
Strict liability	Pigovian tax with indemnification	No	Yes	Yes*
No fault	None	No	Yes	Yes*

*Lower transaction costs will allow transactions toward Ω.

under the common law rule is robust with respect to lower transaction costs and that of the pure Pigovian tax is not. The Pigovian tax, with victim indemnification, like its strict liability rule analog, fortunately is not robust with respect to lower transaction costs; zero transaction costs allow trade from the inefficient equilibrium to the social-cost-minimizing point.

10

Strategic Behavior under Tort Law†

*Alfred Endres**

INTRODUCTION

The economics of tort law have been discussed in the literature within a number of alternative frameworks.[1] It has been shown that liability rules produce efficient incentives to take care only under very restrictive assumptions.[2]

An assumption common to all of the analyses of the economics of tort law given in the literature is that each of the involved parties takes the behavior of the others as given, i.e., there is no strategic behavior. In this paper, equilibrium care levels are analyzed, allowing the decision makers to realize their "oligopolistic interdependence" and to act strategically. A particular case is presented analogous to Stackelberg's oligopoly model.

†Originally published as "Strategic Behavior under Tort Law", 1992, *International Review of Law and Economics,* Vol. 12, pp. 377–80.

*I am indebted to two anonymous referees and to the editors for their helpful comments on an earlier draft of this paper. The manuscript was completed while I was a visiting professor at the University of Florida at Gainesville. Financial support provided by the German Marshall Fund of the United States is gratefully acknowledged.

[1]See the fundamental papers by J.P. Brown (1973); W. Landes and R. Posner (1981); and S. Shavell (1980a). The present state of the art is presented in W. Landes and R. Posner (1987) and S. Shavell (1987). For a brief exposition and analysis of the essentials, see R. Cooter and T. Uhlen (1988), pp. 326–71.

The case of non-pareto optimal standards without strategic behavior is analyzed in S. Shavell (1987) and A. Endres (1989).

Other complications in the economics of tort law, ignored in the paper at hand, are discussed in A.M. Polinsky and D.L. Rubinfeld (1988); S. Shavell (1980b, 1985); and E.A.C. Thomas (1985), among others.

[2]The strict liability rule, in order to be efficient, must be supplemented by a rule of contributory negligence. The standard defining due care for the victim has to be set at a pareto optimal level.

It is shown that firms may behave strategically if due care standards are set at suboptimal levels, and this behavior can help to correct the error made in setting the legal standard.

THE TRADITIONAL MODEL

I begin by describing the traditional model of strict liability with a defense of contributory negligence.

Consider one potential injurer *A* and one potential victim *B* who are strangers to each other. *A*'s (*B*'s) cost of care is $C_A(x)(C_B(y))$, where $x(y)$ is *A*'s (*B*'s) care level. The expected damages are $D(x, y)$.[3] Pareto optimal care levels x^*, y^* are defined by minimizing total expected cost, i.e., by

$$C = C_A(x) + C_B(y) + D(x, y) = \min \tag{1}$$

Denote the legal standard for the victim's care level $\bar{y}$, which may or may not equal y^*. *B*'s costs are

$$\begin{array}{ll} C_B(y) & \text{for } y \geq \bar{y} \\ C_B(y) + D(y, x) & \text{for } y < \bar{y}. \end{array}$$

Let $y(x)$ minimize the second of these expressions. Thus *B* solves

$$\min\,(C_B(\bar{y}), C_B(y(x)) + D(y(x), x)). \tag{2}$$

A's costs are

$$\begin{array}{ll} C_A(x) + D(y, x) & \text{for } y \geq \bar{y} \\ C_A(x) & \text{for } y < \bar{y}. \end{array}$$

Let $x(y)$ minimize the first of these expressions. Thus *A* minimizes costs by choosing

$$\begin{array}{ll} x = 0 & \text{for } y < \bar{y} \\ x = x(y) & \text{for } y \geq \bar{y}. \end{array} \tag{3}$$

An equilibrium is a pair of values for x and y that solves (2) and (3). It is well known that the optimal values x^* and y^* are the unique, stable equilibrium under standard convexity assumptions and under the assumption that the legal standard is efficient, $\bar{y} = y^*$. Furthermore, for modest departures of the legal standard from optimality, which I

[3] The standard assumptions in the literature on the form of these functions are $\delta C_A / \delta x > 0, \delta^2 C_A / \delta x^2 \geq 0,\ \delta C_B / \delta y > 0, \delta^2 C_B / \delta y^2 \geq 0, \delta D / \delta x, \delta D / y < 0,$ $\delta^2 D / \delta x^2, \delta^2 D / \delta y^2 > 0,\ \delta^2 D / \delta x \delta y > 0.$

call "moderately inefficient," it is well known that the equilibrium is $\bar{y}, x(\bar{y})$.[4]

A STACKELBERG MODEL OF STRATEGIC BEHAVIOR

Following the tradition of the literature, it has been assumed that each party takes the behavior of the other party as given. However, the equilibrium activity levels of each party depend upon what the respective other party does. It is possible that the parties involved realize their "oligopolistic interdependence" under tort law and adjust accordingly. Of course, many forms of oligopolistic strategies are possible.

A special case of interdependence is analyzed below. Here, the potential injurer realizes that the potential victim's equilibrium activity levels depend upon the levels of the injurer's activities. *A* is assumed to minimize cost, taking *B*'s reaction to his behavior into consideration. On the other hand, *B* is assumed to take *A*'s behavior as given and to adjust to this behavior in order to minimize cost.

These asymmetrical assumptions about the behavior of injurer and victim are analogous to the classical Stackelberg oligopoly model.[5] The behavior of *A* is the independence (leader) position, the behavior of *B* is the dependence (follower) position in Stackelberg's model. An application might be the case of a large firm whose accident risks threaten many small firms. The consequences of this particular form of strategic behavior under tort law are analyzed below.

I show that moderately inefficient standards may induce strategic behavior in the sense that the Stackelberg equilibrium is not a Cournot–Nash equilibrium, whereas excessively inefficient standards do not induce strategic behavior.[6]

Given the moderately inefficient standard $\bar{y}$ for the victim, there is a level $\hat{x} > 0$ of the injurer's care activity, rendering the victim indifferent between keeping and violating the standard $\bar{y}$. So the 'critical' care level $\hat{x}$ is defined by

[4]See the literature listed in note 1.

[5]H.v. Stackelberg (1934). Stackelberg's model has aroused some interest in the recent literature. See, e.g., S.V. Berg (1988); D. Levin (1988); and A.J. Robson (1990). A more elaborate treatment of the Stackelberg game under tort law is given in the working paper version of this note. See A. Endres (1990).

[6]The analysis is confined to the case of strict liability with a defense of contributory negligence in this paper. However, the conclusions regarding strategic behavior under inefficient due care standards do hold analogously for other liability rules.

$$C_B(\overline{y}) = C_B(y(\hat{x})) + D(\hat{x}, y(\hat{x})). \tag{4}$$

Below, $y(\hat{x})$ is denoted $\hat{y}$.

Since the right hand side of equation 4 is monotonically decreasing in x, it follows for $x \geq \hat{x}$, that B chooses to violate the due care standard $\overline{y}$ and to exercise his care activity at a level of $y(x) < \overline{y}$.[7]

$y = y(x)$ is B's 'reaction function', yielding the equilibrium level of y for any given level of $x \geq \hat{x}$.[8]

Now the potential injurer A considers whether it is worthwhile to induce B to violate the standard by choosing $x \geq \hat{x}$. A decides to do just that if

$$C_A(\overline{x}) + D(\overline{x}, \overline{y}) > C_A(\hat{x}) \tag{5}$$

holds.[9] In the case of (5) holding, the Stackelberg equilibrium $\hat{x}, \hat{y}$ prevails.[10]

The welfare consequences of moving from the traditional Cournot equilibrium to the Stackelberg equilibrium, explained in this paper, can be easily assessed:

Adding up the left hand sides and the right hand sides of (4) and (5) leads to:

$$C_A(\overline{x}) + C_B(\overline{y}) + D(\overline{x}, \overline{y}) > C_A(\hat{x}) + C_B(\hat{y}) + D(\hat{x}, \hat{y}) \tag{6}$$

The left hand side of (6) shows total cost in the Cournot–Nash equilibrium; the right hand side shows total cost in the Stackelberg equilibrium. Thus, according to (6) $\hat{x}, \hat{y}$ is pareto superior to $\overline{x}, \overline{y}$. So if A decides to behave strategically in the sense defined above, he increases welfare by inducing B to reduce B's excessive precaution.

Strategic behavior as analyzed here requires the due care standard $\hat{y}$ to be moderately inefficient. There is no incentive for strategic behavior if the due care standard is pareto optimal, or "excessively inefficient."

[7]Of course, given $x = \hat{x}$, B is indifferent between keeping and violating the standard. In the text above, it is assumed that B violates the standard in this "knife-edge" case. If the reader prefers to assume otherwise, the analysis in the text holds for $x > \hat{x}$ instead of for $x \geq \hat{x}$.

[8]It can be shown that it follows from the conditions specified in note 3 that B's equilibrium care goes down when A's care goes up, i.e., that $dy(x)/dx < 0$ holds for $x \geq \hat{x}$. (Symmetrically, A's equilibrium care goes down when B's care goes up.)

[9]$C_A(x)$ is monotonically increasing in x. Therefore, if A decides to induce B to violate $\overline{y}$ he will do so by choosing exactly $x = \hat{x}$ (and not by $x > \hat{x}$).

[10]It follows from note 8 that comparing the Stackelberg equilibrium care levels to the respective levels of the Cournot–Nash equilibrium leads to $\hat{x} > \overline{x}, \hat{y} < \overline{y}$.

In the case of a pareto optimal standard, the sum of expected costs of the injurer and the victim is minimal by definition. The victim secures compensation by meeting the standard. From this initial situation, it is impossible for the injurer to "strategically manipulate" his care activities in the manner discussed above: to secure *B*'s violation of the standard, strategic behavior would have to decrease *B*'s cost compared to the initial pareto optimal situation. To be attractive for *A*, strategic behavior would also have to decrease *A*'s cost compared to the initial pareto optimal situation. However, both requirements cannot be simultaneously met, since this would contradict the fact that the sum of the two costs is minimal in the initial situation.

On the other hand, if standards are "excessively inefficient," *B* ignores the standards of contributory negligence anyway (Endres 1989). So there is no need for *A*'s strategic behavior to induce *B*'s violation of the standard by "strategically" choosing his care level.

CONCLUSION

It has been shown that errors in setting legal standards in tort law may induce the parties to behave strategically. Furthermore, the equilibrium under strategic behavior is pareto superior compared to the equilibrium without strategic behavior. The improvement comes when strategy induces a party to depart from an inefficient legal standard.

BIBLIOGRAPHY

Berg, S.V. (1988). "Duopoly Compatibility Standards with Partial Cooperation and Standards Leadership." *Information Economics and Policy* 3: 35–53.

Brown, J.P. (1973). "Toward an Economic Theory of Liability." *Journal of Legal Studies* 2: 323–49.

Cooter, R., and T. Uhlen (1988). *Law and Economics, Glenview*. Ill.

Endres, A. (1989). "Liability and Information." *Journal of Institutional and Theoretical Economics* 145: 249–79.

—— (1990). "Strategic Behavior under Tort Law." Technical University of Berlin, mimeo.

Grady, F. (1983). "A New Positive Economic Theory of Negligence." *Yale Law Journal* 92: 799–829.

Landes, W.M., and R.A. Posner (1981). "The Positive Economic Theory of Tort Law." *Georgia Law Review* 15: 851–924.

—— (1987). *The Economic Structure of Tort Law*. Cambridge, Mass.

Levin, D. (1988). "H.v. Stackelberg, Cournot, and Collusive Monopoly." *Economic Inquiry* 26: 317–30.

Polinsky, A.M., and D.L. Rubinfeld (1988). "The Welfare Implications of Costly Litigation for the Level of Liability." *Journal of Legal Studies* 17: 151–64.
Robson, A.J. (1990). "Stackelberg and Marshall." *American Economic Review* 80: 69–82.
Shavell, S. (1980a). "Strict Liability versus Negligence." *Journal of Legal Studies* 9: 1–25.
—— (1980b). "An Analysis of Causation and the Scope of Liability in the Law of Torts." *Journal of Legal Studies* 9: 463–516.
—— (1985). "Uncertainty over Causation and the Determination of Civil Liability." *Journal of Law and Economics* 28: 587–609.
—— (1987). *Economic Analysis of Accident Law*. Cambridge, Mass.
Stackelberg, H.v. (1934). *Marktform und Gleichgewicht*. Berlin.
Stephen, F.H. (1988). *The Economics of the Law*. Brighton.
Thomas, E.A.C. (1985). "On Calculating Optimal Contributory Negligence Rules." *Social Choice and Welfare* 1: 65–85.

Law and Economics of Child Labor

11

Compacts, Conventions, and Codes

Initiatives for Higher International Labor Standards†

*Kaushik Basu**

INTRODUCTION

The International Labor Standards (ILS) movement is meant to be an initiative to promote better working conditions and higher living standards for workers in the Third World. It therefore seems baffling that the most vociferous opposition to ILS comes from the Third World, and not just from elite groups and government, but also from workers and grass roots activists. However, this opinion from the South, encountered all over developing countries gets little representation in international forums and global meetings. Is the dissent from the South based on the South's misperception of its own interests? Or is it founded on a realistic perception of global politics and power? The purpose of this essay is to argue the latter—that the Southern apprehension is understandable and to ignore this while drafting policy for the well-being of the workers will not only be an injustice, but it will give rise to global tensions and instability.

The contemporary world has seen a bewildering number of initiatives for ILS, the latest being the UN's Global Compact, which attempts to make big firms and corporations join hands in a voluntary contract to adhere to certain minimal labor standards. This stands in contrast to the effort of the International Labor Organization (ILO) to make *nations* ratify 'conventions,' which then require them to enforce minimal labor standards within their

†Originally published as "Compacts, Conventions, and Codes: Initiatives for Higher International Labor Standards", 2001, *Cornell International Law Journal*, Vol. 34, pp. 487–500.

*This article originated at the *Cornell International Law Journal* 2001 symposium.

national boundaries; and in even sharper contrast to the proposed plan to introduce a 'social clause' in the World Trade Organization (WTO) agreements, which would allow the international community to place trade sanctions on countries that violated minimal labor standards.

This paper will argue that, on the whole, the existing ILS initiatives are ill-conceived and likely to have undesirable fall-outs. This is true even though global opinion has become more sophisticated and nuanced in recent years and some of the more recent proposals, such as the UN Global Compact, are better than some earlier plans. For any ILS effort to succeed and to actually help those it is meant to help, it is imperative to take account of the opinions of developing nations. Accordingly, the paper ends with a discussion of global democracy.

In summary, it is argued that at this stage ILS is best left to individual nations and only a minimal global coordination, and, further, that this global coordination is best done through the ILO and the UN. The WTO, *the way it currently functions*, is not the appropriate body for enforcing labor standards. In the long run, there must be an effort to democratize global organizations and institutions, such as the WTO. Only when that is done, or at least when the process is reasonably underway, can global organizations be seriously entrusted with the task of promoting higher international labor standards.

I. THE ISSUES AND THE HISTORICAL BACKGROUND

Most people, when they think of labor standards, think of the law as its natural hand-maiden. If workers are to be better off, avoid excessively hazardous work, keep their children out of the workplace, and so on, our natural tendency is to think of the law as the natural instrument for achieving these. Thus we may think of direct laws (such as minimum wage legislation and the legal prohibition of child labor) and indirect laws, which enhance worker power (such as the right to bargain collectively) as essential instruments for raising worker welfare.

A large part of mainstream economics is a warning that this kind of reasoning is faulty. It reminds us that the absence of government action does not necessarily mean that labor standards will remain low. As productivity and the demand for labor rise, workers can achieve higher living standards through the forces of the market. The mere threat that a worker may quit his or her job could ensure that he or she will be paid well and not be exposed to excessive risks, made to work excessive hours, and so on. Of course, some economists go overboard and argue that the well-being of the worker can be left entirely to market forces.

In reality, there are two broad reasons why interventions may be called for. First, markets often fail because of externalities, asymmetric information, or the difficulties of monitoring, and we may need laws to correct for these failures. And even when markets do not fail, the market outcome may be more inequitable than we are willing to tolerate. Second, even when each nation prefers a higher labor standard this may be impossible to achieve unless several nations coordinate their behavior. When this happens, not only do governments immediately come into play, but the need arises for an internationally coordinated effort. The subject of International Labor Standards pertains to this second kind of intervention.[1]

The historical roots of the labor standards movement go far back into history, beginning with Sir Robert Peel's introduction of the English Factory Act of 1802, which is now treated as a landmark. The problem of inter-country coordination in the context of labor standards dates back to 1818, and in particular to the writings of Robert Owen, which were soon followed by the advocacy of numerous French intellectuals and activists.[2] Awareness of the inter-regional nature of the labor standards problem increased through the nineteenth century and early twentieth century as the federal government of the United States battled to curb inter-state competition and adopt common labor standards.[3] The U.S. historical experience nicely mirrors the current global problems.

In the U.S. the first child-labor legislation was enacted by the state of Massachusetts in 1837. Thereafter, different states brought in different legislation, often backing down for fear that firms and capital would leave and go to states where labor laws were more lax. Some of this history is nicely recounted by Florence Kelley.[4] The openness of this inter-government competition is transparent from the following account in her book:

[1]This view of ILS is explicit in Kaushik Basu, *International Labor Standards and Child Labor*, 42 Challenge 80, 89 (1999); Nancy H. Chau & Ravi Kanbur, The Race to the Bottom, From the Bottom (Cornell University, CEPR Working Paper No. 2687, 2000), *available at* http://www.arts.cornell.edu/poverty/Kanbur/ck15.pdf.

[2]*See* Stanley Engerman, *The History and Political Economy of International Labor Standards*, mimeo: Rochester University (2001), *available at* http://www.egdi/gov.se/pdf/study/studyl.pdf; *see also* Steve Charnovitz, *The Influence of International Labour Standards on the World Trading Regime: A Historical Overview*, 126 Int'l. Lab. Rev. 565 (1987).

[3]*See* Florence Kelley, Some Ethical Gains Through Legislation 3–104 (1905).

[4]*See id.; see also* Carolyn M. Moehling, *State Child Labor Laws and the Decline of Child Labor*, 36 Explorations Econ. Hist. 72, 74–78 (1999).

For lack of uniformity, progress has been hindered in many states, notably in the glass industry which, during 1904, successfully represented to the legislature of New Jersey that, if deprived of the privilege of employing boys under the age of sixteen years at night, it would migrate to Delaware and West Virginia, where no such restrictions yet await it.[5]

The inter-state competition came to an end as recently as 1938 with the passing of the first nationwide law in the U.S. to monitor labor standards—the Fair Labor Standards Act.[6]

After the Second World War, and especially in the last one or two decades, as the process of globalization gathered momentum and labor and capital, began to move more freely across nations, the labor standards concern spilled beyond national and regional boundaries and became properly an international matter. Ever since the formation of the International Labor Organization (ILO) in 1919 there has been a forum for these international concerns. But for a long time the ILO was an ineffective body, with some doubts about its survival. Initially it had only 44 member nations. Membership grew slowly until 1946 when the ILO became an agency of the United Nations, and its membership grew rapidly thereafter. By 1969 it had 174 members.[7]

The globalization of these concerns led to the codification of labor standards. The standards were classified under four kinds of "rights": (1) *Basic Rights*, which included the right against involuntary servitude and injunctions against exploitative child labor and discrimination; (2) *Civic Rights*, which gave workers the freedom of association and collective bargaining rights; (3) *Survival Rights*, which ensured a minimum wage, accident compensation, and the right not to be exposed to excessive hazards; and (4) *Security Rights*, which placed restrictions on employers from firing workers and gave workers the right to retirement benefits.[8]

[5]Kelley, *supra* note 3, at 91.

[6]Jagdish Bhagwati, *Trade Liberalisation and 'Fair Trade' Demands: Addressing the Environmental and Labor Standards Issues*, 18 World Econ. 745 (1995).

[7]Engerman, *supra* note 2.

[8]Alejandro Portes, *When More Can be Less: Labor Standards, Development, and the Informal Economy, in* U.S. Department of Labor, Labor Standards and Development in the Global Economy 219 (1990); Keith E. Maskus, Should Core Labor Standards be Imposed Through International Trade Policy? 4–7 (The World Bank, Development Research Group, Policy Research Working Paper, 1997); Nirvikar Singh, *The Impact of International Labor Standards: A Survey of Economic Theory*, mimeo: University of California, Santa Cruz (2001), *available at* http://www.egdi.gov.se/pdf/study/study2.pdf.

Resisting the tendency for proliferating labor standards and recognizing that if the same standards are to be imposed on all regions, from sub-Saharan Africa to Western Europe, the requirements have to be fairly minimal, there has now emerged what is often referred to as the list of 'core labor standards.'[9] These consist of (1) prohibition of forced labor, (2) prohibition of discrimination in employment, (3) right to freedom of association, (4) right to bargain collectively, and (5) prohibition of exploitative child labor.[10]

While the core labor standards are much more reasonable and realistic, the crux of the matter is not the agreement, in the abstract, of the importance of these minimal standards—most reasonable people will accept these—but the practical interpretation of these precepts and the methods used to implement them.

II. EXISTING INITIATIVES AND THEIR SHORTCOMINGS

There are two broad classes of global actions that have been used thus far to promote higher ILS. Following my earlier usage,[11] I shall call these *extra-national* and *supra-national* actions.

Extra-national action is action taken by a nation within its own territory that creates incentives in other countries to improve ILS. An example of an extra-national action is Harkin's Bill, more formally known as the Child Labor Deterrence Act, which has, fortunately, remained a bill.[12] The aim of this bill was to enable the United States to put a ban on any import that has a child labor input. The law works within the United States but creates incentives in other nations to keep children out of the labor force because nations who do not do so will be prohibited from exporting to the United States. One can go further and argue that children should be empowered as actors in the process of decision-making concerning their own rights.[13]

[9]For discussion, see Kenneth A Swinnerton, *An Essay on Economic Efficiency and Core Labour Standards*, 20 World Econ. 73, 76–84 (1997).

[10]*Id.*

[11]Kaushik Basu, *Child Labor: Cause, Consequence, and Cure, with Remarks on International Labor Standards*, 37 J. Econ. Literature 1083 (1999).

[12]S. 613, 103rd Cong. (1993).

[13]This is argued by Jo Boyden & Deborah Levinson, Children as Economic and Social Actors in the Development Process (EGDI Working Paper No. 1, 2000), *available at* http://www.edgi.gov.se/pdf/workpaper.pdf.

The weakness of the bill is its failure to recognize that (1) parents do not typically send their children to work out of sloth but out of desperation, and (2) it is possible for children to suffer a worse fate than labor, such as starvation. In the poorest nations an abrupt halt to child labor is likely to cause children to suffer acute poverty and hunger.[14] Clearly, we must not be so single-minded in eradicating child labor that we are prepared to do so by making children starve. Additionally, this kind of extra-national action is likely to drive children away from the export sector to other sectors, which may be worse for the children's welfare. There is now mounting evidence from Nepal's carpet industry and Bangladesh's garment industry that the anticipation of legislative and other punitive actions by industrialized nations has driven children away from labor to prostitution.[15]

The trouble with such bills is that even if they are inspired by a genuine concern for workers in the South, as they often are, they enable protectionism in the North. Interestingly, while the current versions of the Harkin's bill appeal only to the welfare of the child in motivating the legislation, the early versions of the bill had open reference to the fact that child labor in the Third World may cause unemployment in the North.[16] An implication of the analysis in this paper is that more effective solutions would attack child labor at a nationwide level, rather than in the exports sector alone.[17]

A supra-national action is an action undertaken by a *collectivity* of nations to sanction against the violation of minimal labor standards.

[14]There is a lot of evidence that it is poverty that drives households to send their children to work. For cross-country evidence, see Alan Krueger, *International Labor Standards and Trade, in* The World Bank, Annual World Bank Conference on Development Economics 1996 (Michael Bruno & Boris Pleskovic eds., 1997). And for evidence based on inter-temporal micro data, see Eric Edmonds, Will *Child Labor Decline with Improvements in Living Standards*?, mimeo: Dartmouth College, *available at* http://www.dartmouth.edu/-eedmonds/vnivc.pdf, and see also *infra* note 29.

[15]*See* UNICEF, *Girls in Especially Difficult Circumstances: An Action Report*, Kathmandu: UNICEF; Drusila Brown et al., *US Trade and other Policy Options and Programs to Deter Foreign Exploitation of Child Labor* (University of Michigan, Discussion Paper No. 433, 1999), *available at* http://www.spp.umich.edu/RSIE/workingpapers/wp.html.

[16]A superior extra-national legal action is the Sander's Amendment of the Tariff Act of 1930, which seeks to ban imports of goods that use *forced* child labor. This move towards distinguishing between different forms of child labor is a move in the right direction.

[17]*See* Kaushik Basu & Pham Hoang Van, *The Economics of Child Labor*, 88 AM. Econ. Rev. 412 (1998).

Two prominent examples of supra-national actions are the UN Global Compact and the various ILO conventions. In the case of the Global compact, companies voluntarily agree to abjure certain practices. In the case of the ILO conventions, countries commit to adhere to certain standards. The important difference between these two voluntary schemes is that they place the primary responsibility of ILS on different agencies. The Global Compact places the responsibility on multinationals and big corporations while the ILO conventions place the responsibility on the nations, and primarily the Third World nations since these are the potential violators of the standards.

Perhaps the most potent form of supra-national action contemplated is to have a social clause in the WTO provisions, which would allow the WTO to impose trade sanctions on an erring country.[18] The risk of empowering the WTO thus is that this will become a powerful instrument of protectionism in the North.[19] Powerful lobbies may have already misused similar well-meaning legislation.[20] An interesting case in point is the use of the Sander's Amendment against the Brazilian company Sucocitrico Cutrale.[21] The charge was that the company was using children to pluck oranges. However, as the *Wall Street Journal* pointed out this was probably an act of reprisal headed by the Teamsters Union against Cutrale for downsizing some Minute Maid plants it had bought from Coca-Cola Co. in Florida.[22]

The problem is not just that the power of the WTO will be misused, but that, as things stand, it is likely to be used disproportionately by industrialized nations against developing countries simply because the latter do not have the resources—money or expertise—to fight out cases in Geneva. Hence, the across-the-board negative reaction of developing countries to the idea of empowering the WTO seems to have some basis.

[18]Robert Staiger, The International Organization and Enforcement of Labor Standards, mimeo: University of Wisconsin, *available at* http://www.egdi.gov.se/pdf/study/study4.pdf.

[19]Much has been written about the dangers of giving WTO the power to uphold ILS. E.g., Jagdish Bhagwati, *Trade Liberalisation and 'Fair Trade' Demands: Addressing the Environmental and Labour Standards Issues,* 18 World Econ. 745 (1995); *see also* T.N. Srinivasan, *International Trade and Labor Standards from an Economic Perspective, in* Challenges to the New World Trade Organization (Pitou van Dijck & Gerrit Faber eds., 1996).

[20]Matt Moffett, *Citrus Squeeze: U.S. Child-Labor Law Sparks a Trade Debate Over Brazilian Oranges,* Wall St. J., September 9, 1998, at A1.

[21]*Id.*

[22]*Id.*

Faced with these criticisms, there is a groundswell of opinion in the industrialized nations, at least among the intelligentsia, to use more informal, and therefore flexible, arrangements to raise labor standards.[23] What has caught a lot of the liberal attention is the idea of 'product labeling,' that is, to have stickers on 'suspect' goods that declare these goods are "child labor free" or, more generally, produced under circumstances that meet a minimal ILS.[24] Hence, the ultimate decision whether or not to boycott such a product is left as a decision of individual consumers. In fact the UN Global Compact is likely to have a very similar effect. By publicizing the list of companies that are signatories to this compact it can create a sense among consumers about which companies meet minimal labor standards and consumers can then boycott the others or buy from them only when there is a substantial price advantage.

Such informal schemes can be deeply unfair. There is, first of all, the large question of whether moral judgements ought to be dispensed through the markets. At first sight, this may appear to be an instance of consumer's sovereignty. But a preference against a carpet that uses child labor is not quite the same thing as one's preference for red apples or against green apples. The former is intimately tied to the urge to sanction a certain kind of behavior. It is a moral preference of a particular kind, which may be called a "sanctioning preference."

While social sanctions do play important roles in civic life, it is not obvious that they are always the right method for dispensing justice. And there is good reason for this. When we express an interest in one good over another as a form of our sanctioning preference, our aim is not just

[23]For a very interesting suggestion of how to organize a flexible system, see Archon Fung et al., *Realizing Labor Standards: How Transparency, Competition, and Sanctions Could Improve Working Conditions Worldwide*, Boston Rev., Feb./Mar. 2001, at 4. Their scheme shares the spirit of the UN Global Compact in one respect—they both place the primary responsibility for upholding standards on the corporations. However, the scheme does have important flaws. *See, e.g.*, Pranab Bardhan, *Some Up, Some* Down; Robin Broad, A *Better Mousetrap*?; Mark Levinson, *Wishful Thinking*; David Moberg, *Union and the State*; Guy Standing, *Human Development*; Heather White, *Educating Worker*, and Kaushik Basu, *The View from the Tropics, in id.*

[24]For analyses of product labeling, see Drusilla K. Brown, A *Transactions Cost Politics Analysis of International Child Labor Standards, in* Social Dimensions of U.S. Trade Policy (Alan V. Deardorff & Robert M. Stern eds., 2000); Arnab K. Basu et al., Guaranteed Manufactured without Child Labor (Department of Agricultural, Resource, and Managerial Economics, Cornell University, Working Paper 2000–04, 2000); S.L. Bachman, *The Political Economy of Child Labor and Its Impact on International Business*, 35 Bus. Econ. 30 (2000).

to gratify a personal hedonism, but to punish or reward some people (for instance, those involved in the production of a certain good who, in the process, violate or adhere to certain standards). But what we really want is that those who violate certain standards should be punished to a certain degree, for instance, by losing a certain percentage of their business—say 40%. But there is no way for a *single* consumer to express this preference in the market. If he boycotts the good in an effort to hurt the producer and all those involved in the manufacture of a certain product, how does he know that all other consumers will not do the same and so end up drying up 100% of the business, instead of exactly 40%? Likewise, when a consumer decides to buy a particular brand name to reward the manufacturer a certain amount, there is no way to ensure that the right amount of consumers will do the same and so the reward will be commensurate with the good act. In brief, there is a huge coordination problem in the dispensing of justice that cannot be solved by the atomistic decisions of thousands of individual consumers.

Hence, punishments dispensed through informal social sanctions often turn out to be witch-hunts causing disproportionate pain to some and too little pain to others. Not surprisingly, when it comes to justice, most societies prefer to use a centralized, non-democratic system, namely, that of the courts and the judiciary. The free market is not the right instrument for passing moral judgements.

More specifically, the method of product labeling has the disadvantage of being too blunt an instrument. It treats all countries on par. Take, for instance, child labor. Some sub-Saharan African countries, such as Ethiopia, have a huge dependence on child labor, with close to 45% of all children in the age group 10 to 14 years working. On the other hand, in most Asian countries, including China and India, the participation rates are much lower (respectively 11% and 14%).[25] If consumers in industrialized nations begin to totally boycott goods with a child-labor input, it is arguable that some of these countries where the participation rates are low will suffer, but be able to withstand the boycott. On the other hand, for several African countries and even some Asian and Latin American countries—the poorer ones—there may be a major adverse impact on the economy, causing a disproportionate suffering for all, including the children, who were meant to be protected by this action.

[25]These and other statistics were compiled by the ILO in Economically Active Populations: Estimates and Projections, 1950–2010 (International Labor Organization CD-ROM, 1996).

Additionally, this action is likely to be biased in favor of large manufacturers. Consider a small producer of soccer balls in Pakistan. For him the production unit is likely to double up as factory shed and bedroom. For such a producer to persuade a labeling agency that it does not use child labor and so should get a label will be very hard, since the children are never far away from the areas of production. On the other hand, a large producer can centralize its production and prevent children from even entering the factory. This is in fact exactly what Reebok International has done in Sialkot, Pakistan.

Finally, these informal methods of product boycott share the problem of extra-national action discussed above, which drive bad practices, such as the use of child labor, from the export sector of developing countries to the indigenous sectors where conditions are often worse.[26]

What then are we to do to improve labor standards?

III. RECOMMENDATIONS

One general recommendation for upholding labor standards that economists make is the importance of keeping trade channels from the Third World open. It is the greater demand for goods from the Third World that translates into a higher demand for labor, which raises the bargaining power of workers. This argument has been made so many times[27] that there is no reason to dwell on it beyond endorsement.

A related and more specific recommendation, in the context of child labor, is for policies that improve conditions in the adult labor market. While some early work held parents responsible for child labor, it was argued in Basu and Van that a child's non-work is likely to be a luxury good in a household's decision-making.[28] In other words, parents do not like to send their children to work if they can help it; it is only when

[26]For an interesting study in the context of Bangladesh of how global monitoring can backfire, see Naila Kabeer, The Power to Choose: Bangladeshi Women and Labour Market Decisions in London and Dhaka (2000).

[27]E.g., Avinash Dixit, *Comment on A Transactions Cost Politics* Analysis *of International Child Labor Standards, in* Social Dimensions of U.S. Trade Policy (Alan V. Deardorff & Robert M. Stern eds., 2000); Saqib Jafarey & Sajal Lahiri, Will *Trade Sanctions Reduce Child Labour? The Role of Credit Markets*, mimeo: University of Essex.

[28]*See supra* note 17; *see also* Swinnerton et al., The *Economics of Child Labor: Comment*, 89 Am. Econ. Rev. 1382 (1999). Very different kinds of problems arise with street children, but unfortunately on this there are as yet few studies, an exception being William Myers, *Alternative Services for Street Children: The Brazilian Approach, in* Combatting Child Labor (Assefa Bequele & Jo Boyden eds., 1988).

they are driven by acute economic hardship that they send their children to work.[29] This argument does not deny that there are exceptions in the form of abusive parents who buy their own leisure by making their children work and that other factors, such as the availability of decent schooling, have a large influence on the incidence of child labor. But in general, when child labor is a mass phenomenon, as in contemporary developing countries, it is wrong to equate child labor with child abuse. It follows that a policy for eradicating child labor should treat the parent as an ally in this task rather than an adversary. Hence, if we can intervene to reduce adult unemployment and raise adult incomes, parents on their own will withdraw children from the labor market. There will be no need to use the stick to achieve this. So, somewhat paradoxically, the one policy always worth using to combat *child* labor is to improve the conditions of *adult* labor.

All these policy interventions through the market are desirable but will clearly take a lot of time to implement. Even if we use them in the long run, we have to think of more direct interventions in the short run. What should these be? We have seen above how it is likely to be better to rely on conventions such as the ones adopted by the ILO or compacts such as that of the UN, rather than to use the social clause of the WTO. Yet even these are not good enough. Nor is it a good idea to leave sanctions to the consumers.

As things stand, the main agency for labor standards policy has to be with the national governments, which can tailor the policy to each nation's specific needs and context. Yet this alone is not enough, since labor standards have an important inter-country dimension. The tension is not between the North and the South but between the South and the South, as argued in Basu (1999) and Kanbur and Chau (2000).[30] With globalization it is now easier for capital to move from one country to another. It is only natural that when one developing country contemplates

[29]There is ample evidence for the luxury axiom. For empirical studies that shed light on this axiom see, for instance, Ranjan Ray, *Child Labor, Child Schooling, and Their Interaction with Adult Labor: Empirical Evidence for Peru and Pakistan*, 14 World Bank Econ. Rev. 347 (2000); Sonia Bhalotra, Is *Child Work Necessary?*, mimeo: University of Cambridge (2000); Patrick Emerson & Andre Souza Portela, Is *There a Child Labor Trap? Inter-generational Persistence of Child Labor in Brazil*, mimeo: Cornell University (2000), *available at* http://econ.cudenver.edu/emerson/childlabor/pdf; Samuel Freije and Luis F. Lopez-Calva, *Child Labor, School Attendance, and Poverty in Mexico and Venezuela*, mimeo: Cornell University (2000).

[30]Basu, *supra* note 1; Chau & Kanbur, *supra* note 1.

raising a particular standard it has to worry that it may drive capital to another developing country.

This was borne out quite strikingly when, because of political reasons, the U.S. stopped importing carpets from Iran. With one developing country's exports cut off, another developing country took over the business. In this case, India became the largest exporter to the U.S. It is this very fear that exports will shift to another developing nation that ties the hands of individual governments of developing countries from taking more action. On the other hand, the chances of an export activity shifting from a developing nation to an industrialized nation because of the raising of labor standards are negligible because the two types of nations have such widely differing comparative advantages. There is therefore need for multi-country coordinated action, but the coordination has to be among the developing countries in their own collective interest.

Hence, we need a global organization to do the coordination. The difficulty stems from the fact that there is no organization that adequately represents the opinion and interests of developing nations. A prerequisite for handing over labor standards policy to an international organization is the democratization of the organization. Indeed, the WTO, in principle, could be an enforcer of ILS, *if* developing countries felt it represented their interest adequately. So, though for now we do not have too many options, other than relying on market-oriented policies, such as bolstering the demand for adult labor in developing nations and keeping open trade channels, and for some effort by national governments, there has to be a major effort to democratize international organizations, such as the WTO, so that they can then be entrusted with the important task of crafting and implementing policies for better labor standards.

The democratization of international organizations is a large topic. The concluding section of this essay is a brief incursion into this complicated subject.

IV. RESTRUCTURING INTERNATIONAL ORGANIZATIONS

One concomitant of globalization and technological progress that has either gone unnoticed or been hushed up by those who did notice it is that it has a natural corrosive effect on global democracy. As a consequence of this phenomenon, even if individual countries become democratic, the aggregate of global democracy may well be on the wane. Democracy entails many things—the existence of a variety of political and legislative institutions, avenues for citizens to participate in the formation of economic policies that affect their lives and, in the ultimate analysis, a certain mind-set. Yet at the core of it and in its simplest form, democracy requires (1) that people should have the right to choose those who rule them and (2) the principle that the vote of each person should count as much as another person's vote.

Note that globalization, almost by definition, means that nations and people can exert a greater influence on other nations and the lives of citizens in other nations. Moreover, this power of one nation to influence another is by no means symmetric. The U.S., for instance, can cut off virtually all the trade lines of Cuba. It can do so not only by curtailing its own trade with Cuba but by threatening punitive action against those who trade with or invest in Cuba. This is not just a hypothetical possibility; the Helms-Burton Act in the U.S. is testimony to how this can actually happen.[31] Cuba, on the other hand, can do little to hurt the American economy or polity. Likewise, China can do things to Taiwan, which Taiwan can in no way reciprocate.

As the world shrinks and powerful governments develop a variety of instruments and ways to influence the lives of citizens in other nations, it is no longer enough for people to be able to choose the leaders of their own nations. Since transnational voting does not happen (and even its hypothetical suggestion sounds absurd to us), globalization is bound to cause a diminution of global democracy.

Thanks to globalization there are a variety of instruments that nations can use to influence outcomes elsewhere. For the purposes of the current essay the most important is the cessation of international trade, such as would happen if the WTO were empowered to enforce ILS. International trade (after a slow-down in the years between the two World Wars) has risen steadily. These global linkages have fuelled unprecedented growth rates of national incomes (during the 1990s China grew at around 8% per annum and India 6.5%), but they have also created new vulnerabilities. Governments and international organizations can now use the threat of disrupting these flows (or the lure of releasing greater flows of money or goods) to enforce conformity to certain kinds of behavior. And such threats have been used. International organizations have given money while insisting that the developing countries fulfill certain conditions, many of which have had nothing to do with ensuring repayment. These conditionalities have,

[31] I have discussed the role and consequences of "triadic" threats in my *Prelude to Policital Economy: A Study of the Social and Political Foundations of Economics* (2000).

at times, even been contradictory, such as requiring the debtor nation to practice democracy and to privatize certain key sectors, unmindful of the fact that this may be against the collective wishes of the people.

Some of these conditions have been blatantly in the interest of the donor nation. In 1998, during the Asian crisis, the rescue package put together with money from several industrialized nations, most prominently Japan and the U.S., had clauses that required Korea to lift bans on imports of certain Japanese products (which Japan had long been trying to sell to Korea) and to open up its banking sector to foreign banks (an item that had long been on America's bilateral agenda with Korea). Some of these demands may well be good for the borrower, but that is not the issue here. From the point of view of assessing global democracy what is relevant is that people of the weaker nation have very little say in the imposition of these policies.

Given that the benefits of democracy are ample, as academic research has shown and non-academics always knew, this erosion of global democracy must have negative fall-outs. Indeed, it is arguable that the rise in global unrest and instabilities are a manifestation of this retreat of democracy. And the inchoate demands of the protestors in the streets of Seattle and Washington may be founded in an intuitive but ill-articulated perception of this erosion of democracy.

What can be done about the erosion of global democracy? Utopian schemes, such as a global government or a global bank that is answerable to all nations in the world, are a distant dream. The process of globalization will course on, and inter-country democracy will continue to get bruised. It will be some time before this can bring us to discussing global governance and banking. In the mean time, what is open to us are small measures, namely those of strengthening the democratic structure of global institutions, such as the World Bank, the IMF, and the WTO. These are small measures, but extremely important.

Therefore, the appropriate measures are, ironically, quite different from the dismantling of these organizations, which is what the protestors in Seattle and Washington, and also some arch conservative groups in industrialized nations, want. On the contrary, we need to restructure these organizations and recognize that they have an especially important role to play today. Of course there will be need for vigilance. There is enough evidence that powerful politicians in powerful nations like to think of international institutions as valuable only to the extent that they can use them to their own advantage.

On January 20, 2000, Senator Jesse Helms, arguably the most important congressional voice in the U.S., told the council members of the UN:

If the United Nations respects the sovereign rights of the American people, *and serves them as an effective tool of diplomacy, it will earn and deserve their respect and support.* But a United Nations that seeks to impose its presumed authority on the American people, without their consent begs for confrontation and, I want to be candid, eventual U.S. withdrawal.[32]

Helms went on to express distaste for "supranational institutions," including the international criminal court, which was created in 2000. What is most damaging about this kind of remark is that any organization that meets with Jesse Helms' approval immediately becomes suspect from the point of view of the world as a whole. The last thing that a credible international organization will now want is Jesse Helms' blessing. A WTO or a UN that has Helms' blessing and is entrusted with enforcing international labor and environmental standards will immediately be unacceptable to other nations, especially the developing countries whose interests are often orthogonal to that of industrialized nations.

We need to work to give nations, rich and poor, equal say, at least in international organizations that are supposed to play a mediating role in world economics or international relations. This horizontal equity is violated in most organizations through at least one of two routes. First, there is the open channel, which gives a larger share of votes to the nations contributing more to these organizations. This is certainly true of the IMF and the World Bank. The second route is through the lack of transparency of decision-making. One can see the importance of this for democracy by looking at policy-making within a country. If the process of decision-making is visible to all, it becomes difficult for any group or lobby to hijack the agenda. The same holds true for international organizations. Big and powerful nations, by virtue of contributing senior personnel and money to these organizations have much greater access to them. If decisions occur behind opaque walls powerful nations are much more able to divert the agenda to suit their own interests. Take the case of the WTO. While it does follow the important principle of one-country one-vote, it is widely perceived as a preserve of powerful and rich nations. This is in part because of what some analysts call the 'green room' process, that is, what goes on behind the scenes.[33] It is the green room where the agenda is set and what is to appear on the table for all member

[32]http://www.conservative.org/columnists/helms01202000.htm (last visited Oct. 10, 2001) (my italics—but also my hunch that those would be Helms' italics).

[33]See Jeffrey J. Schott & Jayashree Watal, *Decision Making in the WTO, in* Institute for International Economics, The WTO After Seattle, 283, 285–286 Jeffrey J. Schott ed., 2000).

nations to discuss and vote on is determined. Many of the end results are determined at that stage. If the WTO is to become a more democratic institution, it must not allow its green room to be hijacked by a few.

This problem is nowhere more obvious than in the drafting of international labor standards. These are ostensibly designed in the interests of the workers of developing countries. But the form that these standards are tending to take—and the increasing talk of using trade sanctions to impose these standards—is close to what protectionist lobbies in industrial nations seek. This is not surprising given the greater access that the lobbies of rich countries have in the corridors of power in international organizations.

Most sound surprised by this criticism of global institutions. The fact that the *questioning* of the practice of richer nations (who contribute more funds) exercising more voting power in these organizations sounds outrageous simply shows how far away we still are from *global* democracy. It does not at all seem outrageous that Bill Gates does not have multiple votes in the U.S. elections on the ground that he contributes more to government coffers. In fact, the suggestion that he could have more votes sounds outrageous. This is because democracy within a nation is a much more settled idea.

Fortunately, opinions change. Multi-nationals nowadays talk in terms of environmental responsibility and the importance of respecting labor standards, even when that implies taking a cut in profits. This seems to violate age-old beliefs and also the textbook description of multinational corporations. When the one-person one-vote idea first came about, the rich feudal landlords must have been shocked and cried foul at this blatant injustice and the chaos in the process of decision-making that this would cause. But no longer does this democratic principle *within a nation* seem strange.

Now, with the call for restructuring international organizations ringing out from the streets of Seattle and Washington and also congressional committees, such as the commission headed by Allan Meltzer,[34] this is a good time for us to think through some of these issues. We must consider these issues not just from the point of view of economic efficiency and greater cost effectiveness, but also from the point of view of representation of the poor. It is only when we manage to make these changes in the structure of international organization that we will be able to entrust them with important tasks such as monitoring labor and environmental standards across the globe.

[34] *Report of the International Financial Institution Advisory Commission* (2000), *available at* http://www.house/gov/jec/imf/meltzer.pdf.

12

Child Labor

Lessons from the Historical Experience of Today's Industrial Economies†

Jane Humphries

Fifty years ago it might have been assumed that just as child labor had declined in the industrial world in the late 19th and early 20th centuries, so, too, it would eventually disappear elsewhere. But child labor has not faded away (for estimates of child labor, see the International Labor Organization's LABPROJ database; for data on industrial countries, see Lavalette 1999). Endemic in today's poor countries, child labor seems to have reemerged in industrial countries as well, raising questions about its importance in national and regional economies and in family economic strategies. What have historians of today's industrial countries learned that may help answer these questions?

The first part of this article overviews the extent and settings of child labor in Western Europe and the United States in the past. Historians must rely on a quantitative record that is patchy and difficult to interpret. As a result, it may not be possible to say with confidence whether the era of proto-industry or the early factories saw the high-water mark of child labor, and the nature and time path of decline remains debated. Nonetheless, broad trends emerge that put the experience of today's poor countries into historical perspective and provide an empirical backdrop for the analysis in the second and third parts of the article, which seek to explain why child labor increased during industrialization and declined thereafter.

†Originally published as "Child Labor: Lessons from the Historical Experience of Today's Industrial Economies", 2003, *The World Bank Economic Review*, Vol. 17, pp. 175–96.

Four types of explanation are offered. The first focuses on developments within capitalist labor markets. It examines the effects of technology as well as managerial and trade union strategies on children's work. The second focuses on the parental decision to send children to work. Historical analyses discuss this decision in terms of family strategies and parent-child relations. Economic analyses focus on the possibility of divergent interests within households and the potential for agency problems with implications for underinvestment in children's human capital. Both historians and economists ask whether parents are altruistic or selfish. They seek to determine whether child labor always follows from parental egoism or whether there are conditions in which caring parents would send their children out to work. The third type of explanation relates to the legal and political stance of the state. The fourth focuses on social norms and beliefs about appropriate behavior.

I. CHILD LABOR DURING THE INDUSTRIAL REVOLUTION

How extensive was child labor in Western Europe and the United States in the past? Were children concentrated in particular jobs, or did they work in most occupations and sectors? How important were they to the industries in which they worked, and how much did they contribute to economic growth and development?

Investigating the importance of children's work involves difficult conceptual problems of defining work and determining who is a child. Measuring the extent of child labor in the past is particularly difficult because the data are often inadequate. The summary presented here supplements evidence from early censuses and industrial surveys with material from less conventional sources, such as household budgets and the memoirs and diaries of working people.

The earliest censuses in what are now industrial economies began too late to capture the extent of child labor during industrialization. They measured a phenomenon already in decline, and they undercounted child workers, especially outside child-intensive industries, such as textiles. In 1851, when the British census first recorded the occupations of young people, 97 percent of children age five to nine were without a "specified occupation"; beginning in 1881 the census no longer bothered to count working children in this age group. But by 1851 the Industrial Revolution was already more than 70 years old in Britain, and child labor had been the subject of (albeit imperfect) regulation for almost half a century. Not surprisingly, few very young workers were recorded, although children age 10–14 still often worked. The first relevant censuses in France and the United States were not conducted until the very end of the 19th century, by which point they, too, recorded few young children at work. For the era of industrialization, then, historians must rely on industrial surveys, household data, and other fragmentary evidence. What do such sources suggest?

Child labor was important in the early phases of industrialization, when large-scale production was a novelty, especially in textiles and mining. It was particularly important to the early starters on the path of industrial progress, notably Britain, Belgium, France, the western parts of Prussia, and the United States. For these early starters the intensive use of child labor in the key sectors of the Industrial Revolution was superimposed on children's employment in proto-industry and occurred in a cultural setting predisposed to "making children useful." The reduced wage costs must have played a role in the competitiveness of the key industries in the Industrial Revolution, although no study has measured the exact contribution of child labor.

A recent survey of the evidence on industry and mining in Britain reveals astonishingly high relative employment levels of children (under age 13) and young people (age 13–18) in textiles and coal mining in the early 19th century (Tuttle 1999). Children and young people made up one- to two-thirds of all workers in many textile mills in 1833, and they regularly represented more than a quarter of the workforce in mines in 1842.

Although Britain was exceptional in the intensity of children's work, the evidence for other early industrializers shows that child labor was not uncommon. A study of French workers in 1839–43 revealed that children under the age of 16 made up 12.1 percent of the labor force (Heywood 1988). Another, albeit not necessarily comparable, inquiry for Belgium in 1843 counted 10,514 child workers, or 19.5 percent of the workforce (De Herdt 1996). Goldin and Sokoloff (1982) estimate that in the Northeastern United States, women and children made up about 40 percent of the manufacturing labor force in 1832.

Household budgets for Britain from the precensus era provide further evidence that industrialization was associated with a boom in child labor (Horrell and Humphries 1995). Though children's contributions were always important, their relative contributions and participation rates were highest in the 1820s and 1830s. According to Horrell and Humphries, more than 10 percent of 5–9-year-old children and more than 75 percent of 10–14-year-olds were in the labor force. These participation rates exceed the rates recorded in the mid-Victorian censuses (which covered all children, not just children in working-class families) and those estimated for working-class mothers.

Working-class autobiographies also suggest an increase in child participation rates in Britain during industrialization (Humphries 2003b). Boys age 9–13 were more likely to work if born after 1790 than before and even more likely to work if born after 1820. In contrast, only a small proportion of five-, six-, and seven-year-olds worked in the late 18th and early 19th century. Boys age 14 and older almost always worked, both early and late in the Industrial Revolution.

Child labor was strategically crucial to the transition to factory production. Domestic industry and mining used large numbers of child workers, but it was factory jobs that witnessed the largest increase in child labor (Horrell and Humphries 1995; see also Galbi 1997).

U.S. household data for the end of the 19th century reveal the relatively high incidence of child labor among children of textile workers (Goldin and Parsons 1989). Autobiographical evidence for Britain from the precensus period also suggests that the children of factory workers started work at relatively young ages and had relatively high participation rates (Humphries 2003a). As population and employment in the factory districts grew in the early stages of the Industrial Revolution, the absolute number of children in work and the aggregate child participation rate rose.

Child labor in the early factories in Britain was associated with the apparently large-scale and long-distance movement of pauper apprentices. These wards of the state worked in isolated water-powered mills and endured punishing work and living regimes (Dunlop and Denman 1912). The potential for abuse spurred the passing of the Health and Morals of Apprentices Act in 1802, the first legal protection afforded to child workers (Engerman 2003). Orphaned and abandoned children also figured in the early factory labor force in France (Chassagne 1986) and Japan (Saito 1996). In the United States in the 18th century, the institution of pauper apprenticeship conveyed thousands of destitute and abandoned children into the labor force, although most were destined for agriculture and trades rather than factories (Murray and Herndon 2002).

The importance of child labor in the early mills and mines should not detract from its presence in other sectors, including agriculture, miscellaneous manufacturing, and services, where it was often hidden by the familial and informal nature of employment. Europe and the United

States remained primarily rural and agricultural through the 19th century, and agriculture provided most children's jobs as it did adult jobs (Sjoberg 1997). The most common first job in working-class autobiography was that of farm boy. Bird scarers, shepherds, and ploughboys were also common (Humphries 2003b; Maynes 1995). Where the family farm predominated, children's work was ubiquitous, though often hidden from census enumerators (Heywood 2001). Historians have used school attendance registers to reveal the regularity with which the sons and daughters of small farmers were withdrawn from school to help, as well as the wholesale absence of children in agricultural districts at harvest or haymaking time (Coombs and Radburn 1995). Such work was tolerated, even approved, because of its family context or seasonal duration, and a blind eye was often turned in its direction even after legal prohibition. Farm service, common across Europe, in which young people aged between 12 and 14 were sent to live and work away from home, evaded censure because of its family setting and parallels with apprenticeship. But a rosy interpretation is sometimes at odds with reported experience (Humphries 2003b). Generally, the larger, more commercial, and more capitalist the setting of children's agricultural work, the less tolerant both contemporaries and historians have been in judging it, with the gang work performed in the eastern counties of England in the mid-19th century representing the nadir (Kitteringham 1975).

In industry, too, child labor was entrenched in traditional sectors and small-scale production units as well as factories and mines. A common first job, often taken at a very young age in proto-industrial families, was winding bobbins for hand loom weavers (Humphries 2003b). In miscellaneous manufacturing, children were important in silk, bricks, small-scale metal manufactures, garments, and footwear. In services, boys were employed running errands, delivering messages in offices, and working as monitors in schools. For girls, child-minding and domestic service remained the foremost employment in most European countries in the 19th century (Coninck-Smith, Sandin, and Schrumpf 1997). It remains unclear whether work in these more traditional jobs was less intense or harsh than work in factories or mines.

Although children's participation was not sustained at the levels characteristic of the crucible of the Industrial Revolution, child labor did not rapidly disappear, as some historians have suggested (Nardinelli 1990). Child labor was not a dinosaur, perfectly adapted to early industrial conditions but then driven rapidly to extinction when times changed.

Tuttle (1999) notes that in all British textile industries, the proportion of the workforce under age 18 was close to 50 percent for the entire period 1835–50, long after the initial phase of factory production, when rural water-driven mills relied on child paupers. Children also worked in most mines from 1800 to 1850, often representing 20–50 percent of workers. Children remained an important part of the workforce in more traditional jobs in agriculture, manufacturing, and services as well. Autobiographical evidence suggests that only the cohort born after 1850 was able to delay entry into work.

The decline of child labor began in Britain and other early starters around 1850. As with the boom in child labor, which affected young but not the youngest children disproportionately, the withdrawal of child workers was also age-specific. The youngest child workers, age five to nine, never very common in the labor force, were the first to go, disappearing from the workforce by the time modern census enumeration began. The withdrawal of children age 10–14 came later, accelerating after 1870. In 1851, 30 percent of 10–14-year-olds worked; by 1901 the figure had fallen to just 17 percent (Lavalette 1999). This withdrawal of children by age represents the first stage in the "adulting" of the labor force, as Cunningham (2000) calls it. The systematic undercounting of child workers in the censuses of the mid-19th century means the decline may be underestimated. When the U.S. census finally counted child workers at the end of the 19th century, it found only 17 percent of 10–14-year-olds gainfully employed (Trattner 1970). The French census of 1896 found only 20 percent of children this age working (Heywood 1988). Most of the working children in this age band would have been 13 or 14. The era of extensive child labor was over.

Superimposed on the disappearance of young children from the labor force was a redistribution of older working children. By the late 19th century, children in the industrial economies no longer participated in the key industries in which they had been so important (Winstanley 1995). Children also began to withdraw from miscellaneous manufacturing industries (Schrumpf 1997). They were not involved in the newer industries developing in the early 20th century and the interwar years. But the retreat of children from industry did not signal the death knell of child labor. For one thing, the retreat was uneven; for another children were removed to "a distinct and marginalized children's labor market" (Cunningham 2000: 409; see also Childs 1992; Solberg 1997).

In textiles and mining in the heyday of child labor, although some children did the same work as grown-ups (as Tuttle 1999 notes), most children held distinct jobs. But they were distinct jobs within key industries. By the early 20th century, children had been excluded from such industries and were increasingly confined to the service sector and to child-only jobs. Thus by the 1911 census in Britain, more than one-quarter of employed boys under age 15 worked as messenger boys. As Cunningham (2000) notes, these jobs were not only reserved for children but also marginal to the economy (see also Childs 1992).

It is important not to overemphasize this transition. Earlier censuses had also recorded large numbers of boys in industrial service, many of whom were messengers or office boys (Booth 1886). Messenger boys were also numerous among autobiographers, representing 7 percent of an early industrial sample of 506 boys whose first job was known, the second most commonly recorded job (Humphries 2003b). But there is no doubt that this shift represents a distinct and important second stage in the adulting of the labor force and one not confined to the vanguard economies. In Norway, children worked in agriculture, tobacco, and glass manufacture in 1875; by 1912 they worked mainly as newspaper boys (Schrumpf 1997). By the 20th century much of children's work was part-time and thus not incompatible with school attendance. As half-timers in the mills, they clung on in a traditional industrial job, but most part-timers worked in the service sector, working in shops, delivering goods, and running errands.

The history of child labor illustrates the danger involved in drawing simple parallels between the industrializing economies of the 19th century and developing economies today. Once considered a paradigm case, the British Industrial Revolution now appears to be shot through with peculiarities (Crafts 1985). One such peculiarity is the extent and duration of child labor, which was greater in Britain than in any other 19th-century industrializer or indeed developing area today. Belgium, another early industrializer whose transition was also heavily based on coal and textiles, ranks a distant second (De Herdt 1996).

Historical comparisons are problematic because of the difficulties of measuring child participation and converting 19th-century income levels into 1992 U.S. dollars. Nevertheless, the gap between the level of child labor in 19th-century Britain and developing economies today is sufficiently large as to dominate the likely effects of computational errors (see figure 1, which compares historical and present-day experience). The greater use of child labor in the British case complements current reinterpretations of the Industrial Revolution as involving, at least in its early stages, an increase in labor input ("an industrious revolution") rather than an increase in productivity (Crafts 1985; De Vries 1994). The

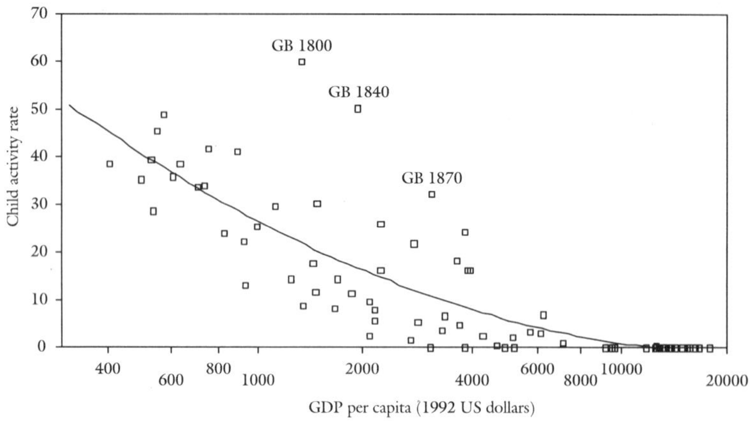

Figure 1: Child Labor and GDP per Capita

Note: 1870 data are for boys only.

Source: Krueger (1997); historical observations based on Crafts (1985), Horrell and Humphries (1995), and Humphries (2003b).

apparent restraint shown by today's developing economies in comparison with the first industrial nation affords grounds for guarded optimism.

II. EXPLAINING THE INCREASE IN CHILD LABOR

What explains the importance of child labor during the Industrial Revolution, particularly for early starters? Why was the phenomenon so widespread in Britain, the first industrial economy?

Development of the Capitalist Labor Market

The older literature, with its fixation on the employment of children in mills and mines, emphasized technology. Steam power and machinery allowed women and children to take over work that had previously required the strength and skill of men (Nardinelli 1990). Industrial technologies differed in terms of opportunities to employ children (Horrell and Humphries 1995; Goldin and Parsons 1989). For some of these technologies, child labor appeared essential. Early wooden textile machinery that had to be close to the ground may have dictated child-intensive employment (Tuttle 1999). The narrowness of underground passages in both British and Belgian thin-seam pits hindered the mechanization of transport and so maintained the demand for child drawers, who dragged the coal from the face to the surface (Humphries 1981). But the child intensity of technology cannot be taken as exogenous. As Bolin-Hort notes, "The relationship between technology and child labor was reciprocal rather than one-sided" (1989: 17). Certainly some early machinery was specifically constructed to be used by children to reduce labor costs, as the study of British patents reveals (MacLeod 1988).

The importance of child labor varied significantly across regions, even when the same technology was used (Bolin-Hort 1989). The Waltham system of textile production in New England in the mid-19th century employed young women rather than children, whereas high proportions of children worked in Lancashire. In a sample of 43 Manchester mills, 22.3 percent of the workforce was under age 14 and 32.4 percent under age 16; in 29 mills in Glasgow, 35.6 percent the workforce was under age 14 and 48.3 percent under age 16 (Bolin-Hort 1989). In Alsace in the 1820s, more than a third of mill workers were under age 16 (Heywood 2001).

Firms combined the same technology with different compositions of adults and children. In the Ghent cotton industry, the large firm of Voortmans recruited women and children (Scholliers 1996). In 1842 just 3.7 percent of Voortmans' labor force was under age 15; by 1859 that proportion had risen to 10 percent. But although Voortmans' use of child labor was exceptional for Ghent, it was modest in comparison with elsewhere. Technology was only one item in a list of important determinants of the proportion of child workers; the list included the availability of children, industrial organization, the employment strategy of manufacturers, and the strength of labor organizations representing men.

The organization of the labor process had both direct implications for the demand for child labor and indirect implications through its influence over technology, employment strategies, and labor relations. Goldin and Sokoloff (1982) argue that in the Northeastern United States, innovations such as a more elaborate division of labor, a more disciplined working environment, and a larger scale may have been just as important as technological change in creating the surge in the demand for female and child labor associated with industrialization. In Britain organizational change promoted the employment of women and children by breaking down customary age and gender divisions in the workplace and undermining the power of labor organizations to defend such customary barriers (Berg and Hudson 1992). The neglect of organizational initiatives in promoting child labor is consistent with researchers' overemphasis on factory production of textiles, for these innovations were particularly important in miscellaneous manufacturing, such as boot, shoe, glass, and paper manufacturing, where children's work has been underestimated.

Far from always following the substitution of machinery for muscle power, children's work was often the consequence of failed or incomplete mechanization. Thus the expansion of child labor in coal mining was the result of increasing output in the absence of changed transport technology. In a swathe of diffused and workshop-based industries outside the celebrated example of textile production, partial mechanization created new jobs for boys and girls. Lathes and presses, along with many simple machines, needed boys to feed them.

Manufacturers' strategies also increased child labor. The older literature documents the turning of British manufacturers to child labor in the context of the labor shortages of the Napoleonic wars (Hammond and Hammond 1925). The bellicose background of early industrialization in Europe may have contributed to the intensive use of child labor. In Britain one in 10 able-bodied men was in military service in 1794 (one in 6 by 1809); in France, Russia, and Austria probably about one in 14 prime-age men was under arms in the early 19th century (Cookson 1997). Military participation on this scale was totally new, and the effect on labor markets must have been substantial.

Manufacturers fended off government regulation of child labor by appealing to the need to keep labor costs low to compete internationally (Engerman 2003). Children's work was a necessary evil, essential to the competitive success of the key industries of the Industrial Revolution. Evaluation of the manufacturers' claim awaits counterfactual analysis of competitiveness without child labor.

Employers' strategies to reduce costs affected child employment levels. If employers had market power and children could be substituted for adults, their employment depressed adult wages. At the level of the household economy, this triggered a vicious circle, with lower adult wages increasing the need for children to work to maintain subsistence. The management of Voortmans pursued just such an employment strategy, making it effective even in a densely populated region, without recourse to paternalism (Scholliers 1996).

Labor relations also deserve mention. An older generation of historians emphasized the role that the emasculation of labor organization played in the boom in child labor. The Hammonds' (1925) chapter "The War on Trade Unions", which ends with the assertion that "the Combination Laws and the employment of children on a great scale are two aspects of the same system" (142), immediately precedes the chapters on child labor. Recent work has emphasized organized labor's resistance to the introduction of women workers and been less inclined to see trade unions as heroic. Perhaps the strategies of adult male workers should be reexamined in the light of the greater threat posed by competition from children and organized labor's inability to contain the surge in child employment (see also Cunningham 2000).

Family Strategies

Economic historians have studied the supply of child labor in the context of the household economy, analyzing the decision to send a child to work as part of a "family strategy." A family strategy involves a family acting as a single unit in the interests of all members. How these interests are identified and how possibly heterogeneous preferences are combined remains unclear. If parents do not care enough about the future welfare of their children, agency problems in human capital formation could occur within the household. In particular, selfish parents would prefer that their children work while the parents are alive and able to benefit from their children's labor. Children would overwork, and there would be underinvestment in their health, education, and training. Intervention to influence the household allocation of child labor and lifetime consumption of parents and children would be justified. Options include bans on child labor, compulsory schooling, or educational subsidies that relax the tradeoff between the current consumption of parents and the current education and future consumption of children.

But even altruistic parents may send their children to work. If the payoff to child labor in terms of the return to the physical investment of their earnings exceeds the return to human capital, the optimal strategy would involve child labor. If parents are too poor to meet the necessary expenditures of the household and cannot borrow against the future earnings of their children, dissavings in the form of child labor may be necessary for survival. Even if the family is not so impoverished, borrowing rates that are higher than lending rates shift the tradeoff between the value of schooling and child labor in favor of work, because the family receives the income flows earlier.

Which of these scenarios holds matters, because the optimal policy intervention differs in each case. If the family is so poor that children have to work, legislation would be difficult to enforce and could reduce children's well-being. In contrast, if parents are selfish, the case for intervention must rest on there being greater private than public returns to education, and subsidies to education would be the preferred policy.

The same would be true in the third scenario, in which subsidies could offset capital market imperfection.

Economists infer the altruism or selfishness of family members from outcomes in consumer goods markets. If parents are unhappy about children working, then controlling for prices, child labor should be associated with lower parental consumption. The intuition is that parents will equate the marginal utility of consumption to the marginal utility of child leisure, which is higher if children work.

Historians lack the household and consumption data needed for econometric investigation of the relationships between parents and children. A few studies have explored the links between child labor and household poverty, but the construction put on the findings depends on the assumptions. Goldin and Parsons (1989) use household data to investigate whether poor parents were altruistic toward their children in the United States in the late 19th century. They assume perfect capital markets, allowing resources to move freely across time and generations, and perfect labor markets, allowing families to move freely from one industrial center to another in response to labor and capital market conditions and parental preferences. Altruism (or costlessly enforceable intergenerational contracts) is combined with the capital and labor market assumptions in the rejected model. The negative correlation found between adult and child earnings can then be interpreted as indicating that parents were willing to accept large reductions in their own wages to secure employment in areas having abundant opportunities for child labor. The high savings out of children's earnings are held to be inconsistent with parents using child labor to offset borrowing difficulties alone. Goldin and Parsons conclude that parents did not have strong altruistic concerns for their children.

> The presence of industries with a high demand for child labor reduced the future wealth position of the offspring. Child labor had the obvious, almost definitional, negative effect on schooling attainment. At the same time the family provided little in the way of offsetting physical asset transfers (in the form of gifts and bequests) to compensate children for their lost schooling and future earnings. The increased family income was apparently absorbed in higher current family consumption. (Goldin and Parsons 1989: 657)

Horrell and Humphries (1995) do not explicitly consider the issue of altruism, though their findings are suggestive. They obtained expenditure data for a subset of families in the budget data set. These families were not saving—indeed, some ran deficits, which they financed by pawning or borrowing. Several received poor relief. Spending on food and rent dominated the budgets (Horrell 1996). These families were closer to subsistence than those in the sample investigated by Goldin and Parsons, and assumptions of perfect capital markets and household mobility are implausible. Thus the finding that fathers' earnings were negatively correlated with the likelihood of participation suggests that poverty was driving child labor. However, the high participation rates of children in the relatively prosperous factory districts suggests that in some situations the desire for consumer goods played a role (Horrell and Humphries 1995).

Traditionally, historians have explored parental altruism by examining evidence on the nature of the parent–child relationship. Parents have received bad press in much of the historical literature. "The further back in history one goes, the lower the level of child care, and the more likely children are to be killed, abandoned, beaten, terrorized and sexually abused," according to Lloyd deMause (1974:1); deMause may have been extreme in his denunciation of child-rearing in the past, but he was not alone in the 1970s and 1980s, when many historians perceived children as badly treated and parental love as fickle (Shorter 1977; Stone 1977; Badinter 1981). These historians considered the 18th century to have been an important turning point in the way in which children were perceived and treated.

Recently, historians have been less hasty to condemn parents and more careful to distinguish between practices that can be unambiguously condemned and those that are considered cruel or harmful today but were considered appropriate in the past. Pollock (1983) uses diaries and autobiographical material on parent–child relations to argue strenuously against any cultural shift or indeed the systematic ill treatment of children in the past. On the basis of working-class evidence given to various public inquiries, she concludes that parents largely did not send children to work for selfish reasons. In her view, poverty lay behind child labor.

In contrast, many observers during industrialization suggested that selfish and greedy parents sent their children to work, often instead of working themselves, using the children's earnings to buy goods such as alcohol and tobacco (for a summary of such views see Pinchbeck and Hewitt 1973; Pollock 1983; Nardinelli 1990). Of course, many of these commentators themselves employed children or shared the background and interests of employers who used child labor. In projecting these views, they sought to exculpate themselves and their peers by shifting the blame for what was increasingly seen as a reprehensible practice.

Working-class autobiographies of the period provide rare evidence from the child's perspective. Few children supported the charge of parental exploitation, instead seeing their parents as kind and caring. What, then, did these children think forced their entry into work?

Custom and practice undoubtedly played a role. Historians have condemned parents for expecting nothing better for their children than they experienced themselves (see Pinchbeck and Hewitt 1973), thereby locking the working class into a low-skill and early work intergenerational equilibrium. But investigation of the autobiographical evidence suggests that the main determinant of children's age at starting work was the family's economic circumstances, with father's earnings crucial (Humphries 2003b). Men in trades and clerical and service occupations constituted an aristocracy of labor, earning more than unskilled workers and enjoying greater regularity of earnings. Predictably, their children were withheld from the labor market longer than those of other workers (Humphries 2003b). Other workers could not always earn enough to ensure their family's subsistence without help from their children. Recent definitive estimates of real earnings show that solid increases did not occur until after 1850 (Feinstein 1998), a finding that is consistent with the apparent maintenance of high levels of child participation well into the 19th century.

Industrialization involved the rise and fall of sectors, technological change, shifts in the location of work, and an intensification of the business cycle. Even for skilled workers, earnings did not go up without interruption, as Feinstein's (1998) data show. Many fathers experienced short-term unemployment and stagnant wages. But it was hard to distinguish a temporary situation from something more permanent and to decide on an accommodation. Responding appropriately to fluctuations was often expensive, involving migration or retraining, and it was hampered by imperfect capital markets and lack of information. A holding strategy involved putting more family members to work, finding jobs for children. When hard times persisted, stopgaps became permanent. Sending children to work became normal and widely adopted by other desperate families. The generation of children sent to work early in response to shifts in the demand for labor had less opportunity to accumulate human capital, therefore becoming less productive and so less able to support its own children. In this way, demand shocks in the labor market echoed through the generations to hold the economy at low levels of productivity and high rates of child labor. Such added-worker effects characterized the prolonged competition between hand trades and factory production, promoting and intensifying child labor (Lyons 1989; Humphries forthcoming).

Mothers were described as caring for their children, though the extent to which their love was manifest in working to help support their children varied across Europe. Child labor may have been more extensive where married women pursued exclusively domestic roles, though children's child care responsibilities surely offset this pattern (Horrell and Humphries 1995; Cunningham 2000). Compared with French and German mothers, few British mothers appear to have contributed to family income by participating in the labor market—in contrast to their children (Horrell and Humphries 1995; Maynes 1995). This substitution of children's labor for that of their mothers was embedded in a family strategy that both responded to local economic and demographic conditions and reflected cultural values. Its potential importance in the modern world makes it deserving of more careful study.

Whether or not they worked outside the home, mothers, unlike fathers, were almost never depicted as consuming the fruits of their children's labor. The custom for children to surrender their earnings to their mothers ensured that children's earnings were recycled through the household accounts, to be spent in children's interests. How mothers weighed the claims of older and younger children and of working and dependent children remains unclear.

In a few cases, children did blame parents, in particular fathers, for contributing to their families' poverty and so to early working. Drinking was a cause of misery for many working families, and alcoholic fathers were often associated with children's early working. But children did not always see their fathers' drinking as selfish. Fathers were driven to drink by their inability to provide, the physical demands of their hard jobs, and the grimness of their working lives. Drinking was also a response to bereavement (Humphries 2003b). Alcohol has addictive and stimulant characteristics, which may explain its overpowering of fathers' altruistic intentions. These links between selfishness and drinking are consistent with evidence associating lack of altruism with stimulant and addictive goods consumed mainly by men.

Abandonment destined families for poverty (Humphries 1998; Horrell, Humphries, and Voth 2001). In contrast to drinking, it was rarely condoned. Being without a father (perhaps even a nonaltruistic father) appears to have had a large and significant effect on the age at which children started working, according to British autobiographies, advancing children's entry into the labor market by more than 15 months (Humphries 2003b).

Family size also affected family poverty and therefore child labor. Large families increased the need for children to supplement fathers' earnings. In Britain industrialization proceeded against a backdrop of historically rapid population growth and increased average family size. In 1821 children under the age of 9 made up 28 percent of the population, and young people 10–19 represented another 21 percent (Wrigley and Schofield 1981). This proportion probably increased throughout the 18th century. The pressure created by the rising dependency rate has been somewhat neglected by economic historians, but its potential as an explanation of the pattern and extent of child labor in Britain is considerable. Many boys cite the presence of large numbers of dependent siblings as having pushed them into the labor force; their impressions appear borne out in the autobiographical evidence on age at starting work (Humphries 2003b). Britain's unusual demographic experience may well have contributed to the exceptional reliance on child labor.

The Role of the State

The state usually enters the story of child labor only as an agent in its decline. But in Britain the state by both action and inaction facilitated the boom in child labor. This is not to suggest that the state adopted a conscious strategy in support of child labor, although several apocryphal stories repeated in the classic British accounts suggest as much (Hammond and Hammond 1925; Mantoux 1928). More likely the boom in child labor was the unintended consequence of policies such as legislation weakening labor organization (the Combination Acts, the repeal of the Statute of Artificers) and the miserly treatment of the wives and children of soldiers. Most important in this context was the operation of poor relief. The Old Poor Law arguably inhibited the indiscriminate growth of child labor by occasionally subsidizing poor families with many children and channeling children into more acceptable forms of work through pauper apprenticeship. It also treated single mothers relatively generously (Snell and Millar 1987). The retreat of the Old Poor Law in the face of rising expenditures in the late 18th century and the transition to the New Poor Law, although not eliminating fiscal transfers, emphasized the conditionality of assistance on children's working with negative implications for human capital formation (Horrell, Humphries, and Voth 2001). In a world in which orphaned and fatherless children are legion, perhaps this is the most pertinent finding from the past.

Cultural Context

The idea of a change in parent–child relations in the 18th century is firmly established in the literature, with harshness in the medieval and early modern periods giving way to kinder treatment later on. Such a shift in values has intriguing implications for the historian of child labor. It suggests that countries that industrialized early, before this transition was completed, might be expected to have used child labor more intensively than countries that industrialized later.

III. EXPLAINING THE DECREASE IN CHILD LABOR

Motivated by the need to discourage child labor in the developing world, economists have looked mainly to the past to understand what caused child labor to decline.

Development of the Capitalist Labor Market

Chief among the usual suspects is technology: the demand for child labor allegedly faded as more advanced industrial technologies replaced the need for unskilled labor of children (Goldin and Parsons 1989; Nardinelli 1990). As Cunningham observes, 'It is assumed that technology has its own in built rationale and that it always acts in favor of adult and in opposition to child labor' (2000:417). But earlier technology had developed to facilitate the substitution of child for adult labor. Why should it suddenly have changed direction unless reversed by a shift in the interests of management or labor? There has to be a motive for its development and introduction.

In France in the 1840s and in some industries in Britain in the mid-19th century, employers campaigned for a reduction in child labor (Humphries 1981; Weissbach 1989; Dupree 1995). Their motives were both strategic and philanthropic. By promoting protective labor legislation, employers who had already dispensed with child labor or who had technology that obviated the need for child labor sought to gain a competitive advantage over other employers for whom child labor remained essential (Marvel 1977; Humphries 1981). Others were convinced that child labor was morally wrong (see Hammond and Hammond 1925, ch. 8) or that it was in the collective interest to develop a healthier and more educated workforce.

But an account of changes in the capitalist labor market, which deals only with employers' strategies, is unbalanced. Managerial strategies may also have shifted toward an intensive labor process in which the strength and power of adults was needed (Cunningham 2000). Moreover, by the mid-19th century male labor had also begun to reorganize defensively within revamped institutions. An extensive literature suggests how strong trade unions, protective labor legislation, and campaigns for family wages led to the rise of the male-breadwinner family. This phenomenon is traditionally presented from a feminist perspective that focuses on the exclusion of female labor. But the timing of women's retreat from the labor market does not coincide with the growing strength of organized labor (Creighton 1996). Reoriented to provide a political-economic explanation of the decline of child labor, male unionists' campaign for family wages slots neatly into the chronology of adulting.

Family Strategies

Clark Nardinelli's influential book (1990) gave family strategies a neoclassical twist. Heavily influenced by the New Household Economics, Nardinelli argued that because working families in the early 19th century had the opportunity not to send their children out to work but chose to do so, child labor must have been the best option. Ignoring the possibility of heterogeneous preferences and agency problems by assuming a unitary household, Nardinelli explained the decline of child labor in terms of families' rational responses to changes in relative prices and incomes. Technology rendered child labor unproductive, and economic growth eventually trickled down to raise adult male earnings. Thus the boom in child labor hinged on a fortuitous coincidence of a transient technology and low adult wages. It declined when technology advanced and adult wages rose, allowing children to attend school instead of work.

The policy implications of this hypothesis are profound. According to Nardinelli, low adult wages cause child labor. There is no remedy to the problem, except to wait for economic growth, which, with Chicago School optimism, Nardinelli believes inevitable provided it is not stymied by well-meaning but inappropriate government intervention.

Nardinelli's analysis of the causes of the decline of child labor is consistent with his chronology of events, which describes a rapid decline in child labor starting before the Factory Acts and coinciding with strong growth in the real earnings of adult males. The decline in child labor, however, is disputed by evidence that children's involvement in productive activities was more extensive and more enduring than Nardinelli suggests. Moreover, Feinstein's (1998) definitive series delays sustained growth in real earnings until the mid-19th century, which is out of sync with Nardinelli's account.

A newer view fits neatly with a later and more gradual decline in children's work and with an explanation that draws on the socioeconomic construction of the male-breadwinner family in the second half of the 19th century. The growth in adult earnings in the later 19th century was not independent of the ongoing struggle—not only in capitalist labor markets but also within Parliament and the press—between opponents and proponents of child labor. This struggle was but one aspect of a campaign to defend the integrity of the working class family.

One variable that emerged as an important determinant of age at starting work that is often forgotten in stories about the decline of child labor is family size. Fertility peaked in Britain in the 1820s, but large families remained standard among some occupational groups and very common among the working class at large.

The Role of the State

An older generation of historians explained the decline of child labor almost solely in terms of the Factory Acts (Hutchins and Harrison 1903). Neoclassical economics is predisposed to deem intervention unnecessary if not mischievous. Is legislation possible only when the majority of powerful employers has already dispensed with child labor? Does it harm children by pushing them into more hazardous but less visible work and reducing family incomes?

Moehling (1999) uses a "difference-in-differences-in-differences" procedure to isolate the effects of child labor laws on children's participation by state in the United States between 1880 and 1930. Child labor fell precipitously during this period, but the decline was not driven by the legislative success of the child labor movement. The occupation rate of 13-year-olds did decline in states that enacted a minimum working age of 14, but so did the occupation rates of children not covered by the restrictions (Moehling 1999). Legal prohibitions emerge as consequences rather than causes of the decline in children's work.

In contrast, other legislation is widely agreed to have had some effect. The classic case is the 1833 Factory Act, whose impact even Nardinelli acknowledges. Cunningham (2000) provides a list of child labor laws that historians have deemed effective, including the 1864 act that reduced children's participation in potteries (Dupree 1995), the 1872 Mines Regulation Act (Church 1986), the 1874 act in France (Weissbach 1989), and the measures taken by the National Recovery Administration in the United States in 1933 (Trattner 1970). Data from the 1960 census suggest that child labor laws and compulsory schooling increased educational attainments of children in the United States between 1915 and 1939 (Lleras-Muney 2002).

Chang (2002) scrutinized the historical record to establish the time it took for legislation to have an effect. He argues that the child labor standards demanded of the developing world require a swifter eradication of children's work than was achieved by today's industrial countries. Chang takes the industrial countries' stance on child labor as an example of his more general argument that today's wealthy countries industrialized and became rich using policies and institutions that were often the opposite of those they now thrust on developing economies. Industrial countries are attempting to kick away the ladder by which they rose to prosperity, denying poor countries the same route to the top.

Although Chang has a point, his description of historical events should not go unchallenged. First, regulation became comprehensive over a shorter time period than Chang suggests, certainly less than the centuries he cites. Second, wealthy countries industrialized at different times and made different demands on child workers, with implications for legislative progression. Third, the early starters made more extensive use of child labor, suggesting that even among the now rich countries, later entry into the race for prosperity involved different standards of acceptable conduct. Yet this did not kick away the ladder to development for Europe's late industrializers. Fourth, though some of the policies and institutions that rich countries now condemn can be linked to economic development (tariffs, for example, may have helped infant industries develop), the contribution of child workers to economic growth has not been established.

An alternative way of curbing child labor is by requiring school attendance. Unlike child labor laws, compulsory schooling does not encourage a move into unregulated and perhaps less desirable work. Case studies suggest that the desire to limit child labor was sometimes a motive for compulsory schooling (Hogan 1985). For several European and non-European countries, the decline in child labor appears correlated with the introduction of compulsory education (Weiner 1991). In Britain, for example, the decline in the participation rate of 10–14-year-olds gathered momentum after the introduction of compulsory schooling in 1870. But the importance of compulsory education has not yet been demonstrated in a study that controls for changes in other possible explanatory variables. Given the important policy implications that ride on the validity of this link, more research is needed.

School subsidies, in principle an attractive option, have not been studied historically. The popularity of charity schools is suggestive, but working-class parents' apparent preference for schools whose curriculum and setting were under their jurisdiction over free state schools implies that they valued the right to control children's schooling (Gardner 1984). Sunday schools, an enormously important deliverer of 19th century education, pose a recurrent dilemma: how to evaluate an educational institution designed to accommodate child labor. Perhaps the considerable achievements of Sunday Schools, part-time and seasonal education, reading rooms and mutual improvement societies, ragged schools (free schools for poor children), and apprenticeships have been undervalued because of a distaste for institutions that remained wedded to children's ongoing involvement in productive activities (Silver 1977; Snell 1999).

Cultural Context

A cultural account of the decline of child labor could be built around the diffusion to the working class of the transition in parent–child relations that historians have documented for the elite (for a dissenting view, see Nardinelli 1990). More specifically, the political-economic campaigns of the later 19th century for protective labor legislation, the integrity of the family, and the family wage could themselves have influenced values and attitudes. The theory of cognitive dissonance suggests that the routine expression of ideas and beliefs is intolerable unless they are adopted. Victorian working men embraced the schooled child along with a nonworking wife as hallmarks of a desirable and respectable family life that went with (indeed required) higher adult male pay. Their wage demands became inseparable from a package of ideas about proper family structure that went to the heart of contemporary views of enlightened and civilized society. Their claim was eventually supported by groups of men from other ranks of society—employers, politicians, journalists, philanthropists—prepared to sacrifice some immediate self-interest to accommodate the diffusion of a family structure that had powerful appeal (Creighton 1999).

IV. CONCLUSIONS

Countries in which child labor is common today bear a greater resemblance to industrial countries on the eve of industrialization than to those same countries 50–100 years later, when child labor began to decline. Among 19th-century industrializers, child labor was more prevalent in early starters, and it appears to have been more prevalent in both early and late industrializers than it is in developing economies today. This difference may be a source of optimism signaling the spread of technologies that have little use for child labor and values that endorse the preservation and protection of childhood. But the historical record warns that technological and cultural developments are not independent of underlying economic conditions. Whether such technology and values can survive the impact of the AIDS epidemic, famines, and civil and regional conflicts on family structures and the supply of child labor remains to be seen.

Child labor is hard to document, let alone measure, particularly in the very sectors and jobs in which it is likely to be prevalent, namely, family farms and businesses, the informal sector, and part-time and seasonal work. Historical experience warns against focusing only on public forms of employment and assuming that as children are removed from the visible sectors they will also withdraw from the darker corners of the economy. On the other hand, historians have been too ready to assume that familial or informal employment is intrinsically more benign than work in factories. What are needed are comparative analyses of forms of child labor, which might provide criteria for a normative ranking of jobs for use in a world in which some kind of economic contribution from children is tolerated. The ways in which learning and work were combined in the past are also worth more attention.

Historians' finding that poverty was the main determinant of child labor should not be cause for resignation. Welfare-improving intervention appears possible at low incomes. Moreover, all poor children are not equally at risk. Orphaned and fatherless children and those in large families are the most vulnerable. Efficient interventions to curb child labor involve fiscal transfers to fatherless children and large families and active policies toward street children.

Historians disagree about whether it is possible to regulate the demand for child labor without harming the very children whose protection was intended. Perhaps the lesson here is that interventions must be customized to suit particular circumstances. Compulsory schooling and legislation banning child labor were successful and apparently welfare improving in some times and places but not others. The discrediting of technological determinism by historians and its replacement with more nuanced accounts of the decline in child labor also suggests the importance of close scrutiny of circumstances and context.

The documentation of the interplay of interests that over time led to the adulting of the labor force has resonance with Basu's theoretical account of a labor market with multiple equilibria, some involving child labor (Basu 1999). Policymakers can try to encourage a movement from equilibria that involve child labor to those that do not. The effectiveness of such policies depends on understanding the institutional configuration of the labor market, including how child labor fits into family strategies—that are themselves embedded in historically and culturally determined ideas about mothers' and fathers' roles—and evolving relations among employers, workers, and the state.

REFERENCES

Badinter, Elisabeth. 1981. *The Myth of Motherhood: An Historical View of the Maternal "Instinct."* London: Souvenir Press.

Basu, Kaushik. 1999. "Child Labor; Cause, Consequence, and Cure, with Remarks on Labor Standards." *Journal of Economic Literature* 37: 1083–119.

Berg, Maxine, and Pat Hudson. 1992. "Rehabilitating the Industrial Revolution." *Economic History Review* 45(1): 24–50.

Bolin-Hort, Per. 1989. *Work, Family and the State: Child Labor and the Organization of Production in the British Cotton Industry, 1780–1920.* Lund, Sweden: Lund University Press.

Booth, Charles. 1886. "On Occupations of the People of the United Kingdom, 1801–81." *Journal of the Royal Statistical Society* 49(June): 314–435.

Chang, Ha-Joon. 2002. *Kicking away the Ladder: Development Strategy in Historical Perspective.* London: Anthem Press.

Chassagne, Serge. 1986. "La Naissance de l'Industrie Cotonnière en France: 1760–1840." PhD diss., Ecole des Hautes Etudes en Sciences Sociales, Paris.

Childs, Michael J. 1992. *Labor's Apprentices. Working Class Lads in Late Victorian and Edwardian England.* Montreal and Kingston: McGill-Queens University Press.

Church, Roy. 1986. *The History of the British Coal Industry.* Oxford: Oxford University Press.

Coninck-Smith, Ning, Bengt Sandin, and Ellen Schrumpf. 1997. *Industrious Children: Work and Childhood in the Nordic Countries 1850–1990.* Odense, Denmark: Odense University Press.

Cookson, J.E. 1997. *The British Armed Nation 1793–1815.* Oxford: Clarendon.

Coombs, Simone and Deborah Radburn. 1995. "Children and Young People on the Land." In Michael Winstanley, ed., *Working Children in Nineteenth-Century Lancashire.* Preston, Lancashire: Lancashire County Books.

Crafts, N.F.R. 1985. *British Economic Growth during the Industrial Revolution.* Oxford: Clarendon.

Creighton, Colin. 1996. "The Rise of the Male Breadwinner Family: A Reappraisal." *Comparative Studies in Society and History* 38(April): 310–37.

——. 1999. "The Rise and Decline of the 'Male Breadwinner Family' in Britain." *Cambridge Journal of Economics* 23(5): 519–41.

Cunningham, Hugh. 2000. "The Decline of Child Labor: Labor Markets and Family Economies in Europe and North America since 1830." *Economic History Review* 53(3): 409–28.

De Herdt, Rene. 1996. "Child Labor in Belgium: 1800–1914." In Hugh Cunningham and Pier Paolo Viazzo, eds., *Child Labor in Historical Perspective, 1800–1985: Case Studies from Europe, Japan and Colombia.* Florence: UNICEF.

deMause, Lloyd B., ed. 1974. *The History of Childhood. The Untold Story of Child Abuse.* London: Bellow.

De Vries, Jan. 1994. "The Industrial Revolution and the Industrious Revolution." *Journal of Economic History,* 54(2): 249–70.

Dunlop, O.J., and Richard D. Denman. 1912. *English Apprenticeship and Child Labor. A History.* London: Fisher Unwin.

Dupree, Marguerite. 1995. *Family Structure in the Staffordshire Potteries, 1840–1880.* Oxford: Clarendon.

Engerman, Stanley. 2003. "The History and Political Economy of International Labor Standards." In Kaushik Basu, Henrik Horn, Judith Shapiro, and Lisa Roman, eds., *International Labor Standards: History, Theory and Policy Options.* Oxford: Blackwell.

Feinstein, Charles H. 1998. "Pessimism Perpetuated: Real Wages and the Standard of Living in Britain During and After the Industrial Revolution." *Journal of Economic History* 58(3): 625–58.

Galbi, Douglas. 1997. "Child Labor and the Division of Labor in the Early English Cotton Mills." *Journal of Population Economics* 10(4): 357–75.

Gardner, Phil. 1984. *The Lost Elementary Schools of Victorian England: The People's Education.* London: Croom Helm.

Goldin, Claudia, and Donald O. Parsons. 1989. "Parental Altruism and Self-Interest: Child Labor among American Families." *Economic Inquiry* 27(4): 637–59.

Goldin, Claudia, and Kenneth Sokoloff. 1982. "Women, Children, and Industrialization in the Early Republic: Evidence from the Manufacturing Censuses." *Journal of Economic History* 42(4): 741–74.

Hammond, J.L. and Barbara Hammond. 1925. *The Town Labourer, 1760–1832.* London: Longmans.

Heywood, Colin. 1988. *Childhood in Nineteenth-Century France: Work, Health and Education among the "Classes Populaires."* Cambridge: Cambridge University Press.

——. 2001. *A History of Childhood. Children and Childhood in the West from Medieval to Modern Times.* Cambridge: Polity.

Hogan, D.J. 1985. *Class and Reform: School and Society in Chicago, 1880–1930.* Philadelphia: University of Pennsylvania Press.

Horrell, Sara. 1996. "Home Demand and British Industrialization." *Journal of Economic History* 56(3): 561–604.

Horrell, Sara, and Jane Humphries. 1995. " 'The Exploitation of Little Children": Children's Work and the Family Economy in the British Industrial Revolution." *Explorations in Economic History* 32(4): 485–516.

Horrell, Sara, Jane Humphries, and Hans-Joachim Voth. 2001. "Destined for Deprivation: Human Capital Formation and Intergenerational Poverty in Nineteenth-Century England." *Explorations in Economic History* 38(3): 339–65.

Humphries, Jane. 1981. "Protective Legislation, the Capitalist State and Working Class Men: The Case of the 1842 Mines Regulation Act." *Feminist Review* 7(1): 1–35.

——. 1998. "Female-Headed Households in Early Industrial Britain: The Vanguard of the Proletariat?" *Labour History Review* 63(l): 31–65.

——. 2003a. "Child Labor in the Industrial Revolution." In Peter Scholliers and Leonard Schwarz, eds., *Experiencing Wages: Social and Cultural Aspects of Wage Forms in Europe since 1500.* Oxford: Berghahn Books.

——. 2003b. "Child Labor in the Industrial Revolution: The Evidence from Working Class Autobiographies." Oxford University Economic and Social History Working Papers.

——. 2003c. "The Parallels between Past and Present." In Kaushik Basu, Henrik Horn, Judith Shapiro, and Lisa Roman, eds., *International Labor Standards: History, Theory and Policy Options.* Oxford: Blackwell.

——. Forthcoming. "Household Economy." In Roderick Floud and Paul Johnson, eds., *Cambridge Economic History of Britain.* Cambridge: Cambridge University Press.

Hutchins, B.L., and A. Harrison. 1903. *A History of Factory Legislation.* London: P.S. King and Son.

Kitteringham, Jennie. 1975. "Country Work Girls in Nineteenth Century England." In Raphael Samuel, ed., *Village Life and Labour.* London: Routledge and Kegan Paul.

Krueger, Alan. 1997. "International Labour Standards and Trade." In Michael Bruno and Boris Pleskovic, eds., *Proceedings of the Annual World Bank Conference on Development Economics, 1996.* Washington, DC: World Bank.

Lavalette, Michael ed. 1999. *A Thing of the Past? Child Labor in Britain in the Nineteenth and Twentieth Centuries.* Liverpool: Liverpool University Press.

Lleras-Muney, Adriana. 2002. "Were Compulsory and Child Labour Laws Effective? An Analysis from 1915 to 1939." *Journal of Law and Economics* 45(2): 401–36.

Lyons, John. 1989. "Family Response to Economic Decline: Handloom Weavers in Early Nineteenth-Century Lancashire." *Research in Economic History* 12: 45–91.

Macleod, Christine. 1988. *Inventing the Industrial Revolution: The English Patent System.* Cambridge: Cambridge University Press.

Mantoux, Paul. 1928. *The Industrial Revolution in the Eighteenth-Century.* London: Jonathan Cape.

Marvel, Howard P. 1977. "Factory Regulation: A Reinterpretation of Early English Experience." *Journal of Law and Economics* 20(October): 379–402.

Maynes, Mary Jo. 1995. *Taking the Hard Road: Life Course in French and German Workers' Autobiographies in the Era of Industrialization.* Chapel Hill: University of North Carolina Press.

Moehling, Carolyn M. 1999. "State Child Labour Laws and the Decline of Child Labor." *Explorations in Economic History* 3(1): 72–106.

Murray, John E. and Ruth Wallis Herndon. 2002. "Markets for Children in Early America: A Political Economy of Pauper Apprenticeship." *Journal of Economic History* 62(2): 356–82.

Nardinelli, Clark. 1990. *Child Labor and the Industrial Revolution.* Bloomington: University of Indiana Press.

Pinchbeck, Ivy, and Margaret Hewitt. 1973. *Children in English Society.* Vol. 2 London: Routledge and Kegan Paul.

Pollock, Linda. 1983. *Forgotten Children: Parent-Child Relations from 1500 to 1900.* Cambridge: Cambridge University Press.

Saito, Osamu. 1996. "Children's Work, Industrialism and the Family Economy in Japan, 1872–1926." In Hugh Cunningham and Per Paolo Viazzo, eds., *Child Labor in Historical Perspective, 1800–1985. Case Studies from Europe, Japan and Colombia.* Florence: UNICEF.

Scholliers, Peter. 1996. *Wages, Manufacturers and Workers in the Nineteenth-Century Factory: The Voortman Cotton Mill in Ghent.* Oxford, U.K.: Berg.

Schrumpf, Ellen. 1997. "From Full-Time to Part-Time: Working Children in Norway from the Nineteenth Century to the Twentieth Century." In Ning de Coninck-Smith, Bengt Sandin, and Ellen Schrumpf, eds., *Industrious Children: Work and Childhood in the Nordic Countries, 1850–1990.* Odense, Denmark: Odense University Press.

Shorter, Edward. 1977. *The Making of the Modern Family.* London: Fontana.

Silver, Harold. 1977. "Ideology and the Factory Child: Attitudes to Half-Time Education." In Phillip McCann, ed., *Popular Education and Socialization in the Nineteenth Century.* London: Methuen.

Sjoberg, Mats. 1997. "Working Rural Children: Herding, Child Labor and Childhood in the Swedish Rural Environment 1850–1950." In Ning de

Coninck-Smith, Bengt Sandin, and Ellen Schrumpf, eds., *Industrious Children: Work and Childhood in the Nordic Countries, 1850–1990.* Odense, Denmark: Odense University Press.

Snell, K.D.M. 1999. "The Sunday School Movement in England and Wales: Child Labour, Denominational Control and Working Class Culture." *Past and Present* 164(August): 122–68.

Snell, K.D.M. and Jane Millar. 1987. "Lone Parent Families and the Welfare State: Past and Present." *Continuity and Change* 2(3): 387–422.

Solberg, Anne. 1997. "Seeing Children's Work." In Ning de Coninck-Smith, Bengt Sandin, and Ellen Schrumpf, eds., *Industrious Children: Work and Childhood in the Nordic Countries, 1850–1990.* Odense, Denmark: Odense University Press.

Stone, Lawrence. 1977. *The Family, Sex and Marriage in England, 1500–1800.* London: Weidenfeld and Nicholson.

Trattner, Walter I. 1970. *Crusade for the Children: A History of the National Labor Committee and Child Labor Reform in America.* Chicago: Quadrangle Books.

Tuttle, Carolyn. 1999. *Hard at Work in Factories and Mines: The Economics of Child Labor during the British Industrial Revolution.* Boulder, Colo.: Westview Press.

Weiner, M. 1991. *The Child and the State in India: Child Labour and Education Policy in Comparative Perspective.* New Delhi: Oxford University Press.

Weissbach, Lee Shai. 1989. *Child Labor Reform in Nineteenth-Century France: Assuring the Future Harvest.* Baton Rouge: Louisiana State University Press.

Winstanley, Michael, ed. 1995. *Working Children in Nineteenth-Century Lancashire.* Preston, Lancashire, U.K.: Lancashire County Books.

Wrigley, E.A. and R.S. Schofield. 1981. *The Population History of England 1541–1871.* Cambridge: Cambridge University Press.

Law, Liability and Regulation

13

Liability for Harm versus Regulation of Safety†

*Steven Shavell**

I. INTRODUCTION

Liability in tort and the regulation of safety represent two very different approaches for controlling activities that create risks of harm to others. Tort liability is private in nature and works not by social command but rather indirectly, through the deterrent effect of damage actions that may be brought once harm occurs. Standards, prohibitions, and other forms of safety regulation, in contrast, are public in character and modify behavior in an immediate way through requirements that are imposed before, or at least independently of, the actual occurrence of harm.

As a matter of simple description, it is apparent that liability and safety regulation are employed with an emphasis that varies considerably with the nature of the activity that is governed. Whether I run to catch a bus and thereby collide with another pedestrian will be influenced more by the possibility of my tort liability than by any prior regulation of my behavior (informal social sanctions and risk to self aside). Similarly, whether I cut down a tree that might fall on my neighbor's roof will be

†Originally published as "Liability for Harm versus Regulation of Safety", 1984, *The Journal of Legal Studies*, Vol. 13, pp. 357–74.

*I wish to thank Bruce Ackerman, Susan Rose Ackerman, Lucian Bebchuk, Paul Burrows, Louis Kaplow, Mark Kelman, and Richard Stewart for comments and the National Science Foundation (grant no. SES-8014208) for financial support. A formal version of the main argument of this article is made in my 'Harm as a Prerequisite for Liability' (1979) (unpublished manuscript, Harvard University, Department of Economics); and in 'A Model of the Optimal Use of Liability and Safety Regulation (forthcoming, *Rand Journal of Economics*). The present article will provide the basis for a chapter in the part on torts of *A Theoretical Analysis of Law*, a book on which I am at work.

affected more by the prospect of a tort suit than by direct regulation. But other decisions— whether I drive my truck through a tunnel when it is loaded with explosives or mark the fire exits in my store, or whether an electric utility incorporates certain safety features in its nuclear power plant—are apt to be determined substantially, although not entirely, by safety regulation. There are also intermediate cases, of course; consider, for instance, the behavior of ordinary drivers on the road and the effects of tort sanctions and regulation of automobile use.

What has led society to adopt this varying pattern of liability and safety regulation? What is the socially desirable way to employ the two means of alleviating risks? These are the questions to be addressed here, and in answering them I use an instrumentalist, economic method of analysis, whereby the effects of liability rules and direct regulation are compared and then evaluated on a utilitarian basis, given the assumption that individual actors can normally be expected to act in their own interest.[1] In making this evaluation, I have not counted compensation of injured parties as an independent factor on the grounds that first-party insurance (augmented if necessary by a public insurance program) can discharge the compensatory function no matter what the mix of liability and regulation. Likewise, for simplicity I ignore the complications that would be introduced by considering interest group theories of regulation.[2] Also, I do not make an explicit attempt to determine the extent to which the conclusions reached may be separately attributable to either of the two dimensions in which liability and safety regulation differ: employed only after harm is done versus beforehand; employed only at the initiative of private parties versus a public authority.[3]

Subject to these caveats and assumptions, this article first discusses four general determinants of the relative desirability of liability and regulation. It then argues in light of the determinants that the actual, observed use of the two methods of reducing risks may be viewed as socially desirable, or roughly so. The article concludes with several

[1]This is the general approach adopted by two influential legal scholars in their analyses of tort law; see Guido Calabresi, The Costs of Accidents, 1970; and Richard Posner, Economic Analysis of Law (2d ed. 1977), ch. 6.

[2]See, for example, George Stigler, The Theory of Economic Regulation, 2 Bell J. Econ. 3 (1971); and Sam Peltzman, Toward a More General Theory of Regulation, 19 J. Law & Econ. 211 (1976).

[3]But the concluding discussion may help the reader to make a judgment about this issue.

qualifying remarks and with comments on how the analysis could be extended to incorporate additional means of social control including the fine and the injunction.

II. THEORETICAL DETERMINANTS OF THE RELATIVE DESIRABILITY OF LIABILITY AND SAFETY REGULATION

To identify and assess the factors determining the social desirability of liability and regulation, it is necessary to set out a measure of social welfare; and here that measure is assumed to equal the benefits parties derive from engaging in their activities, less the sum of the costs of precautions, the harms done, and the administrative expenses associated with the means of social control. The formal problem is to employ the means of control to maximize the measure of welfare.

We can now examine four determinants that influence the solution to this problem. The first determinant is the possibility of a *difference in knowledge about risky activities* as between private parties and a regulatory authority. This difference could relate to the benefits of activities, the costs of reducing risks, or the probability or severity of the risks.

Where private parties have superior knowledge of these elements, it would be better for them to decide about the control of risks, indicating an advantage of liability rules, other things being equal. Consider, for instance, the situation where private parties possess perfect information about risky activities of which a regulator has poor knowledge. Then to vest in the regulator the power of control would create a great chance of error. If the regulator overestimates the potential for harm, its standard will be too stringent, and the same will be the case if it underestimates the value of the activity or the cost of reducing risk. If the regulator makes the reverse mistakes, moreover, it will announce standards that are lax.

Under liability, however, the outcome would likely be better. This is clear enough under a system of strict liability—whereby parties have to pay damages regardless of their negligence—for then they are motivated to balance the true costs of reducing risks against the expected savings in losses caused. Now assume that the form of liability is the negligence rule—according to which parties are held responsible for harm done only if their care falls short of a prescribed level of "due" care—and suppose further that once harm occurs, the courts could acquire enough information about the underlying event to formulate the appropriate level of due care. Then parties, anticipating this, would be led in principle to exercise due care.[4] The situation is altered for the worse if the courts are unable to acquire sufficient information to determine the best level of due care; but the outcome would still be superior to that achievable under regulation if the information obtained ex post at trial would be better than that which a regulator could acquire and act upon ex ante.

These conclusions are reversed, of course, if the information possessed by a regulator is superior to private parties' and the courts'; converse reasoning then shows that the use of direct regulation would be more attractive than liability.

The question that remains, therefore, is when we can expect significant differences in information between private parties and regulators to exist. And the answer is that private parties should generally enjoy an inherent advantage in knowledge. They, after all, are the ones who are engaging in and deriving benefits from their activities; in consequence, they are in a naturally superior position to estimate these benefits and normally are in at least as good a position to estimate the nature of the risks created and the costs of their reduction. For a regulator to obtain comparable information would often require virtually continuous observation of parties' behavior, and thus would be a practical impossibility. Similarly, the courts—when called upon under a negligence system—should have an advantage, though a less decisive one, over a regulator. One would indeed expect courts to adjust the due care level to take into account the facts presented by litigating parties more easily than a regulator could individualize its prior standards or modify them to reflect changed conditions.

Yet this is not to say that private parties or the courts will necessarily possess information superior to that held by a regulatory authority. In certain contexts information about risk will not be an obvious by-product of engaging in risky activities but rather will require effort to develop or special expertise to evaluate. In these contexts a regulator might obtain information by committing social resources to the task, while private parties would have an insufficient incentive to do this for familiar reasons: A party who generates information will be unable to capture its full value if others can learn of the information without paying for it. For parties to undertake individually to acquire information might result in wasteful, duplicative expenditures, and a cooperative venture by parties might be stymied by the

[4]See John Prather Brown, Toward an Economic Theory of Liability, 2 J. Legal Stud. 323 (1973).

usual problems of inducing all to lend their support.[5] Continuing, once a regulator obtains information, it may find the information difficult to communicate to private parties because of its technical nature or because the parties are hard to identify or are too numerous. Thus we can point to contexts where regulators might possess better information than private parties to whom it cannot easily be transmitted, even if the usual expectation would be for these parties to possess the superior information.

The second of the determinants of the relative desirability of liability and regulation is that *private parties might be incapable of paying for the full magnitude of harm done.* Where this is the case, liability would not furnish adequate incentives to control risk, because private parties would treat losses caused that exceed their assets as imposing liabilities only equal to their assets.[6] But under regulation inability to pay for harm done would be irrelevant, assuming that parties would be made to take steps to reduce risk as a precondition for engaging in their activities.[7]

In assessing the importance of this argument favoring regulation over liability, one factor that obviously needs to be taken into account is the size of parties' assets in relation to the probability distribution of the magnitude of harm; the greater the likelihood of harm much larger than assets, the greater the appeal of regulation.

Another factor of relevance concerns liability insurance. Here the first point to make is that a party's motive to purchase liability insurance against damage judgments exceeding his assets will be a diminished one, as the protection will in part be for losses that the party would not otherwise have to bear.[8] A party with assets of $20,000 might not be eager to purchase coverage against a potential liability of $100,000, as four-fifths of the premium would be in payment for the $80,000 amount that he would not bear if he did not buy coverage. Hence, it might be rational for the party not to insure against the $100,000 risk. If this is the case, then the assertion that liability does not create an adequate motive to reduce risk is clearly unrebutted.

[5]See generally Kenneth J. Arrow, Essays in the Theory of Risk Bearing (1971), ch. 6.
[6]See more generally Steven Shavell, The Judgment Proof Problem (1984) (unpublished manuscript, Harvard Law School).
[7]The parties could be made to do this through the exercise of the state's police powers; force could be used to prevent a business from operating that disobeyed safety regulations. Where, however, monetary penalties are relied upon to induce parties to satisfy regulations, the fact that their assets are limited might lead to problems.
[8]See William Keeton & Evan Kwerel, Externalities in Automobile Insurance and the Underinsured Driver Problem, 27 J. Law & Econ. 149 (1984); and Shavell, *supra* note 6.

Suppose, however, that the party does choose to purchase liability insurance covering losses substantially exceeding his assets or is required by statute to do so. What then is his incentive to take care? The answer depends on whether insurers can easily determine risk-reducing behavior—so that they can link the premium charged or the other terms or conditions of coverage to the party's precautions. Where this linkage can be established, the party's incentive to take care should be tolerably good. But if insurers find it too costly to verify insureds' efforts at risk reduction, then their incentives to take care may be insufficient; plausibly, they could be lower than if no insurance coverage had been obtained. Consider a requirement that the party facing a $100,000 risk purchase full coverage against it and assume that the insurer cannot observe anything about the party's exercise of care. Then as the party would not have to pay a higher premium or be otherwise penalized for failure to take proper care, he would have no reason to do this. Yet if he had not owned the liability coverage, at least his $20,000 assets would have been at risk, supplying him with some motive to take care. Thus, it appears that the problem of inadequacy of incentives to take care which arises when parties' assets are less than potential harms can either be mitigated or exacerbated by the (mandatory or voluntary) purchase of liability insurance, depending on insurers' ability to monitor insureds.

An additional factor of relevance in considering the effects of inability to pay for harm done concerns firms and their employee decision makers. What is of special interest in this regard is that the activities of firms are prone to result in liabilities much larger than the assets of their employees—quite apart from whether firms themselves have assets sufficient to cover their liabilities.[9] This means that employees' personal liability or ex post sanctions imposed on them of a firm's devise may not result in proper incentives to reduce risks; an employee with assets of $50,000 might not take suitable precautions to reduce the risk of a $1 million corporate liability if only his assets or his job is at stake.[10] Hence, some sort of regulation of employees may be necessary to reduce risks appropriately.

[9]For a general discussion of closely related issues, see Christopher D. Stone, The Place of Enterprise Liability in the Control of Corporate Conduct, 90 Yale L. J. 1 (1980); and see also Lewis A. Kornhauser, An Economic Analysis of the Choice between Enterprise and Personal Liability for Accidents, 70 Calif. L. Rev. 1345 (1982).

[10]Risk aversion is a qualifying factor here. If the individual is sufficiently risk averse (and does not own liability coverage), he might still take adequate care; but beyond some magnitude of corporate liability-perhaps $2 million if not $1 million-the appropriate level of care would exceed that which the individual would be led to take.

But as firms themselves would wish to avoid large liabilities, they would have good reason to establish, ex ante, internal controls over the behavior of their employees. Thus we cannot conclude that there ought to be social regulation without supplying an argument for why it would be superior to a firm's own form of regulation. Now such an argument can be given in respect to the highest level of management—those individuals whose activities are overseen only by the board of directors and the shareholders—assuming that the board and the shareholders lack the time and the necessary expertise to control management's behavior as effectively as a regulator. This argument cannot be made, however, in respect to members of lower-level management, for they have superiors within the firm who presumably have better knowledge than a regulator and are thus able to set up a better scheme of ex ante controls. On the other hand, the desire of these superiors to regulate lower-level management might be inadequate precisely because the assets of the superiors could be less than the firm's potential liability. Thus, the situation is complex, but especially in relation to the decisions of higher-level management we can see that there exist arguments in favour of social regulation independently of whether firms' assets are large enough to cover their liabilities.

Let us turn next to the third of the four general determinants, the chance that *parties would not face the threat of suit for harm done.* Like incapacity to pay for harm, such a possibility results in a dilution of the incentives to reduce risk created by liability, but it is of no import under regulation.

The weight to be attached to this factor depends in part upon the reasons why suit might not be brought. One reason that a defendant can escape tort liability is that the harms he generates are widely dispersed, making it unattractive for any victim individually to initiate legal action. This danger can be offset to a degree if victims are allowed to maintain class actions, whose application has problematic features, however. A second cause of failure to sue is the passage of a long period of time before harm manifests itself. This raises the possibility that by the time suit is contemplated, the evidence necessary for a successful action will be stale or the responsible parties out of business. A third reason for failure to sue is difficulty in attributing harm to the parties who are in fact responsible for producing it. This problem could arise from simple ignorance that a given harm or disease was caused by a human agency (as opposed to being "natural" in origin) or from inability to identify which one or several out of many parties was the cause of harm.[11]

The problems here are aggravated when the potential liability rests on large firms, where complications analogous to those mentioned before exist. Namely, even if the harms can be attributed to an individual firm, the prospect of a successful suit may exert only slight influence on the behavior of corporate decision makers. With the passage of time, for example, there might be no clear way of determining which were the responsible employees, or those who were responsible may no longer be with the firm. The actual decisionmakers therefore may be beyond both the threat of suit and the prospect of sanctions internal to the firm.

The last of the determinants is the magnitude of the *administrative costs incurred by private parties and by the public* in using the tort system or direct regulation. Of course, the costs of the tort system must be broadly defined to include the time, effort, and legal expenses borne by private parties in the course of litigation or in coming to settlements, as well as the public expenses of conducting trials, employing judges, empaneling juries, and the like. Similarly, the administrative costs of regulation include the public expense of maintaining the regulatory establishment and the private costs of compliance.

With respect to these costs, there seems to be an underlying advantage in favor of liability, for most of its administrative costs are incurred only if harm occurs. As this will usually be infrequent, administrative costs will be low. Indeed, in the extreme case where the prospect of liability induces parties to take proper care and this happens to remove all possibility of harm, there would be no suits whatever and thus no administrative costs (other than certain fixed costs). Moreover, there are two reasons to believe that even when harm occurs administrative costs should not always be large. First, under a well-functioning negligence rule, defendants should in principle generally have been induced to take due care; injured parties should generally recognize this and thus should not bring suit. Second, suits should usually be capable of being settled

[11]Discussion of modifications of the tort system that would alleviate this problem of attribution-notably, imposing liability in proportion to the probability of causation-is beyond the scope of the present article. On this matter, see Comment, DES and a Proposed Theory of Enterprise Liability, 46 Fordham L. Rev. 963 (1978); David Rosenberg, The Causal Connection in Mass Exposure Cases: "Public Law" Vision of the Tort System, 97 Harv. L. Rev. 851 (1984); Steven Shavell, Uncertainty over Causation and the Determination of Civil Liability (1983) (unpublished manuscript, Harvard Law School).

cheaply by comparison to the cost of a trial. A final cost advantage of the liability system is that under it resources are naturally focused on controlling the behavior of the subgroup of parties most likely to cause harm; for because they are most likely to cause harm (and presumably most likely to be negligent), they are most likely to be sued.

Under regulation, unlike under liability, administrative costs are incurred whether or not harm occurs; even if the risk of a harm is eliminated by regulation, administrative costs will have been borne in the process. Also, in the absence of special knowledge about parties' categories of risk, there is no tendency for administrative costs to be focused on those most likely to cause harm, again because these costs are incurred before harm occurs. On the other hand, a savings in administrative costs can typically be achieved through the use of probabilistic means of enforcement.[12] But there is a limit to these savings because there is some minimum frequency of verification necessary to insure adherence to regulatory requirements.[13]

Joint Use of Liability and Regulation

Examination of the four determinants has thus shown that two generally favor liability—administrative costs and differential knowledge—and the other two favor regulation—incapacity to pay for harm done and escaping suit. This suggests not only that neither tort liability nor regulation could uniformly dominate the other as a solution to the problem of controlling risks, but also that they should not be viewed as mutually exclusive solutions to it. A complete solution to the problem of the control of risk evidently should involve the joint use of liability and regulation, with the balance between them reflecting the importance of the determinants.

If, then, some combination of liability and regulation is likely to be advantageous, two questions immediately arise: Should a party's

[12]See Donald Wittman, Prior Regulation versus Post Liability: The Choice between Input and Output Monitoring, 6 J. Legal Stud. 193 (1977), for a discussion of probabilistic enforcement in a setting similar to that of this article.

[13]This minimum frequency of verification is determined by the maximum fine—the size of parties' assets—that can be paid for noncompliance. To induce a party with assets of $10,000 to make a precautionary expenditure of $500, for example, his compliance must be verified with a probability of at least 5 percent; for otherwise, even were the fine to equal his entire assets, the probability-discounted fine would be less than $500. But if the likelihood of harm were negligible or lower than 5 percent, then under liability administrative costs could easily be smaller than under regulation, despite its probabilistic enforcement.

adherence to regulation relieve him of liability in the event that harm comes to pass? On the other hand, should a party's failure to satisfy regulatory requirements result necessarily in his liability? Our theory suggests a negative answer to both questions.

As to the first, if compliance with regulation were to protect parties from liability, then none would do more than to meet the regulatory requirements. Yet since these requirements will be based on less than perfect knowledge of parties' situations, there will clearly be some parties who ought to do more than meet the requirements—because they present an above-average risk of doing harm, can take extra precautions more easily than most, or can take precautions not covered by regulation. As liability will induce many of these parties to take beneficial precautions beyond the required ones, its use as a supplement to regulation will be advantageous.[14] At the same time, just because this is true, regulatory requirements need not be as rigorous as if regulation were the sole means of controlling risks.

A similar analysis is appropriate for the second question. If failure to satisfy regulatory requirements necessarily resulted in a finding of negligence, then some parties would be undesirably led to comply with them when they would not otherwise have done so. In particular, there will be some parties (a) who ought not to meet regulatory requirements because they face higher than usual costs of care or because they pose lower risks than normal and (b) who will not have been forced to satisfy regulatory requirements due to flaws in or probabilistic methods of enforcement. By allowing these parties to escape liability in view of their circumstances, the possibility that they would still be led to take the wasteful precautions can be avoided.[15]

[14]To illustrate, suppose that a $500 expenditure is desirable for typical firms to make to prevent $1,000 in losses, but for atypical firms, an additional $500 expenditure will prevent another $1,000 in losses. If the regulator is unable to tell the atypical firms apart and tailor regulations to them, then only through the deterrent of liability will these firms be led to make the extra $500 expenditure. Note, however, that use of liability alone would not be desirable, as then firms with low assets or ones likely to escape suit might not make even the first $500 expenditure.

[15]Suppose that, unlike in note 14 *supra*, the atypical parties ought not to make the first $500 expenditure because for them it would not reduce losses at all. Then, assuming that the regulator is unable to identify atypical parties, a single regulatory standard must be used, and suppose that it corresponds to the $500 expenditure (as the typical parties for whom this is appropriate are so numerous). Now consider the question whether an atypical party who for some reason was not made to satisfy the standard should be found negligent for that, if he happens to cause an accident. Clearly, if

III. ACTIVITIES CONTROLLED MAINLY BY LIABILITY: THE TYPICAL TORT

In this section and the next I will attempt to show that the theoretically desirable uses of tort liability and regulation correlate roughly with their uses in fact. In speaking first about activities controlled primarily by liability rules, I will for concreteness make reference to two activities mentioned earlier—to my chopping down a tree that might fall on my neighbor's home and to my running to catch a bus and possibly colliding with another person. A consideration of the relevance of the four determinants to activities such as these will suggest strong advantages of the liability system and acute drawbacks of regulation.

As regards the first determinant, there is ample reason to believe that private parties would possess much better information about risks and whether and how to reduce them than would a regulator. Because I would know the precise position of my tree and of my neighbor's home, I would likely have superior insight into the chance of an accident and the opportunity to lower it by use of guy wires, or by cutting down the tree in stages. Likewise, I would presumably be better able to determine whether I should do the work myself or hire an independent contractor to do it. Similarly, my knowledge of the probability of knocking someone down when running for a bus at that particular corner under these particular conditions of visibility and weather would be better than a regulator's, and I would surely know more about the importance of catching the bus.

In these situations private parties possess the better information because they apparently do obtain it as an ordinary by-product of their activities and can take into account the changes in circumstance that influence the risks and the value of their activities. Consequently, parties should make reasonably satisfactory decisions under liability, while costly mistakes would be unavoidable under regulation. Were the regulatory authority to set forth rules on the felling of trees or the pursuit of buses, it is a certainty that the rules would sometimes be too restrictive, imposing needless precautions that would not be taken due to a concern only over

---

such an atypical party were not found negligent, then he would not make the $500 expenditure, the desirable result; but if he were found negligent, he might be led to make the expenditure. Hence it is best for atypical parties to escape liability for negligence if they did not adhere to the regulatory standard. (And note again that the use of liability alone would not be desirable, for without regulation typical parties with low assets or who would escape suit would fail to make the $500 expenditure.)

liability; conversely, the rules would fail to identify desirable precautions that parties would obviously be motivated to take to avoid liability.

Turning next to the ability to pay for harm done, there is admittedly a potential problem, but sometimes not one of great magnitude. The damage to my neighbor's roof, for example, will probably be limited in scope, and I am likely to have assets plus liability insurance sufficient to cover it whether I own or rent my house. While inability to pay for harm counts as a weakness of liability in respect to the typical tort, it does not stand out as a problem of unusual dimension, at least by comparison to many of the situations to be discussed in the next part of the article.

The likelihood that suit would be brought against a liable defendant, moreover, appears to be relatively high for the typical tort, as none of the reasons for failure to bring suit seems to apply. Harms generally will not be dispersed among victims; my tree will fall on one, not many, roofs; I will collide with one or at most several pedestrians. Harms will not take a long period of time to manifest themselves; rather, any injury that I cause to a pedestrian or any damage to my neighbor's roof will be an immediate and direct consequence of my behavior. Further, harms will normally be readily attributed to responsible parties; there will be no mystery over whose tree damaged my neighbor's roof or over how the damage came about. There is thus no argument favoring regulation for fear that proper defendants would systematically escape suit.

Finally, liability should enjoy a significant administrative cost advantage over regulation in controlling the risks of typical torts. One does have the impression that it should be much less costly for society to incur administrative costs only when falling trees happen to descend on neighbors' homes and only when individuals chasing buses happen to collide with pedestrians, fairly unlikely events, than for society to formulate and enforce regulations on when and how trees may be cut down and on when individuals may be allowed to hurry after a bus.[16] Indeed, virtually

[16]Suppose, for instance, that the likelihood of my tree's striking my neighbor's roof is 0.1 percent; that should this happen, the chance there would be a dispute over my negligence is 50 percent; that given this, the probability of a settlement before trial would be 75 percent; that the administrative costs of a settlement would be $100 and those of a trial $1,000. Then the likelihood of a dispute ending in settlement would be 0.0375 percent, of one ending in litigation 0.0125 percent, so that the expected administrative costs associated with my chopping down my tree would be $.000375 \times \$100 + .000125 \times \$1{,}000$, or about 16 cents. It is hard to think of any regulatory scheme that could, ex ante, verify satisfaction of safety requirements at comparable cost.

all our routine activities—walking, mowing a lawn, playing catch—are perfectly innocuous in the overwhelming majority of instances, so that the savings achieved by limiting the bearing of administrative costs to those few occasions when harm occurs must be great.

The notion of effective regulation of the activities of everyday life even seems fanciful to contemplate, particularly because it would necessitate the use of extremely frequent and intrusive verification procedures. This is because what would usually need to be determined by a regulatory authority are aspects of modifiable behavior rather than "fixed" physical objects. While it may be enough to inspect elevator cables annually, because their condition will change little over that period, effective regulation of ordinary behavior such as whether I chase after buses clearly requires much more frequent monitoring.

Also of importance is the tendency for administrative costs to be incurred primarily in controlling the parties most likely to cause harm. Because those who fail to prevent their trees from falling on their neighbors' roofs must be a disproportionately awkward group, it is a good thing that the liability system's costs be concerned only with them; it would be a waste for society to incur costs to monitor the majority of careful individuals whose trees fall safely to the ground; yet that is just what the regulatory approach requires.

Let us now summarize our discussion. Of the four determinants, differential knowledge and the size of administrative costs pointed strongly in favor of use of liability to reduce the risk of the typical tort, while inability to pay for harm done worked with only moderate force against it, and the possibility of escaping suit did not constitute an argument against it. Thus, the use in practice of liability to control the familiar category of risks known as torts seems to be the theoretically preferred solution to the problem.

IV. ACTIVITIES SUBJECT TO SIGNIFICANT REGULATION

This section will argue that it is desirable that society resort to safety regulation where it generally does—in controlling the risks of fire, the production and sale of many foods and drugs, the generation of pollutants, and the transport and use of explosives and other dangerous materials. A consideration of the four determinants in these areas will lead to the conclusion that substantial regulation is not a coincidence but rather is needed, both because liability alone would not adequately reduce risks and because the usual disadvantages of regulation are not as serious as in the tort context.

First, what typifies much of regulation in the areas of concern is that its requirements can be justified by common knowledge or something close to it. Presumably most of us would agree that it is well worthwhile for explosives to be transported over designated routes that avoid the drastic risks of explosions in tunnels or in densely populated locations; that expenditures on very strong elevator cables are warranted by the resulting reduction in the probability of fatal accidents; that milk should be pasteurized to decrease the chances of bacterial contamination. In these and similar cases, the regulatory authority can be reasonably confident that its requirements are justified in the great majority of situations. To be sure, they will not always be justified; there will be some occasions when milk will be consumed soon enough that failure to pasteurize it would lead to no significant risk. But these occasions will be few in number, and the error due to inappropriate regulation will be small.

Furthermore, even where the proper design of regulation must be based on much more than common knowledge, the regulatory authority may not suffer an informational disadvantage, but instead may enjoy a positive advantage relative to private parties. Notably, in dealing with many health-related and environmental risks, a regulatory agency may have better access to, or a superior ability to evaluate, relevant medical, epidemiological, and ecological knowledge. A small fumigating company, for example, might know little about, and have limited ability to understand, the nature of the risks that the chemicals it uses create. The same might be true of a large producer of pesticides; it may be uneconomical for the producer to develop and maintain expert knowledge about the dangerous properties of pesticides, especially where there are economies of scale in acquiring this knowledge and where it would benefit others.

Consideration of the determinant concerning inability to pay for harm done also suggests why we regulate the activities that we do. A fire at a nightclub or hotel could harm a large number of individuals and create losses greater than the worth of the owner. The harm caused by mass consumption of spoiled food or by inoculation with vaccines with adverse side effects could easily exhaust the holdings of even a large corporation, and so too with the losses resulting from explosions, oil spills, or the release of toxic agents or radioactive substances. Clearly, in many areas of regulation, potential liability could exceed the assets of the firms involved (certainly of their employees), and the deterrent effect of tort law is therefore diluted.

Deterrence is similarly diluted by the likelihood that responsible parties would not be sued for a wide class of environmental and health-related harms. Many of these harms are sufficiently dispersed that individual victims do not find it worth their while to bring suit. In addition, these harms often become apparent only after the passage of years, either because ecological damage or the disease process itself is slow (as with asbestosis) or because the substance generating the risk retains its potency for a long period (as with anthrax bacillus or radioactive wastes). In consequence, it may be difficult for victims to assemble the evidence necessary to succeed in a suit, the responsible individuals may have retired or died, or the firms themselves may have gone out of business. Last, it is frequently hard to trace environmental and health-related harms to particular causes and then to particular firms. Many different substances may combine to produce a given type of harm, and the mechanism that links cause to effect may be complex and incompletely understood. There are, then, a variety of reasons to believe that parties responsible for environmental and health-related harms would not be sued, and hence to find the use of regulation attractive.

Finally, regarding administrative costs, several factors may offset the underlying advantage of liability in the major regulated areas. First, what regulation often requires is the presence of particular safety devices—fire extinguishers, guard rails, lifeboats—making enforcement less costly than if regulation demanded particular modes of behavior. And where regulation does demand a type of behavior, there may be features of the situation making lack of compliance hard to conceal. How easy would it be for a dairy to keep secret its failure to pasteurize milk when samples can be tested at low cost and when numbers of employees would be aware of the violation? Second, probabilistic methods of enforcement of regulation are often employed; firms are subject to spot visits by regulatory authorities; products and services are randomly selected and examined. Thus, the administrative costs of verifying adherence to regulatory requirements appear sometimes to be low per party, while other times some savings are realized by verifying compliance on a probabilistic basis.

We conclude that the importance of the four determinants is different for the major regulated areas from what it is for the typical tort. In the regulated areas, there is a larger likelihood that responsible parties will be unable to pay for or will escape detection and suit for harms that they bring about; and the disadvantages of regulation involving administrative costs and differential knowledge are less troublesome. Of course, the relative weights of these determinants will change from one case to the next—the possibility of escaping suit, for example, is of significant concern for harms due to pesticides although of little concern for damage caused by fire. But the overall balance of the determinants in the various cases should indicate the desirability of substantial regulation.

This general claim of theoretical consistency is further supported by considering the "second-order" choices society has made over which *aspects* of an activity to regulate given the initial choice that the activity is one that should be subject to important controls. While fire regulations will often contain requirements concerning the installation of smoke alarms and sprinkler systems, they inevitably will not cover many routine practices, such as whether to store flammable furniture polish in a closet through which a heating pipe passes. Regulating these practices would usually be very expensive (closets would have to be checked frequently) or require a highly contextual sort of knowledge (type of polish and of heating pipe). It therefore appears that the two disadvantages of regulation—the magnitude of administrative costs and the regulator's inferior information about risk—help explain what aspects of a regulated activity are left unregulated.

The claim of theoretical consistency is also confirmed by the observed interrelationship between regulation and imposition of liability, especially in the basic rule that compliance with regulation does not necessarily relieve a party of liability.[17] Moreover, the cases often say that it is 'unusual circumstances' or "increased danger" that makes additional precautions desirable, which is exactly what our theory suggested ought to give rise to liability despite satisfaction of regulation.[18] Similarly, the failure to conform to regulation does not in fact automatically result in liability.[19] And the explanation that is furnished here—that a party's "violation of the [statutory] law" does not imply his negligence if the

[17]See William L. Prosser, Handbook of the Law of Torts (4th ed. 1971), at 203.

[18]See *Id.* at 204. Also, at 203, Prosser writes, "The statutory standard is no more than a minimum, and it does not necessarily preclude a finding that the actor was negligent in failing to take additional precautions. Thus the requirement of a hand signal on a left turn does not mean that . . . a driver . . . is absolved from all obligation to slow down, keep a proper lookout, and proceed with reasonable care." This statement is in perfect agreement with our explanation from Section II, *supra,* where we said that the statutory standard ought to be regarded as a minimum since there would be parties who ought to take greater care and would not do so were they to escape liability on account of simply complying with the statutory standard.

[19]*Id.* at 197.

special circumstances justify the apparent disobedience—again comports with the theory.[20]

V. CONCLUDING COMMENTS

a. The basic purpose of the last two sections of this article has been to demonstrate how the observed use of liability and regulation can be explained by looking to the four determinants discussed at the outset. As would be true of any simple theory, however, the fit between the theory presented here and reality is only approximate.

Indeed, we often encounter the view that major mistakes have been made in the use of liability and regulation. On the one hand, it may be asserted that regulation has proved inadequate, as for instance in controlling the disposal of toxic wastes. This particular claim may well have merit, for until recently toxic wastes were little regulated, while the threat of tort liability probably provided an insufficient deterrent against improper disposal—due to manifold problems faced by victims in establishing causation and to the possibility that responsible parties would be unable to pay for harm done.[21] Conversely, there are frequent charges that certain regulations are too restrictive, as in complaints that various OSHA requirements and antipollution standards are unduly constraining or impose excessive costs on industry.[22]

That there are such examples of apparent social irrationality is to be expected, for the choices actually made about regulation and liability

[20]*Id.* at 198. At 198 and 199, Prosser writes that "it has been held not to be negligence to violate . . . a statute because of physical circumstances beyond the driver's control, as where his lights suddenly go out on the highway at night . . . . Another valid excuse is that of emergency, as where one drives on the left because the right is blocked, or a child dashes to the street . . ." (Prosser 1971: 198–9). Such results obviously agree with what we said in Section II. That is, we do not want the driver to stay on the right-hand side of the road when the child dashes out; holding him liable for being on the left would give him a socially undesirable incentive to drive on the right.

[21]See, for example, Note, Allocating the Costs of Hazardous Waste Disposal, 94 Harv. L. Rev. 584 (1981) and references cited therein; Richard A. Epstein, The Principles of Environmental Protection: The Case of Superfund, 2 Cato J. 9 (1982); and "Public Threat Feared in Loopholes in Laws on Toxic Waste Dumping," New York Times, June 6, 1983, at 1.

[22]See, for example, Stephen Breyer, Regulation and Its Reform (1982), ch. 14; Albert L. Nichols & Richard Zeckhauser, Government Comes to the Workplace: An Assessment of OSHA, 49 Public Interest 39 (1977); and, for a general introduction to the issues, ch. 5 of Environmental Law and Policy (Richard B. Stewart & James E. Krier eds. 2d ed. 1978).

are obviously influenced by factors lying outside the framework of this analysis, and in any event often will not reflect a conscious, careful use of a cost–benefit calculus. Moreover, the complexity of the relationship between liability and regulation and the many unanswered empirical questions also afford ready explanations for differences between observed and ideal results.

b. The theoretical determinants examined here would be of relevance to a more comprehensive analysis of the social control of risk, and specifically to one allowing for the use of public fines measured by harm done,[23] and of the private right to enjoin others from engaging in harmful activities. The general conclusions that would emerge from such an analysis seem clear.

First, the fine is identical to liability in that it creates incentives to reduce risk by making parties pay for the harm they cause. Thus the fine enjoys essentially the same advantages as liability rules—the private parties balance the costs of reducing risks against the benefits, while society bears administrative costs only when harm occurs. Also, the fine suffers from similar disadvantages—inability to pay for harm done dilutes its effectiveness, as does the possibility that violators would escape detection.

But the fine differs from liability in its public nature; private parties do not institute suits to collect fines nor benefit financially when they are paid. The principal implication of this difference is that the likelihood of imposition of a fine may be less than the likelihood of a private suit. Private parties should ordinarily be more likely to know when harm occurs than a public agency and, as just observed, will not profit from reporting harm but may from bringing suit. Nevertheless, in some circumstances the advantage may lie with the fine. A fine could be imposed where suits would not be brought due to difficulty in establishing causation or where harms are widely dispersed, as in many environmental and health cases.

The injunction, unlike the fine, resembles safety regulation, for it works in a direct way to control risk; the injunction prevents harm simply by proscribing certain behavior. Hence the injunction shares the main advantages of safety regulation. Its use is in no way impeded by the possibility that a party would not be able to pay for the harm he does,[24] or by the chance that the harm would be highly dispersed or hard to attribute to him under tort principles. Just as, for instance, the regulation

[23]Thus, from the point of view of parties who pay fines, it is as if they were strictly liable for harm done.

[24]This point is made in Robert C. Ellickson, Alternatives to Zoning: Covenants, Nuisance Rules, and Fines on Land Use Controls, 40 U. Chi. L. Rev. 681 (1973).

of nuclear power plants might be justified by both these factors, so too might enjoining their operations in certain circumstances.

The injunction, however, differs from safety regulation in that it is brought at the behest of private parties. The injunction accordingly has an advantage where private parties would have superior information about the harm they might suffer, as is perhaps true of ordinary nuisances. But safety regulation would be more attractive where parties are not easily able to assess dangers or where many parties are involved and "free rider" and associated problems make it difficult to coordinate a collective action.

As this discussion indicates, the injunction and safety regulation may be viewed as substitutes, but not perfect ones, and similarly with the fine and liability. Thus, although an analysis of all four methods of controlling risk would be complicated, the conclusions would parallel our own. Where the theoretical determinants had indicated a relative advantage of regulation over liability, they would now indicate an advantage of regulation or the injunction over liability or the fine.

14

Standards, Rules, and Social Norms[†]

*Eric A. Posner**

I want to discuss three things: the economic literature on rules and standards, the economic approach to social norms, and the rule of law. The connection between these topics might be hard to see. The economic literature on rules and standards deals with the optimal form of the *law*, whereas the economic literature on social norms deals with *nonlegal* phenomena and the rule of law as a political *ideal*. But I will argue that the three topics are closely related, and that analysis of them together illuminates each.

I. RULES AND STANDARDS

My exposition of the economic analysis of rules and standards relies heavily on a model used by Professor Kaplow.[1] For the sake of brevity, I will skip a number of important details, including the role of precedent; the interested reader should consult the original.

When the legislature enacts a rule, it specifies in advance of some action whether that action will be penalized. When the legislature enacts a standard, it delegates to a court the authority to determine after the action whether that action will be penalized. Rules state that you may not do *A*, *B*, and *C*; a standard typically says that you may not behave "unreasonably," or "negligently," or "unconscionably,"

[†]Originally published as "Standards, Rules, and Social Norms,", *Harvard Journal of Law and Public Policy*, 1997, Vol. 21, pp. 101–17.

*My thanks to Eric Rasmusen and Jonathan Wiener for helpful discussions.

[1]*See* Louis Kaplow, *Rules Versus Standards: An Economic Analysis*, 42 Duke L.J. 557, 624–29 (1992); *see also* citations therein.

leaving it to the courts to determine whether an action meets these criteria.[2]

Suppose a legislature contemplates regulating some action *X*. It does not know whether the action will cause harm but does know the probability that it will cause harm. Should it use a rule or a standard? The simplest case assumes that affected parties do not inform themselves about the law, whether the law is a rule or a standard. The legislature must determine two quantities. The first quantity is its one-time cost of promulgating a rule. The second quantity is computed by multiplying the cost of judicial enforcement by the expected number of accidents (which is itself a function of the number of affected parties and the care they take given the cost of the precautions available to them, their uninformed prediction of the chance of accident, and the expected harm that would result from the accident). If the first quantity exceeds the second, the legislature should enact a standard. The reason is that when few accidents are likely to occur, and the judiciary is efficient enough at evaluating them, the legislature should not bother incurring the costs of engaging in the necessary research into the possible harmful consequences of the action.

If the legislature believes that affected parties will invest in legal advice in advance of their conduct, regardless of whether the law is a rule or a standard, its calculation should change. Initially, to know whether the parties will invest in legal advice, the legislature must know the price of legal advice, and also the difference, for each person, between his total expected costs if informed and his total expected costs if uninformed. To determine the former, the legislature must perform the person's cost-minimization calculations, and *this* involves estimating the marginal value of increased precautions in reducing the probability of harm, a calculation that requires the person (in the model) to know or (more likely) to estimate the level of harm. Having determined that regulated parties will inform themselves of the law, the legislature must now compare the cost of promulgating a rule with the sum of (1) the total amount of legal costs incurred by all regulated parties, and (2) the cost of all the enforcement proceedings that result when informed parties take their optimal precautions.

The legislature might also believe that affected parties will invest in legal advice in advance of their conduct if the law is a rule but not if the

[2]As Kaplow points out, the rule-standard issue should not be confused with the optimal complexity of a rule or standard. *See* Louis Kaplow, A Model of the Optimal Complexity of Legal Rules, 11 *J. L. Econ. & Org.* 150 (1995).

law is a standard. This belief assumes that a person can more cheaply inform himself of a rule than inform himself of a standard, a plausible assumption given that the person (or his lawyer) merely consults the legislative code in order to determine the content of a rule, whereas he would have to study and interpret a body of case law in order to predict how a court would apply a standard. To determine whether to use a rule or a standard, the legislature must take account not only of promulgation and enforcement costs, but also of efficiency gains that result because a rule enables parties to take more efficient precautions than a standard does, precautions that result in an accident rate different from the rate that would exist under a standard.

Finally, if, as is plausible, some people will not inform themselves of rules or standards, some people will inform themselves of rules but not of standards, and some people will inform themselves of both rules and standards, the choice between rule and standard will depend on the fractions of the population that will invest in each level of information, and on the relative gains enjoyed by each population under each regime.

This brief summary does not do justice to Kaplow's argument, but it suffices to illustrate the tremendous amounts of information that even a simple economic analysis requires. Indeed, we have only talked about the question of whether the legislature should choose to use a rule or a standard. Having exhausted itself in making this determination, it still must choose, among other things, the optimal complexity of the rule or standard,[3] not to mention (if a rule) the normative content of the law!

The claim that economic analysis requires superhuman information-processing capabilities is an old and hackneyed criticism of law and economics. One of the economist's responses, one with which I agree, is that models usefully draw our attention to variables that should be taken into account even if they cannot always be taken into account with precision. A slightly more aggressive version of this defense holds that people can actually apply the model to the world by supplying the values for the parameters from guesses based on their rough intuitions.

This response is valid sometimes but not always. The model of rules and standards may be one of those cases in which the response fails. To see why, observe that ideally we want to economize on the total cost

[3] *See* Kaplow, *supra* note 2 (regarding complexity).

of the legal system, including the creation and enforcement of laws. Call this amount *C*. Now *C* is clearly a function of the efficiency of a particular law. If a speed limit of 55 m.p.h. is more efficient than a speed limit of 65 m.p.h., for example, then a legislature that chooses to enact the first speed limit minimizes *C* relative to the choice of the second speed limit. But suppose it is more costly for a legislature to fill in the content of the speed limit than it is for the courts to apply a speed limit standard—for example, requiring people to drive at "reasonable" speeds. Then to minimize *C*, we want the courts to do the work, not the legislatures. C, then, is a function both of the content of the law and of the *process* by which it is created (rule or standard). This is where Professor Kaplow's analysis stops. But we can go further. Suppose it is cheaper for the legislature to determine the process by which a law is created in a particular case by using rough, intuitive guesses of the value of the variables in Professor Kaplow's model rather than by sponsoring hearings and studies for the purpose of obtaining more precise estimates. Then to minimize *C*, we want the legislature to use the rough guess method. *C* is therefore a function of the content of the law, the process by which it is created, *and* the method used to determine which process to use to create the law. But how should the legislature know whether to rely on rough, intuitive guesses rather than sponsor hearings and studies for the purpose of obtaining more precise estimates? Maybe, it should mimic what it did last time it faced a question like the one under consideration, or maybe it should sponsor a study to determine the most efficient method for determining the method used to determine which process to use to create the law. You should get the point by now: there is an infinite regress.

Or to put this another way, notice all of the quantities that the legislature must estimate in order to determine whether to use a rule or a standard: the cost of promulgating a rule, the cost of enforcing a standard, the probability of accident given that people are informed of the law, the probability of accident given that they are uninformed, the expected harm they would suffer in an accident, the cost of legal advice, and so on. Where do the numbers come from? How does the legislature make "rough guesses" about these quantities?

One possible answer to these questions is that the legislature obtains these numbers by holding hearings and funding studies. But what does the legislature learn from these hearings and studies? If "hearings and studies" are defined broadly as activities that supply the legislature with *all* relevant numbers, then when it engages in "hearings and studies" in order to determine whether to use a rule or a standard, it thereby also learns the numbers necessary to choose the optimal content of the law—in which case the legislature should go ahead and issue a rule rather than force a court to duplicate this information gathering. Thus, if "hearings and studies" are defined broadly, legislatures would never issue standards.

If "hearings and studies" are defined narrowly as activities that supply the legislature with just those numbers that are necessary for performing calculations at a particular stage of analysis, for example, the rules-versus-standards stage of analysis, then the infinite regress returns. If hearings and studies would tell the legislature only that, say, a rule would be superior to a standard, the legislature must still (before knowing this) hold hearings and commission studies to determine whether hearings and studies are appropriate, rather than imitation or whatever, ad infinitum.

A second possible answer to the question how legislatures make rough guesses is that they bring with them prior knowledge about the world, and they use this knowledge to estimate the quantities needed to do the rules-standards calculation. But why should we think that they have the right kind of knowledge to make the choice between rules and standards, but not the right kind of knowledge to determine the optimal content of the law rather than deferring to the courts? If this is the case, the rules-standards analysis is irrelevant. And if we do not, then we plunge back into the regress. This time, to be sure, the regress is not necessarily infinite—at some earlier stage the legislatures might have sufficient prior knowledge about the world—but we still do not know what stage that is.

The infinite regress does not arise from any flaw in Professor Kaplow's reasoning, but is a characteristic of the optimizing methodology of economics. It is described as follows:

> Suppose that we first formulate a decision problem as a conventional optimization based on the assumption of unbounded rationality and thus on the assumption of zero deliberation cost. Suppose we then recognize that deliberation cost is positive; so we fold this further cost into the original problem. The difficulty is that the augmented optimization problem will itself be costly to analyze; and this new deliberation cost will be neglected. We can then formulate a third problem, and so on. We quickly find ourselves in an infinite and seemingly intractable regress.[4]

[4]John Conlisk, *Why Bounded Rationality?*, 34 J. Econ. Lit. 669,687 (1996).

This objection has been recognized for a long time, and there is no reason to consider it a decisive blow against economics or law and economics. One should recognize, however, that the problem looms larger in some contexts than in others. It does not seem to be a problem when one tries to determine the relative advantages of different remedies for breach of contract and other questions of substantive law. But the problem becomes hard to ignore in discussions about how laws allow legislatures, courts, and other agencies to economize on their lawmaking costs. If a law seems justified because it allows a lawmaking body to economize on its resources, a claim that the lawmaking body *chose* that law for that purpose by engaging in an optimizing methodology is caught in the snares of the infinite regress.

These objections are not merely theoretical. When one turns from theory to the practices of legislatures or courts, one sees very little of what Professor Kaplow models. This is particularly true of courts. When courts interpret precedents, they face the question whether to treat them as standards or rules. Professor Kaplow's model implies that courts should consider the cost of promulgation, the future cost of enforcement, the legal costs of affected parties, and so on, but courts do not do this or even act "as if" they did this. Instead, courts engage in a kind of practical reasoning. If earlier cases use similar reasoning and come to similar holdings with respect to a recurrent set of facts, a court may derive a rule from them; if earlier cases are inconsistent or sparse or difficult to understand, a court may assert a standard (effectively saying that future courts must determine the rule). Professor Kaplow's model also does not describe legislative behavior. Legislatures like courts generally imitate what came before them: the common law or customary law, which is codified, or earlier statutes, which themselves are based on still earlier statutes, some of them taken from foreign countries, most of which are derived ultimately from the common law or customary law.[5] One might argue that in all these cases the decision-maker is optimizing in the face of its high promulgation costs, but this response makes the rules-standards analysis trivial.

The theoretical objection raised by the infinite regress and the empirical dependence of lawmaking on imitation imply that a proper analysis of rules and standards must approach the subject from a different

[5]For a survey of evolutionary theories of the law, see E. Donald Elliott, *The Evolutionary Tradition in Jurisprudence*, 85 Colum. L. Rev. 38 (1985); see also William Ewald, *Comparative Jurisprudence (II): The Logic of Legal Transplants*, 43 Am. J. Comp. L. 489 (1995) (discussing Alan Watson's theory of legal transplants).

angle. I will suggest an approach in Part III, after what might seem to be a digression on social norms in Part II. But the connection between the two topics will presently be clear.

II. SOCIAL NORMS

In economic models in which rational actors take others' actions as given, individuals cannot cooperate for the purpose of creating collective goods. Everyone would cheat on the cooperative project, because each person does better by cheating if the others cooperate (he then obtains part of the surplus without contributing to it) and each does better by cheating if the others cheat (he avoids incurring the costs of contributing to a surplus that would not be created). Yet people often engage in cooperative activities, including the production of the various standard public goods, in the absence of legal enforcement, sometimes even in the face of legal penalties. Examples include the merchants who resolve disputes among themselves without resorting to the courts; the cattle ranchers who help each other maintain fences; and the diamond dealers who refuse to do business with those who have engaged in bad business practices.[6] One explanation of these phenomena is that "social norms" deter the undesirable conduct, but this explanation is not satisfactory. One wants to know why social norms deter the undesirable conduct, which means understanding how they come into existence in the first place. Why do people create and enforce social norms?[7]

There have been numerous attempts to answer this question, none of them wholly satisfactory but many of them illuminating and useful. I focus on two of them.

The first model uses the theories of repeat games and signaling. It begins by noting that people who cooperate often (usually?) do so over a long period of time during which each can observe the actions of others and decide on the basis of those actions whether to continue cooperating

[6] *See* Robert G. Ellickson, Order Without Law (1991); Lisa Bernstein, *Opting Out of the Legal System:Extralegal Contractual Relations in the Diamond Industry*, 21 J. Legal Stud. 115 (1992); Stewart Macaulay, *Non-Contractual Relations in Business: A Preliminary Study*, 28 Am. Soc. Rev. 55 (1963); *see generally* Eric A. Posner, *The Regulation of Groups: The Influence of Legal and Nonlegal Sanctions on Collective Action*, 63 U. Chi. L. Rev. 133 (1996).

[7] This question has drawn the attention of economists and legal economists. *See* Eric A. Posner, *Signals, Symbols, and Social Norms in Politics and the Law*, 27 J. Legal Stud. (forthcoming 1998), for one effort and for citations to both literatures. The interest among legal economists can be traced to Ellickson, *supra* note 6.

or stop. When each round of play is followed by another, players know that if they cheat in one round they may have no chance of obtaining high payoffs in the next. Some level of cooperation, and a concomitant production of some level of the potential surplus, can be sustained by various strategies, most famously, the "tit-for-tat" strategy in which a player cooperates in every round except those that succeed a round in which the other players cheated.[8] Although the results have to be interpreted with care because of the problem of multiple equilibria—and this is true especially when information is imperfect and the number of players is greater than two—the results are nonetheless highly suggestive of the possibility of nonlegal cooperation.

Although this theory takes great strides toward explaining how people can cooperate in the production of collective goods, it does not explain what a social norm is. In the diamond trade, for example, merchants no doubt refrain from misrepresenting the value of a diamond because if they were discovered, other merchants would stop doing business with them, but the repeat game theory does not explain why the merchants seal their contracts using traditional words and record their contracts in a traditional and consistent way.[9] These practices are norms. One might argue that these practices are the cheapest way to make a record, but this argument is implausible, because it does not explain why *every* transaction takes the same form. Surely, when traders know each other better or worse, or the value of the transaction is higher or lower, the optimal form of the writing would change as well. What needs to be explained is why that does not happen.

This is where the idea of signaling comes in. Suppose that in a merchant community some people are better contractual partners than others. This may occur for several reasons: the "high" types care more about future payoffs, or they feel guilty easily, or they cannot hide their intentions well, and so on. The "low" types are the opposite. When seeking partners in contractual endeavors, high types want to match up with other high types, but low types want to match up with high types. Low types hit upon the strategy of sending "signals" that they think high types will think that only other high types can send. But because a high type who accepts a low type as a contractual partner risks

[8]The literature on this topic is vast; the interested reader should consult standard game theory texts for discussion and citations. *See, e.g.*, Eric Rasmusen, Games and Information (2d ed. 1994).

[9]*See* Bernstein, *supra* note 6, at 122.

being cheated, high types will send their own signals. They might mimic the signals of the low types in order to avoid the impression of being low themselves, or they might send even more costly signals than the low types do. Depending on the cost structures of the various signals, it is possible to obtain equilibria in which only the high types send the signal, or equilibria in which everyone sends a signal. (Other possibilities exist as well.) The latter equilibria are not informative, and do no one any good, but they can be sustained because no one wants to deviate from the equilibrium signal lest as a consequence others believe that he is a low type.

There are many examples of such signaling in everyday life, of which gift-giving is probably the most intuitive. People give gifts to each other in order to show that they care about maintaining relationships: low types find it hard to give gifts, or good gifts, because they are costly and they require a costly inquiry into the other person's tastes.[10] In the example of the diamond community, the peculiar use of the writing may have begun as a signal of one's type. A low type may have introduced the writing as a way of persuading the other person that he was a high type. After all, the writing is costly in the sense that the existence of a record makes it more difficult to cheat one's partner by misrepresenting the transaction to arbitrators or witnesses in case of a dispute. The high types, who may have been happy enough with oral transactions, would hasten to mimic the low types, so that their partners would not think that *they* are the low types. Social norms, then, reflect signaling behavior: unlike efficient behavior in transactions, which one can expect to vary according to the type of transaction, signaling behavior is always patterned, norm-like.[11]

The second theory focuses on coordination games, rather than on prisoners' dilemmas. In a coordination game, both players do better if they engage in a similar or symmetrical action than if they do not. An old example draws on the problem of two people driving towards each other on roads without lanes. If both people drive on the right or both people drive on the left, they receive high payoffs. If one person drives on the right while the other drives on the left, they crash. It can be shown that if people generally imitate people with higher payoffs (those who do not crash), and if enough people start off choosing the same

[10] *See* Eric A. Posner, *Altruism, Status, and Trust in the Law of Gifts and Gratuitous Promises*, 1997 Wis. L. Rev. 567 (1997).

[11] *See* Posner, *supra* note 7 (regarding symbols).

strategy, over time one strategy will drive out the other and result in an equilibrium that is stable against occasional mistakes or experiments with novel strategies.[12] The equilibrium strategy, for example driving on the right, can be called a social norm. What is striking about this result, and what distinguishes it from the earlier model, is that it holds even if people are strangers who are not self-consciously involved in a cooperative endeavor.

In the case of the merchant group, the form of writing could have been a convention in this sense. If some people started using writings at random or as an experiment or as the result of a misunderstanding, and it turned out that they were later involved in fewer disputes, others might have started imitating the first. Notice that the use of the writing may be value- maximizing, but it survives as a result of a kind of natural selection, not because of rational optimization. But this means that people may continue to imitate both the use of a writing and the particular form of the writing long after it ceases to be value-maximizing.

These models do not explain all forms of collective action; indeed, they raise as many problems as they solve. But they appear to have fruitful implications, which I will discuss below. Also, notice that the first model relies on the standard optimizing methodology of economics, whereas the second assumes that people mimic rather than optimize—or, to use the trendy phrase, it assumes that people are "boundedly rational."

III. IMPLICATIONS

A. Positive Implications

It is difficult to interpret Professor Kaplow's model as a positive model, because it puts too heavy an epistemic burden on legislatures and courts, and because the evidence suggests that legislatures and courts do not typically weigh costs and benefits when choosing between rules and standards. The signaling model and the evolutionary model offer some alternatives.

To illustrate the application of the signaling model, assume that legislators, like our merchants and cattle ranchers, have an interest in signaling that they are high types. Space limitations prevent me from defending the assumption, but something like it can be found in various models of the political process. If this is so, time-consuming and expensive legislative studies emerge as signals in equilibrium. The reason is that if

[12] *See* Robert Sugden, The Economics of Rights, Co-operation, and Welfare 34 (1986).

people cannot directly observe the quality of laws, and therefore cannot vote for legislators on the basis of the quality of the legislative product, they might infer the type of a legislator from the energy that he puts into legislation. A legislator might then overinvest in legislation, which could take the form of supporting rules over standards, because by hypothesis standards cost the legislature little. (Legislators might also overinvest by supporting lots of different laws.) They might create standards only (or usually) when the subject of the law is controversial, thus requiring courts to absorb the political costs of taking the wrong position. One might thus expect uncontroversial laws (traffic regulations, tax codes) to appear as rules and unpopular or controversial laws (abortion regulation, affirmative action programs) to appear as standards.

The first model also suggests that if judges want to have influence, they can cause other judges to follow them on some cases if they can commit themselves to following those judges on other cases. One way to commit oneself, if one otherwise cares about the content of an opinion, is to follow another judge even when one does not agree with him or her.[13] If this is true, rules may emerge in areas of law where disputes are common and not in areas of law where they are rare, for only in the former will it be clear enough that a judge is following another judge rather than contradicting him.

To illustrate the application of the second model, assume that legislatures mimic other legislatures. They might do so because the effect of most laws on social behavior is so complex that a boundedly rational legislator could not predict it. Ironically, it is possible that the results of Professor Kaplow's model will be vindicated. For if laws containing optimal rules and standards are more likely to survive (in the sense that legislatures revise rules and standards only when they lead to observable pathologies), then imitation of them will cause them to spread. However, it is also possible that lags will occur.

Finally, assume that courts are also boundedly rational, and imitate prior opinions when the facts underlying those opinions sufficiently resemble the facts of the case before them. When such imitation occurs, observers (or the court itself) will say that the precedent states a rule. When a case is novel, and the court must decide on the basis of the facts, it will appeal to a standard. So when, in a particular area of law, facts vary

[13] *See, e.g.*, Thomas J. Miceli and Metin M. Cosgel, *Reputation and Judicial Decision-Making*, 23 J. Econ. Behav. & Org. 31 (1994); Eric Rasmusen, *Judicial Legitimacy As a Repeated Game*, 10 J.L. Econ. & Org. 63 (1994).

considerably from case to case, that area of law will be more standard-like, whereas in other areas of the law rules will emerge.

These sketchy examples should not persuade anyone that Professor Kaplow's analysis is right or wrong. For one thing, Professor Kaplow's analysis is normative, and these examples are all of positive analysis. For another, the first model relies on the same optimizing methodology that I criticized while discussing Professor Kaplow's model. I do think that the infinite regress is less of a danger in the first model than in Professor Kaplow's model, mainly because the first model does not ask players to economize on deliberation costs, but I do not have the space to defend this argument. The lesson of the discussion is more modest: it is that models that analyze incentives to engage in cooperative action may be helpful for explaining important features of the legal system, including the use of rules and standards.

B. Normative Implications: The Rule of Law

The different models have many normative implications, but I want to focus on the implications for the rule of law. By the rule of law I mean an ideal that law should inflict punishment only on people who engage in actions that conform to general categories identified by that law, and not on people who engage in actions or have characteristics that the authorities conclude are undesirable after the fact. Because the rule of law implies a preference for identification of proscribed actions in advance, it implies (as the name suggests) a preference for rules over standards.[14] Although a legislature, by issuing a standard, announces in advance of the regulated conduct that anyone who engages in that conduct now risks a sanction, in practice this announcement does not amount to much. To announce, for example, that product liability will henceforth be determined by the standard of negligence does not tell people what is permitted and what is not permitted, though it gives them something of an idea. I do not mean to suggest, however, that standards are inherently bad: the rule of law is one among many values, and departure from it on occasions to economize on lawmaking costs may be justified. Indeed, this is one interpretation of Professor Kaplow's analysis.

The signaling model suggests deeper problems with standards, problems that arise because people's behavior may be more sensitive

[14]*See* generally Frederick Schauer, *Rules and the Rule of Law*, 14 Harv. J.L. & Pub. Pol'y 645 (1991).

to standards than to rules. Consider an example from Professor Lessig, which I will quote at length:

Before the 1960s, motorcyclists in Soviet Russia did not wear helmets. In part this was because of a lack of any perceived need to wear helmets; in part it was because the Soviet economy failed to produce any helmets . . . Soon Russians began to wear motorcycle helmets produced in Western Europe. . . .

When these helmets first began to appear, the Soviet government quickly reacted against them. For despite bearing the medical costs associated with cycling accidents, the Soviets perceived a much greater cost to the Soviet state associated with individuals wearing helmets, that is, the invasion of Western style. Because helmets were produced only in the West, wearing them was a political statement antithetical to the message the Soviet government wanted broadcast.

Thus began an extraordinary and self-conscious campaign by the Soviet government to vilify the wearers of motorcycle helmets. Cartoons appeared in the popular (read: government-controlled) press. . . . By the early 1960s, people began wearing helmets only at night, to avoid easy detection.

The night-riding behavior suggests the campaign attacking helmet wearing as "imperialism" had some effect. For no laws were passed banning the wearing of helmets.[15]

When the Soviet Union finally began manufacturing helmets in its own factories, people began to wear helmets again (presumably, during the day): the stigma now was not against wearing any helmet, only against wearing imported helmets.[16]

In the United States, any opinion by the President or other important officials on the desirability of motorcycle helmets would be widely ignored if not ridiculed, just as President Carter's urging that people lower their thermostats was widely ridiculed. It certainly would not influence the frequency with which people wear helmets. The United States, in fact, uses laws to encourage people to wear helmets.

What accounts for this difference? An answer is that in the Soviet Union having a reputation for loyalty to the state was, in the eyes of the authorities, far more important than it is in the United States. In the Soviet Union, a bad reputation could result in expulsion from the Communist Party, and as a consequence in denial of education, desirable jobs, and other benefits. In the United States a bad reputation matters less because the state does not punish you for having it. To put

[15]Lawrence Lessig, *The Regulation of Social Menning*, 62 U. Chi. L. Rev. 943, 964–65 (1995).

[16]*See id.* at 965.

this in terms of the signaling model, it was more important to signal one's loyalty to the state in the Soviet Union than it ever has been in the United States. Thus, in the Soviet Union, people would voluntarily engage in patriotic displays, refrain from criticizing the government, and even refrain from wearing motorcycle helmets when doing so was defined as disloyal or unpatriotic. In the United States this phenomenon is rarer because the commitment to the rule of law generally restricts the ability of legislatures to enact vague standards (for example, "you must be patriotic") that can lead to the pooling behavior that occurred in the Soviet Union.

The conformity-inducing properties of standards, however, do not depend on secret police. In the United States, standards would be enforced by the courts. If people cannot anticipate in advance which actions conform to the standard and which actions violate it, they will engage in actions that serve as signals that they possess the characteristics that they believe courts would look for. The result would be pooling of the sort that occurred in the Soviet Union, though no doubt on a smaller scale. A commitment to the rule of law, in contrast, forces legislatures to specify the desired behavior in advance. Because it is (comparatively) clear what is permitted and what is not permitted, less pooling can be expected. Or to put it in terms of the model, when the signal of loyalty or good behavior is too costly, people will not use it, instead satisfying their nonreputational preferences. People may abide by rules in a casuistic manner, sometimes defeating the policy they implement, but they will overcomply with standards.

Should this bother us? From the perspective of social welfare in the economist's sense, this question is quite difficult. Pooling equilibria can be socially costly because everyone incurs costs in sending signals that do not produce any informational benefits. But if sending a signal (like wearing a helmet) causes less total harm than would exist in a separating equilibrium (in which only some people wear helmets), then the pooling equilibria would be superior on efficiency grounds. This means that, even if some regulated behavior will occur rarely and there will be few enforcements, a standard may be inappropriate, because it may cause overcompliance.

But from a different perspective—from the perspective of *autonomy*—the use of standards is more clearly troubling. When people feel that they must signal in order to avoid inferences that they are low types—unpatriotic or disloyal or careless or unreasonable—then they will engage in various forms of patterned behavior rather than satisfying their tastes or pursuing their goals. The Soviet authorities never had to say that wearing bicycle helmets is a punishable offense: once it had expressed its disapproval, people would overreact to avoid the inference of disloyalty. Vague statements about the undesirability of various jobs, pursuits, hobbies, social relationships, and views would likely cause a similar reaction. Indeed, even if the state expresses no opinion on these issues, but punishes anyone deemed unpatriotic, people will struggle to act in conformity with whatever norms they think the state would approve.

When reputation matters a lot, people will conform to whatever pattern of behavior they believe that everyone else approves. When reputation matters a lot to the *state,* with unpleasant consequences to those who have a bad reputation, people will conform to whatever pattern of behavior they believe that the state approves. The state exploits this phenomenon by announcing standards of behavior (the patriotic citizen, or the good socialist), rather than announcing rules, for rules give people the freedom to choose among the actions that are not specifically prohibited. This is why states in which people have freedom also have a strong commitment to the rule of law, and it may be why the rule of law is such a powerful political ideal that overrides short-term concerns about social welfare.

IV. CONCLUSION

This talk has consisted of a hodgepodge of points, none of them strongly supported, all of them speculative, so let me briefly summarize the most important in a manner that does not exaggerate their strength. First is an uneasiness with the optimizing method in some (but not all) contexts of legal decision-making: one may be able to overcome this uneasiness by embedding the decision in a game in which people spontaneously cooperate, so that legal decisions are an outcome of their cooperative behavior; or one may overcome this uneasiness more directly by modeling bounded rationality. But though the latter approach is exciting and perhaps theoretically more pure, it is hampered by the primitive state of the methodology. Second is the claim that the rule of law is important not because rules are better than standards on efficiency grounds—in fact, Professor Kaplow's analysis plausibly suggests that sometimes rules are better and sometimes standards are better. The rule of law is important if we care about autonomy, because standards, more so than rules, encourage self-reinforcing conformity to the imagined goals of the state rather than actions that reflect one's authentic values and interests.

Law, Governance and Values

15

Conflicting Values in Law†

*Cass R. Sunstein**

I thank you all for coming on a rainy day. Actually, I am a little preoccupied right now because there was in a Fordham colleague's office a chart which said how much Elvis would weigh on every planet and on the Sun. On Pluto, Elvis would weigh a mere thirteen pounds; and on the Sun, Elvis would weigh over 7,000 pounds. This is actually related to my topic.

I have two quotations with which to begin. The first is from the United States Constitution, and it goes like this: "No title of Nobility shall be granted by the United States."[1]

The second quotation is from a recent winner of the Nobel Prize in Economics, the University of Chicago's own Gary Becker. Here is how the second one goes: "An efficient marriage market"—now, this is personally relevant to some people here, I know, so please do listen:

> [A]n efficient marriage market assigns imputed income or "prices" to all participants that attract them to suitable polygamous or monogamous marriages. Imputed prices are also used to match men and women of different qualities: some participants... choose to be matched with "inferior" persons because they feel "superior" persons are too expensive....
>
> [A]n efficient marriage market usually has positive assortative mating, where high-quality men are matched with high-quality women and low-quality men

†Originally published as "Conflicting Values in Law", 1994, *Fordham Law Review*, Vol. 62, pp. 1661–73.

*This essay was presented as the Robert L. Levine lecture at Fordham University School of Law. It has been lightly edited, and footnotes have been added, but it retains the form and style of the oral remarks. For a more formal and detailed presentation, see Cass R. Sunstein, Incommemesurability and Valuation in Law, 92 Mich. L. Rev. 779 (1994).

[1]U.S. Const art. I, § 9, cl. 8.

with low-quality women, although [and this makes it somewhat less depressing] negative assortative mating is sometimes important.[2]

I think there is a connection between the quotation from the Constitution and the quotation from Gary Becker, and I hope this will emerge in the course of my comments.

What I want to do is explore two claims and say something about their implications for law.

The first claim is that we value things in different ways; that is to say, we value things not only in terms of intensity, but in qualitatively distinct ways. It is not simply the case that some things are valued more; it is also the case that some things are valued differently from others. That is my first claim, about different modes of valuation.

The second claim is that human goods are not commensurable. This is to say that there is no available metric along which we can align the various goods that are important to us, and that any effort to come up with a metric, like utility or dollars, while nominally designed to aid human reasoning, actually makes human reasoning worse than what it is when it is working well.

So the first claim has to do with diverse modes of valuation; the second has to do with incommensurability. I do think that these claims have important implications for law, though, unfortunately, it is not the case that these claims lead simply to particular recommendations. So I have to apologize in advance for saying that while these things bear on how legal problems are thought about, it is not true that they lead directly to particular outcomes. But by way of diminishing the level of abstraction, let me say something about the areas of law on which they do bear.

In environmental law, it often seems as if there is a debate between economists and environmentalists, with economists acting as if they value the environment somewhat less than the fanatical environmentalists who value it a lot. It might be more accurate to say that economists and environmentalists value the environment in different ways, with economists thinking that the environment is for human exploitation and use, and environmentalists sometimes challenging that assumption.

In debates over surrogacy and prostitution, I think it is very hard to make sense of very prominent current views within the law without noting the existence of an objection to surrogacy arrangements and prostitution that says that the way in which those transactions value sexuality and reproduction is unfortunate and deserving of disapproval.

[2]Gary S. Becker, A Treatise on the Family 108 (2d ed. 1991).

Many current debates over the role of religion in society have a lot to do with modes of valuation. A big decision the Clinton Administration has to make, I think in the next two weeks, is how to handle the Reagan–Bush Executive Order[3] on federal regulation, which moves cost/benefit analysis to the fore. How cost/benefit analysis is thought about has everything to do with modes of valuation.

The talk will come in three parts: the first will have to do with modes of valuation; the second will discuss commensurability; the third, and longest, will have to do with law; here I will try to bring all of this down to earth. So if the stuff with which I am about to get going seems too abstract, I promise that the examples will come before terribly long.

I. MODES OF VALUATION

I have said that we value things in different ways, that goods are subject to diverse modes of valuation.

Let's begin with a simple distinction between goods that are intrinsically valuable and goods that are instrumentally valuable. I think Scrooge is the only character I know for whom a dollar bill was intrinsically valuable. For the rest of us, a dollar bill is valuable for what it can do; it is not valuable in itself. Education is something that has both instrumental and intrinsic value; that is, it is valuable in itself and it is valuable for what it can do for you. If we knew somebody who thought that education was solely of instrumental value, it would seem quite strange.

Goods like friendships are of intrinsic value; they are valuable for themselves and not valuable because of what they are an instrument to.

So a first distinction is the distinction between instrumental and intrinsic value.

The category of goods that have intrinsic value is itself quite diverse. There are goods that are intrinsically valuable that produce respect—an acquaintance might do that. There are goods that are intrinsically valuable that produce affection—a friendship. There are things that produce wonder or awe, like a great musical work or a mountain. There are things that produce gratitude or love. And there are things that are solely for use—our category of instrumental goods.

So every day we make differences among modes of valuation. This is not simply true of good things; it is also true of bad things. Some things

[3]*See* Exec. Order No. 12,291, 3 C.F.R. 127 (1982), *reprinted in* 5 U.S.C. § 601 (1988).

produce contempt; others produce anger and so forth. There is a wide range of negative and positive valuations.

Somebody who didn't make distinctions among modes of valuation might seem really strange, like a character in a science fiction story, or obtuse. If you saw someone who had just pro or con attitudes without making these distinctions, it would be an odd figure indeed, though if we thought for a bit, we could probably think of fictional characters who fit that bill.

What I want to suggest is that there isn't any super-concept—like happiness, or utility, or wealth maximization, or good—that can make sense out of our reflective evaluations in their diversity. That is to say, there isn't any big thing of which all these things are simply aspects. Any big thing that can be identified must allow room for the qualitative distinctions that modes of valuation embody.

That is basically an outline of modes of valuation. Conflicts among modes of valuation are really pervasive.

You can imagine an economist, let's say, who is working hard on a paper and who has scheduled lunch with an out-of-town friend. Let's suppose the economist would like to cancel the lunch, but feels bad about it because it is kind of disrespectful and inconvenient. Let's suppose the economist says to the friend, "I will compensate you—$20, $40, $80, $100, $160—for the cancellation." This would be an absurd response, though perhaps it has happened, and perhaps the so-called victim was, on balance, happy as a result. It would be an absurd response because the payment of cash as compensation for his cancellation of lunch is inconsistent with the way someone values a friend. It is not, I think, quite right to say that the cash is less valuable than the lunch; in fact, if we are talking about aggregates and amounts, the cash might well be less valuable than the lunch. It is that the payment of cash is inconsistent with the way the lunch is valued, and that's what makes it seem like an insult.

I think that this somewhat absurd example helps with an extraordinary array of cases in which social norms or attitudes or law block the use of dollars as a mechanism for doing some sort of exchange work. Let me just give some examples.

If an adult neighbor asks another adult neighbor to mow his or her lawn for a fee, it would probably be perceived as an insult, as if the adult neighbor is being treated as a servant rather than as a person worthy of respect. To offer the dollars is turning the neighbor into someone for your use.

If someone says to you, "I will pay you a lot of money if you go out of town and leave your family for two months," you might do it, but it would seem awful. On the other hand, if an employer says, "As part of this job you have to leave for a month or two, that is part of what the job is"—it's called employment with a New York law firm, let's say—it might be okay. I think that the difference between the two cases is that in one case, absence from family is being sought by the employer, so-called, as a good to be promoted for its own sake; whereas in the other case, the absence is brought about as a kind of by-product of a job.

The movie "Indecent Proposal" is all about this—the use of dollars as a way of turning someone into a sexual object and what that does to a relationship. To get a little closer to law, suppose that in a case of environmental protection, we are trying to figure out how much to value a mountain. If a certain number of dollars is assigned to protection of the mountain, which is almost certainly a fine thing to do, it might well be jarring to say, in a kind of very simple way, "The mountain is really worth, say, two million dollars." That is jarring, I think, because the way the dollars are valued is different from the way the mountain is valued. The mountain is valued as something worthy of respect for some, or maybe awe and wonder for others, and dollars, though maybe deserving a kind of wonder and awe, get a different kind of wonder and awe from a mountain.

I think this issue is all over the current debate with respect to surrogacy arrangements, so-called "baby selling," and prostitution. Judge Posner has suggested a market in babies in writing that perhaps (in my view unfortunately) disqualifies him for appointment to the Supreme Court of the United States.[4] The argument is very provocative and interesting. One thing it doesn't quite pick up on is the possibility that the way babies are valued is inconsistent with trading them on markets, and that is undoubtedly part of the horror at the public reaction to the proposal.

I have given many examples in which dollar trading of things is inconsistent with the mode of valuation of those intrinsic goods. But this is not simply a problem for money. If someone treated a cat in the same way that ordinary people treat a spouse, or if someone treated a diamond in the way that most people treat an animal, something odd would be going on. Quite apart from the issue of financial equivalence, people make distinctions in modes of valuation in their reactions to goods or events.

In lots of areas involving suggested political or legal changes, there is an issue with respect to modes of valuation. We cannot describe the shift from feudalism to capitalism in a sentence, but one thing that happened

[4]*See* Richard A. Posner, Sex and Reason 409–17 (1992).

in that shift was a transition from one mode of valuation to another. With respect to the legal attack on segregation and slavery, a reform occurred in which people who were formerly for other people's use and control were seen as entitled to equal respect. With respect to the exclusion of religious convictions from the public realm, something that seems to have occurred in the last twenty years, sometimes at least, is that certain modes of valuation are being ruled off limits to politics.[5]

The movement for animal rights presents a lot of puzzles. This isn't at all the place to come to closure on that complicated issue. But the movement for animal rights might be best taken as suggesting that animals are entitled to either respect or consideration, and not to be treated as something for human exploitation and use. What the movement for animal rights is trying to do is to shift the mode of valuation and not only the intensity or quantity of valuation.

I have one more notation on modes of valuation and then we are on to commensurability. It often happens in a first-year class that there will be some question raised about the value of a life or a house, and some student will rebel against the effort to monetize, at which point an instructor or another student will say, "Well, that means you must think the life or the house is infinitely valuable," at which point the debate is over. It works as a laugh line and as a decisive objection. I think that victory—the infinite valuation point—is unearned. Often what the student is saying, in the resistance to monetization, is not about infinite value, but about the fact that things are valued in different ways. If the student says that, he or she has to explain a lot. The conversation is hardly concluded, but at least we can start to understand what it is that he or she is getting at.

So much for modes of valuation.

II. INCOMMENSURABILITY

By 'incommensurability', I mean to suggest that some human goods cannot be aligned along a single metric without doing violence to our considered judgments about how those goods are best characterized and experienced. By this I mean that if you develop a single metric, like dollars, by which to align things, you will often do violence to your own judgments about how those things are best understood.

Here is a story. At an academic conference, a friend of mine was buying a present for his daughter at a bookstore which also had presents for kids. He was somewhat embarrassed to be buying a present for his daughter at an

[5]For a discussion, see Stephen L. Carter, A Culture of Disbelief (1993).

academic conference. He said, "I'm purchasing goodwill." Now, he loved his daughter and he wasn't purchasing goodwill, but he was translating into the terms of commensurability what it was that he was doing; he was acting as if what he was doing was partaking of monetary exchange.

This is a jarring description. By telling the story, I mean to suggest is that sometimes there is no single metric available by which to order our assessments of various different goods. This is not to say that judgments among incommensurable goods are irrational or not subject to reasoned valuation. We decide all the time whether to take a job in one city or another, whether to do one thing or another during the evening, whether to take a vacation or not. Often incommensurable goods are at stake and judgments are made, and they can be reasonable or not. I am suggesting that if these various goods are aligned on a single metric, then we are doing violence to our best characterizations of what those things are.

It would not be conceptually impossible to make things commensurable—to line up, for example, vacation and work, or being with family or not, along a single metric, to use something like utility or dollars in order to get analysis going. Mill, the great utilitarian, was extremely tortured on the commensurability point. But this would be a way of doing violence, I think, to the way we really think about these things.

There is a relationship between my claim that there are diverse modes of valuation and my claim about incommensurability, but I want just to bracket that for a moment; to say a few more words about incommensurability, and then to get to some specifics.

One point about incommensurability is that in its most extreme form, it blocks certain reasons for action completely. Sometimes the existence of incommensurability rules off-limits certain bases for doing things that are on-limits in other places. Consider what might happen if a parent is asked, "For how much would you sell your child?" It is not as if the parent is insulted because the amount is too low; it is not as if one is asked, "Could I buy your suit for a dollar?" It is not as if the amount seems scandalously low. It's as if there is something extremely inappropriate about entertaining the choice at all.

This is also the case, I think, in areas of constitutional rights, where Ronald Dworkin describes rights as "trumps,"[6] and where the Supreme Court says administrative convenience is not a basis for intruding on a fundamental right.[7] I think our notion of what rights are is inflected,

[6]*See* Ronald Dworkin, Taking Rights Seriously at xi-xii, 187–205 (1978).
[7]*See* Goldberg v. Kelly, 397 U.S. 254, 266 (1970).

at least, with an understanding that they cannot be compromised for certain kinds of reasons, as well as that they cannot be compromised unless the reason is very strong. You have to have a certain sort of reason as well as a reason of a certain level of intensity.

Some of the most interesting cases of incommensurability are ones in which the existence of no single metric makes certain reasons for action, like the acceptance of dollars, wholly illegitimate as a basis for action. But incommensurability is not just a barrier to action; it also makes possible certain valuable human relations. Without incommensurability, our understanding of what a friendship is, or what it means to be a parent, or what a beach is, would be compromised badly. So we ought not to think of the existence of incommensurability as simply an obstacle. It is also freedom-promoting, in the sense that it makes possible certain valuable human connections and relationships.

Some people think that claims of this sort—and I am going to stay abstract just for a moment longer—are not so important because it is equally accurate to say that certain things are valued a whole lot more than others. It is just as accurate to say things are valued more than others as it is to say that they are valued differently. The philosopher Donald Regan writes that, "when someone refuses to sell friendship for dollars, I think what such a person is most likely to mean is that friendship is more valuable than any amount of money, or, in other words, that the value of friendship is in comparably greater."[8] Says Regan, "When someone refuses to sell a child, it is closer to the truth to say that we regard the value of parenthood as incomparably greater than the value of money than to say that we regard these values as incommensurable."[9]

Regan is suggesting that these cases are best made sense of by saying that some things we value a lot, and in his view, it clouds things to say that they are valued differently. I think that Regan's challenge to incommensurability—as a description of what people mean and what they experience—is unsuccessful. It is possible to imagine someone who thinks that the value of parenthood or friendship is much higher than dollars and not that the value is different from dollars, but it would be a strange person if his assessment of why the child would not be sold was really, "I just like this child a lot more than even ten million dollars, even ten billion dollars." In other words, part of what it means to be a

[8]Donald H. Regan, *Authority and Value: Reflections on Raz's Morality of Freedom*, 62 S. Cal. L. Rev. 995, 1058 (1989).
[9]*Id.* at 1067–68.

parent is to rule off-limits, even as a consideration, the exchange of the relationship for dollars.

I promised I was going to get more concrete, and I am about to. Now I'm going to talk about law.

Two qualifications. It is not the case that law automatically maps, or translates our best valuations into, legal requirements. We might think, for example, that there is something about prostitution that is debasing to human sexuality, and so it is good to have a social norm that says that prostitution is not the preferred sexual mode. But we might think, at the same time, that the law ought not to ban prostitution. It would be perfectly reasonable to say that surrogacy arrangements are not the best way of producing children, but the law won't ban that. So one might think that the legal system ought not to do what social norms do.

My other qualification is this: I am going to go now over a wide range of areas of law and suggest how these issues might bear on current legal disputes, without attempting at all to resolve these issues. I am going to sacrifice depth for breadth.

The unifying theme has to do with what we might call the expressive function of law. By the expressive function of law, I mean not simply the social consequences of law, which are what are typically described, but also what sorts of values the law expresses. This, I think, plays a tacit role in lots of legal debates.

For example, there is a lot of work among economists and some lawyers about whether the antidiscrimination laws of the 1960s actually changed the world at all. Are the lives of black people better off because of those laws? Some people think that the evidence is not fully in. If what I am about to say is right, it still counts in favor of those laws that they express an appropriate valuation of the role of skin color in human relations—even if we cannot show and do not know whether those laws have resulted in higher welfare for the groups they are intended to benefit. That is to say that the values that the law expresses are themselves of interest independent of the direct social consequences.

We should break up this idea of the expressive function of law into two different notions. The first is that we might care about the expressive function of law because the value the law expresses will itself have consequences for social attitudes. If it is the case that prostitution is regularly admitted into society, it might be that social attitudes will shift in a way that is unfortunate.

I think a lot of debate over such things as affirmative action, capital punishment, surrogacy arrangements, prostitution, and drug legalization have to do with the social effects of the mode of valuation that law expresses. And here we are talking about consequences: Is the expression of an appropriate mode, in a way that will affect social attitudes for the better or for the worse?

But there is another notion which is not quite about effects on social attitudes. Here I have a quotation for you that grabbed me while I was writing this paper. It is a quotation from a civil rights demonstrator in the 1960s:

> If I had known that not a single lunch counter would open as a result of my action I could not have done differently than I did. If I had known violence would result, I could not have done differently than I did. I am thankful for the sit-ins if for no other reason than that they provided me with an opportunity for making a slogan into reality, by turning a decision into an action. It seems to me that this is what life is all about.[10]

Now, this is a very stark version of the expressive function of law—the notion that the valuation that law expresses is worth attention independent of social consequences. In this lies the stuff of fanaticism, so one wants to be cautious about the endorsement of the law's expressive function quite apart from social consequences. But I think it is hard to get a full handle on legal debates without seeing that the expressive function—even in this stark, totally non-consequential sense—is part of what the debates are about.

Now for some specifics. In our society, the law carves up the world into different social spheres: politics, religion, family, labor unions, markets. One way to get a handle on what is done through this legal differentiation is to see it as a way a liberal society—"liberal" in the old sense—makes space for different modes of valuation. The family is typically the sphere for affection and love; religion is the sphere for devotion; the market is the sphere for use; politics is the sphere for the exchange of reasons.

Social criticism often consists of saying that one sphere does not live up to its aspiration; that the family, nominally a sphere for love, is actually a sphere for domination; or that politics, nominally a sphere for the exchange of reasons, is actually a place where money and use are very important. I do not mean to question these possibilities. All I mean to suggest is that social differentiation in this really critical sense is best understood as an effort to make space for different evaluative modes.

The Establishment Clause of the Constitution is very hard to make sense out of. What social work is it doing, in saying that the government

[10]James Miller, "Democracy is in the Streets" 52 (1987).

cannot establish an official religion? As it has come to be understood, one thing that it does is to exclude from the political realm a certain mode of valuation which is perfectly acceptable in the private realm, that is, one of devotion to a deity. That mode of valuation—let's call it worship—is acceptable privately; but it has no role in the public sphere. The Establishment Clause, I think, at its inception and now is best understood as excluding a mode of valuation from political life.

The Equal Protection Clause can be seen as a big generalization of the titles of nobility clause with which I began. It has a similar aspiration. At least one of the things the equal protection clause is trying to do is to say that modes of valuation that reflect inadequate respect for blacks or women are not an acceptable part of political debate. An effort to pass a law because of a belief that one group is below another is systematically out of bounds.

The Supreme Court has placed an emphasis on the legitimacy of reasons for governmental action.[11] A literacy test that is disguised to produce good electors is fine; a literacy test that it supposed to exclude blacks is not fine.[12] If all we cared about is consequences, it might not be extremely easy to make sense out of that. Consequentialists are very agile; but I think we do not make full sense out of what is happening in the area of equality law without seeing that the mode of valuation is crucial to judicial determinations of whether the equality norm is violated.

In the law of environmental protection, there are a lot of puzzles. Recently, Americans were asked whether they agreed with the statement that "the environment is more important than anything and worth protecting regardless of the cost." Guess how many Americans said yes? Eighty percent.[13]

In response to surveys, when people are asked, "How much would you have to be paid in order to allow degradation of a park or the air of a certain percentage?" over half refused to answer.[14] If people are asked, "How much would you pay to allow continued existence of the park, or continued existence of an endangered species?" they will give an amount that it is not always that high. But if they are asked how much would they have to be paid, they say something like, "Get out of here, surveyor. I don't answer those questions."

[11] *See* Washington v. Davis, 426 U.S. 229, 239 (1976).

[12] *See id.* at 245–46.

[13] *See Poll Shows Four of Five Americans Support Environment, Even Over Economy*, 23 Env. Rep. (BNA) 1155 (Aug. 7, 1992).

[14] *See* Daniel Kahneman et al., *The Endowment Effect, Loss Aversion, and Status Quo Bias*, 5 J. Econ. Persp. 193, 202–03 (1991).

If we look at our cost–benefit charts—expenditures per life saved—there are wild disparities, ranging from about zero dollars per life saved to the billions.[15] One regulation apparently cost over a trillion dollars per life saved—a pretty dumb regulation.

I think that it is not easy to make sense out of this without adverting to the fact that people are often saying things that suggest that the way they value the environment is inconsistent with exchange for cash straight up. Now again, this is not a claim for infinite valuation of the environment. It is a claim that one can get some purchase on the seemingly weird results by attending to what people actually say when they start to spell these things out—which has to do not with infinite valuation, but different kinds of valuation of what it is that the environment is for. When they say such things as, "No amount of money would be compensation for the extinction of a species," they are talking quite the way parents would if asked how much they would have to be paid to give up their daughter.

If this is right, the problem with cost–benefit analysis is not that it is distributionally wrong, or that it is inferior to the status quo; it is probably better than the status quo of crazy quilt patterns and irrational regulations. The problem with cost–benefit analysis is that it is obtuse. It is obtuse because it does not disaggregate its various ingredients and allow participants in the democratic process a full picture of the differently valued goods that are at stake. If you are told that the cost–benefit analysis for an OSHA regulation has flunked, you know much too little. What is important to know is what those numbers represent. Do they mean more unemployment, more poverty, or higher food prices? A more disaggregated picture of consequences, while more unruly, would give a better account.

All this does not just relate to public law; it relates to private law, too. In the law of contracts, courts sometimes give specific performance remedies; that is, not dollar damages but a right to the thing itself. I guess Kim Bassinger was almost compelled to do a specific performance for a movie that has been released with another actress.

Here a real puzzle in Anglo-American law: When is specific performance granted? For economists, this quite a puzzle. The conventional answer is that specific performance is granted when the thing in question—let's say it is a painting or a piece of land—has value to the plaintiff that is too hard for courts to assess, so the costs of assessment are so high that the courts will order specific performance.[16]

[15] *See* Stephen Breyer, Breaking the Vicious Circle 24–27 (1993).

[16] *See* Richard A. Posner, Economic Analysis of Law § 4.11 (3d ed. 1986).

There is undoubtedly something to that, but I do not think it is the whole picture. I think part of what is going on when the court orders, "You deliver the painting or the land," is that the court is thinking that the person is entitled not to something that is valued *as much* as the thing for which he or she contracted; the plaintiff is entitled to something that is valued *in the same way* as the thing for which he or she contracted. The insistence on specific performance remedies in various areas of contract law has to do with the difficulty of thinking of compensatory remedies, in terms of dollars, as really restoring a status quo ante.

If that is right, it has large implications for thinking about tort law and contract law, where it is usually thought that the purpose of the law is to restore the plaintiff to the position he would have occupied if not for the injury. It might be the case that this view is not quite accurate; that the restoration of the status quo ante is not feasible; and that what the law is doing if specific performance is not available is something different.

I have two more notations to make. One is about feminism and the other is about legal reasoning.

For feminism, I have two quotations for you. Richard Rorty, the philosopher, has paraphrased Catharine MacKinnon very prominently as saying that "being a woman is not yet a way of being a human being."[17]

Mike Tyson, the boxer, during his rape trial, and this was widely quoted—even more widely quoted than Richard Rorty or Catharine MacKinnon—Mike Tyson said, "I love women." I wanted to find that and cite it, speculating that something more interesting than appears might be at work. I put it in the computer and I got, for just a two-year period, 125 references to the words "I love women," many of them involving men accused of sexual harassment or sexual assault.

I think that there is a connection between the Tyson quotation and the MacKinnon quotation. I do not think Tyson was lying. I think he was reflecting a mode of valuation which is sincere. I think at work in Rorty's paraphrase of MacKinnon is a claim that women are typically valued either for use or through love and not sufficiently through respect or in ways that human beings deserve to be valued, that is, for their dignity.

I think a lot of feminism in law has to do with an insistence that the typical modes of valuation, having to do with intense affection or use, are not adequate and that respect or dignity ought to be the substitutes.

[17]Richard Rorty, *Feminism and Pragmatism*, 30 Mich. Q. Rev. 231 (1989).

This claim obviously bears on—even if it does not resolve—such matters as the distribution of work within marriage, abortion, prostitution and surrogacy, sexual harassment, and much, much more.

Many of the debates over surrogacy and prostitution have to do with the claim that women's sexual and reproductive capacities are being turned into objects for the use and control of others, in ways that are inconsistent with law's appropriate expressive function.

III. LEGAL REASONING

In many places analogical reasoning is not popular. Much more popular is top–down reasoning: here is a desirable end—let's call it efficiency, or utility, or equality, or dignity, or something else—and let's use the specified value to work problems through. Analogical reasoning is not now treated with much dignity, though it is the stock in trade of the lawyer.

A famous if perhaps apocryphal story at the University of Chicago goes like this: Edward Levi was the Dean of the University of Chicago, and his great book is actually a tribute to analogical reasoning.[18] When he was Dean, Levi also helped introduce law and economics into the legal culture. The way he did this was to have a fellow named Aaron Director, who never published much but was really very influential, come in and teach every fifth antitrust class. The way the story goes, Levi would spend four brilliant classes doing analogical reasoning. Did he have a theory? No. But he certainly could manipulate the cases. Director would come in the fifth class and show that what Levi had been doing made no sense. Director had a theory. By the end, the story goes, even Levi was converted.

This is something that has happened in many places in the legal culture, and in many different areas of law. In antitrust, Director may well have rightly converted everyone, but it is not clear that the victory has been earned everywhere. The analogical thinker is unequipped with and unburdened by a unitary conception of the good or the right; he is alert to particulars; and he is able to see the diverse modes of valuation at stake in many legal disputes. It may well be in some areas of the law—torts is a candidate, free speech is another candidate—a plurality of values is at stake. Precisely because the analogical thinker does not have a top-down theory, but instead is open to the possibility of plural and diverse theories of value, the analogical thinker has something to be said on his or her behalf.

[18] *See* Edward H. Levi, An Introduction to Legal Reasoning (1949).

It is time to conclude. I have not said much about the important issue of choice—that is, choice between modes of valuation and among incommensurable goods. I have asserted, and I want to assert it once more, that some decisions are reasonable and others not, so one ought not to identify incommensurability with reasonlessness or indeterminacy.

But I do want to say that the loss of diverse modes of valuation would be for the legal culture as for the political culture, something of a tragedy, not least because it would make the very notion of tragedy puzzling or even incomprehensible.

I have a quotation from Mill and then a final note. The quotation from Mill comes from his "Essay on Bentham." Mill thought that Bentham was like a one-eyed man. Because he had only one eye, he could see farther than anybody else, but he could not see everything that other people see. Wrote Mill:

> Nothing is more curious than the absence of recognition in any of his writings of the existence of conscience, as a thing distinct from philanthropy, from affection for God or man, and from self-interest in this world or in the next....
>
> Nor is it only the moral part of man's nature... that he overlooks; he but faintly recognises, as a fact in human nature, the pursuit of any other ideal end for its own sake. The sense of *honour*, and personal dignity... the love of *beauty*, the passion of the artist; the love of *order*... the love *action*, the thirst for movement and activity, ... the love of ease:—None of these powerful constituents of human nature are thought worthy of a place....[19]

My largest suggestion is that an insistence on diverse modes of valuation may be one of the most important lessons that emerges from the study of public and private law.

[19]John Stuart Mill, Mill on Bentham and Coleridge 66–68 (F.R. Lewis ed., 1962) (1938).

16

Democracy as a Universal Value†

*Amartya K. Sen**

In the summer of 1997, I was asked by a leading Japanese newspaper what I thought was the most important thing that had happened in the twentieth century. I found this to be an unusually thought-provoking question, since so many things of gravity have happened over the last hundred years. The European empires, especially the British and French ones that had so dominated the nineteenth century, came to an end. We witnessed two world wars. We saw the rise and fall of fascism and Nazism. The century witnessed the rise of communism, and its fall (as in the former Soviet bloc) or radical transformation (as in China). We also saw a shift from the economic dominance of the West to a new economic balance much more dominated by Japan and East and Southeast Asia. Even though that region is going through some financial and economic problems right now, this is not going to nullify the shift in the balance of the world economy that has occurred over many decades (in the case of Japan, through nearly the entire century). The past hundred years are not lacking in important events.

Nevertheless, among the great variety of developments that have occurred in the twentieth century, I did not, ultimately, have any difficulty in choosing one as the preeminent development of the period:

†Originally published as "Democracy as a Universal Value," 1999, *Journal of Democracy*, Vol. 10, No. 3, pp. 3–17.

*The following essay is based on a keynote address that he delivered at a February 1999 conference in New Delhi on "Building a Worldwide Movement for Democracy," cosponsored by the National Endowment for Democracy, the Confederation of Indian Industry, and the Centre for Policy Research (New Delhi). This essay draws on work more fully presented in his book Development as Freedom, to be published by Alfred Knopf later this year.

the rise of democracy. This is not to deny that other occurrences have also been important, but I would argue that in the distant future, when people look back at what happened in this century, they will find it difficult not to accord primacy to the emergence of democracy as the preeminently acceptable form of governance.

The idea of democracy originated, of course, in ancient Greece, more than two millennia ago. Piecemeal efforts at democratization were attempted elsewhere as well, including in India.[1] But it is really in ancient Greece that the idea of democracy took shape and was seriously put into practice (albeit on a limited scale), before it collapsed and was replaced by more authoritarian and asymmetric forms of government. There were no other kinds anywhere else.

Thereafter, democracy as we know it took a long time to emerge. Its gradual—and ultimately triumphant—emergence as a working system of governance was bolstered by many developments, from the signing of the Magna Carta in 1215, to the French and the American Revolutions in the eighteenth century, to the widening of the franchise in Europe and North America in the nineteenth century. It was in the twentieth century, however, that the idea of democracy became established as the "normal" form of government to which any nation is entitled—whether in Europe, America, Asia, or Africa.

The idea of democracy as a universal commitment is quite new, and it is quintessentially a product of the twentieth century. The rebels who forced restraint on the king of England through the Magna Carta saw the need as an entirely local one. In contrast, the American fighters for independence and the revolutionaries in France contributed greatly to an understanding of the need for democracy as a general system. Yet the focus of their practical demands remained quite local—confined, in effect, to the two sides of the North Atlantic, and founded on the special economic, social, and political history of the region.

Throughout the nineteenth century, theorists of democracy found it quite natural to discuss whether one country or another was "fit for democracy." This thinking changed only in the twentieth century, with the recognition that the question itself was wrong: A country does not have to be deemed fit *for* democracy; rather, it has to become fit *through* democracy. This is indeed a momentous change, extending the potential reach of democracy to cover billions of people, with their varying histories and cultures and disparate levels of affluence.

It was also in this century that people finally accepted that "franchise for all adults" must mean *all*—not just men but also women. When in

January of this year I had the opportunity to meet Ruth Dreyfuss, the president of Switzerland and a woman of remarkable distinction, it gave me occasion to recollect that only a quarter century ago Swiss women could not even vote. We have at last reached the point of recognizing that the coverage of universality, like the quality of mercy, is not strained.

I do not deny that there are challenges to democracy's claim to universality. These challenges come in many shapes and forms—and from different directions. Indeed, that is part of the subject of this essay. I have to examine the claim of democracy as a universal value and the disputes that surround that claim. Before I begin that exercise, however, it is necessary to grasp clearly the sense in which democracy has become a dominant belief in the contemporary world.

In any age and social climate, there are some sweeping beliefs that seem to command respect as a kind of general rule—like a "default" setting in a computer programme; they are considered right *unless* their claim is somehow precisely negated. While democracy is not yet universally practiced, nor indeed uniformly accepted, in the general climate of world opinion, democratic governance has now achieved the status of being taken to be generally right. The ball is very much in the court of those who want to rubbish democracy to provide justification for that rejection.

This is a historic change from not very long ago, when the advocates of democracy for Asia or Africa had to argue for democracy with their backs to the wall. While we still have reason enough to dispute those who, implicitly or explicitly, reject the need for democracy, we must also note clearly how the general climate of opinion has shifted from what it was in previous centuries. We do not have to establish afresh, each time, whether such and such a country (South Africa, or Cambodia, or Chile) is "fit for democracy" (a question that was prominent in the discourse of the nineteenth century); we now take that for granted. This recognition of democracy as a universally relevant system, which moves in the direction of its acceptance as a universal value, is a major revolution in thinking, and one of the main contributions of the twentieth century. It is in this context that we have to examine the question of democracy as a universal value.

THE INDIAN EXPERIENCE

How well has democracy worked? While no one really questions the role of democracy in, say, the United States or Britain or France, it is still a matter of dispute for many of the poorer countries in the world. This is not the occasion for a detailed examination of the historical record, but I would argue that democracy has worked well enough.

India, of course, was one of the major battlegrounds of this debate. In denying Indians independence, the British expressed anxiety over the Indians' ability to govern themselves. India was indeed in some disarray in 1947, the year it became independent. It had an untried government, an undigested partition, and unclear political alignments, combined with widespread communal violence and social disorder. It was hard to have faith in the future of a united and democratic India. And yet, half a century later, we find a democracy that has, taking the rough with the smooth, worked remarkably well. Political differences have been largely tackled within the constitutional guidelines, and governments have risen and fallen according to electoral and parliamentary rules. An ungainly, unlikely, inelegant combination of differences, India nonetheless survives and functions remarkably well as a political unit with a democratic system. Indeed, it is held together by its working democracy.

India has also survived the tremendous challenge of dealing with a variety of major languages and a spectrum of religions. Religious and communal differences are, of course, vulnerable to exploitation by sectarian politicians, and have indeed been so used on several occasions (including in recent months), causing massive consternation in the country. Yet the fact that consternation greets sectarian violence and that condemnation of such violence comes from all sections of the country ultimately provides the main democratic guarantee against the narrowly factional exploitation of sectarianism. This is, of course, essential for the survival and prosperity of a country as remarkably varied as India, which is home not only to a Hindu majority, but to the world's third largest Muslim population, to millions of Christians and Buddhists, and to most of the world's Sikhs, Parsees, and Jains.

DEMOCRACY AND ECONOMIC DEVELOPMENT

It is often claimed that nondemocratic systems are better at bringing about economic development. This belief sometimes goes by the name of "the Lee hypothesis," due to its advocacy by Lee Kuan Yew, the leader and former president of Singapore. He is certainly right that some disciplinarian states (such as South Korea, his own Singapore, and postreform China) have had faster rates of economic growth than many less authoritarian ones (including India, Jamaica, and Costa Rica). The "Lee hypothesis," however, is based on sporadic empiricism, drawing on very selective and limited information, rather than on any general statistical testing over the wide-ranging data that are available. A general relation of this kind cannot be established on the basis of very selective evidence. For example, we cannot really take the high economic growth of Singapore or China as "definitive proof" that authoritarianism does better in promoting economic growth, any more than we can draw the opposite conclusion from the fact that Botswana, the country with the best record of economic growth in Africa, indeed with one of the finest records of economic growth in the whole world, has been an oasis of democracy on that continent over the decades. We need more systematic empirical studies to sort out the claims and counterclaims.

There is, in fact, no convincing general evidence that authoritarian governance and the suppression of political and civil rights are really beneficial to economic development. Indeed, the general statistical picture does not permit any such induction. Systematic empirical studies (for example, by Robert Barro or by Adam Przeworski) give no real support to the claim that there is a general conflict between political rights and economic performance.[2] The directional linkage seems to depend on many other circumstances, and while some statistical investigations note a weakly negative relation, others find a strongly positive one. If all the comparative studies are viewed together, the hypothesis that there is no clear relation between economic growth and democracy in *either* direction remains extremely plausible. Since democracy and political liberty have importance in themselves, the case for them therefore remains untarnished.[3]

The question also involves a fundamental issue of methods of economic research. We must not only look at statistical connections, but also examine and scrutinize the *causal* processes that are involved in economic growth and development. The economic policies and circumstances that led to the economic success of countries in East Asia are by now reasonably well understood. While different empirical studies have varied in emphasis, there is by now broad consensus on a list of "helpful policies" that includes openness to competition, the use of international markets, public provision of incentives for investment and export, a high level of literacy and schooling, successful land reforms, and other social opportunities that widen participation in the process of economic expansion. There is no reason at all to assume that any of these policies is inconsistent with greater democracy and had to be forcibly sustained by the elements of authoritarianism that happened to be present in South Korea or Singapore or China. Indeed, there is overwhelming evidence to show that what is needed for generating faster economic growth is a friendlier economic climate rather than a harsher political system.

To complete this examination, we must go beyond the narrow confines of economic growth and scrutinize the broader demands of economic development, including the need for economic and social security. In that context, we have to look at the connection between political and civil rights, on the one hand, and the prevention of major economic disasters, on the other. Political and civil rights give people the opportunity to draw attention forcefully to general needs and to demand appropriate public action. The response of a government to the acute suffering of its people often depends on the pressure that is put on it. The exercise of political rights (such as voting, criticizing, protesting, and the like) can make a real difference to the political incentives that operate on a government.

I have discussed elsewhere the remarkable fact that, in the terrible history of famines in the world, no substantial famine has ever occurred in any independent and democratic country with a relatively free press.[4] We cannot find exceptions to this rule, no matter where we look: the recent famines of Ethiopia, Somalia, or other dictatorial regimes; famines in the Soviet Union in the 1930s; China's 1958–61 famine with the failure of the Great Leap Forward; or earlier still, the famines in Ireland or India under alien rule. China, although it was in many ways doing much better economically than India, still managed (unlike India) to have a famine, indeed the largest recorded famine in world history: Nearly 30 million people died in the famine of 1958–61, while faulty governmental policies remained uncorrected for three full years. The policies went uncriticized because there were no opposition parties in parliament, no free press, and no multiparty elections. Indeed, it is precisely this lack of challenge that allowed the deeply defective policies to continue even though they were killing millions each year. The same can be said about the world's two contemporary famines, occurring right now in North Korea and Sudan.

Famines are often associated with what look like natural disasters, and commentators often settle for the simplicity of explaining famines by pointing to these events: the floods in China during the failed Great Leap Forward, the droughts in Ethiopia, or crop failures in North Korea. Nevertheless, many countries with similar natural problems, or even worse ones, manage perfectly well, because a responsive government intervenes to help alleviate hunger. Since the primary victims of a famine are the indigent, deaths can be prevented by recreating incomes (for example, through employment programs), which makes food accessible to potential famine victims. Even the poorest democratic countries that have faced terrible droughts or floods or other natural disasters (such as India in 1973, or Zimbabwe and Botswana in the early 1980s) have been able to feed their people without experiencing a famine.

Famines are easy to prevent if there is a serious effort to do so, and a democratic government, facing elections and criticisms from opposition parties and independent newspapers, cannot help but make such an effort. Not surprisingly, while India continued to have famines under British rule right up to independence (the last famine, which I witnessed as a child, was in 1943, four years before independence), they disappeared suddenly with the establishment of a multiparty democracy and a free press.

I have discussed these issues elsewhere, particularly in my joint work with Jean Drèze, so I will not dwell further on them here.[5] Indeed, the issue of famine is only one example of the reach of democracy, though it is, in many ways, the easiest case to analyze. The positive role of political and civil rights applies to the prevention of economic and social disasters in general. When things go fine and everything is routinely good, this instrumental role of democracy may not be particularly missed. It is when things get fouled up, for one reason or another, that the political incentives provided by democratic governance acquire great practical value.

There is, I believe, an important lesson here. Many economic technocrats recommend the use of economic incentives (which the market system provides) while ignoring political incentives (which democratic systems could guarantee). This is to opt for a deeply unbalanced set of ground rules. The protective power of democracy may not be missed much when a country is lucky enough to be facing no serious calamity, when everything is going quite smoothly. Yet the danger of insecurity, arising from changed economic or other circumstances, or from uncorrected mistakes of policy, can lurk behind what looks like a healthy state.

The recent problems of East and Southeast Asia bring out, among other things, the penalties of undemocratic governance. This is so in two striking respects. First, the development of the financial crisis in some of these economies (including South Korea, Thailand, Indonesia) has been closely linked to the lack of transparency in business, in particular the lack of public participation in reviewing financial arrangements. The absence of an effective democratic forum has been central to this failing. Second, once the financial crisis led to a general economic recession, the protective power of democracy—not unlike that which prevents famines in democratic countries—was badly missed in a country like Indonesia. The newly dispossessed did not have the hearing they needed.

A fall in total gross national product of, say, 10 percent may not look like much if it follows in the wake of a growth rate of 5 or 10 percent every year over the past few decades, and yet that decline can decimate lives and create misery for millions if the burden of contraction is not widely shared but allowed to be heaped on those—the unemployed or the economically redundant—who can least bear it. The vulnerable in Indonesia may not have missed democracy when things went up and up, but that lacuna kept their voice low and muffled as the unequally shared crisis developed. The protective role of democracy is strongly missed when it is most needed.

THE FUNCTIONS OF DEMOCRACY

I have so far allowed the agenda of this essay to be determined by the critics of democracy, especially the economic critics. I shall return to criticisms again, taking up the arguments of the cultural critics in particular, but the time has come for me to pursue further the positive analysis of what democracy does and what may lie at the base of its claim to be a universal value.

What exactly is democracy? We must not identify democracy with majority rule. Democracy has complex demands, which certainly include voting and respect for election results, but it also requires the protection of liberties and freedoms, respect for legal entitlements, and the guaranteeing of free discussion and uncensored distribution of news and fair comment. Even elections can be deeply defective if they occur without the different sides getting an adequate opportunity to present their respective cases, or without the electorate enjoying the freedom to obtain news and to consider the views of the competing protagonists. Democracy is a demanding system, and not just a mechanical condition (like majority rule) taken in isolation.

Viewed in this light, the merits of democracy and its claim as a universal value can be related to certain distinct virtues that go with its unfettered practice. Indeed, we can distinguish three different ways in which democracy enriches the lives of the citizens. First, political freedom is a part of human freedom in general, and exercising civil and political rights is a crucial part of good lives of individuals as social beings. Political and social participation has *intrinsic value* for human life and well-being. To be prevented from participation in the political life of the community is a major deprivation.

Second, as I have just discussed (in disputing the claim that democracy is in tension with economic development), democracy has an important *instrumental value* in enhancing the hearing that people get in expressing and supporting their claims to political attention (including claims of economic needs). Third—and this is a point to be explored further—the practice of democracy gives citizens an opportunity to learn from one another, and helps society to form its values and priorities. Even the idea of "needs," including the understanding of "economic needs," requires public discussion and exchange of information, views, and analyses. In this sense, democracy has *constructive* importance, in addition to its intrinsic value for the lives of the citizens and its instrumental importance in political decisions. The claims of democracy as a universal value have to take note of this diversity of considerations.

The conceptualization—even comprehension—of what are to count as "needs," including "economic needs," may itself require the exercise of political and civil rights. A proper understanding of what economic needs are—their content and their force—may require discussion and exchange. Political and civil rights, especially those related to the guaranteeing of open discussion, debate, criticism, and dissent, are central to the process of generating informed and considered choices. These processes are crucial to the formation of values and priorities, and we cannot, in general, take preferences as given independently of public discussion, that is, irrespective of whether open interchange and debate are permitted or not.

In fact, the reach and effectiveness of open dialogue are often underestimated in assessing social and political problems. For example, public discussion has an important role to play in reducing the high rates of fertility that characterize many developing countries. There is substantial evidence that the sharp decline in fertility rates in India's more literate states has been much influenced by public discussion of the bad effects of high fertility rates on the community at large, and especially on the lives of young women. If the view has emerged in, say, the Indian state of Kerala or of Tamil Nadu that a happy family in the modern age is a small family, much discussion and debate have gone into the formation of these perspectives. Kerala now has a fertility rate of 1.7 (similar to that of Britain and France, and well below China's 1.9), and this has been achieved with no coercion, but mainly through the emergence of new values—a process in which political and social dialogue has played a major part. Kerala's high literacy rate (it ranks higher in literacy than any province in China), especially among women, has greatly contributed to making such social and political dialogue possible.

Miseries and deprivations can be of various kinds, some more amenable to social remedies than others. The totality of the human predicament would be a gross basis for identifying our "needs." For example, there are many things that we might have good reason to value and thus could be taken as "needs" if they were feasible. We could even want immortality, as Maitreyee, that remarkable inquiring mind in the *Upanishads,* famously did in her 3000-year old conversation with Yajnvalkya. But we do not see immortality as a "need" because it is clearly unfeasible. Our conception of needs relates to our ideas of the preventable nature of some deprivations and to our understanding of what can be done about them. In the formation of understandings and beliefs about feasibility (particularly, *social* feasibility), public discussions play a crucial role. Political rights, including freedom of expression and discussion, are not only pivotal in inducing social responses to economic needs, they are also central to the conceptualization of economic needs themselves.

UNIVERSALITY OF VALUES

If the above analysis is correct, then democracy's claim to be valuable does not rest on just one particular merit. There is a plurality of virtues here, including, first, the *intrinsic* importance of political participation and freedom in human life; second, the *instrumental* importance of political incentives in keeping governments responsible and accountable; and third, the *constructive* role of democracy in the formation of values and in the understanding of needs, rights, and duties. In the light of this diagnosis, we may now address the motivating question of this essay, namely the case for seeing democracy as a universal value.

In disputing this claim, it is sometimes argued that not everyone agrees on the decisive importance of democracy, particularly when it competes with other desirable things for our attention and loyalty. This is indeed so, and there is no unanimity here. This lack of unanimity is seen by some as sufficient evidence that democracy is not a universal value.

Clearly, we must begin by dealing with a methodological question: What is a universal value? For a value to be considered universal, must it have the consent of everyone? If that were indeed necessary, then the category of universal values might well be empty. I know of no value—not even motherhood (I think of *Mommie Dearest*)—to which no one has ever objected. I would argue that universal consent is not required for something to be a universal value. Rather, the claim of a universal value is that people anywhere may have reason to see it as valuable.

When Mahatma Gandhi argued for the universal value of non-violence, he was not arguing that people everywhere already acted according to this value, but rather that they had good reason to see it as valuable. Similarly, when Rabindranath Tagore argued for "the freedom of the mind" as a universal value, he was not saying that this claim is accepted by all, but that all do have reason enough to accept it—a reason that he did much to explore, present, and propagate.[6] Understood in this way, any claim that something is a universal value involves some counterfactual analysis—in particular, whether people might see some value in a claim that they have not yet considered adequately. All claims to universal value—not just that of democracy—have this implicit presumption.

I would argue that it is with regard to this often *implicit* presumption that the biggest attitudinal shift toward democracy has occurred in the twentieth century. In considering democracy for a country that does not have it and where many people may not yet have had the opportunity to consider it for actual practice, it is now presumed that the people involved would approve of it once it becomes a reality in their lives. In the nineteenth century this assumption typically would have not been made, but the presumption that is taken to be natural (what I earlier called the "default" position) has changed radically during the twentieth century.

It must also be noted that this change is, to a great extent, based on observing the history of the twentieth century. As democracy has spread, its adherents have grown, not shrunk. Starting off from Europe and America, democracy as a system has reached very many distant shores, where it has been met with willing participation and acceptance. Moreover, when an existing democracy has been overthrown, there have been widespread protests, even though these protests have often been brutally suppressed. Many people have been willing to risk their lives in the fight to bring back democracy.

Some who dispute the status of democracy as a universal value base their argument not on the absence of unanimity, but on the presence of regional contrasts. These alleged contrasts are sometimes related to the poverty of some nations. According to this argument, poor people are interested, and have reason to be interested, in bread, not in democracy. This oft-repeated argument is fallacious at two different levels.

First, as discussed above, the protective role of democracy may be particularly important for the poor. This obviously applies to potential famine victims who face starvation. It also applies to the destitute thrown off the economic ladder in a financial crisis. People in economic need also need a political voice. Democracy is not a luxury that can await the arrival of general prosperity.

Second, there is very little evidence that poor people, given the choice, prefer to reject democracy. It is thus of some interest to note that when an erstwhile Indian government in the mid-1970s tried out a similar argument to justify the alleged "emergency" (and the suppression of various political and civil rights) that it had declared, an election was called that divided the voters precisely on this issue. In that fateful election, fought largely on this one overriding theme, the suppression of basic political and civil rights was firmly rejected, and the Indian electorate—one of the poorest in the world—showed itself to be no less keen on protesting against the denial of basic liberties and rights than on complaining about economic deprivation.

To the extent that there has been any testing of the proposition that the poor do not care about civil and political rights, the evidence is entirely against that claim. Similar points can be made by observing the struggle for democratic freedoms in South Korea, Thailand, Bangladesh, Pakistan, Burma, Indonesia, and elsewhere in Asia. Similarly, while political freedom is widely denied in Africa, there have been movements and protests against such repression whenever circumstances have permitted them.

THE ARGUMENT FROM CULTURAL DIFFERENCES

There is also another argument in defense of an allegedly fundamental regional contrast, one related not to economic circumstances but to cultural differences. Perhaps the most famous of these claims relates to what have been called "Asian values." It has been claimed that Asians traditionally value discipline, not political freedom, and thus the attitude to democracy must inevitably be much more skeptical in these countries. I have discussed this thesis in some detail in my Morganthau Memorial Lecture at the Carnegie Council on Ethics and International Affairs.[7]

It is very hard to find any real basis for this intellectual claim in the history of Asian cultures, especially if we look at the classical traditions of

India, the Middle East, Iran, and other parts of Asia. For example, one of the earliest and most emphatic statements advocating the tolerance of pluralism and the duty of the state to protect minorities can be found in the inscriptions of the Indian emperor Ashoka in the third century B.C.

Asia is, of course, a very large area, containing 60 percent of the world's population, and generalizations about such a vast set of peoples is not easy. Sometimes the advocates of "Asian values" have tended to look primarily at East Asia as the region of particular applicability. The general thesis of a contrast between the West and Asia often concentrates on the lands to the east of Thailand, even though there is also a more ambitious claim that the rest of Asia is rather "similar." Lee Kuan Yew, to whom we must be grateful for being such a clear expositor (and for articulating fully what is often stated vaguely in this tangled literature), outlines "the fundamental difference between Western concepts of society and government and East Asian concepts" by explaining, "when I say East Asians, I mean Korea, Japan, China, Vietnam, as distinct from Southeast Asia, which is a mix between the Sinic and the Indian, though Indian culture itself emphasizes similar values."[8]

Even East Asia itself, however, is remarkably diverse, with many variations to be found not only among Japan, China, Korea, and other countries of the region, but also *within* each country. Confucius is the standard author quoted in interpreting Asian values, but he is not the only intellectual influence in these countries (in Japan, China, and Korea for example, there are very old and very widespread Buddhist traditions, powerful for over a millennium and a half, and there are also other influences, including a considerable Christian presence). There is no homogeneous worship of order over freedom in any of these cultures.

Furthermore, Confucius himself did not recommend blind allegiance to the state. When Zilu asks him "how to serve a prince," Confucius replies (in a statement that the censors of authoritarian regimes may want to ponder), "Tell him the truth even if it offends him."[9] Confucius is not averse to practical caution and tact, but does not forgo the recommendation to oppose a bad government (tactfully, if necessary): "When the [good] way prevails in the state, speak boldly and act boldly. When the state has lost the way, act boldly and speak softly."[10]

Indeed, Confucius provides a clear pointer to the fact that the two pillars of the imagined edifice of Asian values, loyalty to family and obedience to the state, can be in severe conflict with each other. Many advocates of the power of "Asian values" see the role of the state as an extension of the role of the family, but as Confucius noted, there can be tension between the two. The Governor of She told Confucius, "Among my people, there is a man of unbending integrity: when his father stole a sheep, he denounced him." To this Confucius replied, "Among my people, men of integrity do things differently: a father covers up for his son, a son covers up for his father—and there is integrity in what they do."[11]

The monolithic interpretation of Asian values as hostile to democracy and political rights does not bear critical scrutiny. I should not, I suppose, be too critical of the lack of scholarship supporting these beliefs, since those who have made these claims are not scholars but political leaders, often official or unofficial spokesmen for authoritarian governments. It is, however, interesting to see that while we academics can be impractical about practical politics, practical politicians can, in turn, be rather impractical about scholarship.

It is not hard, of course, to find authoritarian writings within the Asian traditions. But neither is it hard to find them in Western classics: One has only to reflect on the writings of Plato or Aquinas to see that devotion to discipline is not a special Asian taste. To dismiss the plausibility of democracy as a universal value because of the presence of some Asian writings on discipline and order would be similar to rejecting the plausibility of democracy as a natural form of government in Europe or America today on the basis of the writings of Plato or Aquinas (not to mention the substantial medieval literature in support of the Inquisitions).

Due to the experience of contemporary political battles, especially in the Middle East, Islam is often portrayed as fundamentally intolerant of and hostile to individual freedom. But the presence of diversity and variety *within* a tradition applies very much to Islam as well. In India, Akbar and most of the other Moghul emperors (with the notable exception of Aurangzeb) provide good examples of both the theory and practice of political and religious tolerance. The Turkish emperors were often more tolerant than their European contemporaries. Abundant examples can also be found among rulers in Cairo and Baghdad. Indeed, in the twelfth century, the great Jewish scholar Maimonides had to run away from an intolerant Europe (where he was born), and from its persecution of Jews, to the security of a tolerant and urbane Cairo and the patronage of Sultan Saladin.

Diversity is a feature of most cultures in the world. Western civilization is no exception. The practice of democracy that has won out in the *modern* West is largely a result of a consensus that has emerged since the Enlightenment and the Industrial Revolution, and particularly in the last century or so. To read in this a historical commitment of the West—over the millennia—to democracy, and then to contrast it with non-Western traditions (treating each as monolithic) would be a great mistake. This tendency toward oversimplification can be seen not only in the writings of some governmental spokesmen in Asia, but also in the theories of some of the finest Western scholars themselves.

As an example from the writings of a major scholar whose works, in many other ways, have been totally impressive, let me cite Samuel Huntington's thesis on the clash of civilizations, where the heterogeneities *within* each culture get quite inadequate recognition. His study comes to the clear conclusion that "a sense of individualism and a tradition of rights and liberties" can be found in the West that are "unique among civilized societies."[12] Huntington also argues that "the central characteristics of the West, those which distinguish it from other civilizations, antedate the modernization of the West." In his view, "The West was West long before it was modern."[13] It is this thesis that—I have argued—does not survive historical scrutiny.

For every attempt by an Asian government spokesman to contrast alleged "Asian values" with alleged Western ones, there is, it seems, an attempt by a Western intellectual to make a similar contrast from the other side. But even though every Asian pull may be matched by a Western push, the two together do not really manage to dent democracy's claim to be a universal value.

WHERE THE DEBATE BELONGS

I have tried to cover a number of issues related to the claim that democracy is a universal value. The value of democracy includes its *intrinsic importance* in human life, its *instrumental role* in generating political incentives, and its *constructive function* in the formation of values (and in understanding the force and feasibility of claims of needs, rights, and duties). These merits are not regional in character. Nor is the advocacy of discipline or order. Heterogeneity of values seems to characterize most, perhaps all, major cultures. The cultural argument does not foreclose, nor indeed deeply constrain, the choices we can make today.

Those choices have to be made here and now, taking note of the functional roles of democracy, on which the case for democracy in the contemporary world depends. I have argued that this case is indeed strong and not regionally contingent. The force of the claim that democracy is a universal value lies, ultimately, in that strength. That is where the debate belongs. It cannot be disposed of by imagined cultural taboos or assumed civilizational predispositions imposed by our various pasts.

NOTES

1. In Aldous Huxley's novel *Point Counter Point*, this was enough to give an adequate excuse to a cheating husband, who tells his wife that he must go to London to study democracy in ancient India in the library of the British Museum, while in reality he goes to see his mistress.
2. Adam Przeworski et al., *Sustainable Democracy* (Cambridge: Cambridge University Press, 1995); Robert J. Barro, *Getting it Right: Markets and Choices in a free Society* (Cambridge, Mass.: MIT Press, 1996).
3. I have examined the empirical evidence and causal connections in some detail in my book *Development as Freedom*, forthcoming from Knopf in 1999.
4. See my "Development: Which Way Now?" *Economic Journal* 93 (December 1983); *Resources, Values, and Development* (Cambridge, Mass.: Harvard University Press, 1984); and my "Rationality and Social Choice," presidential address to the American Economic Association, published in *American Economic Review* in March 1995. See also Jean Drèze and Amartya Sen, *Hunger and Public Action* (Oxford: Clarendon Press, 1987); Frances D'Souza, ed., *Starving in Silence: A Report on Famine and Censorship* (London: Article 19 International Centre on Censorship, 1990); Human Rights Watch, *Indivisible Human Rights: The Relationship between Political and Civil Rights to Survival, Subsistence and Poverty* (New York: Human Rights Watch, 1992); and International Federation of Red Cross and Red Crescent Societies, *World Disaster Report 1994* (Geneva: Red Cross, 1994).
5. Drèze and Sen, *Hunger and Public Action.*
6. See my "Tagore and His India," *New York Review of Books*, 26 June 1997.
7. Amartya Sen, "Human Rights and Asian Values," Morgenthau Memorial Lecture (New York: Carnegie Council on Ethics and International Affairs, 1997), published in a shortened form in *The New Republic*, 14-21 July 1997.
8. Fareed Zakaria, "Culture is Destiny: A Conversation with Lee Kuan Yew," *Foreign Affairs* 73 (March-April 1994): 113.
9. *The Analects of Confucius*, Simon Leys, trans. (New York: Norton, 1997), 14.22, 70.
10. *The Analects of Confucius*, 14.3, 66.
11. *The Analects of Confucius*, 13.18, 63.
12. Samuel P. Huntington, *The Clash of Civilizations and the Remaking of World Order* (New York: Simon and Schuster, 1996), 71.
13. Huntington, *The Clash of Civilizations*, 69.